THE SERMON ON THE MOUNT
THE MODERN QUEST
FOR ITS MEANING

THE SERMON ON THE MOUNT
THE MODERN QUEST
FOR ITS MEANING

BY
CLARENCE BAUMAN

Regis College Library
15 ST. MARY STREET
TORONTO, ONTARIO, CANADA
M4Y 2R5

101537

BT
380.2
B 38
1985

ISBN 0-86554-113-2

The Sermon on the Mount
Copyright © 1985
Mercer University Press, Macon GA 31207
All rights reserved
Printed in the United States of America

All books published by Mercer University Press
are produced on acid-free paper that exceeds
the minimum standards set by the
National Historical Publications and Records Commission.

LIBRARY OF CONGRESS CATALOGING IN PUBLICATION DATA:

Bauman, Clarence.
The Sermon on the mount.

Bibliography: p. 421.
Includes index.
1. Sermon on the mount—Criticism, interpretation,
etc.—History. I. Title.
BT380.2.B37   1985   226′.906   85-2927
ISBN 0-86554-113-2 (alk. paper)

CONTENTS

PREFACE   ix

I. INTRODUCTION   1

II. THE MODERN QUEST FOR ITS MEANING   9

LEO TOLSTOY
The Moral Challenge of Literal Interpretation   11

WILHELM HERRMANN
The Sermon on the Mount as *Gesinnungsethik*   37

LEONHARD RAGAZ
The Sermon as the Magna Charta of Christian Socialism   53

FRIEDRICH NAUMANN
The Irrelevance of an Oriental Impossibility   75

JOHANNES WEISS
The Apocalyptic Understanding of the Sermon   95

ALBERT SCHWEITZER
The Sermon on the Mount as Interim Ethic   111

JOHANNES MÜLLER
The Sermon as Nature's Law of Humanization   129

OTTO BAUMGARTEN
The Sermon on the Mount and Contemporary Culture   139

KARL BORNHÄUSER
A Historicist View of Its Relevance   153

GEORG WÜNSCH
  Creation Ethic versus Jesus' Ethic   163
CARL STANGE
  Lutheran Paulinizing Exegesis   177
GERHARD KITTEL
  The Sermon on the Mount as *Praeparatio Evangelica*   187
RUDOLF BULTMANN
  The Sermon on the Mount in Existentialist Perspective   197
HANS WINDISCH
  Historical Exegesis versus Theological Interpretation   209
MARTIN DIBELIUS
  The Sermon on the Mount as Eschatological Stimulus   229
DIETRICH BONHOEFFER
  The Sermon on the Mount and Paradoxical Obedience   249
EDUARD THURNEYSEN
  Christological Interpretation   275
JOACHIM JEREMIAS
  The Sermon on the Mount as Gospel, Not Law   291
WALTER STÄDELI
  The Cultic Interpretation of the Sermon on the Mount   299
AFFIRMATIONS OF PRACTICABILITY   305
THE CURRENT STATE OF INQUIRY   331
III. RETROSPECT AND PROSPECT   341
IV. THE JEWISHNESS OF JESUS   367
ESCHATOLOGY AND ETHICS   369
JESUS AND THE LAW   383
PRACTICABILITY AND RELEVANCE   397
V. CONCLUSION   415
BIBLIOGRAPHY   425
INDEXES
  Names   437
  Themes   440

DEDICATION

TO ALETHEA

PREFACE

The Sermon on the Mount is an enigma to the modern conscience. Many enlightened minds admire what it says without affirming what it means. They assume, albeit regretfully, that its message does not apply to contemporary life and that the ethic of Jesus is therefore essentially irrelevant—a beautiful, irresistible impossibility, a conspiracy to ensure our failure. My first awareness of this dilemma dates back to early childhood when I pondered—in a painting of *Die Bergpredigt* by Schnorr von Carolsfeld—that perplexed face of the Roman soldier who sat listening to Jesus at the edge of the crowd while firmly clutching his sword. To my dismay I later discovered how widespread and deep-rooted that perplexity is throughout Christendom.

The intention of this book is not to expose all possible misunderstandings but to examine some of the most influential and consequential hermeneutical options to see how the nature of their presuppositions predetermines the logic of their conclusions. To discern HOW one understands WHAT one understands WHEN one understands Jesus we examine three aspects of the Jewishness of Jesus that determine the Sermon's Christian interpretation. These are (1) Jesus' view of the future and its implications for our faith and life, (2) Jesus' relation to the Mosaic tradition and the extent to which Christian ethics fulfills the intentions of the Torah, and (3) Jesus' expectation of his followers and the sense in which his teaching is practicable and relevant for us today.

The inspiration for this book developed in the context of an existential quest for the real Jesus while living in the Old City of Jerusalem on the Via Dolorosa, Statio IV—the place where Jesus fell under the weight of the Roman cross. The rationale for this ongoing encounter with the German mind augments my formative study on *Gewaltlosigkeit* at the University of Bonn. The logic of this investigation evolved as a dissertation at the University of Edinburgh. While the research was pursued in the libraries of Jerusalem and elsewhere, the actual writing transpired in a rustic little hermitage in mountainous British Columbia under nature's awe-inspiring wonder and winter's life-threatening austerity.

By documenting and articulating the typology of ecumenical perspectives on the meaning and relevance of Jesus' teaching this treatise intends to fill an omission in the modern intellectual history of Christian self-understanding and to further Jewish-Christian dialogue on the intentions of Jesus. May this history of interpretation serve the logic of inquiry as prelude to that more demanding exegetical task of examining the text itself to discern what it *says* before declaring what it *means*.

Blessings on those who helped finance this publication, with special thanks to Willard M. Swartley for his initiative and humble gratitude to J. Lawrence Burkholder for his magnanimity.

I
INTRODUCTION

INTRODUCTION

The Sermon on the Mount is the most important and most controversial biblical text.* With incredible ingenuity and astounding diversity, scholars have debated its exegetical meanings, its theological presuppositions, and its ethical implications. In the hope of explaining to whom, when, and how it applies, the Sermon on the Mount has been
either dramatized as *imitatio Christi* (St. Francis)
　　or traumatized as Oriental impossibility (Naumann);
either clericalized as counsels of perfection (Aquinas)
　　or secularized as metaphysical mind science (Fox);
either absolutized as impracticable ideal (Kittel)
　　or relativized as eschatological stimulus (Dibelius);
either characterized as Jewish wisdom (Windisch)
　　or de-judaized as Aryan humanization (Müller);
either universalized as timeless truth (Harnack)
　　or historicized as a temporal event (Bornhäuser);
either categorized as otherworldly (Weiss)
　　or modernized as *Gesinnungsethik* (Herrmann);
either dogmatized as divine grace (Barth)
　　or rationalized as moral imperative (Kant);
either actualized as the Christian way (Miller)
　　or criticized as impossible law (Stange);
either symbolized as Oriental hyperbole (Barton)
　　or moralized as philosophy of life (Jones);
either psychologized as mental health (Ligon)
　　or romanticized as idyllic fantasy (Renan);

---

*Matthew 5–7; cf. Luke 6:17-49.

either allegorized as Christology (Thurneysen)
  or sacramentalized as cultic liturgy (Städeli);
either politicized as Christian Socialism (Ragaz)
  or individualized as impossible ideal (Niebuhr);
either radicalized as *Nachfolge Christi* (Denck)
  or naturalized as ethic of creation (Wünsch);
either literalized as *nova lex Christi* (Tolstoy)
  or demythologized as self-understanding (Bultmann);
either dispensationalized as futuristic (Chafer)
  or spiritualized as illumination (Prabhavananda);
either pragmatized as *satyagraha* (Gandhi)
  or compromised as ethical paradox (Bonhoeffer);
either etherealized as mountain pathways (Waylen)
  or internalized as pietistic experience (Heim);
either eschatologized as Interim Ethic (Schweitzer)
  or idealized as design for living (Hunter).

This many-sided dialogue involving the meaning and relevance of the Sermon on the Mount cannot, however, be reduced to a single-phased polarization between any two divergent points of view. Nor do we create clarity within this profuse diversity by ascribing oversimplified labels to complex positions without taking into account the history and scope of their development, without acknowledging the evident parallels and similarities, or without exploring the basis for differences in emphasis or substance. The more we understand any particular position, the more we come to appreciate its elemental integrity, and begin to realize that any either/or alternative is subject to the fallacy of oversimplification and the presumption of deciding the issues on the basis of a single variant without acknowledging many intrinsic interrelationships.

Each interpretation of the Sermon on the Mount from within a given set of presuppositions constituting a system of thought or frame of reference is an attempt at a reconciliation of sorts between history and theology, an attempt at synthesizing *Heilsgeschichte* and *Kulturgeschichte*. After following the modern analytical mind through the labyrinth of countless pursuits of this goal, the question of whether a logical synthesis of Jesus' history and our interpretation is possible remains open—an anomaly that characterizes both the inspiration of the human quest for meaning and its ongoing inconclusiveness. All these multifarious attempts to analyze, characterize, categorize, criticize, and modernize the Sermon on the Mount invariably appear to be consciously or unconsciously motivated by the same elemental concern: to rediscover oneself in Jesus and his word so as to confirm oneself in one's own point of view and in turn to justify one's own interests and values. The disillusioning arbitrariness of theological interpretation can be transcended only insofar as we discern the meaning of the Sermon on the Mount within its original Jewish context, by allowing Jesus to speak to our time from within his own. Too much theological interpretation of the Sermon on the Mount intends to abstract its universal Christian content from its historic Jewish form. We hope for a time when it will be no longer necessary for Christians and Jews to identify their *Daseinsberechtigung* with their mutual exclusiveness. This study in the modern intellectual history of Christian self-understanding is an expression of this hope for the future of theology and for the theology of the future.[1]

Our history of interpretation extensively documents the representative positions of the modern quest, identifies the theological presuppositions and ethical implications of each approach, analyzes the criteria of integrity and validity inherent in each stance, probes the gaps of faith and reason peculiar to each position, uncovers the hidden inconsistencies of each interpretation, elucidates the intrinsic possibility and liability of each *Anschauung*, and evaluates the nature of the bridge of meaning that characterizes the relevance of each perspective for our time. Following a comparative summary analysis of all points of view in their order and relation, the decisive theological issues that have emerged from this historical investigation are examined in their own right for the purpose of indicating the direction in which their hope of resolution appears to lie.

The justification for the preponderance of German sources lies in the awareness that "nowhere save in the German temperament can there be found in the same perfection the living complex of conditions and factors—of philosophic thought, critical acumen, historical insight, and religious feeling—without which no deep theology is possible."[2] Of

---

[1]"The Church needs the enlightened eyes of Israel to discover for it the full riches of the Gospel of grace, and it may well be that apart from Israel the Christian Church will never be able to find its way out of the present divisions into true wholeness and unity." T. F. Torrance, *Conflict and Agreement in the Church* (London: Lutterworth Press, 1959) I:303.

[2]Albert Schweitzer, *The Quest of the Historical Jesus. A Critical Study of Its Progress from Reimarus to Wrede*, ET. W. Montgomery (New York: Macmillan, 1968) 1. That this same temperament constitutes not only the hope but also the agony of theology is implied in our conclusion.

approximately a thousand bibliographical items on the Sermon in all languages, only those decisive monographs are given detailed consideration that by nature of their thoroughgoing eccentricity have advanced the logic of the quest in a way in which the more mediating and compromising positions have not. The analysis and evaluation of less determinative perspectives are incorporated within a fabric of footnotes. Rather than attempt an exhaustive anthology of all possible points of view, our intention is to chart the course of modern interpretation by highlighting its definitive hermeneutical landmarks in their chronological and logical topographical interrelationship.

Biblical exegesis is a field where many poppies bloom. We can gain perspective on this field by preoccupying ourselves with that subtle science of interpreting the Bible without reading it. Or, we could go directly to the text to discover therein treasures old and new. But to read the text attentively and intensively is to realize that others have read it also and that our hope of improving upon their best insights demands testing them against our own in the broadest possible perspective. The rationale and validity of our historical approach therefore lies in the need to objectify in a comparative way the theological and cultural determinants of exegesis.

The history of interpretation of the Sermon on the Mount has previously received only scant attention. In 1918 Preisker discussed several interpretations.[3] Numerous scholars have provided brief reviews of other viewpoints as introductions to their own.[4] In 1941 Soiron classified and

---

[3]H. Preisker, "Die Art und Tragweite der Lebenslehre Jesu," *Theologische Studien und Kritiken* (1919):1-45.

[4]For example, H. W. Beyer, *Der Christ und die Bergpredigt nach Luthers Deutung* (München, 1933) 5-9; Johannes Schneider, *Der Sinn der Bergpredigt* (Berlin, 1936) 8-14; Hans Windisch, *The Meaning of the Sermon on the Mount*, ET S. M. Gilmour (Philadelphia: The Westminster Press, 1951) 44-61; Eduard Thurneysen, *The Sermon on the Mount*, ET W. C. and J. M. Robinson (Richmond: John Knox Press, 1964) 20-28; Gerhard Heinzelmann, "Das richtige Verständnis der Bergpredigt," *Theologische Studien und Kritiken*, N. F. III, 6. Heft, 108 (1937-38):458-71; S. MacLean Gilmour, "Interpreting the Sermon on the Mount," *Crozer Quarterly* 24 (1947):47-56; Karl Heim, *Die Bergpredigt Jesu* (Hamburg: Furche Verlag, 1959)4-6; A. M. Hunter, *Design for Life* (London: SCM Press, 1965) 99-106; Henlee Barnette, "The Ethic of the Sermon on the Mount," *Review and Expositor* 53 (1956):23-33; Josef Staudinger, *Die Bergpredigt* (Wien: Herder Verlag, 1957) 318-22; E. Fascher, "Bergpredigt II: Auslegungsgeschichte," *Religion in Geschichte und Gegenwart*, 3rd ed, 1:1050-53; Irvin Batdorf, "How Shall We Interpret the Sermon on the

succinctly described the various trees then flourishing in the forest without attempting to analyze, compare, or evaluate, their various characteristics.[5] McArthur's study[6] focuses primarily on the Fathers and Reformers, while Bonham's book,[7] valuable in its own right, plows only a shallow furrow in the deep soil of European thought. Kissinger's survey[8] abstracts the range of authors and movements from patristic to modern times without scrutinizing their conflicting claims to validity, and Berner's treatise[9] documents the current discrepancy between theological and text-critical approaches without resolving the ethical impairment.

Our own analysis begins with Tolstoy because it was through him that the Sermon on the Mount first became a problem to the modern conscience.

Mount?'' *Journal of Bible and Religion* (1959):211-17; Joachim Jeremias, *The Sermon on the Mount*, ET N. Perrin (Philadelphia: Fortress Press, 1963) 1-12; Wolfgang Knörzer, *Die Bergpredigt* (Stuttgart: Katholisches Bibelwerk, 1970) 95-104; Petr Pokorný, *Der Kern der Bergpredigt* (Hamburg: Herbert Reich Evangelischer Verlag, 1969) 56-61; Fred L. Fisher, *The Sermon on the Mount* (Nashville: Broadman Press, 1976) 13-22; D. A. Carson, *The Sermon on the Mount. An Evangelical Exposition* (Grand Rapids: Baker, 1978) 151-57; Robert A. Guelich, *The Sermon on the Mount. A Foundation for Understanding* (Waco TX: Word Books, 1982) 13-22; Eduard Schweizer, *Die Bergpredigt* (Göttingen: Vandenhoeck & Ruprecht, 1982) 101-16.

[5]Thaddäus Soiron, *The Bergpredigt Jesu* (Freiburg i.B.: Herder, 1941).

[6]Harvey K. McArthur, *Understanding the Sermon on the Mount* (London: Epworth Press, 1961).

[7]Tal. D. Bonham, *The Demands of Discipleship* (Pine Bluff, Arkansas: Discipleship Book Co., 1967).

[8]Warren S. Kissinger, *The Sermon on the Mount*, ATLA Bibliography Series No. 3 (Metuchen, NJ: Scarecrow Press, 1975).

[9]Ursula Berner, *Die Bergpredigt. Rezeption und Auslegung im 20. Jahrhundert* (Göttingen: Vandenhoeck & Ruprecht, [1979] 1983) [Göttinger theologische Arbeiten; Band 12]. Cf. also Georg Strecker's ''Auslegungstypen der Bergpredigt,'' *Die Bergpredigt, Ein exegetischer Kommentar* (Göttingen: Vandenhoeck & Ruprecht, 1984) 13-23.

II
THE MODERN QUEST
FOR ITS MEANING

LEO TOLSTOY:
THE MORAL CHALLENGE
OF LITERAL INTERPRETATION

Of all the Gospels, the Sermon on the Mount was the portion which impressed me most. . . . Nowhere else does Christ speak with such solemnity; nowhere else does he give so many clear and intelligible precepts, which commend themselves to everyone.[1]

On reading these precepts, it always seemed to me that they applied to myself, and that I was morally bound to obey them. I even felt convinced that I could, immediately and from that very hour, do all that they enjoined.[2]

I accepted the fact that Christ meant exactly what he said.[3]

I understood that the whole force of the teaching lay in the words, "Resist not evil," and that all the context was but an application of that great precept.[4]

Is not all Christianity summed up in the words, "Love your enemies."[5]

The least that can be required of those who judge another man's teaching is, that they should take the teacher's words in the exact sense in which he uses them. Christ did not consider his teaching as some high ideal of what mankind should be, but cannot attain to, nor does he consider it as a chimerical, poetical fancy, fit only to captivate the simple-minded inhabitant of Galilee; he considers his teaching as work—a work which is to save mankind. His suffering on the cross was no dream; he groaned in agony and died for his teaching.[6]

---

[1]Leo Tolstoy, *What I Believe*, ET C. Popoff [also known as *My Religion*] (London: Elliot Stock, 1885) 7-8.

[2]Ibid., 9.

[3]Ibid., 10.

[4]Ibid., 12.

[5]Ibid., 14.

[6]Ibid., 43.

In the Sermon on the Mount Christ expressed both the eternal ideal towards which it is natural for men to aspire, and that degree of its attainment which mankind can even now reach.[7]

I began by loving my orthodox faith more than my peace; then I loved Christianity more than my Church, and now I love the truth more than anything in the world.[8]

At the age of eighteen Leo Tolstoy[9] observed that religious belief "has no influence on life nor on the relations between men," whereupon he dis-

---

[7]Tolstoy, "The Kingdom of God is Within You," in *The Kingdom of God and Peace Essays*, ET Aylmer Maude, The World's Classics (Oxford University Press, 1951) 445: 4th ed. 121.

[8]*On Life, and Essays on Religion* (1887-1909), Vol. 12 of *The Works of Leo Tolstoy* (Oxford: University Press, 1934) 225.

[9]Count Leo Nikolaevitch Tolstoy was born in 1828 at Yasnaya Polyana near Moscow. His childhood was marked by extreme sensitivity and passionate temperament and his youth by idealistic longing for perfection. He studied at Kazan and Petersburg universities, served in the Crimean War, and married in 1862. Thirteen children were born to the couple during the next 25 years, while Tolstoy wrote his long novels, *Anna Karenina* and *War and Peace* (which his wife painstakingly copied out seven times).

Tolstoy spent most of his life in his country estate looking after his holdings and writing. All along he was haunted by an ever more persistent quest for the meaning of life. Disenchanted with wealth and fame, he turned to science. The ingenious theory of evolution, while offering a partial answer to the question of life's origin, did not, however, address itself to the question of life's purpose. Then he interrogated the priests, but they were as disappointing as the scientists, for they were not open to explore the meaning of life and death apart from the creedal statements they endorsed. With few exceptions, the priests did not object to mass murder in war but sanctioned it in their ministry as chaplains by blessing battleships and imploring God to confound their enemies even without knowing who they were. Tolstoy concluded the church's stance commends itself neither to reason nor to conscience.

Despairing of "what men say," Tolstoy resolved to observe "what men do" hoping thereby to discern the object of life. First, he observed those who lived like animals. They did not understand his quest, and from them he learned nothing. Next, he turned to the professionals in business, literature, and government, but these were either too preoccupied with their work, too hypnotized by the authority of the newspaper, the emperor, or the pope, or too bound in loyalty to church or state to be free to ask fundamental questions. Most contemptible of all were the Epicureans, who, while admitting that their lives were meaningless, continued undisturbed in their hedonism.

Finally, Tolstoy turned to the peasants who, despite poverty, ignorance, and oppression, bore life with patience and death with tranquillity. After studying the Chinese, Buddhist, and Moslem scriptures, he discovered in the Gospels the clearest expression of that

carded all belief in everything he had been taught except for "belief in the possibility of perfection," although he could not determine "what it was in itself or what would be its results." Despite contempt and derision from his contemporaries, he arduously strove to become "a good and virtuous man."[10]

In Europe he learned that the way to perfection was the way of evolutionary progress. But the spectacle of a public execution in Paris shattered his belief in 'progress.'[11] On the basis of his observations and experiences, he concluded that all the resources of culture and learning were totally incapable of answering the one question uppermost in his mind: What is the meaning of life? What is its purpose?

From that point, he determined to live with the peasants. Identifying with them, he found an integrity he had not realized before. He discerned that the meaning of life is "to live after God's Word," that is, to "renounce all the pleasures of life, labour, be humble, endure, and be chari-

---

by which the peasants lived and died, the answer to his own quest for the aim or purpose of life, and the resources to meet death without fear. In the Sermon on the Mount Tolstoy discovered sayings of Jesus that were perfectly clear, simple, easy to grasp "and that agreed with his own experience of life and accorded with his own reason and conscience." (See Aylmer Maude, *Tolstoy and His Problems* [London, 1902] 13.)

Around 1878 Tolstoy became overwhelmingly convinced that the Sermon on the Mount should be applied literally to every phase of human life. Every person, he believed, was given the resources of reason and conscience to discern good from evil, to obey his higher spiritual nature and not yield to his lower animal nature. Tolstoy's religious fervor might be characterized as a mixture of radical Christian socialism, mysticism, and asceticism. His influence upon the world has probably been greater than that of any other Russian through both his artistic and religious works, the most important of which include: *My Confession, A Criticism of Dogmatic Theology, The Four Gospels Harmonized and Translated, What I Believe* (or: *My Religion*), *The Gospel in Brief, What Then Must We Do?* (or: *What To Do?*), *On Life* (or: *Life*), *The Kreutzer Sonata, The Kingdom of God Is Within You, The Christian Teaching, What Is Art?, Resurrection,* and *What Is Religion and What is Its Essence?*

[10]*My Confession* [1879-1882] and *The Spirit of Christ's Teaching* (London: Walter Scott, n.d.) 1, 3, 7, 8.

[11]"When I saw the head divided from the body and heard the sound with which it fell separately into the box, I understood, not with my reason, but with my whole being, that no theory of the wisdom of all established things, nor of progress, could justify such an act; and that if all the men in the world from the day of creation, by whatever theory, had found this thing necessary, it was not so; it was a bad thing, and that therefore I must judge of what was right and necessary, not by what men said and did, not by progress, but what I felt to be true in my heart." *My Confession*, 19.

table to all men.''[12] He desired living in spiritual harmony with the common people, but he could not, for the sacraments of the Church so utterly repelled him.[13] And when he observed all that was done in the name of religion by men who profess to be Christians, he was horrified.[14] Instead of inspiring love and respect for the actual teachings of Jesus, the successions of councils, fathers, popes, and patriarchs had preached doctrines ''most alien to Christ''[15] and had alienated generations of earnest seekers from Jesus because of a ''monstrous parasitic tradition that has fastened about his words.''[16] ''The chief matter is,'' Tolstoy declared,

> not whether Jesus Christ was God, or from whom descended the Holy Ghost, or when and by whom was a certain Gospel written, or if it may not be attributed to Christ; but the light itself is of importance to me, that it still shines upon me after eighteen hundred years with undimmed brightness; but how to call it, or of what it consists, or who gave it existence, is immaterial to me.[17]

For Tolstoy, the roots of the hermeneutical problem lay in claiming equal inspiration for both Old and New Testaments, in equating Paul with Jesus, and in replacing Christ's own teaching with church doctrines to the effect that ''no understanding of the teaching of Christ is admitted which

---

[12]Ibid., 119.

[13]''When I drew near to the altar, and the priest called upon me to repeat that I believed that what I was about to swallow was the real body and blood, I felt a sharp pain at the heart; it was no unconsidered word, it was the hard demand of one who could never have known what faith was. I humbled myself again, I swallowed the blood and the body without any mocking thoughts in the wish to believe; but the shock had been given, and knowing what awaited me another time, I could never go again.'' Ibid., 128-30.

[14]''Russians slew their brethren in the name of Christian love. Not to think of this was impossible. Not to see that murder is an evil, contrary to the very first principle of every faith, was impossible. In the churches, however, men prayed for the success of our arms, and the teachers of religion accepted these murders as acts which were the consequences of faith.'' Ibid., 140.

[15]Such as, ''that it was Christ who declared that it was by his blood he redeemed the world, that God was a Trinity, that the Holy Ghost descended upon the apostles and was transmitted to the priesthood by the laying on of hands, that for salvation seven sacraments are needed, that the communion must be celebrated in two aspects, and so forth; whereas in all Christ's teaching there is no hint at all of this.'' Ibid., 166.

[16]Ibid., 170.

[17]*The Spirit of Christ's Teachings*, 161.

does not accord with that of the preceding and following revelation.''[18] Tolstoy was greatly perplexed to find "that the texts upon which the Church has grounded her dogmas are of an obscure character, whereas those which teach us how to live are the most simple and clear.'' Only in the Gospels could he discover the resolution of his doubts. "The Sermon on the Mount was the portion which impressed me most,'' he wrote. "Nowhere else does Christ speak with such solemnity; nowhere else does He give us so many clear and intelligible moral precepts, which commend themselves to everyone.''[19]

As Tolstoy read the Sermon on the Mount over and over again, he admitted that the words were not clear, for "they seemed to enjoin an impossible self-abnegation, which annulled life itself, and therefore it seemed to me that such abnegation could not be the requirement on which depended man's salvation.'' This understanding was confirmed in the various commentaries he consulted; they explained that the Sermon on the Mount is an indication of the perfection after which human beings must strive but "that man, being full of sin, cannot attain this perfection by his own unaided strength, and that the salvation of man lies in faith, prayer, and the gifts of the grace of God.''

These explanations did not satisfy him:

> Why should Christ have given us such clear and good precepts, applicable to us all, if he knew beforehand that the keeping of them was impossible by man in his own unaided strength? On reading these precepts, it always seemed to me that they applied to myself, and that I was morally bound to obey them. I even felt convinced that I could, immediately and from that very hour, do all that they enjoined. I wished and tried to do so, but as soon as any difficulty arose in the way of my keeping them, I involuntarily remembered the teaching of the Church, that "man is weak, and can do no good thing by himself''; and then I became weak. I have been told that it was necessary to believe and pray, but I felt that my faith was weak and that I could not pray. I had been told that it was necessary to pray for faith— for that faith without which prayer is of no avail. I was told that faith comes

---

[18]Ibid., 162. "The Sectarianism of Christianity has its root in the idea that the Gospels are to be understood, not by themselves, but in accordance with all Holy Writings" much like the Mohammedans who subordinate Moses and Christ to the final revelations of Mohammed, except that they call themselves after the name of Christ "in order to combine the licence of their own teaching with the authority of Christ's." Ibid., 165.

[19]*What I Believe*, 7-8.

through prayer and that prayer comes through faith which, to say the least, was certainly bewildering. Such statements commended themselves neither to reason nor experience.

Consequently, Tolstoy lost all faith in the explanations of learned theology, for he could not abjure the book. Finally, "after many doubts and much suffering . . . in obedience to the words of Christ" inviting us to receive the kingdom of God "like a child (Mark 10:15)," Tolstoy "accepted the fact that Christ meant exactly what he said," whereupon "all that had hitherto obscured the truth cleared away, and the truth itself arose before me in all its solemn importance."[20]

Tolstoy found the key to understanding the Sermon on the Mount in Matthew 5:39: "I say unto you that ye resist not evil. . . . The whole force of the teaching lay in the words, 'resist not evil' and . . . the context was but an application of that great principle." The rest of the Sermon on the Mount simply describes what one might expect to happen to those who actually follow Jesus. "Christ does not require us to turn the other cheek and to give away our cloak in order to make us suffer; but he teaches us not to resist evil and warns us that so doing may involve personal suffering."[21] Tolstoy concluded that the law of nonresistance was indeed the essence of the Gospel and that Jesus had implied that those who live by it are "liable to be persecuted, stoned, and reduced to beggary." Jesus clearly says that "the disciple who does not take up his cross, who is not willing to renounce all, cannot be his follower, and he thus describes the man who is ready to bear the consequences that may result from the practice of the doctrine of nonresistance."[22] Tolstoy felt inwardly compelled to receive the words of Jesus without attempting either to allegorize them or to evade them.

> If my master were to say to me, "Go and cut wood," and I were to answer that I could not do it in my own strength, would it not show that either I had no faith in my master's words or that I did not choose to obey him?

---

[20]Ibid., 8-10.

[21]Ibid., 12: "Does a father, on seeing his son set out on a long journey, tell him to pass sleepless nights, to eat little, to get wet through, or to freeze? Will he not rather say to him, 'Go, and, if on the way you are cold and hungry, be not discouraged, go on.' Christ does not say, 'Let a man smite thy cheek and suffer,' but he says, 'Resist not evil'—whatever men may do to you, 'resist not evil.' "

[22]Ibid., 13.

God has given us a commandment which he requires us to obey; he says
that only those who keep his commandments shall enter life eternal. . . .
He does not say that it is hard to keep this law; he says, on the contrary,
"My yoke is easy and my burden light."[23]

Yet ecclesiastic teachers kept telling Tolstoy that to observe the teaching
of Christ "was impossible on account of the weakness of human nature,"
while secular teachers told him that "the whole order of life proved that
the teaching of Christ was impracticable and ideal and that we must, in fact,
live contrary to his doctrine." The inconsistency of "professing Christ in
words and denying him in deed"[24] greatly perplexed Tolstoy. It appeared
to him that "to consider this rule of life as a precept which cannot be obeyed
without supernatural aid is to annihilate the whole doctrine of Christ completely. How can a doctrine, the fundamental law of which is cast aside as
impracticable, be considered practicable in any of its details?"[25]

Tolstoy could foresee no legitimate way of resolving the tension between "the doctrine of Christ which teaches love, humility, self-denial"
and that "contrary law, both in the history of the past and in the present
organization of our lives—a law repugnant to my heart, my conscience,
and my reason, but one which flattered my animal instincts." Eventually
this irreconcilable dichotomy forced him to choose:

If I accepted the doctrine of Christ, I would be forsaken, miserable, persecuted, and sorrowing, as Christ tells us his followers would be. I knew
that if I accepted the law of man, I should have the approbation of my fel-
low-men; I should be at peace and in safety; all possible sophisms would
be at hand to quiet my conscience, and I should "laugh and be merry," as
Christ says.[26]

Unwilling to suffer any more inconvenience than absolutely necessary,
Tolstoy temporarily avoided any closer examination of Jesus' teaching,
desisting from all further attempts to comprehend it.

---

[23]Ibid., 14.

[24]Ibid., 17.

[25]Ibid., 18. "I was confessing Christ as God and his teaching as divine, and at the same
time I was ordering my life contrary to his teaching. What was left me to do but to acknowledge the teaching as an impracticable one? In word I acknowledged the teaching of
Christ as sacred; but I did not carry out that teaching in deed, for I admitted and respected
the unchristian institutions which surrounded me." Ibid., 19.

[26]Ibid., 23.

Yet his conscience gave him no rest. His membership in the law court which guarded his property and his personal safety began to bother him. It had never before occurred to him that Jesus' saying, "Condemn not," could have any reference to courts of law, district courts, criminal courts, assizes, and courts of peace. But, after examining the meaning of the words in their contexts, Tolstoy concluded

> that human courts were not only contrary to this commandment but in direct opposition to the whole doctrine of Christ and that therefore he must certainly have forbidden them. . . . Christ enjoins us to return good for evil. Courts of law return evil for evil. Christ says: "Make no distinction between the just and the unjust." Courts of law do nothing else. Christ says: "Forgive all; forgive not once, not seven times, forgive without end." "Love your enemies." "Do good to them that hate you." Courts of law do not forgive, but they punish; they do not do good but evil to those whom they call the enemies of society. So that the true sense of the doctrine is that Christ forbids all courts of law.[27]

The immediate objection to this interpretation is that "Christ had nothing to do with human courts of law and never considered them." But, Tolstoy reminds us, we cannot deny that

> from the day of his birth, Christ had to submit to the jurisdiction of Herod, the Sanhedrin, and the high priests. Indeed, we find that Christ speaks more than once of tribunals as being evil. He tells his disciples that they will have to be cited before tribunals; and teaches them how to behave in courts of law. He says that he himself will be condemned and sets us all an example of the way in which we are to treat the laws of man. . . . In the case of the adulteress, he positively rejects human justice and proves that, on account of each man's own sinful nature, he has no right to judge another.[28]

This teaching is further exemplified in the sayings of Jesus regarding the beam and the mote and the blind leading the blind.

Some critics expostulate against Tolstoy's interpretation on the grounds that Jesus only "intended to show us the frailty of human nature in general" and "does not intend to forbid our having recourse to human justice for our protection against evil men."[29] Tolstoy replied that the Sermon on

---

[27]Ibid., 25.

[28]Ibid., 26.

[29]Ibid., 26.

the Mount is addressed to all human beings and that it is for none to presume to distinguish some as evil and others as good as the law courts do. The hypothesis that this teaching "applies only to the relations between private individuals and the public courts of law" is likewise inadmissible, for it denies that Jesus "enjoins all men, without exception, to forgive as they hope to be forgiven." Tolstoy concludes that "according to the doctrine of Christ, a judge who condemns his fellow creature to death is no Christian,"[30] an understanding consistently confirmed throughout the New Testament.

Tolstoy examined the writings of the Early Church Fathers and found "that they all consider the precept never to use force, never to condemn or execute as the one which distinguishes their doctrine from all others. . . . They only submit to the tortures inflicted upon them by human justice. The martyrs all confessed the same, not only in word but in deed." In fact, "all true Christians, from the disciples up to the time of Constantine, regarded courts of law as evils which had to be endured with patience; and the possibility of a Christian's taking part in judging another never occurred to any of them."[31] However, in all the commentaries of the Church Fathers "from the fifth century to the present day, I found that these words are considered as signifying to condemn in word, that is, to speak evil of our neighbour."[32] All the Greek, Catholic, and Protestant theologians whom Tolstoy consulted gave this text the narrow interpretation of not speaking evil of others without any mention of applying it to the death penalty of the law courts. They all concurred "that the exercise of the courts of law in Christian states is necessary and is not contrary to the law of Christ."[33] But, since the same Greek term for "condemn" (κρίνω) is also used to express the execution of Jesus, Tolstoy could find no basis for interpreting the command of Jesus, "Condemn not," to refer only to evil speech and not to the death penalty.

Against those who reject this teaching of Jesus as incompatible with human nature, Tolstoy insists that it is the life of violence that is against human nature wherefore "no judge will ever undertake to strangle with his

---

[30]Ibid., 27.

[31]Ibid., 32.

[32]Ibid., 33.

[33]Ibid., 34.

own hands the man whom he has condemned to death."[34] Tolstoy proceeds to examine in some detail the text of the Sermon on the Mount, beginning with Matthew 5:17-19 regarding Jesus' attitude to the law. He observes that the "law" Jesus came not to destroy but to fulfill is not the written law of Moses but the eternal law of God.[35] If Jesus did not abrogate the Mosaic law by his teaching, why then did the Pharisees, scribes, lawyers, and priests collaborate to crucify him? Tolstoy was convinced that "the contradiction between the whole spirit of the Mosaic law and the doctrine of Christ remains in all its force."[36] But ever since the fifth century, the teachers of the Church have sought somehow to resolve this contradiction in their own interests. "The impossible attempts at uniting what cannot be united are clear proof that this was not an involuntary mental error, but was effected with some definite purpose in view." As a case in point, "John Chrysostom plainly acknowledges the law of a tooth for a tooth to be the Divine Law, and the reverse of that law—that is, Christ's doctrine of nonresistance—to be wrong." Chrysostom reasons: If the law were done away with, "what disasters would then rush in torrents into the lives of men!" But he fails to tell us by what criterion he judges who are the wicked to be restrained.[37]

---

[34]"Who will deny that it is repugnant and harrowing to a man's feelings to torture or kill, not only a man, but even a dog, a hen, or a calf? I have known men, living by agricultural labour, who ceased entirely to eat meat because they had to kill their own cattle. And yet our lives are so organized, that for one individual to obtain any advantage in life another must suffer, which is against human nature." Ibid., 44. Men will argue: "The doctrine of Christ, which teaches us not to resist is—a dream! But the sight of men in whose breasts love and pity are innate, spending their lives in burning their brethren at the stake, scourging them, breaking them on the wheel, lashing, splitting their nostrils, putting them to the rack, keeping them fettered, sending them to the galley or the gallows, shooting them, condemning them to solitary confinement, imprisoning women and children, organizing the slaughter of tens of thousands by war, bringing about periodic revolutions and rebellions; the sight of others passively fulfilling these atrocities, the sight of others again writhing under these tortures, or avenging them—this is no dream! This delirium of madness is indeed a dream from which it is enough to awake once, never to return to it." Ibid., 46, 47.

[35]Otherwise Matthew 5:17 would not read: " . . . the law or the prophets" but rather: " . . .the law and the prophets," ibid., 52.

[36]Ibid., 61.

[37]Ibid., 63. "He ought to have told us who is to take an 'eye for an eye' " if not "the men who were forbidden to do so by the Son of God." The problem, as Tolstoy discerns,

What then is the commandment of Christ? It is not what the theologians suppose, namely, to love God and our neighbor as ourselves, for that was given to the ancient Hebrews—as Jesus himself reminded the scribes (cf. Matthew 22:35-40). The five new and definite commandments of Christ which constitute the Kingdom of God on earth are clearly expressed in the Antitheses of Matthew 5:21-48. Tolstoy paraphrased them in order:

(1) To offend no one, and by no act to excite evil in others, for out of evil comes evil.

(2) To be in all things chaste, and not to quit the wife whom we have taken; for the abandoning of wives and the changing of them is the cause of all the loose living in the world.

(3) Never to take an oath, because we can promise nothing, for man is altogether in the hands of the Father, and oaths are imposed for wicked ends.

(4) Not to resist evil, to bear with offenses, and to do yet more than is demanded of us; neither to judge, nor to go to law, for every man is himself full of faults, and cannot teach. By seeking revenge men only teach others to do the same.

(5) To make no distinction between our countrymen and foreigners, for all men are the children of one Father.[38]

Christ's first commandment is "Do not be angry" (Matthew 5:22-25). Tolstoy noted that the text had been tampered with by redactors. By the fifth century the word εἰκῆ, meaning "needlessly" or "without a cause," had been inserted into the initial unconditional statement of Jesus and thereby modified it to the conditional statement: "Whosoever is angry with his brother *without a cause*. . . . " Tolstoy was amazed to note that the Fathers had concentrated on defining those causes for which anger could be legitimized by citing in support of their opinions instances of the anger of the apostles and saints. As a result, each person became his own judge as to whether his anger was justifiable and hence not "without a cause," each person claiming his own anger to be both lawful and necessary.[39]

---

ultimately reflects a dichotomy in man's knowledge of God: "John Chrysostom and the Church follow the commandments of the Father—i.e., the Mosaic law—and reject the commandments of the Son, while ostensibly professing His doctrine." Ibid., 64-65. Cf. Chrysostom's Commentary on St. Matthew, I:320-23.

[38]Ibid., 186.

[39]Ibid., 68-70.

The second commandment of Christ reads, "Do not divorce" (Matthew 5:27-32). Jesus' law stands in opposition to Moses' law, which allowed a man to put away his wife if he provided a writing of divorcement. Jesus makes no mention of divorce in the sense of legitimizing separation. To interpret the so-called "except clause" ("Except for the cause of adultery," Matthew 5:32) as a qualification to the predicate "putteth away" and thus to accommodate the unconditional commandment of Christ to the sinful condition of man altogether obviates the intended *contrast* of Jesus' law to that of Moses.

> Be the wife guilty or not, by putting her away the husband causes her to sin. . . . [πορνείας] . . . properly implies a depraved state or disposition, and not an action, and cannot therefore be translated by the word "adultery." . . . I saw that there could be no doubt about the word πορ-νείας referring only to the husband. . . . Therefore, the text stands word for word thus: "He who divorces his wife, besides the sin of lewdness, causes her to commit adultery." . . . And thus the meaning is clear that Christ in this passage refutes the notions of the Pharisees that a man who put away his wife, not out of lewdness, but in order to live matrimonially with another woman, did not commit adultery.

Jesus says that putting away one's wife "even if it be not done out of lewdness, but in order to be joined in bonds of matrimony to another woman, is adultery." Jesus commanded, "Take no pleasure in concupiscence; let each man if he be not a eunuch have a wife and each woman a husband; let a man have but one wife and a woman but one husband and let them never under any pretext dissolve their union."[40] This simple and clear teaching has been obscured and misinterpreted, Tolstoy wrote, by the desire to justify existing evils.

Jesus' third commandment is "Swear not at all" (Matthew 5:33-37). But the commentators say "that this precept given us by Christ is not always obligatory, and that in no case does it refer to the oath of allegiance to the existing powers, which every citizen is obliged to take. They choose out texts from Holy Scripture, not with the purpose of confirming the direct meaning of Christ's precept, but in order to prove that it is possible

---

[40]Ibid., 81-84.

and even necessary to leave it unfulfilled."[41] Thus, a soldier solves the problem of inconsistency between his commitment to do evil and the Gospel's forbidding of evildoing by saying that he has sworn an oath of allegiance, that is, sworn "upon the Gospel":

> How can it come into the head of a man who is made to take an oath on the Gospel or the crucifix that the crucifix is sacred for the very reason that he who forbade our swearing was crucified upon it? He who takes the oath perhaps kisses the very passage which so clearly and definitely says,"Swear not at all."[42]

The fourth commandment, "Do not retaliate" (Matthew 5:38-42), is held to be impracticable, for to apply it would destroy "the whole organization of life which we have set up so well. We decide beforehand that the present organization of our lives, which his words tend to destroy, is the sacred law of mankind [though] Christ exhorts us to act otherwise."[43] Tolstoy discerned two opposing ways of seeking to promote the triumph of good over evil. One may witness to the truth clearly and fearlessly as did Jesus and hope thereby to influence others to live by the truth. The opposite approach is to coerce other people by threat and force of violence to do what we think they should do and to justify injuring and destroying others on the grounds that, if we ceased to do so, evil would surely overcome us.

The fifth commandment of Christ is "Love Your Enemy" (Matthew 5:43-48). But, Tolstoy wrote,

---

[41]"It is affirmed that Christ himself sanctioned the taking of an oath in courts of law, by his answer, 'Thou hast said,' to the High Priest's words: 'I adjure thee by the living God.' It is likewise affirmed that the Apostle Paul called upon God to bear witness to the truth of his words and that this was obviously an oath. It is affirmed that oaths were enjoined by the Mosaic law, and that Christ did not abrogate them, and only set useless, pharisaically hypocritical oaths aside." Ibid., 86.

[42]Ibid., 89. Jesus bids us not to contradict our reason and conscience by an oath of allegiance to Czar, Emperor, Kaiser, King, Queen, President, or General, for some day they may require us to kill our fellowmen. Then we will be forced either to break our oath or commit crimes of which we would not otherwise have dreamed. Wilhelm II once addressed some naval recruits who had just taken the oath of allegiance, reminding them that, if commanded to shoot their fathers, they were bound by oath to obey him. As in the Roman Empire of Jesus' day so also in all nations today, people are recruited and trained for wholesale murder called war. They are induced by the swearing of oaths to entrust their consciences to the keeping of others. Cf. Maude, *Tolstoy and his Problems*, 17.

[43]Ibid., 91.

> it is persistently instilled into us that it is our bounden duty . . . to oppose
> our enemy.[44] We have grown so used to calling "a Christ-loving army"
> the men who devote their lives to murder, who put up prayers to Christ for
> victory over the enemy, whose pride and glory are in murder . . . that it
> now appears to us that Christ did not forbid war.[45]

But such chicanery cannot be deduced from the text. Throughout the Gospels, the word "enemy" is used "not of a private, but of a common enemy, a national enemy."[46] Christ speaks of the Mosaic regulations concerning a national enemy. He combines in a single expression "to hate, to wrong an enemy," all the various precepts dispersed through the Scriptures by which the Hebrews are enjoined to oppress, kill, and destroy other nations. And he says: "You have been told that you shall love your own people and hate the enemies of your nation, but I say unto you that you love all without distinction of their nationality."[47]

The establishment of the Kingdom of God on earth depends upon our fulfillment of these five commandments of Jesus. If people would only obey them, there would be eternal peace on earth. But instead of obeying, people say they are too weak and Jesus' commandments are too hard. Instead of doing what Jesus says, people believe that Jesus himself will establish the Kingdom of God quite independently of us when he comes again at his appointed time to judge the living and the dead.[48] Why do we say Jesus' commandments are too hard and impracticable? Because, Tolstoy wrote, we have been indoctrinated by Paul and all the catechism of the Church in the single conviction "that the doctrine of Christ is good but cannot be put into practice."[49] It is asserted everywhere that man has no need "to strive after what is best for himself; he has only to believe that Christ redeemed him from sin to become sinless, that is, perfectly good."[50] "This teaching . . . calls eternal life the true life, that is, a life which nobody has ever seen

---

[44]Ibid.,, 94.

[45]Ibid., 99.

[46]Texts cited include Luke 1:71, 20:43.

[47]Ibid. 96.

[48]Ibid., 104-105.

[49]Ibid., 109.

[50]Ibid., 111.

and which does not exist. And the life which is, the only life which we know, which we lead, and which mankind has ever led, is, according to this teaching, a fallen wicked life."[51] The problem of evil is understood and resolved not in terms of man's intellectual and moral commitment to the eternal law of Christ but is instead defined dogmatically in terms of the metaphysical apple which Adam ate. In short, the problem of evil is defined in such a way that it no longer applies to human beings.

> Adam sinned . . . and we all fell irrevocably, and all our endeavours to live rationally are useless, and even godless. [Theology tells me that] I am irrevocably bad, and I must know it. My salvation does not lie in the fact that I can order my life by my reason and, having learnt to know good from evil, do what is best. No, Adam sinned once for all, and Christ has once for ever set the evil right; and all that is left me to do is to mourn over the fall of Adam and rejoice in my salvation through Christ.

Because of this, all love of good and truth and all endeavors to enlighten life by reason are deemed unimportant, "they are all vainglory and pride."[52]

> The dogma of the fall and of the redemption of man has closed the most important and lawful domain of man's activity to him and has excluded from the whole sphere of human knowledge the knowledge of what man must do to be happier and better. [In fact] the teaching of morality called ethics has quite disappeared from our so-called Christian society. Neither believers nor unbelievers ask themselves how we ought to live and how we must use our reason which is given us; but they ask themselves, "Why is our life here not such as we fancied it to be and when will it be such as we wish it to be?"[53]

What shall we do then? Now that we understand the commandments of Christ, we shall have faith in the truth and commit ourselves entirely to it. "The foundation of faith is a true comprehension of life which enables

---

[51]Ibid., 112.

[52]Ibid., 113.

[53]Ibid., 117. Confucianism deals with moral improvement, Judaism with obeying God's covenant, Buddhism with escaping life's evils, Socrates with improvement in the name of reason, Stoicism with rational liberty,etc., but in Christianity there is, complains Tolstoy, no place for ethics, only for belief in substitutionary atonement and otherworldliness, the hoped-for perfect state of ideal bliss to be brought in by *deus ex machina* at the παρουσία. "If men would but keep from ruining their own lives and expecting someone from outside to come and help them—either Christ on the clouds with the flourish of trumpets or some historical law. . . . No one will help them if they do not help themselves." Ibid., 125.

man to distinguish what is important and good in life from what is unimportant and bad.''[54] ''Faith needs no promise of reward.''[55] ''He who has understood this doctrine of Christ can require no strengthening of his faith. Faith, according to Christ, is based on the light, on the truth.''[56]

''There are only two ways open to us,'' Tolstoy wrote,

> our teachers tell us that ''we must either believe our spiritual pastors and obey them and those that are in authority over us and take an active part in the evil they organize or else leave the world and enter a monastery, deprive ourselves of food and sleep, let our bodies rot on an iron pillar, bend and unbend our bodies in endless genuflections, and do nothing for our fellow creatures.'' Thus, a man must either confess the doctrine of Christ to be impractical and live contrary to it or renounce the life of this world which is but a species of slow self-murder.

The second option is based on the erroneous idea that it is better to leave the world than to submit to its temptations. The monastic escape was the option Jonah elected when he fled from association with the depraved inhabitants of Nineveh. ''But God shows him that he is a prophet—whose one duty is to make known the truth to those who have gone astray and that he must not flee from them but live amongst them.''[57] This was the delusion that Christ overcame in the strength of the spirit before he came back into Galilee to pass his life among publicans, Pharisees, and sinners, teaching them the truth. Those who follow Christ in this way will no more avoid suffering than will the wicked:

> The chances of suffering may be the same for both, with the difference that the followers of Christ will be ready to bear them, while the followers of the world will use all their endeavors to avoid them; the followers of Christ will suffer but will know that their suffering is necessary for the good of humanity, while the followers of the world will suffer without knowing the reason why they suffer.[58]

---

[54]Ibid., 158.

[55]Ibid., 162.

[56]Ibid., 164.

[57]Ibid., 168.

[58]Ibid., 172-73.

The problem with the first option lies in the preoccupation of the Church with the metaphysical side of Christ's teaching to the complete neglect of its ethical requirements:

> And this metaphysical teaching, with the rites which form part of it, losing more and more of its fundamental sense, reached its present point: it has become a teaching which explains the mysteries of life in heaven, gives the most complicated rites for divine worship, but at the same time gives no religious teaching at all concerning life on earth.[59]

Consequently,

> the world, with its social adjustments consecrated by the Church, has now thrown the Church aside . . . and now lives without it. The Church is done with, and it is impossible to conceal the fact. All those who really live and do not drearily vegetate in our European world have left the Church.[60]
>
> The Church, whose members tried to unite men by persuading them that it was necessary for salvation blindly to believe that the truth was in her, is no more. But the Church whose followers are not united by promises of reward but by good deeds and lives will live forever. That Church does not consist of men who cry "Lord, Lord," and live in sin but of men who hear his words and follow his commandments.[61]

Tolstoy's exposition of the Sermon on the Mount has such force because he discerned so clearly the Lukan *Leitgedanken* of love of neighbor and enemy. It seemed obvious to Tolstoy that moral teaching of any kind could not coexist with allowing a person to kill another human being for any reason whatsoever:

> No other command of Christ has been as much neglected, misinterpreted, and belittled as this, for it seems impossible to meet force by anything but force. . . . Yet it is in this point that the deepest wisdom of Christianity is to be found without which all other beliefs remain incomplete. For this command when followed out solves a problem whose abstract solution has defeated the greatest endeavours of all philosophers.[62]

---

[59]Ibid., 204.

[60]Ibid., 207.

[61]Ibid., 236.

[62]Paul Roubiczek, "The Struggle for Virtue," *The Misunderstanding of Man* (London: Routledge and Kegan Paul, 1949) 210-11.

Tolstoy has many critics. Most of them praise him highly for his life but reject his teaching as invalid, often without really saying why.[63] Many critics see in his practical religion nothing but "a destructive intellectual force that undermined all regulations, human and divine."[64] The anarchistic element in Tolstoy's social and political gospel is depicted as an Asiatic penchant for Utopias or as an aristocratic passion for "a bucolic placidity of the soul." This "passim" was inspired by Rousseau's return to the rusticity of nature and exemplified in Tolstoy's pedagogical ideal of "letting all the children out of the benches."[65]

As an officer in Russia's "Christ-loving army," Tolstoy had occasion to observe how men practice violence against their fellows, and, as a member of the court of justice, he had occasion to perceive how people take political advantage of one another. He noticed how the Czarist government oppressed the people and discerned that redemption could come only through the abolition of its misrule.[66] He studied the Gospels and con-

---

[63]To one such critic Tolstoy replied: "The Christian world has been waiting for eighteen hundred years to hear why it should not obey the commandments of Christ. Dean Farrar tells us that he knows why, but he cannot spare the time to inform us.—What a pity!" Cited by Aylmer Maude, "Editor's Note," *A Confession* and *The Gospel in Brief* (Oxford & London, 1933) xviii. (With a few notable exceptions, most of the vast polemic literature against Tolstoy is so lacking in integrity that it does not warrant mention.)

[64]For example, Thomas Mann, "Goethe and Tolstoy," *Three Essays* (London, 1932) 11.

[65]Ibid., 12, 122. In his *Confessions* Tolstoy wrote: "I have read the whole of Rousseau, the whole twenty volumes, including the lexicon of music. What I felt for him was more than enthusiasm; it was worship. At fifteen I wore round my neck, instead of the usual crucifix, a medallion with his picture. I am so familiar with some of the passages in his works that I feel as though I had written some of them myself."

[66]While Tolstoy's sympathies with the peasants clearly identified him with the class struggle of the proletariat to overthrow the bourgeoisie, it would be entirely wrong to misconstrue Tolstoy's "anarchy" as revolutionary in the Marxist sense, for Lenin and Plekhanov most sharply attacked his opposition to the employment of revolutionary means to attain socialist ends and were particularly annoyed by the way his idea of nonresistance discouraged radical political action; cf. Theodore Redpath, *Tolstoy* (London, 1960) 25. What Marx and Tolstoy had in common they got from a common source, as reflected in Marx's indictment of the capitalist ethic in these words: "Does not every moment of your life prove your theories to be lies? Do you consider it wrong to resort to courts when others take advantage of you? But the Apostle writes that to do so is wrong. Do you hold forth your right cheek when someone strikes you on the left or do you not prosecute for injuries? But the Gospel forbids it. . . . does not the greater part of your legal processes and the greater part of your civil laws concern possession? But you have been told, that your treasures are not of this world." Tolstoy, Ges. Ausg. I, S. 246, cited by G. Bornkamm, *Jesus of Nazareth* (London: Hodder & Stoughton, 1963) 202.

cluded that "Christianity in its true sense puts an end to the state. It was so understood from its very beginning, and for that Christ was crucified."[67] Since true Christianity demands conscientious objection to conscription, which constitutes the keystone of the modern state, Tolstoy reasoned that the increase of Christianity implies the decrease of the state until all governments are replaced by the spontaneity of brotherly love without oaths of allegiance, legal proceedings, or war taxes to maintain military defenses. According to Machiavelli, nonresistance would only encourage tyrants to be more tyrannical. But Tolstoy was more optimistic about the triumph of good over evil. Even when that triumph was not exemplified within the ambiguity of the human situation, Tolstoy had no other counsel but to encourage all people everywhere to obey the commandments of Jesus "as far as possible" and not to despair if they could not do so perfectly.

Tolstoy wavered between advocating the Christian ideal on principle—on the grounds that life has no other meaning—and appealing to the pragmatist with the universal wisdom that doing only the truth is really worthwhile. Tolstoy gave the world an ideal towards which all people ought to work, but, given the present state of the world, he did not leave a blueprint for carrying it out. Since we do not criticize explorers for providing maps of territories as yet unexplored, it is perhaps sufficient if prophets behold the land that is very far off even if they overlook the difficulties weaker pilgrims encounter in holding to the true course.

Despite the special feeling of reverence his nation had for him, Tolstoy did not appear to make any allowances for the fact that it might be harder for others than for himself to refuse to wage war, pay taxes, or take oaths. Yet it is clear from his writings that he anticipated persecution and prepared himself for it. In fact, Tolstoy's whole life was an inner struggle to know and do the truth in accord with reason and conscience, a struggle which most of his critics, and especially theologians, regard as foolish. They acknowledge that Tolstoy has bequeathed to us "a precious legacy of profoundly suggestive ethical and spiritual thought" but discredit his precepts as erroneous because they are "born out of due season" and "offered to men before their minds are ripe for their reception."[68] Perhaps the

---

[67]"The Kingdom of God is Within You," in *The Kingdom of God and Peace Essays*, 281.

[68]Alexander H. Craufurd, *The Religion and Ethics of Tolstoy* (London, 1912) 81-82.

minds of those accustomed to adjusting their commitments to the advantages they expect to gain will never be "ripe" enough to receive the radical sayings of Jesus that the prophets of all subsequent ages have felt compelled to echo. Nor does it appear that the maturity of mankind is furthered by silencing or discrediting its prophets, especially those prophets who still hold out hope for progress.

The merit of Tolstoy's practical Christianity lies precisely in his attempt to find a way of living a Christian life in the world as it now is rather than in some otherworldly utopia. It seemed quite clear to Tolstoy that, if people would simply obey the command of love, they would be freed from the political, social, and economic injustices in which they are now caught. If people were only more willing to help than to exterminate one another, if they could overcome their personal selfishness and be guided by a loving and growing sense of human community, the social ideal would be easily accomplished. The chief difficulty lies in one's unwillingness to take Jesus that seriously; hence, his commandments remain unfulfilled and appear remote and impracticable. Tolstoy believed that no individual lacks the divine resources to achieve something constructive and lasting. If he wills to do so and commits himself wholeheartedly to the task of doing what is right, that is, doing what commends itself to his reason and corresponds with his conscience, a person will progressively discover new resources commensurate with this growing venture. Tolstoy never wearied of urging the possibility for everyone to fulfill the commandments of Jesus to a considerable extent even if the ideal is not yet attainable.

> The Christian teaching seems to make life impossible only when people mistake the indication of an ideal for the laying down of a rule. . . . In reality those principles [of the Sermon on the Mount] alone make true life possible, and without them it cannot exist.[69]
> The ideal is love of all men, but what is possible for everyone is not to be angry with men and not to hurt them; the ideal is to have complete trust and to live entirely in the present without wanting security for the future, but what is possible is not to take an oath so as to bind oneself in the future; the ideal is nonresistance, but what is possible is not to hate other nations and not to fight against them. . . . He who wants to swim across a swiftly flowing river will not swim directly towards his goal on the other bank but against the current.[70]

---

[69]*The Kingdom of God*, 117.

[70]Paraphrase of Tolstoy by Roubiczek, "The Struggle for Virtue," 210; cf. *The Kingdom of God*, 120-22.

Merezhkovsky, the great Russian critic, said that the artistic work of Tolstoy "is at bottom nothing else than one tremendous diary kept for fifty years, one endless, explicit confession."[71] Thomas Mann charged that all of Tolstoy's works were inspired by "the impulse a man feels to 'fixate' his life, to exhibit its development, to celebrate his own destiny in set literary form and passionately invoke the sympathy of his contemporaries and posterity."[72] In short, Mann claimed that all of Tolstoy's religious and artistic works were motivated by nothing but self-love and self-pity, a form of self-deception and self-mortification exemplified in "a clumsy attempt at spiritualization" as when Tolstoy refers to his twelve literary volumes as so much "artistic twaddle."[73] Granted that every prophet has something of a Messiah complex, what does it mean to "explain" Tolstoy's self-denial as a form of self-love? And what does it say for the critics who reject the author's self-estimate so as to impose their own self-contradictory judgments upon his personality?[74]

Perhaps Tolstoy was altogether too austere and cold in treating religion exclusively as morality rather than art. If he only could have taken those dogmas of the church which were so offensive to him less literally and more symbolically, he need not have suffered half so much within or without. Why could so great an artist not have adopted a figurative, mythical, or poetic understanding of the divinity of Christ, the fall of man, and the resurrection of Jesus? Then he, with so many others, could have continued to admire the splendor of these truths even without denying those, whose imagination is limited to that option, the intrinsic value of believing in them. Why must everything beautiful and abiding be either literally true or fraudulent and absurd?[75] And why must the uniquely Christian attitude towards

---

[71]Cited by Mann, "Goethe and Tolstoy," 15.

[72]Ibid., 16.

[73]Ibid., 23.

[74]Tolstoy's humility and integrity are reflected in his response to the Synod that excommunicated him: "I do not believe my faith to be the one indubitable truth for all time, but I see no other that is plainer, clearer, or answers better to all the demands of my reason and my heart; should I find such a one, I shall at once accept it." Cited by Maude, "Editor's Note," xxiii.

[75]Leo Chestov, "The Last Judgment, Tolstoy's Last Works," In Job's Balances (London, 1932) 90, accused Tolstoy of being "one of the priests of the supreme lie" for teaching us "to exhibit the beautiful side of existence and to hide the truth" and saw in this dichotomy the basis for his "madness."

life always be defined in negative terms of self-denial? Why is there so little self-acceptance in Tolstoy's plea for universal love?[76] Why should God's
will and human will not be regarded as complementary rather than at odds,
so that one may be fulfilled only at the expense of the other?

By experience Tolstoy observed people to be fundamentally egoistic
and therefore fundamentally bad—quite in accord with the doctrine of
"original sin" which he so vigorously opposed—and yet he advocated belief in the essential goodness of humanity, although this goodness seemed
nowhere in evidence. This unresolved ambiguity within Tolstoy's anthropology is further complicated by his appeal to reason over against faith.
Since the proof for the reasonableness of Christianity as a way of life is
logically hard to establish—even in the face of death—it is a safe premise
to posit that, while egoistic impulses may not always be right, the will of
the infinitely good God can never be false.[77] Yet Tolstoy also knew that
the way in which the will of God becomes relevant for the human situation
is discerned not by reason alone but by that divine faculty within us known
as conscience.

Most of Tolstoy's unresolved tensions and ambiguities somehow relate to his conversion, which has often been characterized as an unhappy
and morbid depression of mystical madness. The ominous description his
wife Sonya gave of his newly converted state has been the source of much
speculation.[78] Of what then did his "madness" consist? Chestov replies:
"His 'madness' lay in the fact that everything which had formerly seemed
to be real and to have a solid existence now appeared illusory, whereas all
that had seemed illusory and unreal now seemed to him the only reality."[79]
Before and especially after his conversion, Tolstoy excelled in contrasting

---

[76]Mann "Goethe and Tolstoy," 64, explains Tolstoy's asceticism in terms of his conscious disgust for his ugly face and uncomely body. According to his *Confessions* Tolstoy
first became aware of his unattractive physique as a small child while being bathed in a
wooden tub and observing his little body with the ribs visible on the breast in front.

[77]Cf. Redpath, *Tolstoy*, 22.

[78]"His eyes are strange and staring, he hardly speaks at all, he is like a being from another world, and is positively not capable of thinking of earthly things . . . he is sunk in his
work. His head pains him all the time. He is very much changed and become a rigid and
practising Christian. But he has got grey, his health is weak, he is sadder and more silent
all the time . . . fallen into a kind of despairing apathy. He ate nothing and did not sleep,
sometimes literally wept." Cited by Mann, "Goethe and Tolstoy," 33.

[79]"The Last Judgment . . . ," 93.

two ways of looking at reality—as he so ingeniously expressed in his un-finished short story, "The Morning after the Ball," written in 1903. Here he obviously intended to confront his youthful conception of life as a fas-cinating "ball" with his new vision of life as the running of a "gauntlet." The social life he once described in such idyllic colors in *Anna Karenina* had become a burden to him; the festivities in which he was once a leading attraction he now loathed.

How really different was Tolstoy's "madness" from that of the prophet Hosea or Jesus?[80] The spiritual vision of even the greatest of the prophets often appears confusing, perplexing, incoherent or even inconsistent.[81] But by what criteria may we therefore reject the prophets as abnormal and the gospel they proclaim under compulsion as irrelevant while acknowledging that they have discerned more clearly and experienced more deeply the ul-timate issues of life? "The minds of God-intoxicated thinkers often seem for a time ill-balanced. Yet are they the world's best regenerators. Leo Tolstoy might have said with Paul, 'Whether we be beside ourselves, it is God; or, whether we be sober, it is for your cause.' "[82] Concerning him-self Tolstoy testified: "There is a Power enabling me to discern what is good, and I am in touch with that Power; my reason and conscience flow from it, and the purpose of my conscious life is to do its will, that is, to do good."[83]

Tolstoy is not merely a great artist gone astray, whose religious fan-tasies deserve little claim to serious consideration, especially by theolo-

---

[80]Cf. Hosea 9:7—"The prophet is a fool, the man of the spirit is mad." Plato held sub-lime madness to be a condition often inseparable from divine inspiration. Cf. *Phaedrus*, 244-45: "There is a madness which is a divine gift, the greatest blessings have come to us in madness . . . for prophecy is madness . . . ;" cited by A. Heschel, *The Prophets* (New York, 1962) 392. Socrates ascribed the wisdom to discern good from evil to personal guid-ance by a spirit (δαιμόνιον), and, if our time possessed a Delphic Oracle, might it not ascribe to Tolstoy a place alongside Tiresias?

[81] Tolstoy sought to live as consistently as possible, yet he could not give all his prop-erty to the poor, for to do so would anger his wife and children and thus violate the first commandment of Jesus. So he had to contend with the reproach of being "inconsistent" even though he lived as simply and frugally as possible and expended much energy and time helping others. During the 1891-92 famine, he was instrumental in procuring and dis-tributing relief to many starving peasants, and later he assisted the emigration of the per-secuted Doukhobors to Canada.

[82]Craufurd, *The Religion and Ethics of Tolstoy*, 154.

[83]Cited by Maude, *Tolstoy and His Problems*, 14.

gians. He who so denigrates him completely fails to discern the vital connection between his art and his religion: the one invariably displaced the other as Tolstoy eventually became the great prophet for the Russian peasants who had so long and so pathetically endured so much. It is not hard to see how his famous novels became a kind of prelude to his passionate and earthy religion. He was such a tortured soul because he identified so deeply with the tortures of Christ.[84] The questions this moral and religious teacher posed to the church during the last thirty-two years of his life demand answers, not just enlightened dismissal or psychological evasion. If Tolstoy has not understood the Sermon on the Mount correctly, it is up to us to say where and how he erred. We may criticize Tolstoy's interpretation, but we cannot afford to ignore it. Even in our critique we ought to remember that "polemic against 'fanatics' is to a large extent polemic against the Sermon on the Mount and criticism of Jesus himself. Such polemic and such criticism may be necessary, but one should know what one is doing."[85]

---

[84]For Répin's famous painting of the scourging of Christ, Tolstoy wrote: "The soldiers are flogging Christ and it is pitiable to see his suffering. It is yet more pitiable to think that they have not yet ended. We, like the soldiers and even worse than they, still torture him. The soldiers did not know who he was, where he came from, or what he had brought to men. But we know who he is, know whence he came, know that he brought us salvation, and yet we torture him as they did and even more cruelly. Every day and every hour we add to his sufferings—the sufferings of him who came to save us. Everything we do to our fellowmen we do to him. When we repulse a hungry beggar or take advantage of a man's need, when we are haughty or lord it over a fellow creature keeping him at a distance and despising him, we torture—more painfully than Pilate's soldiers did—the Christ who told us to be one with himself. When we infringe upon the conjugal law . . . [of] him who said that man should not put asunder what God has joined. . . . When we do violence to men and return them evil for evil, when we torture men and shed human blood—are we not torturing him . . . ? We torture Christ and he will not cease to suffer at our hands until we fulfil his commandment—to love one another as he loved us." Cited by Maude, "Editor's Note," xxiii-xxiv.

[85]Hans Windisch, *The Meaning of the Sermon on the Mount* (Philadelphia: The Westminster Press, 1950) 172.

Thoughts from the Mount of Blessing by Ellen G. White (Mountain View CA: Pacific Press, 1956; first published in 1896) conveys the conviction that Christ the Law-Giver is also the Life-Giver and that "through faith in Him everyone can reach the standard held up in His words" (viii). As in nature "so there are great principles of righteousness to control the life of all intelligent beings, and upon conformity to these principles the well-being of the universe depends'' (48). Consequently, Jesus' mission, according to White, was ''to show the spiritual nature of the law, to present its far-reaching principles, and to make plain its eternal obligation'' (49). ''This standard [referring to Matthew 5:48] is not one to which we cannot attain. In every command or injunction that God gives there is a promise, the most positive, underlying the command. God has made provision that we may become like unto Him, and He will accomplish this for all who do not interpose a perverse will and thus frustrate His grace'' (76).

George A. Barton considered what he designates ''the Royal Law'' of Matthew 5:21-48 to consist essentially in Oriental hyperbole characteristic of the Levant whose forms of speech are ''much more graphic, picturesque, and exaggerated'' than our own (*JBL* 37 [1918]: 54-65). To illustrate his point, he cites the El-Amarna correspondence of a Syrian ruler addressing an Egyptian king as ''my lord, my sun, my sun-god . . . seven times seven I prostrate myself'''—all of which seems quite unrealistic to Barton. ''A Syrian's chief purpose in a conversation,'' explains Barton, ''is to convey an impression by whatever suitable terms and not to deliver his message in scientifically accurate terms. He expects to be judged not by what he *says* but by what he *means*'' (59). Barton regrets Tolstoy's going astray in attempting to take Jesus' words literally and sees himself faced with the duty of thinking more clearly about these matters in applying his hyperbolic ''key'' to the meaning of Jesus' sayings, though he confesses to some ''hesitation and distrust'' lest ''he in some way impair the high ethical standard erected by Jesus'' (59).

''When the world is filled with ideal individuals and the nations have become as ethical as Jesus demands that individuals shall be,'' then, surmises Barton, ''it will be safe to make an extension of the command regarding love of enemies, to imply that it means not to kill,'' as Tolstoy in his 'misunderstanding' did (60). Meanwhile, Barton would have us realize that God not only gives life but also takes life in the ongoing evolutionary process ''carried on by struggles in which many of his creatures have been his agents in taking life'' (59). Barton therefore admonishes us not to shirk the tasks of this evolutionary process ''even if at times they are gruesome.'' (60). Whatever that may involve, Barton knows that so paradoxical a saying, as ''resist not one that is evil,'' is impossible for one to take literally and be a worthy citizen or a decent person'' (63).

WILHELM HERRMANN:
THE SERMON ON THE MOUNT
AS GESINNUNGSETHIK

The most widespread and most serious mistake in the interpretation of these words [of the Sermon on the Mount] is to consider them all to be laws which are to be fulfilled in every case. That is impossible. . . . If he [Jesus] had intended his words to be general rules, he would have been much worse than the teachers of the law whom he attacked. . . . We follow him only if we have the same mind [Gesinnung] and on that basis seek from within our stance—as independently as he did—the direction towards the eternal goal. But, if we follow any particular words solely because they have been transmitted to us as words of Jesus, . . . we then precisely thereby offer resistance to the man who sought to bind us to himself.[1]

Wilhelm Herrmann,[2] in his own unique way, sought to bridge the distance between the ethic of Jesus and the moral demands of contemporary life without succumbing either to the legalism of Tolstoy, on the one hand, or the duplicity of Naumann, on the other. Herrmann is the chief exponent of the so-called *Gesinnungsethik* (or ethic of disposition) which emphasizes attitudes over against acts. As a disciple of Tholuck and Ritschl and a forerunner of Barth and Bultmann, he masterfully and almost convincingly demonstrates how a theologian who assumes the validity of the im-

---

[1]Wilhelm Herrmann, *Die sittliche Weisungen Jesu. Ihr Mißbrauch und ihr richtiger Gebrauch* (Göttingen: Vandenhoeck und Ruprecht, 1907²) 54-55.

[2]Wilhelm Herrmann was born in 1846 near Schönhausen on the Elbe and educated at Halle under the influence of Tholuck and later Ritschl. He taught theology at Halle from 1874 to 1888, after which he was professor of systematic theology for 24 years at Marburg. His major works include: *Mystik und Theologie* (1876), *Die Religion im Verhältnis zum Welterkennen und zur Sittlichkeit* (1879), *Der Verkehr des Christen mit Gott* (1886), *Ethik* (1901), *Die sittliche Weisungen Jesu* (1904), and *Dogmatik*, ed. M. Rade, (1925).

peratives of Kant and the authenticity of the eschatology of Jesus can, by modernizing Jesus, come to terms with his offensive and incomprehensible teaching in the Sermon on the Mount.

At the outset, Herrmann shrewdly deliberates on those sayings of Jesus which prohibit ''cares'' for the economic necessities of life (Matthew 6:19ff.). He dismisses as improbable the suggestion that in the Galilean country of Jesus' day nature may have provided so abundantly as to obviate every necessity for human labor.[3] By defending our means of production we give priority to our future needs over against the present needs of others. In striking contrast, Jesus does not condone self-interest but advocates giving loans without usury and satisfying without question and beyond expectation every claim to our possessions. As Herrmann reasons, ''it is impossible to do business in the economic world on the basis of such principles.''[4]

One might rationalize that, despite the cares of vocational life, one could retain a free heart, but, while Herrmann shares this view, he denies that it is what Jesus meant. His word, ''Do not lay up for yourselves treasures on earth,'' confronts human beings with the decision either to orient themselves entirely to eternal values or to permit themselves to be bound by earthly treasures in such a way as to become enslaved by them. In the final analysis, it is impossible to reconcile with a good conscience our confession that we wish to and need to obey Jesus while continuing in possession of—and, as Jesus would say, in bondage to—capital:[5]

> By his assumption that our possessions belong only to us and that we are free without hesitation to dispose of them, Jesus transgresses the intactness of the social order by which we are bound to others in community. The fact itself that Jesus is so completely indifferent toward the social order separates him from us. But he goes much further. With harsh words he demands that we disassociate ourselves from these orders. Anyone wishing to follow Jesus soon discovers that family ties become bonds which one must tear. Unless one does so, one is separated from Jesus. He who does not discern in Father and Mother that which is to be hated cannot be Jesus' disciple (Luke 14:26).[6]

---

[3] ''Es war dort wie bei uns. Die Saat wuchs von selbst; aber erst mußt sie gesät werden.'' *Die sittliche Weisungen Jesu*, 15.

[4] Ibid., 16.

[5] Ibid., 18.

[6] Ibid.

But Jesus is even more insistent and clear in his rejection of the state. He who cannot condone compulsion and the power struggle not only cannot participate in the state but in his deepest inclination conflicts with it. For him the state is that which ought not to be. In propagating this attitude he works towards the state's dissolution. Thus, Jesus brings us into conflict with the social responsibilities to which we cling. . . .[7]

We can fulfill no political responsibilities without compelling others. . . . But how can we do that in opposition to the word of Jesus, "Among you it shall not be so"? Magisterial Christendom appears merely to admire Jesus' word but in effect to do the opposite. These thoughts have repeatedly inspired passionate attack against the church for celebrating Christ as God but treating his word as though it were impotent over against the world he wanted overcome.

"And," surmises Herrmann, "it is still that way with us: obedience to the words of Jesus and serious moral commitment to cultural responsibilities seek to exclude one another. Whether we hold to Jesus as our *Führer* has become the vital issue of Christendom. . . ." According to Herrmann's diagnosis, "correct insight" into the Sermon on the Mount "is hindered through a misuse of Jesus' ethical counsels (*Weisungen*)." This grave misuse is kept from detection through disregard of the historical situation from which a good deal of the content of Jesus' words is derived and "is supported by an astounding disregard for the person of Jesus Christ himself."[8]

Instead of resolving this ambiguity, the Church delegated the irreconcilable options of obeying Jesus and cultivating our own interests to two distinct classes, so that the laity might amass mammon while the clergy abstains from it. The laity produced earthly goods and received in exchange spiritual goods in order that they too, despite their imperfect obedience, could be saved. "Thus, the very contradiction which at first threatened to make Christian society impossible became the basis for its development." This system had the advantage not only of a division of labor that made sense to the common man but also of perpetuating the impression "that life in the discipleship of Jesus is an exceptionally high thing" quite beyond the potentiality of the average mortal.[9] This ingenious arrangement made possible the existence of a "mixed" society in which

---

[7]Ibid., 19-20.

[8]Ibid., 22.

[9]Ibid., 23.

each contributed according to his ability and received according to his need. Beyond realistically meeting all the demands of nature and spirit, the strength of this social order lay in its political integration; here, it evaded the essense of the moral dilemma. The conflict of commands once left to be resolved within the inner life of the individual was now built into the very constitution of the church by nature of its task to rule the world.[10] Those who resolved the moral dilemma by this political solution thereby ceased to be ethically responsible. In escaping from the world the monk evades the commands of Jesus while the lives of those remaining faithful in their secular vocations are poisoned by the reproach of having rejected the way of perfection. Perhaps they can temporarily console themselves in supposing that before God the way of perfection is optional, not mandatory. But invariably they must acknowledge that such a God is fictitious. The living God of our conscience unequivocally demands that we do what we acknowledge to be perfect. Because the illusion of perfection has put his conscience to sleep, the moral corruption is greater for the monk. Conscience in the Christian laity is much more sensitive and can lead to agonizing insecurity and unrest.[11]

Luther offered no solution to this moral dilemma. In fact, Herrmann claims that the success of the Reformation resulted in moral regression as the contrast between the words of Jesus and the affirmation of life in the world became progressively disguised.

> That we today still allow ourselves to be confused by the contrast between the meek and compassionate Jesus, on the one hand, and our desire and need for power, on the other hand, has to do with the fact that Luther never overcame this barrier. He also considered it to be self-evident that the Christian is at least obligated to obey every transmitted word of Jesus not expressly addressed to some individual, without asking whether what is demanded really also concerns him in his particular situation. But such obedience amounts to a flagrant misuse of Jesus' words, allowing a viable Christendom no other option than to divide into clergy and laity as a result of which both morally deteriorate.[12]

---

[10]"An die Stelle des Gegensatzes von Aufforderungen, der in dem inneren Leben des Einzelnen durchgekämpft werden sollte, war ein Gegensatz von Einrichtungen getreten, der durch die Weltherrschaft der Kirche vermittelt wurde. Die Menschen, die sich mit dieser politischen Lösung einer sittlichen Frage zufrieden geben, hören nun damit auf, sich sittlich zu verhalten, nicht bloß die Leichtsinnigen, sondern auch die Ernsten." Ibid., 24.

[11]Ibid., 25-26.

[12]Ibid., 27-29.

Jesus demanded unconditional obedience of his disciples. But never, argues Herrmann, did he demand that one should blindly obey his words without understanding them.[13] Luther failed to comprehend the meaning of many of Jesus' words simply because critical scholarship was still so undeveloped. Unless one learns to see Jesus in historical perspective, one invariably assumes that his words are all addressed to contemporary people in a modern situation.

It is a painful resignation, Herrmann admits, to be forced to realize that we have no word from Jesus telling us how to manage our economy and politics. Yet the one actual benefit of historical criticism is precisely that it frees us from this pain![14] Historical scholarship has established Jesus' oblivion concerning social responsibilities. Reflection upon the limits of state intervention in the economy of a people, for example, never occurred to Jesus. His apocalyptic *Weltanschauung* made him quite indifferent to the concerns of the future of society because, in his opinion, "society had no future at all, only an imminent end. Jesus saw that the beginning of world catastrophe had come and lived in the imminence of the final judgment."[15] Consequently, Jesus freed himself from what continues to bind us. Demanding the same detachment of those whom he sought to prepare for the new glory, he prohibited all accumulation of earthly treasure and in quiet resignation allowed cultural life and its social responsibilities bypass him.[16] In him we sense nothing of the zeal of a social reformer. Left without guidance from Jesus for our own situation, we are forced to fall back upon ourselves, "for the loosing of earthly attachments, to which Jesus urged his disciples, is impossible for us because our world is different." What was authentic for them would be self-deceit for us, since we are confronted not with the end of the world but with endless responsibilities with which it confronts us.

The eschatological mood of Jesus compels us to concede that we are removed from him to the extent that we do not genuinely share his pre-

---

[13]Ibid., 29.

[14]"Die Versagung des Möglichen kann uns schmerzen; mit der von uns selbst eingesehenen Unmöglichkeit finden wir uns ab." Ibid., 31.

[15]Herrmann holds the finality of the judgment rather than its imminence to be the primary motivation underlying Jesus' ethic. Cf. ibid., 53.

[16]Ibid., 32-33.

dominant belief in imminent world catastrophe and do not see in the future
of history only forebodings of doom:

> Because historical research has made this distinction clear to us, it ex-
> cludes for us a following of Jesus (*Nachfolge Jesu*) as the perfect ones of
> the Roman Church want to effect it. This is a great gain. For in the last
> analysis, this presumed *Nachfolge Jesu* ends in dishonesty.[17]

Manly energy is expended to ensnare people in childish ways. In the quest
to be freed from the world one sinks into a monastic barbarity constituting
the most flagrant secularization of humanity. By seeking to escape earthly
conflicts and goals so as to serve God in freedom, one exchanges the
boundless opportunities for serving God worthily in the world for the petty
rivalries of clerical confinement. Herrmann rejoices that historical research has finally exposed the impropriety and impossibility of following
Jesus on the false assumption that our present relation to the world could
either be identical with or derived from Jesus' own particular misson in
it.[18]

It is evident that Herrmann does not idealize Tolstoy for having shown
us how to apply the teachings of Jesus towards the destruction of *Kultur-
Christentum*. According to Herrmann, Tolstoy's anarchism has neither established nor proven the ethical possibility of applying Jesus' teaching as
the norm of life. Too many Protestants have praised Tolstoy as the path-
finder of ethical thought without diagnosing his misuse of Jesus' words as
a basic sickness within Christendom. Herrmann acknowledges the strength
of Tolstoy's individualism in dispensing with the dogmatic ballast of the
Church and in holding only to the words of Jesus, but he rejects Tolstoy
as naïve for not realizing that chaos would result if the principle of "nonresistance to evil" were adhered to as a general rule. Herrmann accounts
for Tolstoy's indifference toward the state by contending that Russia had

[17]Ibid., 35.

[18]"Die Versuche, Jesus in demjenigen nachzufolgen, was an seine besondere Aufgabe
in der Welt und an seine uns nicht gegebene Stellung zur Welt verknüpft war, - diese Be-
mühungen ohne allen Ernst des Notwendigen, haben die Sache so lange geschädigt, daß
unsere Freude sich nicht wird dämpfen lassen, wenn nun endlich wissenschaftliche Arbeit
die Unmöglichkeit eines solchen Unterfangens vor aller Augen stellt." Ibid., 35-36. "Wie
sinnlos . . . die Haltung moderner Christen ist, die die eschatologische Stimmung Jesu tei-
len zu müssen meinen, aber sich wohl hüten, die Dinge dieser Welt als gleichgültig zu be-
handeln. . . . " Ibid., 56.

not yet reached the point of historical development at which political power acquires moral dignity.[19]

Not only have we been freed from the yoke of the historical past,[20] but we are bound to the person of Jesus himself in order that we might discern his "mind" or attitude (*Gesinnung*). True righteousness concerns not so much the outward act as the true *Gesinnung*.[21] The Pharisees sought to keep the law in order to achieve their own righteousness, and in so doing they lost out on the essential intent of the law which was to establish true community (*Gemeinschaft*). By their slavish legalism to the letter of the law, they confessed that they had no eyes of their own to discern what is good. Jesus wanted us to realize "that we do not at all experience what is good through a word from outside, but that we must produce the unchanging direction of our volition from within ourselves."[22]

It is a most serious misunderstanding to interpret Jesus' sayings as universally applicable legal prescriptions or general rules to be kept by all people at all times in all circumstances. When we lack the *Gesinnung* of Jesus, we are tempted to fall back upon the legalism of imitating him by seeking to apply to our modern circumstances words he spoke for situations thousands of years ago. We may even find comfort and solace in the manifest awkwardness and difficulty encountered in that self-righteous endeavor known as *Nachfolge Jesu* without realizing that this impotent game has nothing to do with the spirit of Jesus. "The most widespread and most serious mistake in the interpretation of these words [of the Sermon on the Mount] is to consider them all laws which in every case are meant to be fulfilled."[23] It is most unlikely that Jesus would have desired his followers throughout all succeeding generations to cling legalistically to his transmitted words (the meaning of which, taken out of context, has become quite unintelligible) as if the *Gesinnung* he advocated were some dark mystery compelling blind obedience without understanding.

---

[19]Cf. ibid., 37-38.

[20]"des Einmaligen und Vergangenen."

[21]Ibid., 39-40.

[22]"Jesus hat uns vielmehr zu der Erkenntnis bringen wollen, daß wir überhaupt durch kein Wort von außen erfahren können, was gut sei, sondern aus uns selbst die unveränderliche Richtung unseres Wollens erzeugen müssen." Ibid., 44.

[23]Ibid., 54.

"Jesus did not demand of all his followers renunciation of possessions," Herrmann wrote. "Had he done so, he would indeed be a lawgiver
who reduces persons to slaves."[24] From Jesus' *Gesinnung* it does not follow, surmises Herrmann, that we should disregard God's good economic
gifts rather than employ them in his service. For us to "sell all" and not
"lay up treasures" would, as Herrmann concludes, surely deny the true
Gesinnung. Jesus does confront us with the decision to relinquish possessions and honor. But the decisive factor is not *what* we do but whether we
do whatever we do in joyful obedience to God rather than out of fear or
piety. What matters is not the act but the attitude.[25] This rules out the Roman Catholic misunderstanding of Jesus' teaching as a legalistic morality
intended to ensnare people and limit their free movement by exceptionally
harsh determinations known as "counsels of perfection."[26] People can
introspectively[27] discern for themselves what is morally right and necessary in any given situation. Jesus expects us to be morally responsible free
agents who discern the truth in any circumstance.

"Out of the independence of the true *Gesinnung* follows the boundlessness of the ethical task":[28] love of God and love of humanity.

> By love Jesus means the pure power of the spirit understood to be the
> highest energy of will.[29]. . . The love of the enemy [*Feindesliebe*] which
> Jesus demands is not an exceptional accomplishment, admirable but in-
> comprehensible, but a visible example of the will to personal communion
> [*Gemeinschaft*]."[30]

In contrast to justice, love is not determined by prescriptions but provides
its own guidelines. One cannot be commanded to love, for love is a state
of being, not a mode of action. The activity of love is rooted in itself and

---

[24]Wilhelm Herrmann, *Ethik* (Tübingen u. Leipzig, 1901) 127.

[25]"Er hat . . . nichts als Gerechtigkeit anerkannt, als die Gesinnung, die ihren eigenen
Weg geht." Ibid., 128.

[26]"Er [Jesus] hat nicht die großen Kinder heranbilden wollen, die als Heroen des Ab-
sonderlichen angestaunt werden, wie der heilige Franz, sondern er hat ernste Menschen
dazu anleiten wollen, sich klar zu machen, was für sie sittlich notwendig sei." Ibid., 131.

[27]That is, through *Selbstbesinnung*.

[28]Ibid., 130.

[29]*Die sittliche Weisungen*, 48.

[30]Ibid., 49.

is boundless.[31] According to the *Gesinnung* of Jesus, the "good" is the will to communion on the part of independent beings, the will to love.[32]

True love of neighbor is not based on common interests or mutual advantage. Herrmann explains how this misunderstanding resulted in the moral perversion of the foremost commandment to imply, "love your neighbor and hate your enemy," a possibility excluded by Jesus who insisted that we heap goodness upon our enemies, not with the intention of shaming them, but in an endeavor to establish genuine relations of communion with them. Rapprochement presupposes the willingness to overcome barriers. Apart from the will to communion, one experiences only a sense of guilt or duty that one ought to help others, an awareness readily limited by the rationalization that a person is obligated to love others only to the extent that he feels so inclined and insofar as his life's goals and duties are not thereby thwarted. Otherwise, "the commandment of love acquires the implicit meaning that, apart from our neighbor, we should also love ourselves,"[33] a rationalization the intention of which is to make the command of Jesus more reasonable and respectable. The love Jesus intends, however, does not seek its own nor does it conceive self-interest to be an independent concern.[34]

To seek to fulfill the commandment of *Feindesliebe* by an outer bearing of mutuality which veils an inner attitude of antipathy is sheer hypocrisy. This commandment can be obeyed only by a man of whose own volition it is the expression.[35] It is possible only as one exalts the value of the person of the enemy over against the nature of his offense. Jesus never overpowered people by the sheer force of his authority but sought to lead them to the insight that becoming one in *Gesinnung* constitutes human goodness. As we cultivate within ourselves this positive intention of true

---

[31]"He who knows only limited tasks has not yet achieved the inner dynamic and freedom of the ethical *Gesinnung*" qualified as love. Ibid., 51.

[32]"Für den Gerechten ist das gute Werk nicht etwas ihm abgerungenes, sondern die Frucht, die aus seinem eigenen Innern stammt." *Ethik*, 130.

[33]Ibid., 134.

[34]"Die Liebe, die Christus meint . . . wohnt nicht in einem geteilten Herzen, sondern ist selbst die höchste Einheitlichkeit der Gesinnung." Ibid.

[35]Wilhelm Herrmann, *The Moral Law. As Understood in Romanism and in Protestantism* (London, New York, 1904) 179. (ET of *Römische u. Evangelische Sittlichkeit*).

community with neighbors, strangers, and enemies, our whole life, like his, becomes a service to others.

This intention of winning the enemy for the common task is possible only as we within ourselves overcome the natural tendency to maintain our own life over against that of others. We accomplish this not by exterminating nature—for nature does not allow itself to be destroyed—but by confident commitment to God, who compensates us in the future for any impoverishment we may suffer now.[36]

> To give up entirely the struggle for honor among men; to be ready for unlimited acts of forgiveness for all vileness; to renounce all revenge, even showing oneself willing to suffer further from the insulting one—he, it seems, is no Christian who is not *able* for that. To love one's neighbor as oneself—that is to say, to set all one's hopes in life on attaining hearty and spiritual fellowship with the persons whom circumstances have placed near us—he is no Christian who does not *do* that.

But the commandments of Jesus

> can be fulfilled only by one who has them in his heart as the object of his own will. If, for instance, Jesus had required nothing more than that on being struck by a malicious person you should declare yourself ready to receive further blows, that would of course be easily fulfilled. . . . But by the commandment[37] Jesus asks for something quite different. You may easily allow yourself to be repeatedly struck and yet all the time be bitterly resenting it and wishing evil to the offender. The Christian is to stand to such an evildoer in a relation of spiritual freedom; he is not to allow himself to be forced by him into a longing for revenge, but he is to feel himself so united to him as to be even ready to suffer still further at his hands. What Jesus requires is not the weakness of a person who sets no value on himself but the highest superiority and strength. But this superiority of goodness towards an offender can evidently be evinced only by a man to whom the moral necessity for such behavior has been so disclosed that his moral sense is filled with it. The will so to act must arise in himself; that is, he must be subject in his inmost soul to what the commands require.[38]

After insisting that "we should always be filled with the disposition out of which springs readiness of mind to bear further indignities from the

---

[36]*Ethik*, 137.

[37]Matthew 5:39: "Resist not evil; whosoever strikes you on the right cheek, turn to him the other also." Cf. Luke 6:29.

[38]*The Moral Law*, 180-82.

offender,'' Herrmann cautions that ''we are by no means to exhibit that readiness in every case'' and most certainly not ''when it would not be an expression of love to our neighbor . . . but weakness or outer obedience to a mere rule.''[39] It appears that, despite all his idealistic sentiment about the true *Gesinnung*, Herrmann leaves us with a very subjective and indeed dubious criterion of inner discernment as to when it is necessary and when it is not necessary to act ethically. If we actually ''feel'' like loving our enemy and experience within our true self that irresistible urge of the pure energy of spirit and will to love and bless him, then, Herrmann allows, we might as well do so. But, cautions Herrmann, let him who wishes to follow Jesus seriously consider whether he really has the resources to go through with it.[40] Those not so compelled by their own independent will or not so convinced of their own resources ought not parade as paragons of virtue by making overtures of rapprochement towards others out of duty, guilt, or piety when within themselves they have not yet fully overcome the powerful competitive drives of nature which neither should nor could be suppressed.

One has the impression that the true *Gesinnung* which must precede any ethical action is, for Herrmann, a rather uncommon phenomenon among mortals. We are not actually given any indication by this champion of *Gesinnungsethik* as to whether this situation should or could be changed. In fact, on the dubious assumption that everything in our power somehow serves the cause of love, Herrmann appears to reflect a *Gesinnung* quite different from that of Jesus in holding that God ''compels us into conflict with others in order that we might really be something and accomplish something.'' Having justified the necessity of man's desperate struggle against his fellows as a natural phenomenon, Herrmann then claims Jesus as the one who gives man a good conscience.[41] The Christian may be appalled at the exercise of violence, but, when it becomes his vocation to practice it, he is instructed to do so with good conscience and constancy of mind (*Gesinnung*!) in the realization that the peace which guarantees our independence is not derived from ethical *Gesinnung* but necessarily

---

[39]Ibid., 182.

[40]*Ethik*, 134.

[41]*Die sittliche Weisungen*, 69.

established by force which is a product of nature and therefore cannot be changed.[42]

"War and love of neighbor stand in glaring contrast," Herrmann wrote. "Nothing appears more obvious than the Christian necessity to reject war and everything associated with it." But, according to Herrmann, since the final goal of ethical *Gesinnung* is the *Kulturstaat*, "it is hypocrisy to will the state but not admit that one wills war." Herrmann resolves the dilemma by concluding that, because war is necessary, it cannot therefore be unchristian.[43] After maintaining that the state is not Christian but "natural" and that to defend it Christians must not do what is ethical but what is necessary, Herrmann concludes his Ethics with the alleged confidence that "once the Christian comprehends the *ethical significance* of the state" (the reality of which he disclaims) "he will consider his vocation to consist, above all else, in obedience to the governing powers . . . and in promotion of patriotism among the people."[44]

Herrmann found the essence of Jesus' ethical *Gesinnung* in those counsels (*Weisungen*) "in which unconditional love is directly required,"[45] yet he discounted the desirability and feasibility of expressing such love by giving priority to the natural instinct and national necessity for self-defense. Against Schweitzer, Herrmann insisted that the *Feindesliebe* Jesus demands is not eschatologically conditioned by the expectation of an imminent end of history, for then such love could not be the will to *Gemeinschaft* within history and therefore it could not be true love. Instead of dismissing the ethic of Jesus on eschatological grounds, Herrmann found it more expedient to discredit the logic of discipleship by redefining Christian vocation as consisting "above all else" in unconditional obedience to

---

[42]"Es ist sinnlos, von einem Staat zu verlangen, dass er sich im Dienst anderer Staaten selbst verleugne. . . . Er ist eine Naturerscheinung, an der man arbeiten kann, um die sittlichen Zwecken dienstbar zu machen, an deren Natur aber Niemand etwas ändern kann." *Ethik*, 181.

[43]"Der Krieg an sich ist weder christlich noch unchristlich, weder sittlich noch unsittlich. Er ist in einer bestimmten geschichtlichen Lage die unabweisbare Äusserung der in der Kulturbewegung entwickelten Menschennatur. Für den Christen aber ist der Krieg sittlich gerechtfertigt, wenn er politisch richtig ist, als ein Akt der Selbstbehauptung eines Volkes in der Kulturaufgabe. . . . Den Krieg überhaupt zu negieren, kann aber nicht die Aufgabe des Christen sein. Ibid., 186.

[44]Ibid., 186-87.

[45]*Die sittliche Weisungen*, 57.

the state and in promotion of German patriotism. He despised Tolstoyan *Nachfolge Jesu* as naïve, impossible, irresponsible, and presumptuous; he quite discounted the feasibility of deducing from Jesus' teaching abiding ethical norms.

Despite his emphatic insistence that what really matters is whether one has the true *Gesinnung*, Herrmann has, however, failed to indicate what difference the true *Gesinnung* actually makes, how the *Gesinnung* of Jesus could be identified, or what makes it so admirable. Herrmann reproved Naumann for relinquishing the relevance of the Gospel and for resorting to a dual ethic, but his own attempt to span the gap of history has not elucidated the criteria on the basis of which Christians must at all costs identify with the modern *Kulturstaat* while in effect leaving their Jesus together with his *Gesinnung* out there on the other side of the bridge. Herrmann urges us to consider our historical removal from Jesus as a special grace which frees us from the sentimentality of relic worship. He might have said the bridge is love, but for that he would have been decried a *Schwärmer*. As it is, his *Gesinnungsethik* is insufficient basis for a hermeneutic and differs from Naumann's duplicity only by virtue of its lack of consistency and realism.

Herrmann's ethic is purely formal, entirely void of content.[46] From Kant he learned that a good will makes a good person and that the end of ethics is personal freedom. That is a meaningful insight, derived from Kant and not from Jesus, which illustrates the unchallenged assumption of his modern approach to the Sermon on the Mount that the *Gesinnung* of Jesus of Nazareth was identical with the *Gesinnung* of Herrmann of Marburg. Since Herrmann rejects all ethical precepts and all concrete demands of external authority, he assumes Jesus could have intended his Antitheses only as antitheses of legalism, formal ''expressions of energy,'' void of all material content. But Jesus' Sermon on the Mount originated not in Marburg but in Galilee, where Herrmann's antithesis between *Gesinnung* and *Gesetz* hardly applies. Obviously, Jesus intended a new attitude, but every Jew knew this

---

[46]''Nun müsste Herrmann konsequenterweise in seiner Ethik über Staat, Wirtschaft, Familie usw. schweigen. Aber das tut er nicht, weil er doch die Notwendigkeit empfindet, darüber etwas zu sagen. . . . Dieses Verhalten ist voller Widersprüche. Schließlich läuft es doch darauf hinaus, in der Kulturgemeinschaft zu bleiben und sie zu 'bessern.' Dann aber erhebt sich die Frage: *Wie* bessern? In welcher Richtung? Nach welchen Kriterien?'' Georg Wünsch, *Evangelische Wirtschaftsethik* (Tübingen: J. C. B. Mohr, 1927) 11.

meant a new obedience, not a new gnosis! True *Gesinnung* manifests itself in right behavior toward God (for example, almsgiving, prayer, fasting) and humankind (for example, reconciliation with neighbor, love of enemy). "Each tree is known by its fruit" (Luke 6:44). "Those who *do* God's will shall enter the Kingdom" (Matthew 7:21). "Why call me Lord and not *do* what I say?" (Luke 6:46). Herrmann has not convinced us that Jesus did not intend his commands to be understood and fulfilled literally. That we are intellectually or morally unwilling or unable to follow Jesus does not justify ascribing our own approach to life to Jesus' *Gesinnung*.[47]

---

[47]"Aus der Gesinnung heraus, in der wir mit Jesus einig sind, wollen wir den nationalen Staat, dessen Wesen und Aufgaben Jesus noch nicht kannte, und lassen uns dadurch nicht irremachen, wenn manches an diesem Gebilde der menschlichen Natur mit der Lebensführung und Stimmung Jesu in so grellem Widerspruch steht, wie die Waffenrüstung und ihr mutiger Gebrauch." *Die sittliche Weisungen*, 66.

Comparable to Herrmann, Ernest F. Scott interprets *The Ethical Teaching of Jesus* (New York: Macmillan, 1925) as true inwardness. "Hence he declares that the good or evil of an act consists wholly in its motive and that the moral task is nothing else than the right ordering of the inner life" (19). "If his words were taken literally, they would lead to dangerous consequences" (69). That pertains especially to Jesus' teaching on nonresistance which, says Scott, "may possibly be explained as little more than a prudential maxim" and applies only "to the case of an individual." According to Scott, Jesus was silent on political issues to avoid diverting attention from his religious message (78). "His concern is always with the inward principles of man's life, not with the framework" (81). Quite in keeping with his restriction of ethics to religious inwardness of the individual, Scott finds "no inconsistency" in waging war among Christian nations, "for Christianity is essentially a religion of courage." Furthermore, "it has always thought that men must be faithful unto death in what they conceive to be their duty and that compromise and submission are unworthy of the disciple of Christ" (107). In Scott's opinion most of Jesus' teaching is either too dangerous, too exaggerated, or too apocalyptic. The remainder is "plainly unwarranted" or must be limited either to the individual case or to the inner life. It appears that Scott and Jesus have very little in common.

"Das Problem der Bergpredigt" as defined by Friedrich Traub (Zeitschrift für Theologie und Kirche. N. F. 17. Jg. 1936. Tübingen: J. C. B. Mohr [193-218]) is whether the Sermon constitutes a legitimate basis for Christian ethics (209). After rejecting the answers provided by Catholicism, Tolstoy, Naumann, the eschatologists, the rabbinists, Dibelius, and Windisch, Traub proceeds, in dependence on Kant and Herrmann, to define the two basic requirements of ethics as (1) consistency and (2) universality. From the former, Traub concludes one cannot identify simultaneously with Tolstoy's pacifism and Naumann's patriotism. On the same grounds, he rejects the assumption that as a Christian one may sometimes act from non-Christian motives (210), for God demands our whole obedience. The second principle, that of universality, implies that no realm of life may be excluded from the norms of Christian ethics. While the Sermon on the Mount qualifies as a basis for Christian ethic by Traub's first criterion, he concludes that it falls far short of the second, for it has nothing explicit to say regarding the domain of family, society, law, state, capital, culture, art, science, sport, and whatever else makes up our modern civilization. "Therefore, the Sermon on the Mount cannot be the sole foundation of Christian ethics" (213). Consequently, we "cannot feel bound by individual words of Jesus but only by his *Gesinnung* on the basis of which one may conclude the very opposite of what Jesus concluded in his time" (215). This may not even be necessary, for, as Traub infers, Jesus' warning, "Do not gather treasures," does not challenge but presupposes the intactness of the capitalist order. Jesus, says Traub, was indifferent to Jewish culture or else his gospel would have perished with it. "Therefore it survives, independent of any culture, ancient or modern" (216).

"Behind the Sermon on the Mount stands the person of Jesus himself, and this person is—what his words cannot be—the foundation for Christian ethics. For he is the basis of the Christian faith upon which the Christian ethos rests" (216). "The person of Jesus as the personal revelation of God . . . enables us to recognize in the social orders of the world— which have no place in the Sermon on the Mount—God's orders of creation *(Schöpfungs- ordnungen)*" (217). By this logic Traub rationalizes that belief in Jesus' person justifies rejection of his teaching. "The nation to which we belong," says Traub, "is the highest earthly value that we know, and as believing Christians we cannot help think of this value as rooted in the Creator's will" (217). "Faith has an absolute meaning and as such it affirms the national life as a divine given to which one is bound for God's sake" (218). This reasoning also explains why for Traub the national ethos replaces the Sermon on the Mount as a basis for ethics.

LEONHARD RAGAZ:
THE MAGNA CHARTA
OF CHRISTIAN SOCIALISM

The Sermon on the Mount is no utopia or fantasy. It is thoroughly realistic. It is indeed the only true realism. It is the reality which holds if God exists.[1]

The Sermon on the Mount is the unprecedented message of the revolution of the world through God. It is being moved anew into the foreground by the world catastrophe and world revolution and introduces the radical renewal of the cause of Christ which is the ultimate meaning of our time.[2]

It is thoroughly practicable. . . . Jesus' demand is to be fulfilled here and now as his promises apply here and now.[3]

The demands of Jesus intend not a moral aristocracy but a moral democracy which, like every true democracy, has about it an element of aristocracy.[4]

It is never to be forgotten that everything which the Sermon on the Mount says applies, never just to the private life, but constitutes a comprehensive order.[5]

Kingdom of God is essentially also a political and social matter.[6]

The whole Gospel, and Christ himself, must be understood from the Sermon on the Mount.[7]

---

[1]Leonhard Ragaz, *Die Bergpredigt Jesu* (Bern: Verlag Herbert Lang & Cie, 1945) 7.

[2]Ibid., 9.

[3]Ibid., 28.

[4]Ibid., 79.

[5]Ibid., 88.

[6]Ibid., 146.

[7]Ibid., 194.

Leonhard Ragaz,[8] the father of Christian Socialism, sought to develop the practical implications of the Sermon on the Mount as a basis for a comprehensive program of social reform. The Sermon on the Mount was to be the guiding light providing the spirit and the principles for a new economic and political order. Ragaz advocated with unflagging zeal an idealist ethic oriented not to what is but aspiring to what ought to be, to that transcendent power claiming man's obedience of mind and deed.[9] Realizing the impossibility of escaping the world of nature for the realm of spirit, Ragaz defended a relative monism according to which—in contrast to positivism—spirit is not subjected to nature but nature to spirit. Ragaz believed (1) that there is an unconditionally binding moral obligation not derived from instinct and (2) that man has an innate capacity both to comprehend and to obey it.[10] In effect Ragaz advocated a return to Kant—"Du kannst denn

---

[8]Leonhard Ragaz was born in 1868 at Tamnis in Graubünden in the Swiss Alps, as the fifth of nine children of a poor but noble peasant family. The economic struggle and the democratic independence of these mountain villagers deeply impressed young Leonhard. He studied theology at Basel, Jena, and Berlin and entered the pastorate at the age of 21. In 1908 he became professor of systematic and practical theology at Zürich, a post from which he resigned in 1921 to devote himself entirely to the ethical and political concerns of Christian Socialism. In his formative years he was particularly influenced by Spinoza, Nietzsche, Richard Rothe, F. W. Robertson, Albert Bitzius, and Friedrich Naumann, and later he was much preoccupied with Marx, Kierkegaard, Tolstoy, Ritschl, Zwingli, Calvin, Carlyle, Alexander Vinet, Henri Bergson, Pestalozzi, Grundvig, and especially Blumhardt.

The bibliography of Ragaz totals some 1260 published titles of which 67 are books. Of these the most important include: *Du Sollst. Grundzüge einer sittlichen Weltanschauung* (1904), *Das Evangelium und der soziale Kampf der Gegenwart* (1906), *Dein Reich komme!* (1908), *Die neue Schweiz...* (1920), *Weltreich, Religion, und Gottesherrschaft* (2 vols., 1922), *Der kampf um das Reich Gottes in Blumhardt, Vater und Sohn* (1922), *Von Christus zu Marx—von Marx zu Christus* (1929), *Reformation nach Vorwärts oder Rückwärts? Eine Kampfschrift* (1937), *Das Reich Gottes und die Nachfolge. Andachten* (1938), *Die Geschichte der Sache Christi* (1945), *Die Bergpredigt Jesu* (1945), *Die Bibel—eine Deutung* (7 vols., 1947ff.), *Mein Weg* (2 vol. autobiography, 1952).

[9]That is, "Gesinnung und Tat."

[10]*Du Sollst, Grundzüge einer sittlichen Weltanschauung* (Freiburg i. B.: Paul Waetzel, 1904) 66. If conscience were synonymous with custom, Ragaz reasoned, why then do the bearers of custom crucify the prophets of conscience? How can one explain the conscience of Socrates, Amos, Jeremiah, Jesus, Luther, Tolstoy, and that of all the martyrs as merely the reflection or echo of custom? To him who prefers death to compromising his conscience, the positivist argument that the good is that which furthers our well-being apparently does not apply. Man may err in his conscience, but he cannot disregard his conscience and be a real individual.

du sollst"[11]—affirming the freedom of the will and the independence of the human spirit. Just as the phenomenon of Jesus cannot be explained on the basis of time and circumstances as a product of his environment (for he became what he was in reaction against it), so it is with ethical man today: the mystery of his person is his freedom transcending all naturalistic and mechanistic determinations. The power upon which all depends does not stand over us but works mightily within us.

What Jesus demands, says Ragaz, is not a new legalism but a new *Gesinnung*.[12] But Ragaz goes beyond Herrmann in insisting that having the *Gesinnung Jesu* implies participation in the Kingdom of God,[13] a participation that consists not in cultic ritual, ecstatic mysticism, or creedal dogmatism but in that unity of morality and religion exemplified in Jesus.[14] But "how shall such morality be considered practicable when one wishes to remain alive?"[15] Ragaz replies: "The Speech of Jesus is full of paradox. Literalism is often entirely excluded. . . ."[16]

---

[11]"Wir haben die Predigt der Verpflichtung nötig, des Gewissensernstes, der Abkehr von einer Genuß- und Erfolgsethik zu einer Ethik, die im Tun des Guten des Lebens Inhalt erkennt. Wir müssen unser Leben wieder auf den Felsengrund des Heiligen stellen und in Zucht und Gehorsam die verlorene innere Freiheit und Freudigkeit wiedergewinnen." Ibid., 89.

[12]"Die lebendige Gesinnung ist alles...Das ist der große Sinn der Bergpredigt....Aus dieser Gesinnung heraus, die in jedem entstehen muß, der mit der sittlichen Wahrheit Ernst macht, sollen wir selbst in jedem einzelnen Falle das rechte Verhalten finden. So entspricht es dem Geiste Jesu. Er hat uns ganz frei gemacht, im Innersten frei, indem er uns gebunden an uns selbst, an die göttliche Stimme in uns." Ibid., 121.

[13]"Durch die Gesinnung, die Jesus von seinen Jüngern fordert, gelangen sie zur Teilnahme am Reiche Gottes." Ibid., 123. "Gottesdienst ist Erfüllung des göttlichen Willens." Ibid., 129.

[14]Cf. ibid., 125ff.

[15]"Ist die Moral durchführbar? In concreto: geht es an, demjenigen, der mich auf den rechten Backen schlägt, auch den linken zu bieten? Könnte ihn das nicht vielleicht in seiner Brutalität bestärken, so daß mein Tun sogar gegen die Liebe ginge? Darf ich dem geben, der mich bittet und mich nicht abwenden von dem, der mir abborgen will? Das wäre Züchtung des Bettels—also wieder Lieblosigkeit. Ist es recht, wenn ich dem, der den Rock nehmen will, auch den Mantel gebe? Wo bliebe da der Kampf ums Recht, der zur Erhaltung der Gesellschaftsordnung nötig ist? Muß ich alle meine Habe den Armen geben? Wer sorgt denn für meine Kinder? Und kann ich mich der Sorge für Nahrung und Kleidung entschlagen, wenn ich für eine Familie verantwortlich bin?" Ibid., 156-57.

[16]"Niemand wird Jesus zutrauen, daß er uns wirklich auffordere, das rechte Aug auszureißen und von uns zu werfen, wenn es uns ärgerte oder Vater und Mutter wirklich zu hassen um seinetwillen." Ibid.

He who is unable to comprehend the paradox of such imagery should admit that he fails to comprehend Jesus. Thus it depends on the intention [*Sinn*]. But that does not mean a weakening of the demand of Jesus. And what is the intention of these unprecedented demands of Jesus? They shall clarify for us the boundlessness of the ethical demand, especially that of practicing love.[17]

"Do not care for tomorrow" does not mean "be idle" but rather "become free of the enslaving anxiety about earthly things." "If your eye offends you pluck it out" really means "save your own moral integrity at all costs." To "turn the other cheek" implies that the community of love may not be dissolved through offense; the brother who strikes you must be led back into the ways of love that evil be overcome with good. "Give him who asks" indicates that we owe our brother everything except our personality. "But surely he who would mechanically observe these sayings would hardly be acting in the spirit of Jesus." Jesus made no law out of his demands, not even for himself. When at his trial he was struck on the cheek, he did not turn the other, from which Ragaz concludes:

One can do the literal opposite of what Jesus requires and all the more abide in the *Gesinnung Jesu*. It is easier to give alms to a beggar in order to get rid of him than to refrain from doing so because it is his ruin. The latter alone is the Spirit of Jesus, the latter alone is love.

Jesus does not require of everyone what he required of the rich young ruler, namely to give all his possessions to the poor, nor does he require everyone to leave his family in order to follow him. "Some of these demands are of a fortuitous nature occasioned by the particular circumstances." Our task is not to reduce these words of Jesus to an unintelligible and disgusting legislation but rather to let them illumine our lives

as a reminder of the heights of moral truth. We should heed the voice of conscience which at the appropriate time will say: "now is the hour where this word of Jesus indicates your way."[18]

The extent to which Ragaz differed from Naumann and Herrmann in his understanding of and identification with *die Sache Christi* ("the cause

---

[17]Ibid., 157.
[18]Ibid., 158-59.

of Christ'')[19] can best be discerned in his last book, an interpretation of the
Sermon on the Mount as "the Magna Charta of the Kingdom of God."[20]
According to Ragaz, the Sermon on the Mount is misunderstood whenever
it is (1)elevated to a fantastic utopia as in Roman Catholicism; (2) reduced
to the level of the commonplace as in Protestantism where the dogmas of
Paul have consequently replaced the message of Jesus; (3) legalized as the
nova lex Christi as in the sectarians preceding and following Wycliffe, Hus,
the Anabaptists, and Tolstoy; or (4) individualized, that is, limited to the
private sphere to the exclusion of its social intentions or *Sozialen Sinn*.[21]
Furthermore, the Sermon was meant to be realized here and now on earth,
not at some earlier or later time or in some otherworldly "heaven." The
Beatitudes proclaim a complete "transvaluation of values" through the
impending (Socialist) world revolution as a result of which the "poor" will
inherit the Kingdom, a promise which includes the proletariat[22] and all those
whose anticipation and hope differ from the mentality and security of the
rich. "He who lives for God instead of for the world becomes infinitely
poor and infinitely rich."[23] That is the way of Jesus, and that must also
become the way of our world as it is transformed into a new creation.[24] The
world revolution which effects this transvaluation of values can happen only
in a nonviolent way. In the last analysis, the world belongs to the spirit, to
freedom, to truth, and to love. And he who seeks to conquer it by violence
defeats his purpose. Violence only separates man from God and his brother.
"He who knows God knows another power and trusts in it. Only he can
use violence who does not honor God."[25]

---

[19]The extent to which Blumhardt inspired the vision and terminology of Ragaz can be
discerned in the latter's book, *Der Kampf um das Reich Gottes in Blumhardt Vater und
Sohn—und weiter!* (Erlenbach-Zürich: Rotapfel-Verlag, 1922).

[20]*Die Bergpredigt Jesu* (Bern: Verlag Herbert Lang & Cie, 1945),10.

[21]Ibid., 7-9.

[22]"Es sind die kleinen Leute, die in bescheidensten Verhältnisse Lebenden, die Be-
drückten und Belasteten, auch oft genug Vergewaltigten und Enterbten...den auf Gottes
Kommen Wartenden." Ibid., 14.

[23]Ibid., 15.

[24]"...was man einmal mit einem freilich ungenügenden Ausdruck proletarische Kultur
nannte." Ibid., 16.

[25]"Wer Gott ehrt, der ehrt auch das heilige Recht des Andern, des andern Menschen,
des andern Volkes, der anderen Rasse, der anderen Religion." Ibid., 19.

Blessed are the peacemakers who speak truth to power and suffer for it. This is the line of promise that runs through the Beatitudes and proclaims the revolution of the Kingdom of God who overcomes the world. "The Beatitudes are only a few important *examples* to illustrate this fundamental fact of all spiritual reality."[26] The Beatitudes are intended for all, for God desires to be Lord over all, and his Kingdom shall come to all. But now they apply only for his disciples who alone live for (*aus*) God, having acknowledged and accepted his Kingdom or rule:

> For others the Beatitudes—like the entire Sermon—have no meaning. But all can here and now become disciples. Therefore the Beatitudes—like the entire Sermon—are the invitation to all: choose between the world and God, between nonblessing and blessing."[27]

What the Beatitudes proclaim applies today. Today the Kingdom belongs to the poor. Today the mourners shall be comforted and those who hunger and thirst after righteousness shall be satisfied. Today we must strive for peace. Today those who are persecuted for righteousness' sake shall rejoice and be consoled. In the perfected Kingdom all that is no longer needed.[28] But in the meantime those who are the salt and light of the world spread this revolution of the Kingdom of God throughout the world. The *Sache Christi* is the salt of the world and can never become the sanction of the world.

But can we actually do these good works? Is it not quite beyond the ability of sinful man to do anything but believe—as Paul and the Reformers emphasized? Ragaz replies: "Christ is more than Paul and the Reformers." While they did not intend to suppress works, their one-sided emphasis has done much damage:[29]

---

[26]Ibid., 26.

[27]Ibid., 27. "Die Forderung Jesu ist zwar bloß für die Jünger gedacht weil sie allein die Voraussetzung für ihre Erfüllung in sich tragen, aber alle sind zu Jüngern berufen." Ibid., 79.

[28]Ibid., 28.

[29]"Er [Paulus] wird einseitig, gerät ins Theologisch-Systematische hinein und damit in die Nähe des Künstlichen, des Konstruierten, während Jesus in göttlicher Einfachheit verharrt. Sodann: Bei Jesus tritt das Element der *Werke*, die aus dem über dem Gesetze stehenden Leben mit Gott fließen, entsprechend einfacher und mit unvergleichlicher elementarer Gewalt hervor. Darum kann auch Paulus in Bezug auf den Kampf gegen das Gesetz nur ein *Hinweis* auf Jesus sein, nicht ein Ersatz für Jesus....Jedenfalls hat sich nicht die Bergpredigt dem Römerbrief unterzuordnen...[sondern] der Römerbrief der Bergpredigt." Ibid., 50-51.

Therefore we must return to Christ. The good works which he intends derive not from the law but from the true source, from God. We can and shall do such works. He says so and demands it. We are able to do them in the light of the Kingdom and shall do so.[30]

Our works indicate whether we have the Kingdom and whether we represent *die Sache Christi* in accord with Jesus' saying: "Let your light so shine before men, that they may see your good works and give glory to your Father who is in heaven" (Matthew 5:16):

Deeds are the true word of God. God speaks through deeds, and we are to speak of him through deeds. . . .Create a world of the righteousness of the Kingdom of God and humanity will believe in God. To the Kingdom belongs discipleship.[31]

"The Sermon on the Mount is," Ragaz wrote, "the fulfillment of the Decalogue and only in its fulfillment its dissolution."[32] The first commandment which Jesus said he came not to abolish is "You shall not kill" (Matthew 5: 21-26). Ragaz understands this quite categorically: "A disciple of Christ may not and cannot kill, neither the so-called enemy nor the so-called criminal." Jesus applies this to the political as well as the civil order, for "the Kingdom of God is not a private matter but an all-inclusive order." To the questions—"Does not the Sermon on the Mount apply only to those who wish to be disciples of Christ? How then can one expect those to keep it to whom it does not apply? Is it the Magna Charta of the Kingdom but not of politics?"—Ragaz replies: "Politics shall also be subject to the Kingdom of God. In the first instance the Sermon on the Mount is understood and acknowledged only by the disciples and the Christian community, but the Christian community shall conquer the world in their unique way," so that the order of God may also become the order of the world.[33]

In a chapter concerning purity, Ragaz specifies how a legalistic misunderstanding of any of the commandments denies their intention and contradicts their purpose. The commandment, "Do not commit adultery" (Cf. Matthew 5:27-32), when perverted into a legalistic form, becomes a sanction of covenant-breaking under certain circumstances. Even the intention

---

[30]Ibid., 37.

[31]"Zum Reiche gehört die Nachfolge." Ibid., 38.

[32]Ibid., 51.

[33]Ibid., 56.

of the commandment to pluck out the offending eye "is much more severe than if just taken literally! . . . It is the severity of the surgeon who cuts deep in order to heal" lest coveteousness ruin man's body and soul. "The severity of Jesus is mild, it saves. But the severity of sheer legality only causes distress and hypocrisy and increases coveteousness."[34]

On the matter of swearing oaths (Cf. Matthew 5:33-37) we have inherited a whole legalistic and casuistic structure of distinctions between what is and what allegedly is not permitted, all of which betray the attempt to derive the truth from an external authority—be it that of church or state with their respective rules of the game. Instead of being in the truth and doing the truth, we evade it or exploit it in the service of some power and thereby reduce the truth to a lie. Jesus confronts this lie, as did all the prophets before him, with the unconditionality of the truth of God, who recognizes no compromise. Ragaz holds this word of Jesus to be particularly applicable to theologians who seek to evade the truth by conflicting statements called paradox.[35]

And, as for Jesus' teaching on retaliation (Matthew 5:38-42), is that not sheer utopia? It is utopian, says Ragaz, only when Jesus' prohibition of litigation, retaliation, and resistance is elevated to such an impossible heavenly height as to be entirely unattainable for the mass of humanity and accessible only to those ethical mountaineers who, like the disciples of St. Francis, make a profession of scaling such towering peaks of perfection with their severe asceticisms. The fulfillment of this commandment, claims Ragaz, was not intended as a professional sport for a select few but as the work of all.[36] This obligation is not a law but a new freedom, not a compulsion but a privilege. And the very fact that it is valid for all does not discount its idealism but establishes its actual relevance without relegating it to an ascetic utopia which, in the last analysis, proves to be nothing but an illusion—as every honest monk will admit with regard to his own self-acquired perfections.

Jesus abolished the *lex talionis* because the legalistic misuse of the law of God failed to fulfill its intention: to preserve what is holy, namely, life and property. Jesus abolished the law in order to fulfill it. He knew that

---

[34]Ibid., 62.

[35]Cf. ibid., 70, 76-77.

[36]Cf. ibid., 79.

mere defense of every person's legal rights does not necessarily sanctify humanity but often occasions anger, bitterness, hatred, strife, and war. To accomplish its intention, justice must transcend the balance or superiority of power. Therefore, Jesus advocated going the second mile when pressed into service by the Roman post. Jesus advised that a person should, when personally affronted, give the offender something better than his legal due, namely a material and spiritual measure of grace and love as becomes a child of God; for in God we have all things in common, including our rights.[37] A free son of God does not claim the right to retaliate but mediates instead holy righteousness which is never without grace and forgiveness. The force of evil must be withstood with the power of truth. Truth is never without love; nor is love ever without the power of truth.

This is the spirit which Jesus' word "Resist not..." intends. This non-literal understanding does not imply a weakening but rather a radicalization of the demand. It is easier to pilgrimage to some holy place with dried peas in one's shoes—or even to pluck out one's eye—than constantly to give God the glory and to sacrifice whatever stands in the way of full commitment and obedience to his will:

> This command also is no literalism but a principle. Perhaps you should not literally offer your left cheek when you have been struck on the right one—Jesus himself did not do that before the high court, and you may never be in such a situation—but you should offer the offender more: God's right in which your own wrong is somehow included. Perhaps in a legal suit you should not offer also your cloak to him who wants your coat, but in such a dispute over material things you should meet him more than half-way. You may never be required to render transport-duty, but in similar situations it is better to do too much than too little.... You should not simply give financial aid to everyone who requests it of you...but you must give him more...perhaps by assuming responsibility for a better social welfare. . . . These paradoxes of Jesus are not literalisms but symbols. They have an all-inclusive meaning. They represent the freedom of the Kingdom of God but in radicalness go far beyond the righteousness of the scribes and Pharisees—into a new world.[38]

Everything Jesus says applies not merely to the personal realm but also holds unconditionally for the public domain of political and social life in

---

[37]Ibid., 82.
[38]Ibid., 87-88.

terms of national and international freedom, justice, and peace which can only be realized to the extent that the Kingdom of God is realized. To proclaim its coming and to strive for its fulfillment is therefore the mission of the people of God.

While the Old Testament nowhere explicitly commands hatred of the enemy, it reflects the law of society in respecting ethnic, racial, religious, and national barriers according to which concessions are granted to members of the same tribal, racial, or religious group but not to outsiders. Over against such natural morality Jesus demands: ''Love your enemies and pray for those who persecute you'' (Matthew 5:44). Ragaz reminds us that it is not self-evident for Jews to love Germans who interned their families in gas chambers, for Chinese to love Japanese who bombed out their homes, and for Czechs to love Germans who destroyed their villages, killed their husbands, and deported their wives. Love under such extraordinary circumstances, claims Ragaz, is precisely what Jesus demands. Love of the enemy is not a natural love, as within the filial bond, but a deeper kind of covenant love. It arises not from nature but from one's relationship to God. It is therefore neither sentimental nor utopian but quite realistic. Such love is not an idealism that overlooks the faults of others but a commitment to overcome hatred and evil by establishing reconciliation and brotherhood.

Jesus' command frees us from the necessity to hate those who hate us and thereby frees us from the mutual self-destruction implied in that necessity. Those who hate do what is natural, but those who love do what is supernatural and bear the image of God as sons of God.[39] This is the sense in which Jesus asks that we become not ''perfect'' but complete (Matthew 5:48), that is, unconditionally committed to the greatness, goodness, holiness, and love of God. Thus the difficult becomes easy and the extraordinary self-evident, effecting the abolition of all war and establishing rapprochement amongst all people in the mutual endeavor to overcome all conflict of interest and all hatred. Ragaz is optimistic and hopeful that the many Christians in the world will be pioneers who set a precedent that will transform the world.[40]

---

[39]Ibid., 96-98.
[40]Ibid., 101.

Next, Ragaz explores the economic implications of Jesus' transvaluation of values on the basis of Matthew 6:19-34. Money separates man from God and his brother,[41] creates classes and class conflict and causes strife and war from the sphere of private life to the international plane. St. Francis is alleged to have said that, if one has possessions, one requires weapons to defend them, for they are the source of all strife and litigation and therefore a great hindrance to love of God and neighbor.[42] People crave security to overcome their anxiety or *Angst*.[43] Since their insecurity is boundless, their *Angst* becomes a demonic obsession which compels them towards the abyss—whether in the form of capitalism, imperialism, militarism, Fascism, or Nazism. Jesus seeks to redeem us not from the cares of earning an honest living but from the compulsive power of this *Angst*.[44] With his whimsical saying about the birds and lilies (Matthew 6:26ff.), Jesus admonishes us to cultivate a divine indifference to money and possessions. As long as we live only for ourselves, we are caught up in the bonds of *Angst*, but, if we live for God, we become as free as his birds and lilies.[45] To imitate St. Francis would be wrong, as every imitation is. In capturing the spirit and intention we embody not the form but the life which proceeds from God and overcomes the world. The poverty Jesus demands is not an institution but a principle, not a new form but a new atmosphere. The blessing is upon the poor who overcome Mammon through the riches of God within the new community of man.[46]

---

[41] "Man kann Gott und sein Reich nicht anders haben als in der Haltung und Gesinnung der Armut, als im Hungern und Dürsten nach der Gerechtigkeit. Besitz aber macht satt. Besitz macht hochmütig. Jeder Besitz, besonders aber der von Geld. Und von dem hängt ja meistens alle andere Besitz, auch der kulturelle, ab. Denn weniges macht erfahrungsgemäß die Herzen so hart, so kalt, wie dieses harte, kalte Metall. Und nichts so gierig." Ibid., 133.

[42] Ibid., 133.

[43] "Es ist die Angst vor dem Schicksal, die Angst vor dem Tode, die Angst vor der Not, die Angst vor der Leere." Ibid., 137.

[44] "Die Sorge, von der uns Jesus erlösen will, ist nicht die Sorge als Fürsorge, auch nicht die Sorge als Bürde, die wir zu tragen haben, die Sorge als Schicksal oder Schickung, sondern die Sorge als "Macht," die Sorge als Götze und Mutter der Götzen, die Sorge als die Angst der Welt." Ibid., 142.

[45] Ibid., 144.

[46] Ibid., 149.

Having indicated in what sense Jesus opposes natural morality,[47] Ragaz proceeds to show us that Jesus was also the greatest opponent of religion by replacing both the law of morality and the law of religion with the reality of God. Jesus' word, "Do not judge..." (Matthew 7:1-5), is directed against that cancerous sore of religious piety and churchianity, the tendency to condemn those who differ—a tendency that leads to fanaticism and eventually to the inquisition, that torments and utterly destroys the freedom and life of the spirit. The tendency to condemn others for unbelief is proportional to one's own weakness; it is a legalism that seeks to exterminate the freedom of true faith in others.[48] That we are to discern but not to condemn implies a complete transformation of interhuman relationships.

The "broad way" (Matthew 7:13-14) includes, according to Ragaz, the way of the Church or religion over against the narrow way of the Kingdom. Religion provides comfort and consolation, forgiveness of sins and satisfaction, and costs little or nothing. One can enjoy religion without encountering God and without becoming involved in conflict with the world. But the lonely way of the Kingdom—as the fate of the prophets and Jesus exemplified—often involves death but nevertheless leads to real life.[49] In

---

[47]Ragaz objects to speaking of the teaching of Jesus as "ethics." "Das hieße die Bergpredigt in ein Gesetz und die Botschaft vom Reiche Gottes in eine Wissenschaft verwandeln. Der Begriff der 'Ethik' wie die Sache selbst stammen aus Griechenland, also aus einer Welt, welche den lebendigen Gott und sein Reich nicht kennt. 'Ethik' bedeutet ein geschlossenes wissenschaftliches System, das eine ähnliche Rolle spielt, wie das Gesetz der Pharisäer und Schriftgelehrten. Der Bürger des Reiches Gottes aber lebt in allem reichsunmittelbar aus dem lebendigen Gott, seinem Herrn und Vater. Gerade darin besteht auch die Revolution der Moral durch die Bergpredigt, die neue und bessere Gerechtigkeit, die das Gesetz erfüllt, indem sie es aufhebt und das Gesetz aufhebt, indem sie es erfüllt, indem sie über das Gesetz hinaus in die Weiten Gottes weist." Ibid., 102.

[48]"Wer seiner Sache gewiß ist (so wie man das in Demut sein kann), der lässt den Andern Freiheit; wer aber selber schwankt und zweifelt, der ersetzt die eigene Festigkeit durch die Härte gegen die Andern." Ibid., 152-53.

[49]"Man kann Gott nur als Einzelner wirklich haben....Im Reich Gottes spielt der Einzelne eine entscheidende Rolle. . . .Der Einzelne muß voran gehen, der Einzelne bricht Bahn. Der Einzelne muß leiden. Der Einzelne kann eine kleine Gemeinschaft sein oder ein einziger Mensch, ein Moses, ein Elias, ein Amos, ein Jeremias, ein—Jesus. Darum muß wer Gott recht dienen will, nicht nur einsam, sondern auch allein sein können, ganz allein, mit Gott allein. Immer wieder, wenn die Masse gottfern wird, muß der Einzelne aus der Einsamkeit des Gottesberges her zu ihr kommen. Und immer wieder muß der Einzelne der Masse widerstehen. Das ist schwer, aber es ist doch auch herrlich." Ibid., 179.

essence the Kingdom of God is both universalistic and individualistic, for it is intended not only for the "little flock" but also meant to be realized amongst the many. However, the individual or "single one" must lead the way. Everyone must become an individual before God, so that he can lead others to God.

Ragaz interprets the pericope on "saying Lord, Lord" (Matthew 7:21-23) as Jesus' categorical indictment of religion, an indictment which implies that God and religion are mutually exclusive:[50]

> God is there where his will is done in truth, freedom, humanity, and love in the righteousness of the Kingdom. Everything depends on that, not on the Creed. He hates the Creed, hates theology, hates scribal learning, hates piety, hates ritual where his will is not done in the righteousness of the Kingdom. God is there where his will is done even though he himself is not known or named. He avails himself of unbelievers to judge believers. He avails himself of pagans to shame Christians. He identifies not with a creed, a theology, a confession, nor with the religion of Christendom but with the Kingdom and, within the Kingdom, with man.[51]

Finally, the Sermon on the Mount is not a theory but the proclamation of the Kingdom of God through Jesus Christ. "Apart from him it would be mere utopian philosophy, through him it becomes message, it becomes promise and demand of God who speaks by him and through him." But this identification of the Sermon and Jesus may not be exploited to recast the Sermon into the framework of Pauline Christology so that human beings are denied free access to the Sermon and to Jesus. The Sermon on the Mount leads beyond Christology, dogmatics, and ethics to a mountain whose sunshine and Alpine air excel that of the Acropolis and Sinai and at which height one's encounter with God is characterized by freedom from all theology. Therefore, the Sermon on the Mount signifies the revolution of God against the world with all its morality and religion.[52]

Ragaz described his own spiritual development as a series of transitions "from Pantheism to the personal God, from God to the Kingdom of

---

[50]"Gott kann dort sein, wo die Religion nicht ist, und er kann dort nicht sein, wo die Religion ist." Ibid., 188.

[51]Ibid., 188-89.

[52]Ibid., 194.

God, and from the Kingdom of God to Christ, his incarnation."[53] Under the influence of Weiss and Schweitzer, Ragaz rejected the idealism of *Kulturprotestantismus*, but, in reaction against the despair of hope and meaning for this aeon implied in their interpretation of Jesus' eschatology, Ragaz's own understanding of the Kingdom expresses the renewal of the biblical hope for the world. Parallel with this shift from cultural idealism to biblical hope, his understanding of revelation becomes disassociated with the evolutionary process of history as such and identified with the Christ event of "Cross and Resurrection" on the assumption that here alone the intention of history becomes transparent.[54]

For Ragaz, Kingdom of God and society are directly interrelated, since God is alive and active in his dynamic *creatio continua* not as self-evident evolutionary development but in the existential struggle between chaos and cosmos, creation and fall.[55] The Kingdom of God is conceived as realistic and dynamic history borne by God and man and moving towards a definite goal. God is the prime mover in this Kingdom-of-God movement.[56] However, man also plays a decisive role as colaborer with God since he is captivated and claimed by the power of the inbreaking Kingdom and continually experiences—in *"der Nachfolge Christi"*—new breakthroughs towards the goal. When a person falls from this vision and aspiration, the revolution of God becomes the revolution of the world or, in its utter perversion, the revolution of the Devil. God warns and beckons every individual to become a free and moral person, but God does not

---

[53]"Meine geistige Entwicklung," Markus Mattmüller, *Leonhard Ragaz und der religiöse Sozialismus* (Zollikon: Evangelischer Verlag AG., 1957) I:244.

[54]"Der Gerechte muß leiden für den Ungerechten, nur durch Ideale und Opfer wird die Welt erlöst—dieses sittliche Weltgesetz ist am Kreuz entdeckt." L. Ragaz; "Karfreitag und Ostern," *Religiöses Volksblatt* (St. Gallen, 1892) 134, quoted in Hans Ulrich Jäger, "Die sozialische Funktion des Reichgottesglaubens bei Leonhard Ragaz," *Evangelische Ethik,* (Juli/Sept. 1968):228. Fifty years later Ragaz wrote: "Das Göttliche darf nicht sein wie die Welt und darf nicht auf die Weise der Welt siegen: durch Weltmacht und Weltglanz; es muß ganz anders sein als die Welt. Gerade um sie besiegen zu können. Es muß ohnmächtig sein, um allmächtig zu werden. Erst das Kreuz führt zu Ostern." *Die Botschaft vom Reiche Gottes, ein Katechismus für Erwachsene* (Bern, 1942) 308, quoted in Jäger, ibid., 228.

[55]"Das Reich Gottes . . . ist nicht eine Theorie, ein System . . . , sondern eine Bewegung, eine Geschichte." *Neue Wege* (1919) 548, quoted in Jäger, ibid., 221.

[56]"It is God himself who goes before us, who comes nearer us, always new yet always the same God." *Dein Reich Komme. Predigten,* I:63, quoted in Jäger, ibid., 222.

compel man in this movement from theonomy to autonomy. Man can be redeemed only within the context of his environment, and therefore the Kingdom of God always concerns history. Jesus does not teach us to pray, "take Thy Kingdom from us," but "bring it to us."[57]

Ragaz's Christology (or absolute hope in Christ) induced him to see the world as directly *"von-Gott-her"* while his eschatology (or relative hope for history) influenced him to see the world as indirectly *"zu-Gott-hin."* He shared the former perspective with Kutter, but in the latter he moved beyond the limits of liberalism in his endeavor to ascribe to social, political, and cultural hope a Christological foundation. Despite progressive historical disappointments such as the outcome of the Boer War, the perversion of Socialism into Bolshevism, the failure of the League of Nations, the outbreak of World War II, and, finally, the explosion of the hydrogen bomb shortly before his death, Ragaz never despaired of proclaiming the coming of the Kingdom of God. He insisted, in contrast to Schweitzer, that the *Sache Christi* was never meant to be realized beyond history but rather in and through history. It was a relative hope but never merely a consolation to endure the contradiction of hope until one's redemption out of history into eternity. In contrast to Naumann, who despaired of reconciling political realities with gospel ideals, in Ragaz, relative hope for history at times tends to merge with absolute hope in Christ.[58] The reason for this tendency in Ragaz is his firm conviction that a hope for the future which does not manifest itself as a world-changing power cannot affirm itself in the present with credibility. On the other hand, Ragaz held that real hope invariably expresses itself as absolute hope by the very fact that it does not resign itself to the realm of the penultimates within the relativities of history. It was this ultimate dimension of his hope that enabled Ragaz to take upon himself the odium of utopianism in an endeavor to make credible his testimony that the Kingdom of God is a reality already being realized in the revolutionary effect of the salt of the earth.

Rejecting both the duplicity of the Roman Catholic two-level ethic and the dichotomy of the Lutheran *Zwei-Reiche-Lehre*, Ragaz judged the *ordo politicus* by the absolute measure (that is, *"von-Gott-her"*). He wanted to

---

[57]Cf. *Neue Wege* (1909) 299.

[58]"Die relative Hoffnung wächst sich in mir beinahe zu einer absoluten aus." *Leonhard Ragaz in seinen Briefen* (Zürich, 1966) I:217, cited by Arthur Rich, "Leonhard Ragaz, Eine Skizze von seinem Denken und Wirken," *Evangelische Ethik*, (Juli/Sept. 1968):200.

indicate both how radically political reality must be called in question by the claims of God and how revolutionarily the coming Kingdom of God relates to the political order as both judgment and promise. Ragaz's absolute hope expressed itself in political and national ideals as he worked toward an international basis for peace and good will, justice, and brotherhood. Apart from his political engagement, Ragaz was above all a radical Socialist who worked for a structural reform of the social order to alleviate the injustice suffered by the poor and to defend the rights of workers. Ragaz was not an uncritical Socialist, for he distinguished between the revolution of the world and the revolution of God, that work of God in the world to which the Church is committed. Yet, when the revolution of God fails, then, he believed, the revolution of the world takes on the form of judgment that—as when force becomes the determining principle in politics—becomes the revolution of the Devil. In this way Ragaz qualifies both positively and negatively the presence of God in revolution.[59]

While Ragaz did not confuse the Kingdom of God with Socialism, he did consider the Socialist movement a form of *Nachfolge Christi* that in the deepest sense sought to bring about the rule of God and the brotherhood of humankind. For Ragaz, Christian existence is always revolutionary existence because it is always "inner-worldly" existence which never makes peace with the imperfections of this world. Inspired by absolute hope, it always risks the hazards of seeking the new that threatens the old and will eventually replace it. Although the extent to which this goal is achievable within history is forever debatable, we are obliged to concede Ragaz's insistence "that it belongs to the essence of Christianity to work for its accomplishment."[60]

The pacifism of Ragaz illustrates how he aspired to the absolute goal of history while identifying with the relative as the imperfect means of bringing it about.[61] Ragaz was no absolute pacifist (in the Tolstoyan sense

---

[59]Ibid., cf. Rich, "Leonhard Ragaz," 193-209.

[60]*Schweizerisches Protestantenblatt* (1903) 132, cited by Jäger, "Die sozialische Funktion," 227.

[61]"Wir haben ein absolutes Ziel: die neue Welt, worin auch der Krieg nicht mehr ist. Von diesem absoluten Ziel aus beurteilen wir auch die Menschen, Parteien, Losungen, Ereignisse der Zeit. Wir stehen zu ihnen oder bekämpfen sie, je nach dem Verhältnis zu diesem absoluten Ziel, worin sie sich nach unserer Meinung befinden. Dabei stehen wir so,

of despairing with the political struggle for a constructive peace), although he did upon occasion defend the conviction of conscientious objectors who renounced participation in warfare. In reality Ragaz was an eminent political thinker who, while holding to the absolute demands of the rule of God as the ethical basis for orientation, was deeply involved in the relativities of politics not governed by such ideals.[62] To the alarm of many of his friends, Ragaz defended military resistance even though he never envisioned power as a means of resolving political or social problems. His own passion lay neither in the defense of national autonomy nor in pacifistic resignation of national claims but rather in the creation of international justice, collective guarantees of peace, and the League of Nations. He did not confuse these objectives with the Kingdom of God but saw in them something of the historical movement in the right direction. Ragaz's relative pacifism exemplifies how, as the father of Religious Socialism, he always had his eye on both God and the world, the *civitas dei* and the *civitas terrena*. He was able to hold both in focus because proleptically he already saw them unified in Christ, not as a present fact, but as a future promise—in such a way that this revolution of the new enlists the enthusiastic engagement of every believer.

Throughout his life Ragaz sought somehow to hold together the absolutist clarity of conviction and the relativist sense of social responsibility in a painstaking endeavor to avoid an unrealistic one-norm monism, on the one hand, and an unidealistic two-realm dualism, on the other. Though an idealist at heart, he was compelled by reason to reject on pragmatic grounds

---

daß wir nicht alles, was eine diesem absoluten Ziel nicht völlig angemessene Wirklichkeit bedeutet, kurzerhand verwerfen. Wir erlauben uns, daran einen relativen Maßstab anzulegen, und zwar gerade im Dienst des Absoluten. Gewisse Erscheinungen können uns freuen, nicht weil sie schon das Höchste darstellen, was wir wollen und hoffen, sondern weil sie wenigstens eine Annäherung daran bedeuten und im Gegensatz zu anderen Erscheinungen stehen, die wir unbedingt ablehnen, ja hassen. Wir sehen darin Vorbereitungen, Weissagungen, Anstrengungen auf das Höchste hin. So können wir uns unter Umständen selbst daran beteiligen." *Neue Wege*, (Jg. 1918):345, cited by Rich, ("Leonhard Ragaz,") 206-207.

[62]"So sehr er den totalen Gewaltverzicht 'für bestimmte Naturen' und 'für bestimmte Umstände' als individualistisch geboten erachtete, so wenig hat er ihn zu einer Maxime der politischen Ethik erhoben. Nein, dieser Pazifist ging sogar so weit, zu sagen, daß 'unter bestimmte Voraussetzungen...Einzelne und Völker ihr Land mit den Waffen verteidigen' müßten." Rich, ("Leonhard Ragaz,") 207, citing Ragaz, *Neue Wege*, (Jg. 1918):345.

the "all or nothing" perfectionist mentality.[63] He profoundly respected the Christian pacifist conscience, but patriotic sentiment and political ambition kept him from personally assuming so nonconformist an identity. He boldly proclaimed "The Magna Charta of the Kingdom of God" as a "transvaluation of values" that applies today rather than to a future ideal. But when his public image was at stake for sympathizing with a school teacher imprisoned for resisting induction, Ragaz cleared himself with the assertion that national disarmament "might be an ideal for the future but cannot be considered a criterion of ethical discernment for the present."[64]

On the one hand, Ragaz categorically maintained that "a disciple of Christ may not and cannot kill, neither the so-called enemy nor the so-called criminal."[65] On the other hand, he diplomatically explained that "one can do the literal opposite of what Jesus requires" without contradicting his intention.[66] He pleads for a return to Jesus' emphasis on "deeds" over against Pauline "creeds" on the assumption that "we can and shall do such works"[67] as Jesus demands. But then we are informed that Jesus' demands were fortuitous in character and occasioned by circumstances which no longer apply[68] and that everything depends upon the "lebendige Gesin-

---

[63]"Es gibt eine religiöse Denkweise, die Ibsen durch das Stichwort 'Alles oder Nichts' charakterisiert hat. Auf das Allerhöchste und Allerletzte: Gott allein, Sein Kommen und Herrschen, geplannt, verschmäht sie alle bloßen Einzelfortschritte. Sie fürchtet sich vor allen Sich-Einlassen ins Relative eine Schädigung des Absoluten, von allem Arbeiten in menschliche Formen und mit menschliche Kategorien eine Verhüllung des Göttlichen." *Neue Wege* (Juli 1918):337, cited by Mattmüller, *Leonhard Ragaz* (1968) II:325.

[64]*Neue Wege* (Juli 1918):341, cited by Mattmüller, ibid., 326. This ambiguity is documented in Ragaz's autobiography: "Was aber seine [Tolstoys] Lehre von der Gewaltlosigkeit, oder besser, dem Nichtwiderstehen, betrifft, so habe ich sie für einige Zeit angenommen und vertreten, wenn auch nie ganz in seinem Sinne, sie aber nie doktrinär verstanden und schließlich um des passiven und quietistischen Charakters, den sie leicht annehmen kann, ganz aufgegeben. Namentlich habe ich seine gesetzliche Art, die Bergpredigt auszulegen, nie geteilt. Auch habe ich schon früher erklärt, daß ich den Einfluß den er lange auf meine Haltung in geistigen Kämpfen, im Sinne eines Nichtwiderstehens, ausgeübt hat, als Irrtum und schweren Schaden erkannt habe." *Mein Weg* (Zürich: Diana Verlag, 1952) II:18. See also this note, from the same source: "Der wahre Sachverhalt ist der: Ich habe nie mit einem Worte zur Dienstverweigerung aufgereizt. Das hätte ich nicht verantworten können. . . ." Ibid., 22-23.

[65]*Bergpredigt, 56.*

[66]*Du Sollst, 158.*

[67]Ibid., 137.

[68]Cf. ibid., 158.

nung.''[69] He indicts theologians for their sophisticated duplicity called paradox[70] when he himself insisted that ''the speech of Jesus is full of paradox'' and that he who fails to comprehend this fails to comprehend Jesus.[71] We are told that Jesus' demands were intended only for his twelve disciples and apply only ''to those who can comprehend them.'' However, in the same breath Ragaz universalizes this category to include all humankind. Since God wills that all people become disciples, Ragaz concludes that all of the Sermon is unconditionally binding for national and international politics.[72]

Most of Ragaz's apparent contradictions relate to this underlying ambiguity. On the one hand, he addresses himself to committed Christians. On the other hand, he identifies not with religion but with politics, not with the clergy but with the proletariat, and not with Christendom but with Socialism. Ragaz progressively disassociated himself from the Church. First, he left the pastoral ministry, then he resigned from his post as instructor of religion in schools, and later he relinquished his professorship on the theological faculty of Zürich. ''God cannot be where religion is'' and hates everything associated with it. Can it be assumed that Ragaz actually found in the Swiss Socialist Movement—then under Bolshevist influence—the integrity he so much missed in the Church?[73] Perhaps the more fundamental question is: What does it really mean to proclaim ''The Magna Charta of the Kingdom of God'' at large—that is, in general, theoretical, universalistic terms—when there is no nucleus within which *die Sache Christi* is realized, however imperfectly, in specific, concrete, and particular terms?[74]

---

[69]Ibid, 121.

[70]*Bergpredigt, 70.*

[71]*Du Sollst*, 157.

[72]Ibid., 160. *Bergpredigt*, 79, 88.

[73]Hans Ulrich Jäger, ''Die Begründung der Sozialethik bei Leonhard Ragaz,'' *Reformatio* (Oktober 1965):623, credits Ragaz with resisting Lenin's plan in 1919 to annex the Swiss Social Democrats with the Third Communist International. Cf. also ''Meine Beziehung zu den Russen.'' *Mein Weg* II:75-84.

[74] In his book, *Die Geschichte der Sache Christi. Ein Versuch* (Bern: Verlag Herbert Lang & Cie, 1945), Ragaz addresses himself to the task of establishing the sociological and spiritual interrelation between Democracy, Socialism, and Communism as progressive dimensions of man's freedom from the bondage of idols within a cosmic order of world revolution and redemptive evolution—largely a visionary and apocalyptic view of the meaning of history.

Ragaz sought to recover *die Sache Christi* from Schweitzer's apocalyptic in an endeavor to establish directly the contemporary relevance of
Jesus' message of the Kingdom without recourse to its original *Sitz-im-Leben*. He cautioned against replacing the deeds of Jesus with the creeds of
Paul, but the self-evidence with which he makes the leap from oriental
Galilee to modern Helvetia without any hermeneutical qualifications also
accounts for the incongruity of founding the Magna Charta of Political Socialism upon the "hard sayings" of Jesus. Even if one rejects Paul's interpretation of the Cross, one cannot ignore the fact of the Cross together with
its political implications and gain even an elemental understanding of Jesus' teaching. One sometimes has the feeling that the Christian Socialist
Movement claimed the pre-Capitalist Jesus from oriental Galilee so as to
exploit him to full advantage as an advertising label for socialist ideology.
Then, when literal application of the Sermon on the Mount for obvious
reasons altogether fails to fit the scheme of things, the intention is readily
qualified as *Gesinnungsethik*—always an innocuous way of relativizing the
skandalon. For the rest, the text is—in the absence of any hermeneutical
criteria—largely open to any random application, no matter how self-contradictory. Consequently, "Do not swear" (Matthew 5:33-37) suddenly
becomes an indictment of Orthodoxy and all dogmatism including pacifism and antimilitarism.[75] "Do not retaliate" (Matthew 5:38-42) is one of
those "paradoxes" Jesus intended as "symbols."[76] "Do not judge"
(Matthew 7:1-5) has no bearing on litigation—for Tolstoy's interpretation
"is the opposite of the spirit and bearing of Jesus"[77]—but is really directed
against the basic evil of religion. For two thousand years scholars have
searched for the meaning of these words. Ragaz knows exactly what they
mean! It is a great pity he has not revealed the criteria by which he arrived
at his insights. Ragaz admonished us to trust the voice of conscience. At
the right moment this "law within" is to reveal precisely what a particular
word of Jesus means for our situation.[78] For those whose conscience re-

---

[75]*Bergpredigt*, 76-77.

[76]Ibid., 88.

[77]Ibid., 151.

[78]Ibid., 158.

mains unenlightened by Kantian-Socialist presuppositions, this hope provides small comfort.

Rudolf Hermann (*Die Bergpredigt und die Religiös-Sozialen*. Leipzig/Erlangen: A. Deichertsche Verlagsbuchhandlung [W. Scholl], 1922) concluded that the Sermon on the Mount is no Interim Ethic and that the world with which it reckons was not expected to disappear in the twilight of the last things. The people to whom the disciples are to be a light are real people. The law, the Pharisees, and the courts which condemn murder and demand the oath are realities with which to reckon. Marriage is a factual institution. The poor are dependent on alms. Prayer and fasting are regulated by the cult, and the gathering of treasures constitutes a live temptation. "It is into this very world of ours that the bearers of the coming Kingdom have been placed, and it is in this world, its social institutions and private relations, that they shall strive after the Kingdom of God and God's righteousness" (6, 7). This is Jesus' social mandate to his disciple-church to be realized in their "walk" and by their "good works" (Matthew 5:13-16) which constitute the visible signposts of the divine.

The Sermon on the Mount concerns the reality, life, and work of the Creator with his creatures, a reality of love and goodness. Loving one's enemy is therefore no wanton perversion of the natural and no visionary escape from empirical reality. "It is the uplifting of man not into an idea of the absolute but to a comprehension of the creation of the personal God. And this creation has a meaning and a plan, namely, the realization of the Kingdom of God which happens as his will is done on earth as in heaven" (12). Jesus' disciples are the bearers of this history and are to transform it in accordance with its intended destiny. To consider the other person not merely as friend or enemy but "to learn to see him as the creation of God for whom the Father in heaven intends that he participate in his coming Kingdom" constitutes the "perisson," the extraordinary, the uniqueness of being Christian (13).

Hermann's optimism in holding to the Sermon on the Mount as God's design for the life of Christians is based on the implicit trust that, if we really seek God's Kingdom first (Matthew 6:33), the Creator will really provide our actual needs (15). However, adds Hermann, this personal trust and obedience cannot be exploited as a political platform for the politics of Christian Socialism (31).

FRIEDRICH NAUMANN:
THE IRRELEVANCE
OF AN ORIENTAL IMPOSSIBILITY

Those who would keep the precepts of the Sermon on the Mount . . . are bound to complete patience, complete meekness, a perfect fullness of love, to be absolutely without a mind for gain, without self-love, a ready and forward sacrifice for all.

In the full sense of its words, this Sermon has been fulfilled by Jesus alone, but he came to the cross just because he lived according to this new gospel law. . . . He who is ready to follow out this rule of life according to its letter will lose his life as Christ did.[1]

The words of Jesus were originally meant to be taken literally, but they regrettably cannot be literally fulfilled by us.[2]

Let us openly confess that none of us fulfills the requirements of the Sermon on the Mount. . . . Even the best and godliest of men in their transactions with others lose sight of the thread which binds them to the spiritual law of the Gospel.[3]

Not only are we incapable of transferring into our time the exact wording of the Sermon on the Mount, but we do not even manage to consider the spirit of Jesus as normative principle of our economic endeavor.[4]

Of what significance is the Sermon on the Mount to us if we do not follow it? . . . It keeps the feeling alive that we cannot attain to the right moral height here on earth. But at the same time it strengthens us to take up as much as possible of this moral ideal amidst the battle of life around us.[5]

---

[1]Friedrich Naumann, *Aspects of the New Theology containing selections from "Die Hilfe,"* ET J. Miller (London: Elliot Stock, 1915) 27-28.

[2]Friedrich Naumann, *Briefe über Religion mit Nachwort "Nach 13 Jahren,"* 6. Aufl. (Berlin: Druck und Verlag Georg Reimer, 1916) 57.

[3]*Aspects*, 28.

[4]*Briefe*, 62.

[5]*Aspects*, 28-29.

Friedrich Naumann's spiritual pilgrimage[6] from rapturous identification with the social ideals of Jesus' Sermon on the Mount to resolute affirmation of the nationalist aspirations of Kaiser Wilhelm II's *Realpolitik* exemplifies the emotional pathos and intellectual trauma of a whole generation in transition from Lutheran Orthodoxy to National Socialism. In a sense, Naumann speaks for all those who are unable to relinquish or reconcile the claims of God and Caesar within their own *Selbstbewußtsein* and whose agony of conscience in quest for a *modus vivendi* constitutes the *Weltschmerz* characterizing "Christian civilization."

The first stage of Naumann's religious development is marked by his publication, *Jesus als Volksmann* (1894), the object of which was to portray Jesus as a dedicated reformer who alleviated all of man's external needs by effecting spiritual and social change from within. Our time, says Naumann, altogether fails to understand Jesus because it is so rich in knowledge and so poor in feeling. Jesus, on the contrary, was simply overwhelmed by the social and economic inequity between rich and poor and filled with compassion for the needy and with moral indignation towards the wealthy who exploited their misery. Jesus ministered not as a specialist in national economy, social statistics, or civil jurisprudence but as a *Volksmann* who identified with the misery of the *am ha-aretz* and as a social reformer sought to alleviate their plight. Naumann sought to recover for our time Jesus' exemplary ethic of the Sermon on the Mount so

---

[6]Friedrich Naumann (1860-1919) was born in Störmthat near Leipzig, where he also studied theology with one intermission at Erlangen. Through the writings of St. Francis and Tolstoy, he was early attracted to the ideals of Christian Socialism and, while a pastor at Frankfurt, sought to found an independent labor party. In 1898 he resigned the ministry for journalism in Berlin, where he published the socialist weekly *Die Hilfe* and eventually became a staunch advocate of German power politics. His transition from "Christian" to "National" Socialism and the deep personal struggle this entailed are vividly documented by three publications marking the respective stages within this development: *Jesus als Volksmann* (1894), *Asia* (1899), and *Briefe über Religion* (1903).

Under the influence of Max Weber's realism, Naumann committed himself totally to the social, technical and industrial problems of the national economy, the establishment of a European common market, and the development of a strong German naval defense which he considered absolutely essential for the future of the German race though he fully realized the incompatibility of its aspirations with the ideals of Jesus. Naumann became leader of the German Democratic Party, participated in the drafting of the Weimar constitution and achieved distinction for his realistic conception of "responsible social order." To that end he helped found a political academy and published numerous works on political and economic affairs.

that millions of workers in this century might be inspired and captivated by these social ideals—a pious rhapsody for which he expected to be ridiculed as a mystic, romanticist, or dreamer. Nevertheless, Naumann claimed to know what he was saying and assumed that "he who drinks golden wine can afford to put up with the mockery from the drawers of water."[7]

In 1899 Naumann, the Christian Socialist "political pastor," joined one hundred of his countrymen on a Holy Land expedition to witness the dedication of the Erlöserkirche in Nazareth by his majesty Kaiser Wilhelm II and to discern more clearly the life and times of the world's greatest social reformer, Jesus of Nazareth, in his native environment. How deeply Naumann was moved by what he saw and experienced during these weeks is evident from his vivid travelogue *Asia*, which was serialized in the German press for the benefit of less fortunate compatriots eager to participate vicariously in this historic event. While rocking ever so gently on the upper deck of a mighty German steamer proudly churning the calm dark waters that shimmered in the balmy oriental twilight, Naumann would join the hearty chorus of German voices echoing across the Mediterranean the ever recurrent "Deutschland, Deutschland über alles!" which so readily and so deeply stirred the warmest sentiments of every loyal German soul. Or he would be sitting with his travel companions in a casino in Constantinople sipping priceless German beer at only two piastra per glass and trolling the same patriotic refrain for the entertainment of resident German tradesmen and in turn endorsing the logic by which they justified the Turkish massacre of 100,000 Armenians as an act of self-defense.[8] For Naumann the

---

[7]Theodor Heuss, *Friedrich Naumann, der Mann, das Werk, die Zeit* (Stuttgart und Tübingen: Rainer Wunderlich Verlag Hermann Leins, 1949) 137.

[8]Naumann records *in extenso* the argument of the German master potter: "Ich bin ein Christ und halte die Nächstenliebe für das erste Gebot, und ich sage, die Türken haben Recht gethan, als sie die Armenier totschlugen. . . . " *Asia* (Berlin-Schönberg: Verlag der "Hilfe," 1899) 31-32. Naumann himself approved of the Armenian massacre on the grounds that any threat to the sovereignty of Turkey would invariably serve the purposes of England more than those of Germany. "Hier liegt der tiefe sittliche [*sic*] Grund, weshalb wir gegen die Leiden der christlichen Völker im türkischen Reich politisch gleichgültig sein müssen, so schwer dieses unserem Gefühle werden mag." Ibid., 145. Naumann's counsel to German "pioneers" abroad read: "Das Bild Bismarcks, das in euren Stuben hängt, soll euch an eurer nationalen Aufgabe festhalten. Aber das Bild des Gekreuzigten braucht ihr. Ohne treues Festhalten am christlichen Glauben der deutschen Heimat seid ihr gerade im Orient nur Spreu im Winde." Ibid., 162.

entire excursion was a quite overwhelming experience highlighted by the
Kaiser's impressive address at the altar in Nazareth about which Naumann
reflected concern lest the personal piety of the Kaiser affect—even if ever
so slightly—the sagacity of his *Nationalpolitik*.[9]

Anxiously clinging to the remnants of his string-patched saddle pre-
cariously perched on the sore backbone of his decrepit Arab nag as it hob-
bled insecurely over the uneven cobblestones of the old Nablus Road toward
Jerusalem, Naumann, the last man of his company, choked by the persistent dust of the road, exhausted by the relentless heat of the day, and dis-
gusted by the conspicuous absence of any semblance of German character,
discipline, or order in the Orient, experienced a cultural and in turn religious shock from which he never recovered. It suddenly occurred to him
that Jesus himself had walked or ridden at least twice on this same road
without doing anything whatsoever to improve it despite the fact that the
social well-being of the whole country depended then as now upon the
condition of its roads. Surely anyone who has learned to think in sociological terms must consider the condition of the roads an object of practical
Christian concern. And it is evident that in Jesus' day these roads were in
no better condition. What then, surmised Naumann, did Jesus actually say
about these roads? Did he counsel patience or urge renewal? Did he wish
to remedy the poverty of the country or only intend to alleviate its most
dire grievances by charity and miracles? Naumann had always considered
responsible social welfare the embodiment of the spirit of Jesus, but, having seen Palestine, he now began to doubt the correctness of this conception. It slowly dawned on him that the Jesus of the New Testament belongs
not to Germany but Galilee and that it is very hard to do what Kierkegaard
advised: to think of one's self as a contemporary of Jesus. The very manner in which Jesus followed the impulses of his heart seems so strange to
our modern humanitarian age. Naumann had always thought of Jesus as
living in a well-ordered country in the context of which he demanded the
equality of rich and poor in the spirit of human brotherhood. That he lived
in a country lacking the elemental foundations of social progress—namely,

---

[9]"Wir brauchen einen Kaiser der fromm ist bis in die Knochen, aber uns würde bang
sein, sobald das Religiöse im engeren Sinne die politische Leistungskraft auch nur im ger-
ingsten berühren würde. Der Gottesdienst der Könige ist eine große, weitschauende, gerechte und straffe Politik. In diesem Ton war Karl der Große gottesfürchtiger als Ludwig
der Fromme." Ibid., 72.

good roads—became clear to him once he began to read the New Testament with the eye of a Palestinian. "I had to relinquish what had been very dear to me: the earthly Helper who sees all manner of human need."[10]

The image of Jesus Naumann brought with him to Palestine somehow failed to fit the context. This Jesus belonged neither amid the slopes of Galilee nor the lands and roads of Judea. He continues to be the object of pious worship throughout Christendom, but he is not the original Jesus and, in fact, bears little resemblance to him. Naumann had always thought Jesus was too big, too strong, too demanding for Orientals under Roman bondage, for a people lacking self-consciousness and creative drive. Consequently, oriental Christianity compromised the teachings of Jesus as a result of which it eventually disintegrated. By this logic Naumann had always explained that Jesus, in contrast to undeveloped Orientals, was a radical social reformer. But now, compelled by new insights gained during that miserable journey along the Nablus Road, Naumann, however reluctantly and regretfully, relinquished his image of Jesus as economic and social reformer, for by all indications Jesus had cared nothing about the improvement of those neglected roads. Consequently, Jesus had cared little about the economy of his country which then as now depended upon the condition of the roads, and, in turn, it has now become doubtful whether Jesus really cared as much about the social well-being of the people of his land and time as we had always thought.

Naumann's idealistic conception of Jesus as socialist was shattered. All the old familiar Schnorr von Carolsfeld paintings of Jesus in the German Bible likewise had to go. Blessed are the fathers of the German nation who were spared this moment of truth, for who can imagine what this Son of Nazareth has meant for the Germans. "They made him one of their own. All the deeper cultural values of our nation derive from him."[11] Now that the air has escaped the balloon, the whole structure has to collapse. The dead idols can never be resurrected. No new religion is possible, only further decay. These were the sentiments and insights that overwhelmed Naumann as he wearily plodded along that dusty Nablus Road.

In the course of these introspective and somewhat sentimental reflections, Naumann eventually arrived at Jerusalem. What did he find there?

---

[10]Ibid., 114-15.

[11]Ibid., 119.

A miserably impoverished and undernourished remnant of beggarly Jews whose deplorable state of existence Naumann could hardly bear to behold. He began to ask himself: Are these really the same people to whom Jesus addressed his Sermon on the Mount with incomprehensible meekness? How could Jesus have demanded of them: "Give to him who begs from you, and do not refuse him who would borrow from you" (Matthew 5:42)? To one who stands surrounded by a crowd of hungry beggars from the Mount of Olives that most certainly appears an intolerably hard word. Would Jesus really say the same thing to these people today? Would he advise them: "Consider the lilies of the field, how they grow; they neither toil nor spin; yet I tell you, even Solomon in all his glory was not arrayed like one of these. . . . Therefore do not be anxious, saying, 'What shall we eat?' or 'What shall we drink?' or 'What shall we wear?' For the Gentiles seek all these things; your heavenly Father knows that you need them all" (Matthew 6:28-29). Naumann wondered:

> Could Jesus have spoken thus to a people who should instead have been told: Go to the colonies of the German Templars and see how they toil! Your heavenly Father nourishes them for they labor in the sweat of their brow, they till deeply, construct irrigation canals, build roads, provide healthful nourishment, improve bad water, and clothe themselves properly! Or were the people Jesus had before him already so preoccupied with these pursuits that they needed Jesus' strong anti-cultural emphasis? Does one believe Jesus could be a friend of today's Turkish customs poacher as he was a friend of the Roman tax collector? Or was the Master of love indifferent to the condition of the land and the people?[12]

These are the questions to which Naumann sought answers. But all he found were ruins of stone and ruins of people who no longer spoke the language of Jesus. Here, where he sought Jesus, he lost him.

Modern man cannot imagine Jesus as other than the historical son of Mary who lived in Nazareth, Capernaum, Tiberias, Jerusalem, and Jericho, Naumann concluded. One cannot construct a viable image of him solely out of dogmatics.[13] Before we can make Jesus the focal reference for our scale of values, we must comprehend the historical nature of his person. This is what theology by every conceivable means endeavored to

---

[12]Ibid., 114.

[13]Mann "will und muß sich seinen Heiland irgendwie vor Augen stellen. . . . Aus bloßen Glaubenssätzen baut sich keine Gestalt auf, mit der unser Geist reden kann." Ibid., 112.

do; but the more we reached out to him the more we realized how far he is removed from us and how difficult it is to grasp him historically. We seek to comprehend Jesus by understanding the milieu in which he lived as one understands a hero against the background of his time and from within the context of his environment. "What good can come from Nazareth?" One sees nothing but deficiency. How could one construct from such defect an image of Jesus? The soil of Palestine offers the seeker stones instead of bread. "We have visited all the important locations in Jesus' life," reports Naumann,

> and what do they say to us? Nothing! Just the scorching sun on dead rock, that is all. Palestine takes from us our German Jesus and gives us no oriental Jesus in exchange. . . . Protestant theology is in a dilemma: it must press on to the historical Jesus, and yet it has not strength enough to so smite the mountains of Palestine that they yield water.[14]

Naumann acknowledged that

> it is not easy to have seen Palestine and to keep faith. . . . A progressive optimistic nation like ours is inclined to produce its own *Weltanschauung*. "Why," they say, "should we cling to an Asiatic religion with Constantinopolitan dogma? Arise, let us cast off what is foreign and return to the naturalistic thought of our ancestors still unaffected by the waters of Jordan." Such ideas of a pure Teutonism are at times very powerful especially at the Jordan. Inwardly one feels so forsaken in the land of the lost grave of Jesus that one remembers with affection the old sacred shrines of Germany.[15]

In the course of this excursion to the Orient, Naumann had made the transition from Christian Socialism to National Socialism with the confirmed intention of serving the economic and political aspirations of his *Vaterland* with unmatched loyalty and unreserved devotion. Even before his return, a stopover at a German home in Genoa provided the atmosphere and leisure to articulate the implications of his insights for Germany's progressive internal and external *Nationalpolitik*. Naumann fully realized that his political recommendations—to strengthen the German navy,[16] reject

---

[14]Ibid., 115-16.

[15]Ibid., 119-20.

[16]"Jede Flottenverneinung ist unbewußter oder bewußter Dienst für die Flottenherrschaft Englands." Ibid., 145.

international peace treaties,[17] annex Austria,[18] and establish a dictatorship throughout the Orient[19]—implied "a radical solution to a very difficult internal conflict" between national duties and human obligations. When caught within a conflict of loyalties, some may seek a compromise solution in only partially satisfying either claim, but Naumann held that, while doing so is understandable from a human point of view, "it is only seldom morally right." For him it was essentially a matter of determining "on which side the greater, morally more significant responsibility lies. Once one has decided, there can be no more vacillation."[20] Kaiser Wilhelm II made his choice. He believed in a larger independent Germany, and so did Naumann. His final ethical counsel was that "in politics one may not underestimate spiritual forces. Long and hard battles are not won without moral energy."[21] In many avid readers of the *Asia* travelogue Naumann will have evoked a tender touch of empathy by his concluding comment that it was not easy for him as a sincerely convinced Christian to accept from the stony documents of the Holy Land the preaching of this hard truth.[22] No warmth of pious sentiment should, however, obscure for anyone the obvious fact that Naumann's "hard truth" is none other than the Aryan dictum "Deutschland, Deutschland, über alles!" and that the determinants comprising Naumann's *Lebens- und Weltanschauung* derive not from Palestinian but Teutonic soil.

Naumann's critics did not comprehend how one could simultaneously claim to be a conservative Christian, a progressive economist, and a patriotic enthusiast for German naval defense.[23] In his *Briefe über Religion* (1903), Naumann consequently undertakes to expound his new theology within the context of naturalistic philosophy and political ethics.

---

[17]" . . . international ist englisch!" Ibid., 156.

[18]"Wir brauchen Österreich, es mag sein wie es will . . . " Ibid., 153. "Unsere Parole heißt: Mit dem ganzen Kontinent gegen England; mit Österreich gegen Rußland; mit Frankreich, wenn dazu die Zeit gekommen ist." Ibid., 154.

[19]Im Orient "muß also eine Art freundschaftlicher Diktatur angebahnt werden, bei der es bisweilen heißt: 'Vogel, friß oder stirb!' " Ibid., 163.

[20]Ibid., 149.

[21]Ibid., 155-56.

[22]Ibid., 165.

[23]Theodor Heuss, *Friedrich Naumann. Der Mann, das Werk, die Zeit* (Stuttgart und Tübingen: Rainer Wunderlich Verlag Hermann Leins, 1949²) 140.

Naumann explains how the religious doctrine he inherited failed to stand the test of experience; only the person of Jesus stood firm in the midst of everything. Theology is no finished system—except for the dead. *Theologia viatorum* is a matter of following the person of Jesus however difficult it is to distinguish—even within the New Testament—between the Jesus of history and the Christ of faith.[24] The problem with religious influence of the pietist type is that it awakens religious feelings and ambitions to which one can give no practical expression in life.[25] Pietism clings to Jesus' person, not to his teaching. The Pietist proclaims the Lamb of God that bears the sins of the world while the so-called modern Christian hardly knows what to do with the preaching of the Cross[26] and focuses instead on the actual life of Jesus. But what can his life mean for those who no longer view his death as a sacrifice? The history of art indicates how different people of different times have seen Jesus in a thousand different ways. To see only a moral example in him is too little for those who seek to know him personally. "His morality is only a part of his soul and what is actually important about his soul is the penetration of all its movements with divine sonship."[27] Jesus was son of God in Galilee, not Athens, Rome, Berlin, London, or Chicago. While divine sonship is essentially always and everywhere the same, it *manifests* itself differently in different environments, reasons Naumann. When different substances are burned, the process of combustion is essentially the same, but the brightness, temperature, and color of the spectrum vary greatly with the substance being consumed. Everything therefore depends on our correct understanding of Jesus' divine sonship in *Galilee*.

---

[24]"Einige sehen die Sonne zeitiger als andere. Diese Wenigen sind die, die schon bald nach Mitternacht aufgestanden sind, um auf die Höhe zu gehen." Friedrich Naumann, *Briefe über Religion (Mit Nachwort nach 13 Jahren)* (Berlin: Druck und Verlag v. Georg Reimer, 1916⁶) 21.

[25]"Man redet von der Liebe Christi, und dann sammelt man Geld für das Gehalt eines Mannes, der diese Liebe für uns ausüben soll. . . . Ist das die letzte Form der Liebe des Evangeliums?" Ibid., 26-27.

[26]"Diese haben sehr wenig Möglichkeit, sich den Gedanken des versöhnenden Todes auf Golgatha innerlich anzueignen, denn in ihren Seelen fehlen die Vorbegriffe: Schuld, ewige Strafe, Zorn Gottes, Sühne, Stellvertretung, Zurechnung, Rechtfertigung." (Ibid., 44.) And yet, observes Naumann, more people than we suppose are not inwardly free from the silent fear: "daß man schließlich aus lauter Hunger der Seele das härteste Klosterbrot essen werde, um überhaupt etwas zwischen den Zähnen zu haben." Ibid., 46.

[27]Ibid., 50.

How shall we then interpret his words?[28] He says: Care not for tomorrow. But what does our whole economy demand if not planning? Jesus says: Sell all and give to the poor. But who wants to liquidate his real estate, his home, or factory and give the proceeds to charity? "Is it only our hardness of heart and original sin if we do not apply everything literally?"[29] The clergy of all times have by devious ways sought to evade the judgment of these words and say that they were not at first meant literally. But Jesus did indeed demand literal obedience and acted accordingly. "The words of Jesus were originally meant to be taken literally, but they regrettably cannot be literally fulfilled by us."[30] The impossibility of translating Jesus' style of living directly into our time and circumstances constitutes the agony of our troubled Christian conscience. Jesus says: You cannot serve God and Mammon, whereas, we, in our capitalist era, live in the midst of a productive economy that is entirely speculative. How then can we keep from condemning ourselves? Naumann seeks the solution to this moral dilemma in the realization that the Galilean economy of Jesus' day was pre-capitalistic. Economic incentive and its accompanying evils infiltrated the country only from without, and hence it was to these foreign influences threatening to corrupt natural conditions in Galilee that Jesus was so opposed.

The error of Christian Socialism lay in wanting to find in Jesus the highest authorization of our political and economic aspirations. However, "every time we seriously tried to make specific deductions from the gospel, it failed. The gospel was simply Galilean"[31] while our *Klassenkampf* is a modern conflict for which we cannot claim Jesus as defender of the working classes. Our economic problem, observes Naumann, is—quite unlike that of Jesus' time—not so much due to inequity between rich and poor as it is the result of the struggle for supremacy between an agricultural or industrial economy. We cannot extricate from our capitalist economy the built-in axioms of competition and speculation. We, in contrast to Jesus, must learn to live with the fact that business is a law unto itself, gov-

---

[28]"Diese Worte sind nicht totzumachen. Man kann ein guter Psycholog sein und doch hier völlig ratlos stehen. Diese Ratlosigkeit aber gehört zur Religion selbst." Ibid., 42.

[29]Ibid., 56.

[30]Ibid., 57.

[31]Ibid., 59.

erned by cause and effect balance systems of the profit motive—a system that keeps the successful entrepreneur from dissolving his material investments and donating the proceeds to charity. One is not a slave to Mammon when one drives a hard bargain—only when one transgresses the code of acceptable practice. "That a Christian in business must be polite and always seek to act correctly is self-evident." But Naumann failed to discover "how one can realize in business the special spirit of Christ." To christianize the economy is beyond our capacity.

> Not only are we incapable of transferring into our time the exact wording of the Sermon of the Mount, but we do not even manage to consider the spirit of Jesus as normative principle of our economic endeavor.[32]
>
> Let us openly confess that none of us fulfills the requirements of the Sermon on the Mount. Who in the present complicated environment of life can comprise the full content of it in his daily conduct so that his inner and outer self is molded by it? When you go to a merchant, do you not in the meantime leave this Sermon out of doors upon the street? Or, when you strive with your landlord, do you not forget that the meek shall inherit the earth? Or, when importuned by any one, do you always "give to him who asketh you, and do not turn yourself away from him who would borrow"? . . . Even the best and godliest of men in their transactions with others loose from the hand the thread which binds them to the spiritual law of the Gospel.[33]

Our entire capitalist economy is founded on coveteousness. To get anywhere in life we must covet our neighbor's possessions. Covetousness expanded on principle constitutes the competitive world market upon which the economy of every contributing nation thrives. In this world we have only two options: either disassociate ourselves from the creative processes of life or acknowledge the limitation of our Christianity while continuing to confess our desire to be Christian to the extent that it is practicable,[34] realizing that our actual life is not governed by exclusively Christian motives. However serious and committed we are in our Christian discipleship, we must openly and freely admit, says Naumann, that certain aspects

---

[32]Ibid., 62.

[33]Friedrich Naumann, *Aspects of the New Theology containing selections from "Die Hilfe,"* ET J. Miller (London: Elliot Stock, 1915) 28.

[34]" . . . so viel und so gut es in der Welt möglich ist." *Briefe über Religion,* 63.

of life are not subject to Christian rules[35] simply because we have our own lives to live in our own time and place, and that in itself is not an admission of hypocrisy.

We have become accustomed to portraying Jesus as Lord of the lost and poor, who stands among begging, deformed idiots in his majestic heavenly transcendence like a royal princess on a hospital tour. But to realize that the milieu of the poor is actually his own proper environment is absolutely shattering. To see Jesus of Nazareth in his actual habitat with the rags and nooks and filthy poverty of those indescribable slums simply shatters the propriety, decency, and etiquette of Christianity. The insight that Jesus also is the product of his environment[36] only compounds the problem: how can we as cultured Europeans hold solely to him when we have so little in common with his actual environment? Once one has seen the Galilean Jesus in all his harshness and one-sidedness, one intuitively knows that only few can hold to the whole Jesus:

> One cannot hope to base the whole of human progress on sympathy and the spirit of brotherhood. . . . World remains world, and power comes before sympathy.[37]
> Not our whole morality roots in the gospel. . . . Besides the gospel, there are demands of power and of justice without which human society cannot exist. . . . I personally know no other way of resolving the conflict between Christianity and the other responsibilities of life except to discern the limitation of Christianity. That is difficult but better than the burden of half-truths, the pressure of which I have also borne.[38]

Sympathy and chastity are the two focal elements of the gospel ethic Jesus proclaimed in a world full of hardness and uncleanness. The world will always be imperfect and therefore the preaching of this gospel will always be appropriate, and he who hears it will always experience its cleansing effect since man at his best yearns with a holy longing for the blessed eternity of true love and ascetic purity. But the greatest and hardest problems of life are not resolved by the New Testament with its eschatological

---

[35]Ibid.

[36]"In den Tagen des Augustus wuchs das Licht der Welt in Nazareth! Das Heil im Stall, die Perle im Kalk, Jesus unter den Plebejern." Ibid., 65.

[37]Ibid., 65.

[38]Ibid., 66.

otherworldly outlook.[39] The state is guided by quite different instincts than those Jesus cultivated. It is constituted not by sympathy but authority; it is motivated not by fraternal love but by military might. The state is a part of the natural struggle of being—like the protective armor that grows out of the body of a crab. The presuppositions for culture as we know it derive not from the slums of Nazareth but from the nexus of Roman civilization. Either we disassociate ourselves from the state, as Jesus did, or we somehow incorporate into its civil ethos our Christian ethic.

Naumann reasoned that one cannot find the basis for all morality in the gospel, for, if that were so, one would have to argue that the state with its cannons and prisons was an instrument of the Kingdom of God and that Bismarck's preparation for the Schleswig-Holstein war was a service in the Kingdom of Jesus Christ. Naumann found no basis for criticizing that act as such, and yet he could not justify war from the gospel. Consequently, he concluded that not every fulfillment of duty is Christian. Nevertheless, our duty we must do—each in his vocation—even if in so doing we have to break the tenderest emotions of the soul. To the duplicity implied in this necessity Naumann found no alternative.

Conflict is the principle of progress as is seen in children at play. "He who has the better blood lives longer." Shall we subdue the fighting instinct until it is no longer able to assert itself? Or shall we strengthen natural human drives and the human will to live on the assumption that it is through this strength of will that God accomplishes his purposes with us? Is it God who lets nations rise and fall in their historic struggle for survival against one another? They say no sparrow falls from the roof against His will. How is this belief to be reconciled with the fact that half the sparrows die prematurely?

> Following the god of this world produces the morality of the struggle for existence, and serving the Father of Jesus Christ produces the morality of compassion. However they are not two Gods but one. Somehow their arms interlock; only no mortal can say where or how.[40]

Naumann compared his own Christian *Weltanschauung* to the Bamberger Dome. Built over centuries, this dome reflects a variety of architectural styles which in spirit and effect clash with one another; yet taken

---

[39]Cf. ibid., 68.
[40]Ibid., 72.

all together the creation is somehow a majestic whole. The uneducated observer is oblivious to the variety of style and sees only the total effect. The half-educated critic fanatically justifies one style over against others, while the connoisseur appreciates the uniqueness of each style in its own right and in its contribution to the whole. Analogously, Naumann envisions the relation of Christianity to the struggles of life. Some people have no difficulty in seeing harmony in every conflict, reconciling power with love. That God loved Jacob but hated Esau never disturbs such souls nor does the fact that they thank him for their own salvation at the cost of another's destruction. Others, unable to resolve within their knowledge and being this conflict between the ideal and the real, either define the meaning of life simply on the basis of self-interest in terms of nature's struggle for the survival of the fittest or they identify with the principle of compassion as the highest norm of truth and let the rest of the world go by. Either they howl with the wolves or die with the lambs. They give us only two options: either to dominate or to suffer. "Either to go with Bismarck or Tolstoy. Either the gospel of the armed fist or the gospel of the Brothers of the Common Life."[41]

He who has been confronted with this decision knows from the turmoil of his soul how acute this tension between God and history and between heaven and hell really is. Apostles, missioners, and defenders of principles can, observes Naumann, somehow exist in this existential suspension by thriving on the paradox of truth and being in all its mystery and agony. But whoever wills to contribute to the actual process and real stuff of life is compelled to find a practical way out of this paradox. For him, life is greater than principles, even as the Bamberger Dome is higher than the pillars which support it. Naumann concludes that life demands *both*, the clenched fist and the hand of Jesus, each in its time and place. The beatitude of the Psalmist "Blessed shall he be who takes your little ones and dashes them against a rock!"[42] is an ethic much inferior to that of the Sermon on the Mount. However, it is still with us. Why? "Because it is upon this foundation that natural life is built and because no Christianity can remove this natural life."[43] Every state still manifests this raw paganism, for

---

[41]Ibid., 74.

[42]Ps. 137:9.

[43]*Briefe über Religion*, 77.

its ethic is not that of universal love, and its highest goal is not the well-being of mankind.

In the Middle Ages all aspects of life were wedded to the sanctions of the monolithic *corpus christianum,* but, since that has in fact broken up, man's loyalties are divided by the conflicting claims of the labor union, the state, the church, and the home, each making their rightful demands upon his allegiance, but none commanding the totality of the self. In this situation the priorities of commitment are balanced not within a monolithic totalitarian collective but within the responsible individual, and to arrive at this balance with integrity comprises the meaning of being Protestant, according to Naumann.[44]

One must realize that militarism is the foundation of all social order and welfare in Europe:

> Say whatever you know against militarism! It will all be true, for no one can describe the battles more horribly than they are. [Nevertheless] all the damages of military power are minor compared to the plight of a land in which there is no such dominion. . . . Armed peace is not nice, but it is better than all the historical circumstances we have known. . . . The future, especially that of Teutonism, depends on the maintenance of the military spirit of the population. . . . The struggle for existence has taught nations to be armed brutes.[45]

If one can sanction only what is directly supported by Jesus' sayings, one must dispense with the maintenance of the state through the military. Even so, Naumann questions whether the Christian idea of fraternal love could be realized other than upon the foundation of political order. And, since there is no state without a military backbone, either one risks the hazard of being stateless, abandoning one's self to the arbitrariness of anarchy, or one decides to hold to a political confession alongside the religious one:

> He[Jesus] said that his Kingdom is not of this world, but people who wish to live and work in this world must be as clear about the basic conditions of world culture as about the relations of their souls to God.[46]

Jesus did not create Graeco-Roman culture, but neither did he abolish it:

---

[44]Cf. ibid., 76-79.

[45]Ibid., 80.

[46]Ibid., 82.

He was not an enemy of the state on principle. What he offers is a supplement to the culture of his time, a supplement whose worth, power, and goodness cannot be evaluated high enough, but still simply a supplement.

The purer the proclamation of Jesus the less useful it is for the state:

> We do not construct our government house with the cedars of Lebanon but use the building blocks of the Roman capitol. In this house Jesus must today proclaim his gospel as at one time in the Roman house. Therefore, we do not ask Jesus about matters which belong to the realm of political and economic construction. That may sound hard and harsh for every person brought up as a Christian but appears to me to be good Lutheranism. . . . Political matters are, according to Luther, not to be decided on the basis of the gospel but can just as well be determined by Jews and pagans as by Christians, since their regulation requires nothing but reason, not revelation.[47]

We are all slaves to circumstances like animals in a cage. We are all products of our traditions and environments, while Jesus, wandering about Galilee in the dawn of history before the development of civilization as we know it, could afford to be without tradition or society, have the audacity to set himself up against Moses, take the liberty to sit at table with tax collectors and sinners, and be free of all anxiety about tomorrow.[48] Naumann intensely desired to know something of this inexplicably boundless personal freedom to live in accord with the highest ideal, but he could not realize it. He was bound by a thousand insoluble involvements essential for the maintenance and perpetuation of the values of civilization and culture which he felt personally obligated to guarantee. The struggle for existence demands total military mobilization. This presents to the religious soul the problem of personal duplicity. Naumann concludes that as individuals we may be either militarist or pacifist but ''the nation as a whole must simultaneously embody both: Jesus and Caesar! That is hard for the disciples of the Sermon on the Mount, but that is how it is.''[49] In a day when the theo-

---

[47]Ibid., 85.

[48]Ibid., 86.

[49]Ibid., 115. ''Ich sprach mit Offizieren: sie achten ihre Gegner. Manchmal erscheint verstohlen und scheu etwas, was an das Wort Jesu erinnert: liebet eure Feinde. Man kann

logical moorings of Christian Europe yielded to the swelling tide of international imperialistic conflict, a generation of Germans recognized in Naumann's largely individualistic confessions of religious disillusionment and attempts at ideological reconstruction their own quest for a credible existential self-image and a viable teutonic self-identity. So regrettable about Naumann's personal pilgrimage from Christian Socialism to national realism are the losses he—together with his countrymen—suffered, outweighing the reconstructions he realized.

The shattering of Naumann's idealistic vision of following Jesus is so tragic not because it happened while he was following the footsteps of Jesus along the Nablus Road but because Naumann speaks for countless others who, having inherited the Western Christian tradition, somewhere along the way of their spiritual pilgrimage conclude that as far as they are concerned life's meaning and destiny must be radically disassociated from the way of suffering. Abruptly they resolve to take another course. With uneasy conscience they seek to salvage the sentiments of a personal attachment to Jesus but find no way of reconciling his call to faith with the demands of life. Naumann concluded that Jesus' way was not a sufficiently responsible one—neither for his time nor for ours. Not unlike Schweitzer, Naumann exempted Jesus from the obligation of assuming full responsibility for the historical destiny of his nation on the grounds of apocalyptic disillusionment: having been completely captivated by an otherworldly fanaticism, Jesus was unable to discern right from wrong and hence resolved to sacrifice himself for a lost cause rather than fight for a noble one. That exemption cannot, however, be claimed by modern man.

Naumann, the culturally enlightened observer of the Bamberger Dome, realizes that the oriental sentiments of Jesus, King of Beggars, clash with the *Realpolitik* of Wilhelm II, Kaiser of Germany. But, on the strength of his belief in national historical destiny, Naumann resolves that, in the providence of God, both must somehow go together. Then it occurs to him that symbiosis is, after all, the order of nature. That insight suffices to provide the rightful place for the German military under the Bamberger Dome

---

sie nicht schonen und erwartet keine Schonung, solange der Kriegszweck es verbietet, aber eigentlicher unversöhnlicher Haß entsteht nur in Ausnahmsfällen nach Verrat oder Niedertracht. Fast möchte ich vom moralisch geläuterten Kriege sprechen, wohl wissend, das Krieg ein wildes Tier bleibt. Im losgebundenen Kampfe ums Dasein klingt etwas von den Harfen der Ewigkeit, von der über allen Kampf hinaus unauslöschlichen Menschlichkeit.'' Ibid., 128.

of Naumann's "Christian" *Weltanschauung*. The majestic solidity of this "dome"—thanks to its stable Roman pillars—provides the assurance that somehow God defends his own interests in allowing the compassion of Jesus to serve the cause of Caesar. Those who stand perplexed at this moment of truth might realize that for Naumann "perplexity belongs to the essence of religion!"[50]

Naumann's image of Jesus was too fragile to withstand the rigors of the Nablus Road. Through his iconoclastic trauma he suffered a double loss: his Socialist ideal and, in turn, his personal Jesus. Despite his new theology of the bad roads, he hoped to recover the spirit of Jesus for the realm of Caesar without questioning the autonomy of the state from the thread which binds men to the gospel. Unlike Luther, "the great doctor of German faith," who resolved the gap between the Two-Kingdoms by the doctrine of predestination, Naumann, though always hoping to make the best of both worlds, found—apart from his belief in the destiny of the *Vaterland*—no vital connection between the will of God and the *raison d'être* of the state.

Naumann believed that the ethical teachings of Jesus must be understood literally; he realized, however, that the Sermon on the Mount cannot be fulfilled within the order of our civilization and, therefore, concluded that it is no longer authoritative for us. Naumann unsettled the restive conscience of Christendom by exposing with convincing pathos and almost naïve simplicity its inherent dilemma for which he found no theological resolution. Those who seek resolutions must—in the hope of working out their own salvation—move beyond Naumann. What further alternatives there are remain to be seen.

---

[50]Ibid., 42.

Professor Bachmann of Erlangen observed in 1904 that it is commonly said, "The ethic of the Nazarene is orientally inactive, is an escapist monk-ethic which locates man's goal in a visionary beyond" and which only hinders and restrains the cultural process (*Die Sittenlehre Jesu und ihre Bedeutung für die Gegenwart* [Leipzig: A. Deichertsche Verlagsbuchhandlung. Nachf. Georg Böhme, 1904, 14-15). Wishing to allay this critique, Bachmann asks how one can identify with the cultural process when Jesus prophesied its doom (32). Since state and war are inseparable for Bachmann, he considers the central question not "What did Jesus say about war?" but rather "What is Jesus' stance towards the gross national product of human culture?" (42). It does not seem likely to Bachmann that Jesus would consider discipleship and possession of worldly goods as mutually exclusive options

(48). And as for Jesus' saying about loving one's enemy, according to Bachmann, that was meant as an "illustration" which does not encompass the whole relationship (49). The good is not always accomplished through passivity; it may also be good to resist evil. "Only when and where justice is in force is the renunciation of justice a free act of love. Where justice no longer exists, there quiet endurance is no longer the virtue of the strong but the hard lot of the weak" (50).

Jesus was not only an enthusiast for an otherworldly kingdom but identified with the culture of Israel as a "prototype" of the Kingdom of God. Therefore, one cannot deduce from Jesus' silence regarding culture his negation of it. Somehow, somewhere, the stream of culture ought to make its way into the Kingdom of God on earth, alleges Bachmann, though he does not venture to suggest how or where. He bases his cultural optimism on the claim that "Jesus provides the assurance that not only the end of all things but all that is great, good, beautiful, and true constitutes the goal and the peace of the Kingdom of God" (58).

Ludwig Schneller's 20 sermons delivered in 1915 on *Die Bergpredigt* (Leipzig: H. G. Wallmann, 1924) tediously re-echo the nationalist sentiments preached from most pulpits of all lands in times of war. Being Lutheran, he has reservations regarding the oath only in a mixed marriage to a Catholic, in which case the oath must be broken to avert the greater sin of raising heathen children. As for Jesus' prohibition of swearing, the military oath of allegiance is indispensable, insists Pastor Schneller, to uphold the integrity of a nation and to "sustain millions of armed Germans or enable them to endure death out of love for their Vaterland" (50). He respects the sincerity of Quakers and Mennonites in refusing military service but knows their conviction rests on a gross misunderstanding of Jesus' words which, says Schneller, have no bearing on just wars of national defense (55). Schneller commends the German army for its religious devotion and lauds the German idealism of Ernst Moritz Arndt, whose war lyric so beautifully expresses the national sentiment that God provides iron to equip brave men with daggers, swords, and spears because he wants not slaves but heroes who with fiery wrath defend their honor with blood (57).

JOHANNES WEISS:
AN APOCALYPTIC UNDERSTANDING
OF THE SERMON ON THE MOUNT

*To apply the Sermon on the Mount as precept for the daily life of everyone is to
violate its enthusiastic mood. . . . Most certainly Jesus meant it literally and would
have been the first to prove such an attitude with deeds, for his heart is . . . so
inspired with renunciation, deprivation, and self-sacrifice that even the strongest
forms of self-expression scarcely suffice him. . . . There were moments in his life
when he was so overwhelmed by the awesome seriousness of the situation that the
utmost sacrifice seemed trivial to him. And so he simply expressed what he felt—
unconcerned whether it might be rightly understood. . . . Mighty, turbulent sen-
sations dictated the Lord's words which then often enough turned out harsh and
one-sided. All those accomodations, middle axioms and moral conflicts, all those
individual concessions which guide our modern ethic are nonexistent for the
greatest of the prophets. . . . In the time of great crisis in which he lives there
invariably is only an either/or. . . .*

*One may never ask about the literal meaning or significance of the words of Jesus
for the future. Only the intense, impetuous, passionate and hence often prejudiced
religious feeling that breaks forth in them is historically perceptible.*[1]

*If in the Kingdom of God the elect are to sit at table with Abraham, Isaac, and
Jacob, then an entirely otherworldly bliss without analogies to this world is intended.*[2]

---

[1]Johannes Weiss, *Die Predigt Jesu vom Reich Gottes* (Göttingen: Vandenhoeck und
Ruprecht, 1900²) 51-53.

[2]Ibid., 72.

Johannes Weiss[3] determined that Jesus' intentions were altogether otherworldly. He saw thoroughgoing eschatology as the exclusive key to de-
code the mystery of the Kingdom of God and its ethical implications in the
teaching of Jesus. Weiss mustered impressive scholarly evidence for his
singular conviction that, once modern presuppositions are eliminated from
the study of the gospels, one must conclude that Jesus understood the
Kingdom of God to be entirely a future event—as in his prayer: Thy Kingdom come. "If in the Kingdom of God the elect are to sit at table with
Abraham, Isaac, and Jacob," Weiss wrote, "then an entirely otherworldly
bliss without any analogies to this world is intended."[4]

---

[3]Johannes Weiss (1863-1914) was born in Kiel, studied in Marburg, Berlin, Göttingen,
and Breslau and became—as had his father Bernard W.—professor of New Testament and
taught in Göttingen, Marburg, and Heidelberg. His *konsequente Eschatologie* conflicted
with his father-in-law Albrecht Ritschl's completely spiritual and purely ethical understanding of the Kingdom of God. The main works of Weiss include: *Die Predigt Jesu vom
Reiche Gottes* (1892) (1900²), *Die Nachfolge Christi und die Predigt der Gegenwart* (1895),
Das älteste Evangelium (1903), *Die Offenbarung Johannes* (1904), *I. Korinther* (Meyer
Kommentar, 1910), *Das Problem der Entstehung des Urchristentums* (1913), and *Das Ur-
christentum* (1914/17).

[4]Matthew 8:11-12. Johannes Weiss, *Die Predigt Jesu vom Reich Gottes* (Vandenhoeck
und Ruprecht 1900²)72. Weiss understands the ἤγγικεν of Matthew 4:17, 10:7, and Mark
1:15 to mean "das ganz nahe und unmittelbar Bevorstehen der Gottesherrschaft," implying that it is imminent but not already taking place. (In these texts the RSV translates this
Greek perfect with "is at hand" but in Luke 10:9, 11 and 12:31 with "has come near.")
"Das Wesentliche an der Verkündigung," argues Weiss, "ist nicht die grössere oder ger-
ingere Nähe der Krisis, sondern der Gedanke, dass das Reich Gottes jetzt *ganz gewiss*
kommt. . . .Im Vergleich mit dieser erschütterlichen *Gewissheit* ist es unwesentlich, dass
bald gesagt wird, es sei nahe, bald, es sei bereits da. Es kommt auf die Gelegenheit, auf
die jeweilige Stimmung an, ob dieser oder jener Ausdruck bevorzugt wird." When a thundercloud makes its appearance and lightening is already striking on the horizon, one may
say that a thunderstorm is coming. But one can also proleptically say that it thunders. Similarly, while the first sign of spring merely indicates that spring has come near, who would
resist the less objective temperament proclaiming jubilantly that spring is here. In view of
his overwhelming assurance and the freshness and vividness of his impressions, Jesus now
and then in his prophetic enthusiasm proleptically spanned that brief chasm of time separating the old from the new world with expressions almost implying that the goal had already been reached.

In this way, Weiss explains the occasional occurrence of ἔφθασεν (as in Matthew 12:28
and Luke 11:20) to the effect that "the Kingdom of God *has come* upon you" as evidenced
by Jesus' miracles of healing and exorcism. Weiss insists: "Es handelt sich um eine Nu-
ance in der Stimmung, nicht um verschiedene dogmatische Anschauungen," and supports
his claim with philological evidence which minimizes the temporal distinction between these

The Kingdom of God cannot therefore be reduced to a subjective quality "within" one's self. Nor does Jesus in any sense "realize" or "establish" the Kingdom. He declares God will bring it about by supernatural means in his own time. At first, Jesus thought that time was very near and therefore urged his disciples to proclaim the good news throughout the land to call all men to repentance. However, the persistent impenitence of the people convinced him that God could not work this miracle until the guilt of the people had been atoned for by his own death, after which God would

---

two Greek verb forms. Weiss likewise refutes the logic of those who interpret some of Jesus' parables to mean that the Kingdom of God gradually "grows," "develops," or "spreads" and concludes that all attempts to compromise the futuristic meaning are purely arbitrary; cf. ibid., 68-72. Accordingly, Jesus' parable of the mustard seed (Matthew 13:31-32) does not imply that the Kingdom of God grows slowly. The point of the parable is the contrast between the smallness of the cause (or seed) and the greatness of the effect, between the unassuming beginning of the Kingdom of God and the overwhelming impact of the victory and glory of God when he will establish his rule in the messianic age to come; ibid., 82-84.

By questioning the authenticity of those expressions in the gospels which imply a realized eschatology, Weiss establishes his claim that for Jesus the Kingdom of God was entirely a future hope, not a present reality. This eschatological assumption constitutes Weiss's criterion for discerning what of the gospel tradition actually derives from Jesus and which parts reflect the development of the Kingdom of God motif within the Early Church. Certain Matthean formulations which distinguish between "the Kingdom of the Son of Man" and "the Kingdom of the Father" (Matthew 13:41) are thought to originate not with Jesus but with Paul, who conceived of a "Kingdom of Christ" which would eventually be replaced by "the Kingdom of God" (cf. 1 Cor. 15:24). Similarly, the Mark 9:1 reference to "the Kingdom of God come with power" is thought to reflect not so much the mind of Jesus as the self-understanding of the pentecostal church which already claimed to live "in the power of God" through him who "was crucified in weakness" (2 Cor. 13:3-4). The messianic Kingdom, which for Jesus was an object of future hope, was claimed by the Early Church to be present reality and consequently superimposed upon the record its own interpretation by inadvertently ascribing to Jesus an expression (namely, "in power") by which these believers defined their own experience; ibid., 40-42.

In a similar way, Weiss reasoned that the form of the last blessing and woe according to Luke 6:22 and 26 reflects the evangelist's identification of the persecuted ones with early Jewish Christians who eagerly anticipated their reward in the Kingdom about to be realized, while Luke's omission of Jesus' blessings upon the meek, the merciful, and the peacemakers (according to Matthew 5:7, 8, 9) is explained on the grounds that they do not really fit the eschatological context! "Sie fallen durch ihre ermahnende Haltung aus der Gesamtstimmung heraus." These examples suffice to illustrate how Weiss, having once established futuristic eschatology as the sole criterion for determining what is and what is not authentic within the synoptic tradition, excludes by the sheer logic of presupposition any other point of view.

exalt him to heavenly splendor as the "Son of Man."[5]

Jesus was not interested in this world but in the next. His only moral counsel for the old aeon was: Repent! That is why Jesus' ethic, if judged by constructive concerns to maintain this world, appears so entirely negative in character.

Weiss shows how deeply Jesus' idea of the Kingdom is rooted in the theocracy and messianism of the Old Testament. There the kingship of God is viewed either actively—when the emphasis is on the lordship of God exercising his mighty hand and rule—or passively—when the emphasis is upon Israel's obedient submission to the will of God. In the first instance, God is king over his people, judging them and leading their battles. This theocratic motif (exemplified in Deuteronomy 33) is the basis upon which the tribes of Israel were constituted as a people of God. Man's response in total submission to God's rule is essentially passive, an understanding reflected in Jesus' word that "whoever does not receive the Kingdom of God like a child shall not enter it."[6] The Kingdom of God presupposes the repentance of human beings and their instruction and training in humility and obedience. The proclamation of this new *Lebensweise*[7] was the sole intention of the prophets, of John the Baptist, and of Jesus.[8] At every impending crisis the prophets proclaimed the Lord's intention to reassert his kingship over his opponents. These prophecies often contain apocalyptic or cosmic overtones which transcend the plane of history.[9] This transcendent under-

---

[5]Cf. Dan. 7:13. Weiss considers Jesus' use of the "Son of Man" title to be a purely eschatological self-designation without present historical implications. It had always been held that Jesus assumed this title to "veil" for whatever reason whatever was understood to constitute his messiahship until whatever time it was to be "revealed." Weiss articulates this insight by insisting that Jesus' messianic self-designation was not a present claim but a future hope to be actualized when God would realize his Kingdom through and, hence, after the death of Jesus. How else except in a futuristic sense could one now walking on earth describe himself as coming from the clouds of heaven? The question is whether reference not only to exaltation but also to humiliation was associated with the use of this title in the mind of Jesus despite the fact that the disciples rejected the latter implication while disputing with each other over the benefits to accrue to them by the former one.

[6]Mark 10:17 = Luke 18:17.

[7]that is, ὁδός or "way" of life.

[8]Jesus did not differ from John in his proclamation but only in his self-consciousness, according to Weiss.

[9]For example, Isaiah 24-27; cf. ibid., 16-17.

standing of the way God manifests his kingship became the dominant element in Jesus' proclamation.

Jesus did not envision the coming or realization of the Kingdom as his own creation or plantation. Unlike the worldly kingdoms envisioned in Daniel, the Kingdom of God would resemble neither "the tree [that] grew and became strong, with its top reaching to heaven" nor the "four great beasts . . .that came out of the sea."[10] Rather than grow and develop from earth to heaven, the Kingdom of God—like that stone which destroyed the mighty colossus of Daniel's image—would come down from above "by no human hand."[11] Borne upon the clouds, the "new Jerusalem, coming down out of heaven from God,"[12] was to coincide with the appearance of the Messiah "like a son of man."[13] As was the deluge in the days of Noah and the destruction of Sodom and Gomorrah when "fire and brimstone rained from heaven" so the coming of the Kingdom was to be a sudden, unprecedented, overwhelming, supernatural event[14] affecting all of nature including the astronomical bodies.[15] The Kingdom of God will constitute not merely a stage, however significant, in the organic development of all things but a complete break with history as we know it. The Kingdom of God is the "new creation,"[16] a new aeon, a new world. "Behold, I make all things new."[17] Jesus assumed the collapse of this world to be followed by a new world in which he would drink again of the fruit of the gloriously renewed wine in the Kingdom of God.[18]

In contrast to the rabbis who understood Israel's hope primarily in historical and political terms, identifying the realization of the Kingdom of God with the restoration of the kingdom of David, Jesus proclaimed an

---

[10]Cf. Daniel 4:11,7:3.

[11]Daniel 2:34.

[12]Revelation 21:2.

[13]Daniel 7:13.

[14]Luke 17:26f.

[15]Mark 13:24-25.

[16]Galatians 6:15.

[17]Revelation 21:5.

[18]Mark 14:25; cf. ibid., 105-108.

otherworldly Kingdom to be realized by supernatural means.[19] Because there will be no place within the Kingdom of Heaven for the imperium of Rome, therefore, Jesus' proclamation of the Kingdom has no political implications for the state whose institutions and values are of this aeon and not of the coming order. The two realms are so disparate that there is simply no overlapping or conflicting of loyalties. Jesus was not unaware of nor unmoved by the ruthless political oppression and economic exploitation of his people under foreign rule, but what distinguished him from the nationalist zealots of his day was the firm conviction that the messianic Kingdom is not of this world and cannot therefore be taken by carnal force.[20]

The transcendent character for Weiss of the Kingdom of God is exemplified in the Beatitudes. What Jesus promised the poor,[21] the hungry, and afflicted is a future reality compensating their present poverty. In pronouncing them blessed, Jesus does not mean that they now experience the fulfillment of promise but rather that they are the elect of God to whom the Kingdom of Heaven[22] will be given. Weiss ascribed much importance to

---

[19]For this radically antithetical motif Weiss finds no Old Testament equivalent, hence he ascribes it to Iranian influence upon late Jewish apocalyptic. What constitutes the greatness of Jesus is not that he used the idea of the Kingdom of God but that by his life and death he was so totally committed to its realization. "Was im Parsismus und Spätjudentum als Ahnung und Hoffnung für eine späte Zukunft lebt, dass ist für Jesus unmittelbare Gewißheit: Gott ist dennoch der einzige Herr und König der Welt. Jetzt ist die Zeit gekommen, wo er es zeigen und alle seine Feinde vernichten wird. Jesus ist der Herold dieser neuen Zeit, sein Wort ist nicht Lehre, sondern Evangelium, sein Werk ist Kampf für Gottes Sache, sein Ausgang Bürgschaft für den Sieg Gottes." Ibid., 35.

[20]Matthew 11:12, Luke 16:16. As for the meaning of βιάζεται, in these texts Weiss concludes: "Jesus beschreibt—und in der Form der Beschreibung liegt die Ablehnung—eine stürmische, zelotische messianische Bewegung, die seit den Tagen des Täufers im Gange ist." Ibid., 197-98.

[21]Weiss identifies the "poor" as "sinners" who are in a permanent state of uncleanness and hence "accursed" (John 7:49) because they do not know the law and hence cannot fulfill its precepts or gain access to the temple cleansing ritual. "Normaler Weise ist der 'Gerechte' in guter Lage, der Sünder nicht; es ist darum nur natürlich, wenn die Sünder sich auch teilweise mit den eigentlichen Armen decken. Aber es überwiegt, wie gesagt, die gesellschaftliche Betrachtung"; ibid., 130. "Wie Matthäus 5:8 καθαροὶ τῇ καρδία der Gedanke an aüssere, levitische Reinheit ausgeschlossen wird, so hier die Vorstellung leiblicher Armut." Ibid., 183.

[22]"Heaven" is substitute for "God" (cf. Luke 15:18,21), whose name it was the popular Jewish custom to avoid. "Kingdom of heaven" is to say not that the Kingdom is in heaven (as the gen. locative would imply) but that the rule of God is transcendent. Ibid., 43.

the observation that the verbs conveying the blessings are predominantly future in tense.[23]

"Hungering and thirsting" (Matthew 5:6) is not to be confused with moral striving. "How could the Kingdom of God be the object and result of human action," Weiss asks, "when it is equated with 'eternal life'?"[24] The "righteousness of God" (Matthew 5:6,20;6:33) cannot be aspired to as man's "highest good" since it is the gift of God: God's doing and not man's work. The grace of God is not to be confused with just wages as Jesus' parable of the laborers in the vineyard (Matthew 20:1-16) meant to illustrate. The "righteousness of God"—the key concept in Matthew's version of the Sermon on the Mount—constitutes least of all a positive ideal for secular morality, for it is a purely eschatological concept. The one whose conscience acquits him is not righteous, as Kant had held, but the one whom God acknowledges. That verdict will not be pronounced at some indefinite future "day of the Lord" but at any moment and with compelling force. Therefore, Jesus urged all who have ears to hear to "seek first the Kingdom of God and his righteousness" (Matthew 6:33), thereby implying a corresponding indifference to the orders, treasures, and concerns of this world.[25]

In view of the critical nature of the times, Jesus urged those who sought legal arbitration in the courts to be reconciled with their accusers "on the way" lest the thundercloud of messianic judgment overtake them. Rather than human justice, the essential matter now is divine righteousness. Let those who realize the impending crisis turn the other cheek and leave their cloak to those who would still haggle over personal and property rights (Matthew 5:25-26,39-40; Luke 12:54-55). In the Kingdom of Heaven they will be compensated a hundredfold for their earthly loss. Since Jesus was intensely antagonistic towards petty Jewish legalism and overwhelmingly enthusiastic for renunciation, asceticism, and self-sacrifice, even his strongest expressions—such as the saying about the offending eye (Matthew 5:29) or his word about eunuchs (Matthew 19:12)—barely sufficed

---

[23]Cf. Matthew 5:4-11. Weiss argues that the future form of these verbs establishes the sense in which ἐστίν (Matthew 5:3,10)—for which there is no Aramaic equivalent—is used and not vice versa; ibid., 73.

[24]Ibid., 75.

[25]"Ein himmlischer Schatz gilt es zu sammeln . . . .Da treten andere Maßstäbe in Kraft, als bei einer irdischen Sittlichkeit." Ibid., 147.

to express his radical emotions. He was so overpowered by the holy earnestness of the situation that even the greatest sacrifices seemed negligible. Overwhelmed by the turbulent awareness of the imminent end of the world, Jesus' words sometimes proved harsh and one-sided. For the greatest of the prophets there were no halfway measures, no middle axioms, no divided loyalties, no personal concessions, only an ultimate either/or.[26] Whoever wished to be his disciple and anticipated a place within the new aeon had to burn the bridges and break all ties with this world—even hate father and mother—to prepare himself for the world to come. Under the circumstances, Jesus could not tolerate a compromising position. Whoever loves Mammon hates God. Salvation of the rich is as impossible as forcing a camel through a needle's eye. Jesus was so shattered by the soul-destroying influence of the rich who rejected his warning that it never occurred to him one might reconcile responsible use of money with religion![27]

The "new morality" Jesus proclaimed, Weiss wrote, was not intended for the Kingdom itself—that God's will would be done there was self-evident—but was meant to indicate the conditions for entering it. While his commandments were not founded upon the ideal of a perfect human community nor derived from universally valid ethical norms, they were grounded in the awesome seriousness of a moment in which the greatest event of history was about to happen. The most blessed salvation and most terrible damnation were hidden in the darkness of the immediate future. It is the last hour. The remaining time is very short. The final call to decision is just being issued. Very soon the eternal fate of everyone will be finalized. The crucial intervening moments demand the ultimate test of one's values and claim the maximum effort of one's resources. This is the eschatological situation out of which the teaching of Jesus in the Sermon on the Mount is created and to which it is addressed:

> In time of war martial law takes effect which is not applicable to peaceful times; similarly, this part of the ethical teaching of Jesus has a peculiar

---

[26]Ibid. 51ff.

[27]"An die armen guten Reichen, denen solche Worte Seelenqualen bereiten mögen, hat er sicherlich nicht gedacht. In dieser Art des Empfindens hat er keinen ihm ähnlicheren Jünger gehabt, als den Verfasser der Johannes-Schriften." Ibid., 53.

character. His demands are overwhelming, in part superhuman, and, in fact, under normal circumstances would be simply impossible.[28]

Had he not been captivated for the messianic movement by that call at the Jordan, he might possibly have become the founder of a very serious but nevertheless world-affirming "evangelical" ethic commensurate with a healthy, enlightened nature. However, his soul, apart from a few restive periods, was tuned to a different melody farther and farther removed from such interests. . . . At the height of this religious disposition he will have been little inclined to project a moral legislation for life in the world. He has nothing more in common with this world; he already stands with one foot in the world to come.[29]

For example, examine his saying on *Feindesliebe*: "Love your enemies, do good to those who hate you, bless those who curse you" (Luke 6:27-28). We cannot doubt that Jesus felt and acted in that manner as the highest test of his freedom from the world and his longing for heaven.

But who wants to follow him in this? Only one thing is certain: this commandment did not arise in a normal mood and does not reckon with the average disposition. . . . These words were spoken to people who no longer have an abiding city on earth and seek an otherworldly kingdom.[30]

Theologians may surmise what implications this precept, if abstracted from the historical sphere of first century Jewish apocalyptic thought, might have for a modern social ethic. "But without reinterpretation and adjustment it

---

[28]Ibid., 139: "Wie sich ein gefrorener Springquell in seiner wunderbaren regellosen kühnen Schönheit von dem Spiegel einer Eisfläche unterscheidet, so wollen diese Ergüsse einer kampf- und sturmbewegten Seele, die uns in zufälligen und unzusammenhängenden Resten erhalten sind, mit anderem Mass gemessen werden, als das harmonisch abgeklärte System eines friedlichen Ethikers." Ibid., 53.

[29]Ibid., 145.

[30]Ibid., 149. By contrast Weiss puts Jesus' saying about loving God and neighbor (Matthew 22:37, Matthew 12:30, Luke 10:27) in an entirely different category: "Zu den Parteien der Ethik Jesu, die von der eschatologischen Grundstimmung seines Wirkens nicht durchtränkt sind, gehört vor allem seine Äusserung über das Doppelgebot der Liebe. . . . Diese ganze Erörterung (hängt) mit seinen eigensten Ideen, mit der grossen Aufgabe seines Lebens nicht sehr eng zusammen. . . . Es liegt hier eine Kundgebung vor, die ganz von der messianischen Predigt losgelöst werden kann und darum unter allen Worten Jesu am meisten Aussicht hat, als regulatives Prinzip der christlichen Ethik für alle Zeiten weiter zu leben"; ibid., 137-38. The observation that this saying is not at all dissimilar to that concerning *Feindesliebe* undermines Weiss's central thesis: that eschatology is the determining factor prompting Jesus' sayings and therefore our criterion for discerning their authenticity and order of priority.

cannot be done. For in their original intention the words of Jesus lack a social sphere of reference."[31]

Jesus was not concerned about a lasting coexistence or indefinite accommodation of opponents. He meant only to give expedient guidance for that brief time before the divine judge puts an end to all human strife. Under the stress of the circumstances, evil is no longer to be resisted. One is to turn the other cheek, sacrifice one's cloak, and go the second mile (Matthew 5:38ff., Luke 6:29-30),[32] injustices which no large human community could afford to tolerate very long. Nor did Jesus ever assume that for generations to come nations would do so, and Christians have, in fact, not done so.[33] The average person from another era who does not experience the eschatological urgency so dominant in Jesus' whole disposition should, reasons Weiss, not have any scruples of conscience about adapting the teaching of Jesus to correspond with the level of his own religiosity.[34]

Jesus fully expected that God would almost immediately establish his Kingdom.[35] How else can we explain the urgency with which he sent forth his disciples to proclaim the good news with instructions not to waste a moment of time over any unrepentant town—except on the basis of his firm expectation that they "will not have gone through all the towns of Israel before the Son of Man comes" (Matthew 10:23)? Eventually, the com-

---

[31]Ibid., 149-50.

[32]"Diese heroischen Worte, die ohne Weichheit und Sentimentalität zahllose Gemütsbände zerreissen, kann man nicht anders verstehen, als von dem Standpunkte aus, dass alle Dinge dieser Welt, wie hoch und göttlich sie an sich sein mögen, ihren Wert verloren haben, wo jetzt der Untergang der Welt und das Gericht bevorsteht. Jetzt können sie nur lähmen und hemmen. Werft sie von euch, und greift mit beiden Händen nach dem, was von oben kommt!" Ibid., 143.

[33]Ibid., 151.

[34]Ibid., 52. "Wer auch nur ein wenig geschichtlichen Sinn hat, wird durch diese Erwägung ein für alle Mal geheilt sein von der ziellosen Quälerei vermittlungsfreundlicher Theologen, welche diese kühnen und gewaltigen Worte durch Umdeutung abschwächen, d.h. ihnen ihre Seele rauben, um ihre dauernde und wörtliche Gültigkeit für alle Zeiten behaupten zu können." Ibid., 139.

[35]"The whole tenor of Jesus' early proclamation, that is, his joyful enthusiastic manner in contrast to the pessimism of John the Baptist, does not create the impression that he entered his ministry from the start with resignation and the anticipation of his death. The overwhelming charm of his personality and above all the powerful attraction which those who were despairing and lost had for him would be incomprehensible had he at the outset been burdened with dark determinations of death." Ibid., 99-100.

pounded effect of a long chain of negative impressions and experiences convinced Jesus that God was postponing his Kingdom because the fruit of true repentance was not yet sufficiently in evidence. Too much seed had fallen on infertile ground (Matthew 13:1-23). Those whom the king invited to the marriage feast would not come (Matthew 22:3). Everywhere Jesus encountered the hopeless obduracy of the rich, the persistent arrogance of the righteous, the fanatical perversion of the legalists, and the discouraging indifference of the masses. Overwhelmed by resistance on every side, his once bright and joyful disposition develops a dark and deep pessimism. "Many are called but few are chosen" (Matthew 22:4). "Unless you repent you will all likewise perish" (Luke 13:3). His mood changes from joy to grief, his disposition reverts from hope to despair, his manner shifts from invitation to condemnation, his message degenerates from blessing to woe. Judgment will come when the sons of those who murdered the prophets fill up the measure of their fathers (Matthew 23:31-32). Then the owner of the vineyard will come and destroy the tenants who killed his son (Mark 12:1-12). Meanwhile, they will do to Jesus what they did to John the Baptist. Jesus' death is inevitable although not meaningless, for in the providence of God its human certainty constitutes a divine necessity:

> His death cannot mean the failure of his work but the sole means of bringing about the Kingdom of God. Since the sin which brings about his death simultaneously constitutes the prime hindrance to the coming of God's Kingdom, Jesus keenly grasps the paradoxical thought—or is grasped by it—that precisely through his death he must render his people that unique service of love. He must sacrifice his life in behalf of his doomed people. The ransom which the masses are not in a position to provide [Enoch 98:10,Psalm 49:8-9] he pays with his person.[36]

As a result, the coming of the Kingdom has been postponed until the intended effect of Jesus' death becomes evident. When the Kingdom will be realized "no one knows" (Mark 13:32), but it is expected at the latest within "this generation" (Mark 9:1,13:30). No wonder the disciples of Jesus expected the Kingdom soon after his death. Paul reassured his impatient brethren that "the appointed time has grown very short" (1 Corinthians 7:29ff.), wherefore he in the spirit of Jesus enjoined them not to become involved in "worldly affairs." But soon scoffers everywhere were saying:

[36] Ibid., 103.

"Where is the promise of his coming? For ever since the fathers fell asleep all things have continued as they were. . . ." The author of 2 Peter explained "that with the Lord one day is as a thousand years" (2 Peter 3:4-8)—an explanation not soon to be outdated though not easily reconciled with Jesus' promise that "some standing here will not taste death before they see the Son of Man coming in his Kingdom" (Matthew 16:28).

Along with the postponement of Christ's return in the glory of God's Kingdom there occurs in the Pauline letters the idea of a "Kingdom of Christ" realized in the Church (Colossians 1:13).[37] Weiss does not object to this shift from a futuristic to a realized eschatology provided it is validated in its own right and not ascribed to Jesus. Exactly that, however, is what happened. In the Gospel of John the Church's self-understanding in the light of Easter and Pentecost is superimposed upon the historical Jesus, thus blurring the distinction between his unfulfilled hope and their realized faith. For the witness of John this distinction was irrelevant. For the logic of Weiss everything depends upon its discernment. In the Sermon on the Mount Jesus proclaimed world and life negation because he expected an imminent otherworldly Kingdom. But Jesus was mistaken. The Kingdom for which he hoped and died has not come. Therefore, the Sermon on the Mount is invalidated.[38]

Since the logic of Weiss's conclusion discourages, if it does not altogether invalidate, recourse to the historical Jesus, it appears at first a little surprising that Weiss later published a treatise on discipleship.[39] With this work the author intends, however, to further dependence not on the historical Jesus of Nazareth but on the heavenly Christ of the Church.[40] Weiss begins by documenting the centrality of *Nachfolge Jesu* in the Early Church. Turning to the book of Hebrews, he observes historical and transcendent perspectives combined and intertwined in the thought of the early Christians. Therefore, Weiss concludes, although the exemplary influence of the historical Jesus upon the life of these believers should not be underesti-

---

[37]Ibid., 176.

[38]"Nur ein verknöcherter Dogmatismus kann sich an dem 'Irrtum' Jesu stossen." Ibid., 105.

[39]*Die Nachfolge Christi und die Predigt der Gegenwart* (Göttingen: Vandenhoeck und Ruprecht, 1895).

[40]Cf. ibid., 1-2.

mated, "it would be an unpardonable historical error to assume that the faith of primal Christendom were founded upon this impression of his [Jesus'] image. . . [rather than] upon the transcendent experience of Pentecost and the power manifestations of the exalted Lord.''[41] Particularly for Paul, faith in Jesus' death and resurrection as the focal axis of the cosmic drama of redemption was based not on the historical revelation in the life of Jesus but on the supernatural appearance of the exalted Christ.

Weiss concedes the fundamental principle of Jesus' ethic was to be undivided love of God and man, commandments he intended to be kept. But he observes that "Jesus' individual commandments can be applied to our time only with great difficulty and therefore also for the most part simply have not been observed by Christendom.''[42] Most Christians do not in fact turn the other cheek or sell their possessions and give the proceeds to the poor. Somewhat ironically, Weiss comments:

> for what indeed do we have exegesis if by its means we could not dispose of such inconvenient matters. . . .Even with the best intentions, making the commandments of Jesus normative for the Christian life of the individual as well as for all, remains an unsolvable task. . . .Moreover, the ethic of Jesus as a whole is saturated with an attitude towards the world which stands in deep-seated conflict with the attitudes we hold since the Reformation.[43]

Weiss illustrates the nature of this conflict by referring to Jesus' outright prohibition of divorce (the "except" clause is a later concession) but never intending his absolute command to serve posterity as a regulative principle. Expecting the imminent end of the world, Jesus gave no thought to the distant future:

> Therefore, it is neither a transgression nor an observance of Jesus' statement for Christian society to introduce divorce. Society has done so in its own highest moral interests, precisely for the sake of the sanctity of marriage. Whether that corresponds to the mind of Jesus is a question one cannot answer by taking recourse to the "historical Jesus" as the highest norm. For this issue he gave no answer.[44]

---

[41]Ibid., 83.

[42]Ibid., 160.

[43]Ibid., 161.

[44]Ibid., 162.

The same applies for economic considerations. Jesus expected his disciples to relinquish property ownership and take no thought for tomorrow. But we consider it our moral duty to make provision not only for the next day but for the following year. How ridiculous it would be, on the one hand, to preach to an assembly of unemployed fathers with dependents, "do not be anxious for tomorrow," when, on the other hand, we ascribe the development of workingmen's insurance and retirement schemes specifically to the Christian spirit. Again, it is not a matter of acting in accord with the words of Jesus since these were addressed to people who expected nothing more of this world. For them, this world—despite its lilies—was valueless and about to be destroyed. It no longer mattered whether one starved or feasted, went two miles or one, was well or ill. "We just cannot imagine," Weiss wrote,

> what change in attitude and thought has occurred since it became clear to mankind that this world is to be prepared as the place of the Kingdom of God and that one is obligated to leave for the coming generations a better world than one received.[45]

We are not contemporaries of the first disciples, and therefore we are not able to participate in their asceticism and obedience. Christian discipleship can happen today only under changed psychological conditions. Originally, Weiss thought, Christian discipleship meant faith in the exalted Lord of the Church. This exalted ruler identifies with the destiny of his own and, through his spirit, directs them in their work and conflict, imposes his cross on them, enables them to bear it, leads them through the valley of the shadow of death to the throne of God and, finally, obtains through his intercession for them the abiding love and favor of God. Yet, where the abiding presence of the transcendent Christ has been lost, a purely spiritual relationship to Christ can take place, says Weiss. We can still cultivate thoughts about Christ and ask what he would do were he with us today.

But we should not allow our piety to degenerate to a purely mechanical *imitatio Christi*.[46] The historical image of Jesus is no longer normative. Were he to appear in our time, he would probably come as a statesman or general rather than as a carpenter's son or wandering preacher. "Nor could

---

[45]Ibid., 163.

[46]Ibid., 166.

we assume that he would have nothing else to say but the Sermon on the Mount. On the contrary, he would be the most modern of all, expressing himself in entirely new thoughts and words. . . .Surely he would wish to become involved in the course of history and this time not wait for the collapse of the world and the era of the Messiah."[47] We infinitely diminish the treasure of the Person of Christ by limiting him to the image of the gospels. Furthermore, it is morally and religiously dangerous

> to idolize the carpenter's son of Nazareth, the king of beggars, or the harsh judge of the rich and denouncer of the Pharisees as the Christ for our time. No wonder Nietzsche denounced that "ascetic" together with his apotheosis of the cross as essentially *the* corrupter of mankind.[48]

In order that *Nachfolge Christi* might not be confused with *imitatio* of the Franciscan type, Weiss proposed to incorporate the idea of "following Christ" into the concept of the Kingdom of God. In the language and thought of Jesus, the world and the Kingdom of God admittedly represented two irreconcilable poles, but we understand the work of Christ in us as the expansion of the Kingdom which God predestined to encompass the entire world. Our world view differs so much from that of Jesus that we have no point of contact in the gospels for our religious and ethical life, except for this concept of the Kingdom of God as an ever expanding covenant of brothers extending from that original nucleus of Jesus' disciples. This ongoing work of Christ through the expansion of God's Kingdom is not furthered by selling all our possessions and distributing the proceeds among the poor. Nor would we follow Christ by remaining single, but rather by founding exemplary homes. Nor is renunciation of civil service and indifference towards the state the way to build the Kingdom of God today. Instead of relinquishing these claims, the "disciple of Christ will exert redoubled energy to conquer new realms for his Lord."[49]

Weiss's attempt to allay our misgivings about following an allegedly mistaken Jesus and his concern to re-establish a certain validity for *Nachfolge Christi* by replacing imitation of the historical Jesus with attachment to the transcendent Christ fail to convince. For if it were wrong to follow Jesus then, what can it mean to believe in Christ now? How in the provi-

---

[47]Ibid., 167.

[48]Ibid., 167.

[49]Ibid., 170.

dence of God can the error of Jesus become the ground of our faith? How can historical discontinuity become the basis for spiritual identity? And how shall we meaningfully work for the realization of the Kingdom of God, the true nature of which Jesus himself failed to comprehend?

Weiss left us with a problem he never satisfactorily resolved, namely: to whom shall we go, if we cannot follow Jesus? In the hope of finding a better resolution to this impasse, we turn to Albert Schweitzer who, in his own ingenious way, sought to provide an answer to that question.

ALBERT SCHWEITZER:
THE SERMON ON THE MOUNT
AS AN INTERIM ETHIC

The historical Jesus sees the Kingdom as a supra-ethical entity and therefore proclaims only Interim Ethics.[1]

Jesus was expecting a completely supernatural Kingdom of God. [2] *He hurled the firebrand which should kindle the fiery trials of the Last Time, [but] the flame went out.*[3] *Instead of bringing in the eschatological conditions, He has destroyed them.*[4] *This imperious forcing of eschatology into history is also its destruction; its assertion and abandonment at the same time.*[5] *We have been obliged to . . . acknowledge . . . that paradoxical statement: "If we have known Christ after the flesh yet henceforth know we Him no more." . . . It is not Jesus as historically known, but Jesus spiritually arisen within men, who is significant for our time and can help it.*[6]

What bearing does expectation of a supernatural Kingdom have on the ethics of Jesus? It is responsible for a depreciation of the existing transient and imperfect world in comparison with the eternal and perfect world to come.[7] *Jesus even considers that with the Kingdom of God so close at hand the earning of one's living has lost its justification. Concern about the necessities of life should now be left entirely to God.*[8] *The ethics of Jesus . . . have nothing to do with the achievement*

---

[1]Albert Schweitzer, *Geschichte der Leben-Jesu-Forschung* (München und Hamburg: Siebenstern Taschenbuch, 1966) 2:628.

[2]*The Quest of the Historical Jesus* (London: Adam & Charles Black, 1910) 92.

[3]Ibid., 387.

[4]Ibid., 369.

[5]Ibid., 389.

[6]Ibid., 399.

[7]*The Kingdom of God and Primitive Christianity* (London: Adam & Charles Black, 1968) 96.

[8]Ibid., 97-98.

of anything in the world. His expectation of the supernatural Kingdom of God which is coming in the very near future puts Jesus in a position to disregard everything that ethics can achieve in this world.[9]

Albert Schweitzer's[10] *Leben-Jesu-Forschung* was prompted by his awareness of an unreconciled antithesis within Christendom—between the claims of the historical Jesus and the faith in a heavenly Christ. Schweitzer noted that the Early Church sensed this underlying contradiction and left us no history of Jesus apart from a few sentences about his life, miracles, death, and resurrection. That Paul had no desire to know Jesus κατά σάρκα "was the first expression of the impulse of self-preservation by which Christianity continued to be guided for centuries."[11] Gnosticism and the

---

[9]Ibid., 98.

[10]Albert Schweitzer (1875-1965) was born in the little town of Kaysersberg, Upper Alsace. After studying philosophy, theology, music, and medicine at the Universities of Strasbourg, Paris, and Berlin, he spent most of his life after 1913 in the hospital he founded at Lambarene, in what is now Gabon. As philosopher of religion and ethicist, Schweitzer is known for several works: *Die Religions-philosophie Kants* . . . (1899), *Verfall und Aufbau der Kultur* (1923), *Kultur und Ethik* (1923), *Das Christentum und die Weltreligionen* (1924), *Die Weltanschauung der indischen Denker, Mystik und Ethik* (1925), *Goethe* . . . (1950), *Das Problem des Friedens* . . . (1954).

As theologian Schweitzer was curate of St. Nicolaus in Strasbourg and lecturer in New Testament at the University; he is well known especially for the "consistent eschatology" of his famous Jesus and Pauline studies: *Das Abendmahlsproblem* (1901), *Das Messianitäts- und Leidensgeheimnis* (1901), *Von Reimarus zu Wrede* (1906, later known as *Geschichte der Leben-Jesu-Forschung* . . . *1911*), *Geschichte der Paulinischen Forschung* (1911), *Die psychiatr. Beurteilung Jesu* (1913), *Die Mystik des Apostels Paulus* (1930).

Schweitzer is respected also for his musicianship, knowledge of the organ, and interpretation of Bach exemplified in his studies on *J. S. Bach* (1905), and *Orgelbaukunst* (1906). His autobiographical works include: *Zwischen Wasser und Urwald* (1921), *Aus meiner Kindheit und Jugend* (1924), *Briefe aus Lambarene* (1925-28), and *Aus meinem Leben und Denken* (1931). All of these books have been reprinted and translated, some in many languages.

[11]Albert Schweitzer, *The Quest of the Historical Jesus. A Critical Study of its Progress from Reimarus to Wrede*, ET W. Montgomery (London: Adam & Charles Black, 1910) 2. "Paul shows us with what complete indifference the earthly life of Jesus was regarded by primitive Christianity. The discourses in Acts show an equal indifference, since in them Jesus first becomes the Messiah by virtue of his exaltation. . . . So long as theology had an eschatological orientation and was dominated by the expectation of the Parousia the question how Jesus of Nazareth 'had been' the Messiah not only did not exist, but was impossible. Primitive theology is simply a theology of the future, with no interest in history! It was only with the decline of the eschatological interest and the change in the orientation of Christianity which was connected therewith that an interest in the life of Jesus and the 'historical Messiahship' arose." Ibid., 342.

logos Christology of John "agreed in sublimating the historical Jesus into the supra-mundane Idea." The line that extends from Paul found its culmination in Chalcedon, whose creedal formulation

> dissolved the unity of the Person and thereby cut off the last possibility of a return to the historical Jesus. The self-contradiction was elevated into a law. But the manhood was so far admitted as to preserve, in appearance, the rights of history. Thus, by a deception the formula kept the life prisoner and prevented the leading spirits of the Reformation from grasping the thought of returning to the historical Jesus. This dogma had first to be shattered before men could once more go out in quest of the historical Jesus, before they could even grasp the thought of His existence.[12]

As had Tolstoy, Schweitzer turned to the Jesus of history "as an ally in the struggle against the tryanny of dogma,"[13] a struggle for truth "so full of pain and renunciation"[14] if pursued in the "courageous freedom of investigation"[15] which the subject demands.

The central issue of Schweitzer's *Quest* was the riddle of Jesus' eschatological sayings: what theological and ethical conclusions must we draw from the observation that the synoptic tradition ascribes to Jesus the erroneous expectation of an imminent end of the world? Schweitzer could endorse neither the rationalist exclusion of the supernatural so central to the mind of Jesus nor the evangelical escape into the spiritual by attempts to construct the bridge of meaning on unconditional universals, as modern ethics following Kant presumed to do. Schweitzer began with historical particulars. Instead of interpreting Jesus' messianism either in a crudely nationalistic context (as Zealotism then and Zionism now) or as a purely

---

[12]Ibid., 3.

[13]Ibid., 4.

[14]Ibid., 5.

[15]Ibid. "The organized political, social, and religious associations of our time are at work to induce the individual not to arrive at his convictions by his own thinking but to make his own such convictions as they keep ready for him. And any man who thinks for himself and at the same time is spiritually free is to them something inconvenient or even uncanny. He does not offer sufficient guarantee that he will merge himself in their organization in the way they wish. All corporate bodies look today for their strength not so much to the spiritual worth of the ideas which they represent and to that of the people who belong to them, as to the attainment of the highest possible degree of unity and exclusiveness. It is in this that they expect their strongest power for offence and defence." Albert Schweitzer, *My Life and Thought, An Autobiography*, ET C. T. Campion (London: Allen & Unwin, 1933) 179-80.

spiritual ideal (as do most Christians), Schweitzer followed Weiss[16] in defending a thoroughgoing eschatology realized not through human effort but by supernatural intervention.[17] Schweitzer rejected the rationalist-liberal dichotomy between an entirely historical versus a purely spiritual interpretation and validation of Jesus' teaching and combined both categories by investing them with realistic Jewish eschatology. He understood Jewish apocalyptic not as a *Vergeisterungsprozeß* ("spiritualization") but rather as a projection into a future heaven of unfulfilled earthly hope.[18]

John the Baptist and Jesus were the culminating manifestations of Jewish apocalyptic thought:

> They themselves set the times in motion by acting, by creating eschatological facts. . . . There is silence all around. The Baptist appears, and cries: "Repent, for the Kingdom of Heaven is at hand." Soon after that comes Jesus and, in the knowledge that He is the coming Son of Man, lays hold of the wheel of the world to set it moving on the last revolution which is to bring all history to its close.[19]

His miracles of healing and exorcism attest the reality of imminent eschatological redemption. His feeding of the multitudes at the Sea of Galilee (like his last supper in Jerusalem) was meant to signify the anticipated messianic festival in the Kingdom of Heaven.

In parables Jesus propounds the mystery of the Kingdom. This "mystery" lies not in its nearness—that the Baptist already had proclaimed openly and loudly—but in its miraculous character, analogous to the mys-

---

[16]Schweitzer's theological conclusions are not the *de novo* product of his fertile imagination, as is sometimes supposed, but, for the most part, represent the ripe fruit harvested from the soil prepared by Johannes Weiss the thoroughgoing implications of whose consistent eschatology Schweitzer unflinchingly exposed. Schweitzer blamed the eschatological school for not being sufficiently *konsequent* and showing "a certain timidity in drawing the consequences" by not applying the eschatological explanation to the *whole* of Jesus' ministry in word and deed; cf. *Quest*, 349. The genius of Schweitzer lies in his endeavor to find a reasonable resolution of the ethical dilemma posed by unrealized eschatology.

[17]"Als zukünftiges ist es [das Reich Gottes] jetzt rein überweltlich." Albert Schweitzer, *Von Reimarus zu Wrede, Eine Geschichte der Leben-Jesu-Forschung* (Tübingen: Verlag von J. C. B. Mohr [Paul Siebeck], 1906) 236.

[18]"Die Apokalyptik ist so wenig eine Vergeisterung der Zukunftserwartung, daß sie im Gegenteil nur die Verzweifelungstat einer kraftvoll eudämonistischen Volksreligion ist, die die Güter, von denen sie sich nicht trennen kann, in den Himmel erhebt." Ibid., 244.

[19]*Quest*, 368-69.

tery of nature. By reason of the same logic that harvest follows seeding, judgment follows proclamation:

> And he who knows this sees the corn growing in the fields and the harvest ripening with different eyes, for he sees the one fact in the other and awaits along with the earthly harvest the heavenly, the revelation of the Kingdom of God. . . . The coming of the Kingdom of God is not only symbolically or analogically but also really and temporarily connected with the harvest. The harvest ripening upon earth is the last! With it also comes the Kingdom of God, which brings in the new age. When the reapers are sent into the fields, the Lord of Heaven will cause His harvest to be reaped by the holy angels. . . . The eager eschatological hope was to regard the natural process as the last of its kind, and to see in it a special significance in view of the event of which it was to give the signal.[20]

"Like the Baptist, Jesus sees his task as consisting above all in teaching men the outlook required for participation in the Kingdom and instilling it into them." The pious in Judaism held that faithful observance of the Law assured eventual entry into the Kingdom. "Jesus, however, teaches that this righteousness is not enough, but a higher righteousness, consisting in keeping the spirit of the commandments, is required." Accordingly, in the Sermon on the Mount Jesus expounds the nature of the new righteousness which exceeds that of the scribes and Pharisees:

> In the Beatitudes he mentions the qualities which are an indication of inward membership of the Kingdom. [21]
> Blessed are the poor in spirit! Blessed are the meek! Blessed are the peacemakers!—that does not mean that by virtue of their being poor in spirit, meek, peaceloving, they deserve the Kingdom. Jesus does not intend the statement as an injunction or exhortation, but as a simple statement of fact: in their being poor in spirit, in their meekness, in their love of peace, it is made manifest that they are predestined to the Kingdom. By the possession of these qualites they are marked as belonging to it. In the case of others (Matthew 5:10-12) the predestination to the Kingdom is made manifest by the persecutions which befall them in this world. . . . The Kingdom cannot be "earned"; what happens is that men are called to it, and show themselves to be called to it.[22]

---

[20]Ibid., 354-55.

[21]Albert Schweitzer, *The Kingdom of God and Primitive Christianity*, ET L. A. Garrard (London: Adam & Charles Black, 1968) 81.

[22]*Quest*, 353.

The anticipated sufferings signify the eschatological "birthpangs" of the Messiah as does also the expected outpouring of the Spirit in the last days of history preceding the παρουσία of the Son of Man. "All the promises introduced by the words 'for they shall be' . . . refer to participation in the Kingdom." As Israel inherited Canaan, so the meek shall inherit the Kingdom. In the Kingdom those who hunger and thirst for true righteousness will find satisfaction. In the Kingdom the pure in heart will see God, and the peacemakers will be manifest as his children.

> The poor in spirit are those who have retained the simplicity of heart which is necessary in order to understand the message of the coming of the Kingdom. . . . [23]
> All judging of other people must be renounced in view of the coming Judgment to which everyone will be subject. [24]
> The higher righteousness demands not only love of our neighbour but also love of our enemy. [25]

"The entire thought of those who are looking for the Kingdom of God must be directed towards doing God's will. This is the only thing that counts. A resolution of this kind creates a sense of solidarity among men surpassing any other. . . . This is the profound, spiritual, inward-looking ethic required for entry into the Kingdom." [26] Jesus' expectation of a supernatural Kingdom accounts for his "depreciation of the existing transient and imperfect world in comparison with the eternal and perfect world to come," especially since "the time allotted to the present world is now very short indeed." [27] "The aim at which to strive is therefore not greatness and power but insignificance and service" [28] in contrast to "the rulers of the Gentiles [who] lord it over them" (Matthew 20:25). Whoever exalts himself now will be humbled in the Kingdom, and whoever humbles himself now will be exalted in the Kingdom (cf. Matthew 23:12):

---

[23]*Kingdom*, 81-82.
[24]Ibid., 84; cf. Matthew 7:1-5.
[25]Ibid., 85; cf. Matthew 5:43-45.
[26]Ibid., 86.
[27]Ibid., 96.
[28]Ibid., 97.

Jesus even considers that with the Kingdom so close at hand the earning of one's living has lost its justification. Concern about the necessities
of life should now be left entirely to God.[29]

The ethics of Jesus . . . have nothing to do with the achievement of
anything in the world. His expectation of the supernatural Kingdom of God
which is coming in the very near future puts Jesus in a position to disregard
everything that ethics can achieve in this world. . . . The establishment of
better conditions in the world does not enter the picture.[30]

Jesus did not call disciples to improve the world. He chose them as those
who are destined to hurl the firebrand into the world and then "to be His
associates in ruling and judging it.''[31] The mission of the twelve was to

let loose the final tribulation and so compel the coming of the Kingdom. . . . By sending forth the disciples with their message, he hurled the
firebrand which should kindle the fiery trials of the Last Time, [but] the
flame went out.[32]

The coming Son of Man lays hold of the wheel of the world to set it
moving on the last revolution which is to bring all ordinary history to a
close. It refuses to turn, and He throws Himself upon it. Then it does turn;
and crushes Him. Instead of bringing in the eschatological conditions, He
destroys them. The wheel rolls onward, and the mangled body of the one
immeasurably great Man, who was strong enough to think of Himself as
the spiritual ruler of mankind and to bend history to His purposes, is hang-
ing upon it still. That is His victory and His reign.[33]

This imperious forcing of eschatology into history is also its destruction; its assertion and abandonment at the same time.[34]

Those in quest of the historical Jesus

loosed the bands by which He had been riveted for centuries to the stony
rocks of ecclesiastical doctrine and rejoiced to see life and movement come
into the figure once more, and the historical Jesus advancing, as it seemed

---

[29]Ibid., 97-98; cf. Matthew 6:19-21.

[30]Ibid., 98.

[31]*Quest.* 369.

[32]Ibid., 387.

[33]Ibid., 369. This quotation is omitted from the 6th German edition of 1950, along with
pp. 364-69.

[34]Ibid., 389.

. . . straight into our time as a Teacher and Saviour. [Instead] He passes by our time and returns to His own.[35]

As a water plant is beautiful so long as it is growing in the water, but once torn from its roots, withers and becomes unrecognisable, so it is with the historical Jesus when He is wrenched loose from the soil of eschatology and the attempt is made to conceive Him "historically" as a Being not subject to temporal conditions.[36]

To our time the historical Jesus remains a stranger and an enigma. He can claim no authority over our knowledge, only over our will.[37] "We possess him [only] to the extent that we allow him to preach to us the Kingdom of God."[38]

According to Schweitzer, Jesus is so strange to our time because he takes for granted the late Jewish apocalyptic view[39] which sees the Son of Man-Messiah as a supernatural being appearing in the clouds of heaven with his holy angels (Matthew 25:31) to hold judgment over men and fallen angels (Matthew 13:41-43, 25:31-32). "In the Kingdom everyone exists in the supernatural form of those who have risen from the dead."[40] Jesus said: "Many will come from east and west and sit at table with Abraham, Isaac, and Jacob in the Kingdom of Heaven" (Matthew 8:11). "There is no escaping the conclusion from these passages that Jesus was expecting a completely supernatural Kingdom of God of the kind described in the prophetic writings of the late post-Exilic period."[41]

---

[35]Ibid., 397.

[36]Ibid., 399.

[37]"In Wirklichkeit vermag er für uns nicht eine Autorität der Erkenntnis, sondern nur eine des Willens zu sein." *Geschichte der Leben-Jesu-Forschung* (1966) 624.

[38]Ibid., 627.

[39]This is why Jesus does not reprove his disciples for their materialistic outlook when they dispute about who will be greatest in the Kingdom (Matthew 18:1-4). He does not object to Peter's inquiry about the reward for having left everything but replies: "You who have followed me will sit on twelve thrones, judging the twelve tribes of Israel" (Matthew 19:27-28). He is not offended when James and John request places of highest honor but only replies that this request "is not mine to grant" (Mark 10:35-40).

[40]*Kingdom*, 92.

[41]Ibid. "Jesus shares with Enoch the peculiar views that it is not God, as in the later post-Exilic prophets and in Daniel, but the Son of Man, assisted by his angels, who holds the judgment . . . "; cf. Malachi, Joel, Isaiah 24-27, Zechariah 9-14, Daniel, Enoch.

Because it is supernatural, Schweitzer argues, the Kingdom is beyond ethics. Our modern concept of morality is based on the triumph of good over evil within history. For Jesus, the Kingdom of God "lies beyond the borders of good and evil: it will be brought about by a cosmic catastrophe through which evil is to be completely overcome. Hence, all moral criteria are to be abolished. The Kingdom of God is supramoral." For us the Kingdom of God is the realization of ethics. For Jesus, it was the end of ethics:

> When we think of the Kingdom of God, our thought stretches forward to the coming generations which are to realize it in ever increasing measure. Jesus' glance is directed backward. For him the Kingdom is composed of the generations which have already gone down to the grave and which are now to be awakened unto a state of perfection.[42]

When they rise from the dead they will be "like angels in heaven" (Mark 12:25) having no need of sexual, political, or any other type of ethic.

Jesus might have held the view of the early prophets for whom "the Kingdom is essentially a spiritual and ethical identity"[43] and whose ethics "not only prepare men for the Kingdom, but are also valid in it when it comes, and indeed make it what it is."[44] Jesus rejected the spiritual and ethical interpretation of the prophets because it limited the Kingdom to the righteous of the last generation of mankind excluding all earlier generations. Jesus took for granted that "all who had ever lived belonged to the Kingdom."[45] For both the resurrected dead and the present generation to be in the Kingdom together "they must all be supernatural beings, the one through the resurrection, the others through a transformation which they will undergo at the appearance of the Kingdom." The supernatural state of the participants requires that the Kingdom itself be supernatural as does the necessity of recognizing the Kingdom to be a new world in which the powers of evil and death no longer prevail:

> The faith which sets its hopes highest and dares to expect that God will shortly make an end to the present era and bring in an age of perfection can

---

[42]Albert Schweitzer, *The Mystery of the Kingdom of God. The Secret of Jesus' Messiahship and Passion*, ET W. Lowrie (London: A. & C. Black, Ltd., 1925) 102.

[43]*Kingdom*, 93.

[44]Ibid., 94.

[45]Ibid.

entertain no other view but that of a supernatural and super-ethical Kingdom of God. That is why Jesus adopted the outlook of late Judaism.[46]

Nevertheless, Jesus, in contrast to Buddha, demands "not a total, but
only a provisional denial of life and the world."[47] This inconsistency in
Jesus is explained by Schweitzer in this way: When the later post-Exilic
conception of the supernatural Kingdom of God replaced the earlier idea
of a spiritual and ethical messianic Kingdom to be realized in history, one
would have expected a corresponding transition from prophetic life- and
world-affirmation to apocalyptic life- and world-negation. Life- and world-
denial did not, however, become the dominant motif of Jewish ethics

> because the supernatural Kingdom was still regarded as something in the
> remote future. Jesus, however, expects it to come immediately. For him,
> consequently, the far-reaching denial of life and the world that goes with
> this doctrine completely overshadows the spirit of affirmation that under-
> lies his ethic as a continuation of that of the prophets.

Great as the late Jewish apocalyptic influence is upon Jesus

> it does not entirely change the nature of his ethic. There remains in it a
> strain of life- and world-affirmation. Dissociation from the world and ac-
> tive love exist in it side by side. Though in the main it comes down on the
> side of denial of life and the world, yet it also retains some affinity with
> the spirit of affirmation. This continuing influence of life- and world-af-
> firmation explains not only how Jesus can still find a place for ethical ac-
> tivity but also his rejection of every kind of asceticism. Although he calls
> for the limitation of desires, his ethic concedes to man everything that be-
> longs to a natural way of living. The claims of marriage are in no way called
> in question: it is regarded as part of God's will. Fasting is not to be ac-
> counted necessary: Jesus allows himself and his disciples freedom not to
> practise it.[48]

However difficult it appears to reconcile life- and world-negation with
life- and world-affirmation in the eschatology of Jesus, the task is made
even more perplexing by Schweitzer's repeated insistence, on the one hand,
that "the teaching of the historical Jesus was purely and exclusively world-

---

[46]Ibid., 95.

[47]Ibid., 99.

[48]Ibid., 100-101.

negating''[49] and his tacit admission, on the other, that Jesus' ethic "concedes to man everything that belongs to a natural way of living.''[50] Schweitzer despised the "qualifying-clause theology" of his opponents and claimed that "progress always consists in taking one of two alternatives, in abandoning the attempt to combine them.''[51] Since Wrede, there were only two options, either thoroughgoing skepticism or thoroughgoing eschatology. *Tertium non datur.*[52] Schweitzer boldly staked his claim on *konsequente* eschatology with its premium on consistency. However, fifty years later we learn to our amazement that this hard line has indeed been qualified by allowing that Jesus himself was "*in*konsequent" to the extent that he advocated active love and rejected asceticism.[53] This inconsistency is not inconsequential! If Jesus' belief did not altogether change his ethic, by what logic is it to affect ours? And, if Jesus was mistaken about the theological basis of his life- and world-negation, how are we to know the basis for our life- and world-affirmation? Must we bypass Jesus and return to the early prophets of Judaism? Or, shall we validate only that in the thought of Jesus which can be modernized? If not, how are we to relate historical insights to spiritual ideals?

First, we must explore the logic of Schweitzer's paradoxical *via negativa* and then discern whether he leaves us two options or none. The ambiguity of Schweitzer's thought is compounded by his vacillation in the use of the terms "optimistic" and "pessimistic" in characterizing the *Weltanschauung* of Jesus and his own. When he eventually claimed to have found the right definition,[54] he ascribed to Jesus a pessimistic disposition in marked contrast to his own qualified optimism. Nevertheless, he maintained his own *Weltanschauung* to be essentially identical to that of Jesus! How can this be?

---

[49]"Die Lehre des historischen Jesus war rein und ausschließlich weltverneinend." *Von Reimarus zu Wrede* (1906) 247.

[50]*Kingdom,* 100.

[51]*Quest,* 237.

[52]Ibid., 331, 335.

[53]Cf. *Kingdom,* 99f.

[54]"Only when I was working at my Philosophy of Civilization did I eventually find the right definition," Schweitzer wrote Feb. 5, 1926, to Oskar Kraus. *Albert Schweitzer, his work and his Philosophy* (London: Adam & Charles Black, 1944) 79.

Jesus' *Weltanschauung* is optimistic because it is otherworldly and transcendent, although Jesus manifests a pessimistic view of man's natural disposition and capacity to realize the Kingdom. Hence Jesus expected the Kingdom to be realized supernaturally. The essential ambiguity lies in the consideration of whether the repentance which enforces the coming of the Kingdom is itself natural or supernatural. Schweitzer argues that "with Jesus the value of the optimistic element in his world-view is impaired by the fact that he looks forward to a perfected world as the result of a catastrophic end to the natural one."[55] Jesus' *Weltanschauung* is fundamentally optimistic because it is theistic. But, since it is "biased by the expectation of the end of the world, it is indifferent to all attempts made to improve the temporal, natural world . . . and concerns itself only with the inward ethical perfection of individuals."[56]

Because the ethic of Jesus is oriented entirely to imminent supernatural consummation of the world, [57] we may not "tune his denial of the world to our acceptance of it" by leaving his greatest sayings "lying in a corner like explosive shells from which the charges have been removed" so as to prevent them "from conflicting with our system of religious world acceptance."[58] We must not seek to harmonize the *Weltanschauung* of Jesus with our own "which can only be done by a lowering of its demands" with the effect that "it loses its primordial character and is no longer able to influence us in the same elemental way."[59]

> Why . . . abolish the conflict between modern life, with the world-affirming spirit which inspires it as a whole, and the world-negating spirit of Jesus? Why spare the spirit of the individual man its appointed task of fighting its way through the world-negation of Jesus, of contending with him at every step over the value of material and intellectual goods—a conflict in which it may never rest?[60]

Nor may we for the sake of our peace deny the world-negation in Jesus'

[55]Albert Schweitzer, *The Philosophy of Civilization* (New York: Macmillan, 1950) 110.
[56]Ibid., 111.
[57]Cf. *Mystery*, 103.
[58]*Quest*, 398.
[59]*Geschichte*, 624.
[60]*Quest*, 400.

sayings by ascribing them to the redactionary influence of the Early Church as modern theology has done.[61]

How is this "conflict" resulting from our opposition to Jesus to be evaluated? Are we to validate the tension between his life- and world-negation and our life- and world-affirmation with a "good" conscience or accept the inevitability of living with a "bad" conscience? Is this tension inherent in the very structure of being or ought we to seek the meaning of our being in its resolution? Must we contend with Jesus "at every step over the value of material and intellectual goods" or should we simply obey him and follow him?

Instead of providing rational answers, Schweitzer refers us to the paradox that Jesus,

> in spite of his pessimistic attitude towards the world, proclaims an ethic of active devotion to one's neighbor. This activistic ethic is what is wanted to provide the cardinal-point of an evolution from a Christian-pessimistic to a Christian-optimistic philosophy.[62]

In Jesus "an ethic of enthusiasm seemingly focused upon an optimistic world-view! This is the magnificent paradox in the teaching of Jesus"[63] which in turn makes it possible for us to modulate from a pessimistic to an optimistic world-view:

> What we at the present time have to do is to go through the critical experience of being obliged to think as modern men with a world-view of world- and life-affirmation, and yet let the ethic of Jesus speak to us from out of its pessimistic world-view.[64]

Schweitzer was convinced that the future of civilization depends on man's capacity to evolve an optimistic *Weltanschauung*: "Optimism supplies the confidence that the world-process has somehow or other a spiritual and real aim and that the improvement of the general relations of the world and of society promotes the spiritual-moral perfection of the indi-

---

[61]Ibid., 401.

[62]*Philosophy*, 159.

[63]Ibid., 146.

[64]The modern age overlooked this paradox while blindly "assuming in Jesus an optimistic world view." Though this error accounts "for the progress of spiritual life in Europe," historical criticism, by revealing this mistake, finally put an end to a false modernizing of Jesus' personality; ibid., 146.

vidual.''[65] But it is not an optimism based on natural evolution, for ''in the world we can discover nothing of any purposive evolution in which our activities acquire a meaning.''[66] The universe is an appalling spectacle of inner conflict and the ethical principles of the world-process are quite indiscernible. The meaning of the universe evades our comprehension.[67] Despite his belief that ''there is no knowledge and no hope that can give our life stability and direction,''[68] Schweitzer confessed: ''I have to hold fast to world- and life-affirmation and deepen it. My life carries its meaning in itself.''[69] Unable to supply a rationale for his own geocentric optimism in regard to civilization, Schweitzer concluded that ethics is independent of an optimistic or pessimistic point of view. He admitted, however, that the range of ethical action is infinitely widened if one's *Weltanschauung* is optimistic and can include the hope of a purposeful goal for the world as well as infinite progress.[70] But when that is not the case and we cannot harmonize our life-view with our world-view, we should not try to bridge this abyss with a forced logic.[71] When an optimistic world-view can no longer be kept afloat and threatens to sink our life-view with it into the depths, ''necessity bids us cut the tow-rope and try to let life-view continue its voyage independently.''[72]

---

[65]Ibid., 58.

[66]Ibid., 76.

[67]''The hopelessness of the attempt to find the meaning of life within the meaning of the universe is shown first of all by the fact that in the course of nature there is no purposiveness to be seen in which the activities of men, and of mankind as a whole, could in any way intervene. On one of the smaller of the millions of heavenly bodies there have lived for a short space of time human beings. For how long will they continue so to live? Any lowering or raising of the temperature of the earth, any change in the inclination of the axis of their planet, any raise in the level of the ocean, or a change in the composition of the atmosphere, can put an end to their existence. Or the earth itself may fall, as so many other heavenly bodies have fallen, a victim to some cosmic catastrophe. We are entirely ignorant of what significance we have for the earth. How much less then may we presume to try to attribute to the infinite universe a meaning which has us for its object or which can be explained in terms of our existence!''Ibid., 273.

[68]Schweitzer quoted in Kraus, *Albert Schweitzer*, 9.

[69]*Philosophy*, 79.

[70]Cf. *Philosophy*, 57.

[71]Ibid., 78.

[72]Ibid., 274.

The two fundamental attitudes of optimism and pessimism remained unresolved in Schweitzer's own soul. We cannot, he says, get rid of this dualism. No reconciliation is possible: "We are ever wandering on slipping rubble above the abyss of pessimism."[73] Only to the extent that we can come to terms with our embarrassment that, contrary to Jesus' expectation, the world has not come to an end, can we find in the will-to-live a life-affirmation free of the necessity of having to understand the world. This mystical

> life-affirmation exerts itself to take up life-negation into itself in order to serve other living beings by self-devotion, and to protect them, even, it may be, by self-sacrifice, from injury or destruction.[74]
>
> General affirmation of the world . . . must in the individual spirit be christianized and transfigured by the personal rejection of the world which is preached in the sayings of Jesus. It is only by means of the tension thus set up that religious energy can be communicated to our time.[75]

This truly mysterious process is exemplified in Paul. In contrast to Jesus,

> Paul the thinker recognized [that] the essence of the Kingdom of God which was coming into existence consists in the rule of the Spirit. We learn from this knowledge which comes to us through him that the way in which the coming of the Kingdom will be brought about is by the coming of Jesus Christ to rule in our hearts and through us in the whole world. In the thought of Paul the supernatural Kingdom is beginning to become ethical and with this to change from the Kingdom to be expected into something which has to be realized. It is for us to take the road which this prospect opens up.[76]

What then is the nature of our historical connection with the original disciples of Jesus? According to Schweitzer, "the new moral community which Jesus formed about himself was in his thought organically connected with the Kingdom which was supernaturally to appear,"[77] but the nature of this connection remained a divine secret illuminated only by analogies to metamorphosis in the processes of nature. Since the dead were to be resurrected and the living elect metamorphosed into supernatural

---

[73]Ibid., 284.

[74]Ibid., 290.

[75]*Quest*, 400.

[76]*Kingdom*, 183.

[77]*Mystery*, 104.

beings, Jesus could not have envisioned the realization of the Kingdom as the gradually widening circles of disciples throughout the centuries. Whatever, therefore, the nature of the connection in the mind of Jesus between his historical disciples and the supernatural Kingdom, our inclusion lies beyond its intention.

Schweitzer uncritically adopted the eschatology of Johannes Weiss, followed his assumptions to their logical conclusion, and then sought to reaffirm, by resorting to paradox, the relevance of Jesus for ethical mysticism.

Yet how can one hold to Jesus when one cannot believe what he believed? According to Schweitzer, Jesus is to us a stranger and an enigma. He is authoritative not for our knowledge but only for our will. He cannot guide our reason, but only our faith. Our only recourse to the mystery of his spirit is through Paul. Paul reasoned: If Jesus is the bringer of the Kingdom, then there is no reason why it should not come at once:

> Dominated by this conviction, he experienced in the spirit its present reality in the imagery of his time.[78]
> By his doctrine of the spirit he has himself thrown a bridge from his world-view to ours.[79]
> It is only by way of Christ-mysticism that we can have the experience of belief in the Kingdom of God and in redemption through Jesus Christ as a living possession.[80]
> It is not Jesus as historically known, but Jesus spiritually risen within men, who is significant for our time and can help it.[81]

Schweitzer sought to resolve the antithesis between the claims of the historical Jesus and the "tyranny of dogma," but the irrationality of his thought failed to repair the credibility gap of *konsequente Eschatologie* and gives one no reason to believe Paul when one cannot believe Jesus.[82]

---

[78]*Kingdom*, 183.

[79]Albert Schweitzer, *The Mysticism of the Apostle Paul*, ET W. Montgomery (New York: Henry Holt & Co., 1931) 386.

[80]Ibid., 395.

[81]*Quest*, 399.

[82]Schweitzer's whole life exemplified a profound sense of direction and depth of commitment. His eminently ethical character, exceptional degree of moral strength, and deep feeling of compassion are evidently not inspired by a process of reasoning but rather mo-

tivated by the profound impression the personality of Jesus made upon him from earliest childhood, particularly by the way Jesus was moved with compassion for suffering people. It is not hard to see how from this awareness Schweitzer concluded: "Ethics are pity. All life is suffering. The will-to-live which has attained to knowledge is therefore seized with deep pity for all creatures. . . . What is called in ordinary ethics 'love' is in its essence real pity. In this overpowering feeling of pity the will-to-live is diverted from itself. Its purification begins." *Civilization and Ethics*, 167. In his childhood and youth, while reflecting on the vast amount of pain and suffering in the world and on the fact that he himself had been spared, it became clear to him that he had no moral right to assume his own privileges, health, happiness, and ability to work as self-evident; cf. *Memoirs of Childhood and Youth*. Consequently, Schweitzer, in imitation of Jesus, resolved to spend his life relieving the torment suffered by countless Africans deprived of medical aid.

Lewis Sperry Chafer (*Systematic Theology*. Vol. 4 [Dallas TX: Dallas Seminary Press, 1948] 207) says of Jesus' teachings regarding the Kingdom: "Since they anticipate the binding of Satan, a purified earth, the restoration of Israel, and the personal reign of the King, they cannot be applied until God's appointed time when these accompanying conditions on the earth have been brought to pass." "As a rule of life, it [the SM] is addressed to the Jew before the cross and to the Jew in the coming kingdom, and is therefore not now in effect" (5:97). Chafer considers the entire Sermon on the Mount a literary unit from which one may not select one portion as applicable while rejecting another portion as inapplicable. Since the text expresses concern with the danger of hell fire (Matthew 5:22, 29-30) from which Christians have been saved, Chafer argues that the entire Sermon cannot therefore apply to believers during the present dispensation of grace but only to unbelieving Jews in a preceding and following dispensation of law. "The Sermon on the Mount both by its setting in the context [of law] and by its doctrinal character . . . belongs for its primary application to the future kingdom age" (99).

JOHANNES MÜLLER:
THE SERMON AS NATURE'S
LAW OF ''HUMANIZATION''

As moral law, the Sermon on the Mount is a torture rack upon which people use-lessly torment themselves or a supernatural relic which one humbly reveres but does not obey. . . . The most convincing evidence of its impracticability as ''moral law'' is the oldest manuscripts themselves which modified these ''insane demands'' and ''subtle paradoxes'' ''so as to make them acceptable.'' The same is proven by the universal practice of the Church which since earliest times silently agreed not to consider any of Jesus' ''exaggerated demands'' as binding.[1]

The ''way to a lively understanding'' of the Sermon on the Mount involves three fundamental transpositions: First, one must Germanize the Sermon to remove its Jewishness; second, one must contemporize it to abstract from it the ballast of historical tradition; finally, one must individualize its universal truth so that it becomes a personal event.[2]

The de-Judaized, modernized, and individualized essential kernel of universal truth in the Sermon on the Mount must be understood as the natural principles of authentic humanization.[3]

Die Bergpredigt verdeutscht und vergegenwärtigt (''The Sermon on the Mount Germanized and Contemporized'') by Johannes Müller[4] be-

---

[1]Johannes Müller, *Die Bergpredigt verdeutscht und vergegenwärtigt* (München: Oskar Beck, 1906) 9.

[2]Ibid., 11-17.

[3]Cf. ibid., 20.

[4]Dr. Johannes Müller (1864-1949), editor of *Grüne Blätter* 1914-41, published *Vom Geheimnis des Lebens*, Erinnerungen I, II, 1937-38 and zealously supported Hitler's ''national rebirth'' campaign.

came one of the most popular and influential books of its kind. It was first published in 1906 to capture the consciousness of contemporary seekers and to enable them to recognize in the Sermon on the Mount their own aspirations and expectations. Müller felt that these goals would not be realized through critical, intellectual discourse about the Sermon on the Mount:

> He alone understands who personally experiences it. . . . "To the wise and learned these things remain hidden," but to the simple, who comprehend it directly from experience, they are revealed.[5]

According to the author's foreword to the second edition, literary critics and the intelligentsia did not understand his book, while many "who experienced in it the unrest of their own souls found in it the path of their own deepest longings."[6] Reviewers echoed this emphasis, claiming that "such a book cannot be discussed—one must read it." The author claims historical-philological research has led up to but not into the teaching of Jesus. Research has not enabled the sayings of Jesus to become "overwhelming events in our personal lives and guideposts for the particular way of life of the individual."[7] On the other hand, mere pious sentimental reflection about the Sermon on the Mount only leads around its content and meaning back to one's own religious feelings and experiences, thereby hiding the kernel of truth instead of allowing it to sprout and grow.[8]

To find the way to a "sure and lively" understanding of the Sermon on the Mount, Müller argues, we must first rid ourselves of all prejudice about Jesus. We may no longer see him as the founder of a religion, for he was crucified as the enemy of religion and gave rise to a movement which, by its original self-designation, was no church or religion but "the way" (Acts 24:14). Nor should we see in him a founder of a unique culture, an apostle of reform who upsets human circumstances and social values, nor an ascetic prophet of world doom whom the course of history has proven wrong nor a guide through personal problems nor a revealer of the hidden mysteries of life's redemptive resources.

---

[5]*Die Bergpredigt*, vi.
[6]Ibid.
[7]Ibid., 4.
[8]Ibid., 5.

Often the Sermon on the Mount has been mistakenly considered the tables of a new covenant and the fundamentals of a new morality the depth and purity of which are unsurpassed. The Sermon on the Mount, says Müller, is no moral law. Though it contains elements that could thus be conceived, ethical precept is not its intention and meaning. Conceived as moral demands, its counsels are unfulfillable:

> Tolstoy's consistent radicalism has shown that, if the norms of the Sermon on the Mount were really universally applied, they must lead to the dissolution of civil life. Military service, jurisprudence, and social welfare would disintegrate; economic competition and the natural law of opposites would be eliminated. . . . Can one really place upon a person of flesh and blood the moral burden of Jesus' teachings? No, as moral law the Sermon on the Mount is a torture rack upon which people uselessly torment themselves or a supernatural relic which one humbly reveres but does not obey.[9]

The most convincing evidence of its impracticability as generally valid morality lies in the corrections of the oldest manuscripts which modify these "insane demands" and "subtle paradoxes" so as to make them acceptable. Furthermore, the church by its universal practice has since earliest times silently agreed to consider all exaggerated demands as nonbinding:

> One simply refused to put up with everything, [as] blessing one's persecutor, taking the prescribed stance towards possessions, or even simply following Jesus' instructions about prayer. And one is fully aware that one does so in contradiction to Jesus' words.

In order to universalize the Sermon on the Mount one had to denigrate it to its lowest common denominator. Instead of relinquishing the prejudice of misunderstanding it as moral law, one tried to evade or cover up the difficulties while simultaneously proclaiming that Jesus redeemed us from the law![10]

Following this argument against understanding the Sermon on the Mount as *nova lex Christi*, Müller introduces his own approach: A "lively comprehension" of the Sermon on the Mount involves, says he, three elemental steps or transpositions. First, he would *verdeutsch* (Germanize) everything so as to get rid of the Jewish element. This is necessary because the Sermon on the Mount originated on Jewish soil and was addressed to

---

[9]Ibid., 9.

[10]Ibid., 10.

Jews whose thought patterns are as foreign to modern Europeans, Müller believes, as are those of Mongolians or Indians:

> The more we preoccupy ourselves with this difference [between Germans and Jews], the more irreconcilable it becomes. If the difference between Germanic and Semitic thinking appears immaterial, then it is only because the Jewish mentality for hundreds of years has been unsuspectedly injected into the German spirit and, however actively the latter reacted against it—most vigorously in Luther—it was hitherto hardly aware of what was actually at stake.[11]

The German spirit either must reject Christianity altogether on account of its failure to distinguish the universally human from its Jewish frame of reference or it must reject this foreign element that has so confused the spirits. Müller recommends the latter. Responding to concern that the purification process might discard essential gospel elements, Müller claims it is only as one rids the gospel of foreign elements and then comprehends it "with German feeling" that one recovers its true essence.[12]

Second, having processed this purge, Müller would contemporize what has been Germanized so as to jettison the ballast of century-old traditions which only hinder progress. One must radically and courageously reinterpret Jesus' words for one's own time, since it is impossible for one either inwardly or outwardly to regress to the cultural plane of Jesus' time. Descending into the catacombs of the past in no way benefits modern Europeans, who recover life only as Jesus arises from the tomb of his time to appear to them today.

The resultant Germanized and contemporized substance must at last be individualized so each "on the basis of his own experience" can discern the particular implications Jesus has for him and how this affects his inner and outer circumstances. "That no one can discern for another."[13]

Having shown the way to a "lively" understanding of the Sermon on the Mount, Müller next elaborates on its underlying presuppositions. The Sermon on the Mount, he asserts, has to do with the natural principles of "humanization" (*Naturgesetze der Menschwerdung*):

---

[11]Ibid., 12.

[12]Ibid., 14.

[13]Ibid., 17.

If one has not seen this, one has not yet penetrated through the surface of spacial and temporal considerations to the genuine essence within; one is still clinging to the transient: personal attitudes, life-styles, and cultural conditions.[14]

Just as the laws of botanical life remain constant for all times and places though producing different shapes, blossoms, and fruits, depending on climatic and soil conditions,

so there is no change in the laws of human beings, though in differing circumstances their manifestation and outworking vary and are comprehended, if at all, according to the level of intellectual development. Therefore, the content of the Sermon on the Mount retains lasting significance and remains in effect irrespective of how one relates to Jesus, to his person, and his undertaking.[15]

These fundamental principles of humanization must be transposed into the national uniqueness, otherwise, one retains only the transient and superficial externals but loses the creative power of the essential kernel.[16] Paramount is the quest to become fully human, yet no one knows the way:

To all the prophets of the future . . . these natural laws and natural processes that lead to the goal are an impenetrable mystery. They proclaim and foretell how it must happen, but no one can lead to it. . . . In the entire intellectual history of mankind one looks in vain for the answer to the question which preoccupies every thoughtful person: How do I become truly human, how do we achieve a common life together that creatively leads on towards the perfection of mankind, and how do we achieve the new order of all things that satisfies us and is worthy of us? The Sermon on the Mount alone points the way to this highest goal and reveals to us the mystery of its happenings within the heart of man. . . . That is the reason why all searching spirits, whether they realize it or not, are attracted to it with such magical power. Whether they intend it or not, the scent of truth and well-being invariably lead one after another onto this track, and, if one does not wish to helplessly disintegrate in skepticism and spend all of life going astray, one must follow it. Therefore, the Sermon on the Mount is much more than a wonderful document of the past. It is the compass for man's

---

[14]Ibid., 18.

[15]Ibid.

[16]Ibid., 18-19.

future and . . . must come to life as the password for the redemption of the world.[17]

Our era, as no other in history, Müller claims, is determined to comprehend the Sermon on the Mount and to realize its life-force. But, if this is to happen, it is not enough to have the Sermon on the Mount impressed upon our reflective consciousness.

> In the final analysis, we must personally experience what we would personally know. . . . We understand this hidden truth, which in times past found attestation and expression, only in the measure that it becomes our own innermost experience.[18]
> It is a disastrous error to assume that understanding Jesus is a theoretical matter and that one could through industrious study acquire a right conception of his views and then make appropriate reflections corresponding to the spiritual interests of our time. . . . Understanding Jesus is only possible experientially.[19]
> Our goal is not to discern what Jesus thought then—that is only the means to our end—but what we must think today if we understand him in a vital way and what we accordingly must do if we consider ourselves personally addressed.[20]

Jesus, like John, preached repentance, but we, according to Müller, are completely incapable of comprehending the content of that familiar expression. Its mysterious otherness completely evades us until we comprehend that the Sermon on the Mount deals with "the mystery of transformation: wherein it consists and how it comes about. It is the guidepost toward that divine 'newfoundland' and shows us how it can happen."[21]

Turning then to the content of the Sermon on the Mount itself, Müller notes that Jesus pronounced his first blessing upon the "seekers" who restlessly aspire to truth, righteousness, freedom, and all that is authentically human and worthy of humanity:[22]

---

[17]Ibid., 21.
[18]Ibid.
[19]Ibid., 22.
[20]Ibid., 24.
[21]Ibid., 36.
[22]Ibid., 41.

How this quest comes to consciousness, what it brings about, what re-
percussions it has, to what movements it leads—all that is essentially immaterial. Whether one yearns for redemption or a supernatural life, whether
one aspires to authentic German culture or to a future state worthy of human existence, as long as aspiration springs from the depth of a strong
feeling of inadequacy, it is that poverty of spirit which Jesus had in mind.[23]

"Whether Christians or Jews, atheists or materialists, spiritualists or
whatever is altogether immaterial with respect to the Kingdom,"[24] which
means, explains Müller, that the Kingdom is the goal or future of humanity. The realization of the Beatitudes is not merely a promise, but rather an
event governed by natural laws. It is an event giving expression to our
original being, the "eternal kernel" and "divine idea" within us, and the
"destiny of humanity" that desires to take shape in us. "The Kingdom of
God consists in actual being, in abiding values and real strengths."[25] The
subsequent Beatitudes are criteria of the Kingdom's strength and depth, its
authenticity and purity.[26] The mourners are comforted with the messianic
consolation of Israel which naturally in Israel took a peculiar shape and
color. The disciples of Buddha understood it differently than those of Jesus, and we today understand it differently still.[27] The blessing upon the
meek who shall inherit the earth was also originally an expression of messianic felicity, but now it applies to those who thrust ahead against the
stream. Luther lost sight of the heroic strain in this promise to those who
quietly resolve to transform all things.[28] The promise for those who seek
righteousness applies to those committed to transforming humanity from
its subhuman degradation to its incomprehensibly glorious destiny. In
Müller's interpretation of the blessing upon the pure in heart, one recognizes the influence of Nietzsche's "transvaluation of values" to establish
the harmony of being. These promises apply not to a particular group of
disciples or to the crowds in general but to those authentic seekers who an-

---

[23]Ibid.

[24]Ibid., 42.

[25]Ibid., 44.

[26]Ibid., 45.

[27]Ibid., 47.

[28]Ibid., 48-50.

ticipate the future destiny of realized humanity and who are committed to that vision.

Since Jesus left the law and prophets intact (Matthew 5:17-20), that signifies, in Müller's opinion, that the "new" Kingdom does not come by social, political, or cultural reform nor by a change in the external order of things as Tolstoy had surmised.[29] Jesus brings essentially a new morality for one's personal life—a morality of positive fulfillment illustrated in various aspects in Matthew 5:20-48. The emphasis in these "Antitheses" is not on Jesus but on the seekers who are to establish the basis for authentic coexistence; they are not to strive against one another, mislead or degrade one another, or to betray commitment (Matthew 5:21-30). The intention throughout is not pedantic legislation in casuistic form but the inspiration of a great ideal to which humanity should aspire. Jesus' saying forbidding swearing (Matthew 5:33-37) is not about that indispensable legal practice. Once we abstract it from its irrelevant Jewish context which has no bearing on European tradition, it becomes clear, according to Müller, that Jesus intends the truthfulness of our whole being. He does not challenge the social conventions without which community life could not function. The sayings about nonresistance and love of enemies are also signposts pointing the way to the new humanity and the new being. In his final reference to perfection (Matthew 5:48), Jesus is pointing ahead to the new morality that applies to the coming Kingdom rather than to human life as it is lived now. He signals no command but a call to a new quest for those who seek to recover the fountain of true being within themselves and thus lead humanity toward the fulfillment of its destiny.

In what manner are Jesus' demands fulfilled? Fulfillment transpires as the instinctive being-against one is replaced by the new being of unwavering good will for one another so that the life and well-being of the other is no longer threatened or denied but wholeheartedly affirmed. This positive outgoing disposition is much more than mere restraint or omission of evildoing.[30] In the present state there predominates among people "an opposition of interests, a hostile disposition, and an instinctive struggle for existence." Consequently, people live together in a state of constant tension and friction. This inner irritation readily ignites indignation, anger,

---

[29]Ibid., 109.
[30]Ibid., 123.

slander, or spite, giving rise to murder in some form. As Müller understands the counsel of Jesus, this tension, more than merely being repressed, is inwardly resolved. This happens as the tension-unto-death is replaced by a fundamental togetherness in the life-urge with and for one another "that alone is able to heal the irritation of the neighbor against us."[31] This transcendence is essentially implied in Jesus' saying on murder and wrath in particular and in the fulfillment of the six Antitheses in general. As for the command to "be perfect" (Matthew 5:48), Müller believes that perfection "cannot be expected of anyone. For imperfection belongs to the essence of man. . . . If we strive in religious exaltation after sinlessness, we will only betray ourselves with our perfection and miserably come to ruin."[32] It is not people that are designated as perfect but the new morality of the Kingdom of God which Jesus inspires. "Be ye perfect" is no command. It is the challenge directed to seekers to ignite the spark of true being within their inmost selves.[33]

Müller's book was issued in a remarkable eight editions. Could it be that its appeal lay in the liberal optimism that characterized its time? Or was it the fresh breeze of enthusiastic religious psychologizing in contrast to the traditional pessimism of the Christian doctrine of man? The book is filled with constructive insights that raise the level of consciousness in self-understanding and human relations. Though not artfully written, it had its special appeal, not only to the introspective conscience, but also for all children of the new age who at the dawn of the twentieth century were captivated by the evolutionary vigor of life and caught up in the idealism of fulfilling the human potential with fanatical nationalistic zeal.

Müller's underlying premise is that, since modern man cannot identify with the whole gospel of the ancient Christ, he must separate the kernel from the husk. First and foremost, the offensive Jewishness of Jesus must be exposed and eradicated as the foreign element contaminating the purity of the German *Geist* and threatening the superiority of the Aryan self-consciousness. Next, the abstracted and purified universal essence is cut loose from all historic roots (which only hinder progress) and self-consciously contemporized as "the natural principles of humanization." This opera-

---

[31]Ibid., 125.

[32]Ibid., 172.

[33]Ibid., 173.

tion eliminates both Schweitzer's apocalyptic and Tolstoy's legalism. Finally, this Germanized and contemporized lotus-blossom is psychologically individualized as correction to the euphoria of Ragaz's Socialism and as safeguard against Naumann's disillusionment. In this way Müller avoids the perils of either modernizing Jesus or overidentifying with him.

Müller's methodology of abstracting from the accidental facts of history the universal truths of reason betrays the influence of Harnack's masterpiece, *Das Wesen des Christentums*, except that it short-cuts that ingenious redefinition of Jesus' aims by simply disregarding what Jesus thought. The timeless aroma that remains after Müller has peeled the onion in quest of its universal essence appears to have more in common with Unity, Theosophy, and Bahai than with the original *Bergpredigt* of Rabbi Yeshua of Nazareth.

OTTO BAUMGARTEN:
THE SERMON ON THE MOUNT
AND CONTEMPORARY CULTURE

[The Sermon on the Mount exemplifies] a totally otherworldly orientation which despises cultural questions and focuses on a small circle of disciples. . . . Free of all history and culture, [Jesus] lifts his Kingdom of Heaven ethic beyond all time and national boundary. One should, however, not demand that it be what it does not intend: a Kulturethik.[1]

[Jesus] was a sunny, blissful, good-natured, and sentimental person who here judges his whole environment from the perspective of his own being. . . . Our experience of life demands a restriction of this happy confidence to the inner, personal life.[2]

Jesus was essentially concerned about the relation of the soul to its God. . . . There never has been greater one-sidedness of religious interest.[3]

A boundless and unconditional individualism predominates here which finds its measure in itself, in its sanctification before God, without any reflections about its social consequences and implications for society.[4]

Let us therefore not underestimate the difficulty of finding a compromise between the ethos of the Bergpredigt *and the* Kultur der Gegenwart.[5]

The only way out of this dilemma is energetically and radically to limit the applicability of the Sermon on the Mount.[6]

---

[1]Otto Baumgarten, *Bergpredigt und Kultur der Gegenwart*. Religionsgeschichtliche Volksbücher für die deutsche christliche Gegenwart, VI. Reihe 10/12. Heft, begründet von Friedrich Michael Schiele; herausgegeben von Karl Aner (Tübingen: Verlag J.C.B. Mohr [Paul Siebeck], 1921) 34.

[2]Ibid., 96, 97.

[3]Ibid., 118.

[4]Ibid., 49.

[5]Ibid., 83.

[6]Ibid., 10.

Otto Baumgarten's[7] *Bergpredigt und Kultur der Gegenwart* documents a national crisis of conscience. It was November 1918, and the armistice ending the Great War had just been signed. From then on strife between nations was to be resolved beyond the battlefield at the conference table of an international court for arbitration which would guarantee every people the freedom to exercise their right of self-determination. To adapt itself to this new era, the Prussian mentality was to undergo a decisive conversion: its politic of violence, deception, and secret diplomacy was to be replaced by a socializing and democratizing process. The cunning, selfish, and brutal national ethos was to be succeeded by international rapprochement and concord among Europe's states.

A few weeks earlier, Professor Baumgarten was still investing his persuasive talent to free the Christian conscience of his nearly defeated people by urging them to make the ultimate sacrifice to effect the triumph of those values upon which the *Vaterland* was grounded. To do so with ultimate integrity demanded that he, as professor of theology, take issue with the Sermon on the Mount. Upon analyzing the text, however, he could not—to his great dismay—evade the impression that not only isolated clear sentences of Jesus but the whole tenor of the *Bergpredigt* appeared at first glance irreconcilable not merely with wars of aggression but indeed with all forms of self-defense. This realization presented for Professor Baumgarten a dilemma of conscience. Only a few days prior to Germany's acceptance of Wilson's dictates, Baumgarten in a public address challenged his people to remain true to the premises of Bismarck's *Realpolitik* even if the nation should be compelled outwardly to concede to the demands of Wilson, that humanitarian apostle from across the sea.

Meanwhile, Baumgarten was asking himself serious questions: Had not Nietzsche rightly discerned the keynote of Jesus' ethic to be self-renunciation, forfeiture of all honor, *Gelassenheit* (imperturbability), passive submission, and outright compliance? Is it then not a meaningless perversion of Jesus' unequivocally clear teaching to claim that his *Bergpredigt* is not incompatible with war? How can a man who feels himself bound to the national ethos proclaim from the Christian pulpit the right and duty to hate one's national enemy? If the Sermon on the Mount is really the Magna

---

[7]Otto Baumgarten (born 1858) taught at the University of Jena (1890) and was appointed Professor of Practical Theology at Kiel in 1894. He is the author of *Die Voraussetzungslosigkeit der protestantischen Theologie* (Kiel, 1903).

Charta of evangelical ethics, do we then not find ourselves in terrible contradiction unless we affirm absolute pacifism?

> Who dares reinterpret such unequivocally clear teaching until it applies only to one's relation to an altogether personal, private enemy? Surely it violates the respected integrity of a historically and critically educated interpreter to pursue so dubious an art however much one's piety towards Jesus might entice one to do so.[8]

Not without some trepidation, Baumgarten articulates the crucial issue:

> Must we now unlearn our past and break our national ethos in favor of a conjoint humane and humanitarian commitment which evidently stands infinitely closer to the ethos of the Sermon on the Mount than the proud Bismarckian national spirit?[9]

In the course of these deliberations, he confronted his students with the decisive question: How shall we bridge the contradiction between the morality of the state and the ethics of the *Bergpredigt*? Does not this conflict underlie all aspects of our existence? And do we not cut off the branch upon which we sit when we realize that all art and science, all industry and commerce, in fact, everything that comprises our contemporary culture is essentially irreconcilable with the ethics of the Sermon on the Mount? "And so it appears," Baumgarten declared, "that the only way out of this dilemma is to delimit energetically and resolutely the sphere of applicability of the Sermon on the Mount"[10]—an insight which was to constitute the keynote of his entire premise and, in its consistent and erudite development, was to calm the troubled water of an awakened conscience. Had not Luther, that greatest doctor of all German theology, helped himself out of this dilemma by distinguishing the Christian person as individual (*Einzelperson*) from the Christian as official person (*Amtsperson*)? Had not Luther found support for his theory not merely in Paul but also in the teachings of Jesus?

With anxious expectation Baumgarten had looked to the League of Nations to effect "the resolution of the tension between the Sermon on the

---

[8]*Bergpredigt*,4.

[9]Ibid., 7.

[10]Ibid., 10.

Mount and contemporary culture.''[11] Meanwhile, in the hope of finding his own way to the ethical meaning of this crisis, Baumgarten challenged his students with the crucial task of thoroughly investigating the ethics of the Sermon on the Mount against the background of the ancient culture of the New Testament era. In the process two years had elapsed, and Baumgarten observed that the fundamental problem underlying the international contention, far from being resolved, had become only more explicit:

> We Germans have learned at our own expense that our confidence in Wilson's disposition, alleged to be congenial with the Sermon on the Mount, has been betrayed by a false light (*Irrlicht*) which has led us into the mire of total impotence and injustice.[12]

Germans have not fallen for the error of pacifism and antinomianism, Baumgarten added, for the current international politic, in stark contrast to the morality of the Sermon on the Mount, leads further and further towards the brutal dehumanization of Germany. With existential difficulty Baumgarten, as a man of his time, wrestled with the dilemma of reconciling the prevailing political ethics of *"die Kultur der Gegenwart"* with the ethic of Jesus.

In reviewing Baumgarten's scholarly and erudite treatise, we are at once impressed with the ingenuity of his one-sided mentality which enabled him to establish with almost convincing thoroughness a single dominant insight as the exclusive key to unlocking the enigma of the *Bergpredigt*. To one not so convinced, he appears to force every other reality or thought into the service of that singular truth. His thesis, tediously reiterated throughout, is that the *Bergpredigt* exemplifies a socially irresponsible, anticultural religious individualism and constitutes a transworldly, otherworldly pilgrim ethic.[13]

First, we are informed, on the credentials of Troeltsch, that, contrary to enthusiasts like Ragaz, the teaching of Jesus in the *Bergpredigt* had nothing whatsoever to do with any social movement of antiquity. Early Christian missions and devotional literature know nothing of the modern social question and preoccupy themselves exclusively with soteriology. In Christian self-understanding "the values of redemption are purely inward,

---

[11]Ibid.

[12]Ibid., 11.

[13]"eine überweltliche, jenseitige Pilgrimsmoral."

ethical, and spiritual.''[14] The origins of Christianity do not go back to an ancient socialism or communism, as Kautsky thought, for this construction denies the independence of meaning of religious ideas.

The Early Church's attitude towards slavery documents its purely introspective religious disposition. Religiously, master and slave were held to be equally eligible for church office, but this religious equality had no social intentions whatsoever. Slavery in society would not be abolished. The whole class struggle of the proletariat is a social consciousness foreign to the New Testament. Early Christians were not given to such reflections because, in contrast to intellectualized philosophical movements, such as Platonism and Stoicism, believers constituting the dynamic Early Christian communities for the most part represented the lower classes for whom unshattered fantasy, simplicity of emotion, unreflectiveness of thought, native strength, and keenness of desire were predominant characteristics.

It is more difficult to sublimate Luke's frequent reference to sickness, weakness, misery, and poverty to the interests of a soteriological perspective than it is in Matthew. It appears, therefore, that Luke's "blessed are the poor" is his commendation of poverty for its own sake in anticipation of the due recompense offered by the coming Kingdom of God. Matthew is, by contrast, free from such value judgment regarding material involvements, and, therefore, reasons Professor Baumgarten, Matthew's version of the *Bergpredigt* stands invariably closer to the original thought of Jesus, who never tired of proclaiming the inestimable worth of the human soul. Matthew in no way involves Jesus in the class struggles of his day but depicts a Saviour who is altogether oblivious to social and cultural goals and ambitions. For Jesus, neither science nor art, commerce nor industry, jurisprudence nor politics constituted the focus of his reflective interest. His inner disposition was totally preoccupied with the realm of religion. And the one-sided internalization of his reflective disposition was compounded by the fact that the Roman imperium thwarted all independent Jewish social, political, and economic initiative, thus compelling the reflective nature of its occupied people to withdraw into an introspective religious world to focus on private morality, to transpose social ideals into an otherworldly beyond, and to find religious consolation in the cultivation of peace of the soul in its love of fellowman and in its sweet communion with God:

---

[14]Ibid., 12.

> Jesus' Sermon on the Mount has nothing whatsoever to do with social
> and cultural questions. It is purely religious, developed around particular
> thoughts about God and God's will with man.[15]
>
> In contrast to all national, legal, and cultural ethics, the ethic of Jesus
> bears the character of a pure ethic of intention (*Gesinnungsmoral*).[16]
>
> Thus develops that unconditional and unlimited individualism which
> overcomes all cultural barriers and distinctions through the ideal of the re-
> ligious worth of the soul. . . . One sees immediately that for such radical
> individualism no relation to culture can be essential or significant and that
> it has nothing to do with worldly interests and distinctions and cannot make
> any compromises with them.[17]

For God's children there is no right and no duty, no war and no conflict, only endless love and overcoming of evil with good. There is no social or human ideal in view, and there are no thoughts about the
development of culture toward such ideals. The context of Jesus' ethics is
an unequaled cultural and historical indifference. Jesus does not challenge
the thinking capacity of people but appeals instead to authority and revelation, a fact which explains his indifference to all scientific knowledge
and growth in comprehension of truth.[18] Rather than bringing a new social
order and renewal of social institutions, the coming Kingdom Jesus proclaims will bring to an end the state, society, and the family.

Introducing the text itself, Baumgarten immediately poses that the
Bergpredigt is addressed not to the multitude as such but only to a small
circle of disciples. The masses mentioned at the conclusion of the Sermon
do not come into consideration as actual hearers but as stage props for
background in the construction of Matthew.

As for the Beatitudes, promise of their fulfillment redirects the disciples from the present and its culture to those treasures preserved for them
in the Kingdom of Heaven beyond. As a last resort, one might consider
the first and second blessing upon the poor and the mourners to have some
allusion to an earthly future as well. But the promise that they who practice
mercy shall obtain mercy could not even by the greatest optimist be applied to an earthly reference; nor can the promise of seeing God refer to

---

[15]Ibid., 15.

[16]Ibid., 16.

[17]Ibid., 17.

[18]Ibid., 18.

our earthly lives, for no mortal has ever seen God. "The blessedness that is here promised the comrades in the new Kingdom is future, other-worldly, and beyond culture."[19] Jesus' praise of the pure in heart presupposes a naïve optimism untouched by the cultural distinction of even his contemporaries. It appeals to that naïve and undeveloped soul of the child in primitive mentality. "But to contemporary culture the pure heart forever remains a stranger."[20] As for Jesus' promise to the peacemakers, "it is fairly certain that Jesus' nonpolitical stance, so far removed from national life, could not here in any sense have considered international peace."[21]

Baumgarten senses in all the Beatitudes the acute tension between national, self-assertive and self-established culture and the mentality of Jesus which consistently praises the passive disposition. Here Baumgarten remarked, we see the sense in which Nietzsche was justified in criticizing Christianity in his *Genealogy of Morals*:

> This Jesus of Nazareth as the living gospel of love, this "Redeemer" who brings salvation and triumph to the poor, the sick, and the sinners— was he not indeed corruption [Verführung] in its most uncanny and irresistible form, the misdirection and deviation from exactly those Jewish values and revivals of the ideal?[22]

The similes of salt and light (Matthew 5:13-16) are passed over lightly since there is "here no mention of a gradual progressive ferment and illumination of the world" but only of that otherworldly idealism of the disciples.[23] The pericope about Jesus' relation to the law (Matthew 5:17-20) "also interests us very little," for within the expansive soul of Jesus there could not have been room for such a clinging to iotas.[24] The passage attests a

> totally otherworldly orientation which despises cultural questions, focusing on a small circle of disciples who have been loosed from all love of the world and whose souls have been directed to the heavenly Jerusalem. [To them] he gives consciously, explicitly, and exclusively a pilgrim morality

---

[19]Ibid., 22.

[20]Ibid., 25.

[21]Ibid.

[22]Ibid., 28.

[23]Ibid., 29.

[24]Ibid., 32.

[*Pilgermoral*] with overwhelmingly fantastic force and self-confidence. . . .Free of all history and culture, he lifts his Kingdom-of-Heaven ethic beyond all time and national boundary. One should, however, not demand that it be what it does not intend: a cultural ethic.[25]

In the saying on murder and wrath (Matthew 5:21-26), Baumgarten holds that Jesus clearly rejected all juridical order and law enforcement, for he wants to offer only a true *Gesinnungsethik* and therefore takes issue with the entire spirit of Judaism. As for the asceticism implied in Jesus' word on adultery and divorce (Matthew 5:27-32), a contemporary culture feels obliged to reject it. To consider marriage indissoluble would imply reverting to the cultural level of the Catholic Middle Ages.[26] In his teaching about oaths (Matthew 5:33-37), Jesus presents an unsurpassable ideal but certainly no precept.[27] One should not denigrate his high and noble statement by applying it to our justifiable oaths of allegiance and of office. A Christian person will swear only those oaths required on account of the general mendacity but will leave to the respective authorities the decision regarding which oaths are obligatory.[28] Characteristic of his cultural estrangement, Jesus in his prohibition of retaliation (Matthew 5:38-42) altogether disregards the public aspect of life. Consequently, Baumgarten argued,

> it is undeniably correct, as Troeltsch maintained, that a boundless and unconditional individualism predominates here which finds its own measure in itself, in its sanctification before God, without any reflection whatsoever about its social consequences and implications for society.

This individualism is joined with a complete disregard for the "nature of things"—for the natural limitations and differentiations within the mixture of human society.[29] To concede Jesus' counsel to go the second mile when impressed to such injustice would imply that we must forego every defense against ruthless exploitation and likewise forego every just im-

---

[25]Ibid., 34.

[26]Ibid., 43.

[27]Ibid., 46.

[28]Ibid., 48.

[29]Ibid., 49.

provement of the social condition.[30] Baumgarten counsels his students not to preach from this text nor refer to it in catechistical instruction.[31]

Even more serious are the problems encountered in correctly understanding Jesus' word on loving one's enemies (Matthew 5:43-48). We are told that Jewish hatred of the Romans was as common then as German hatred of the French is now but that it would not do to limit the reference of this text to the national enemy when indeed the private enemy is clearly meant. In using the concept ''enemy'' interchangeably with ''persecutor,'' the evangelist is obviously thinking of enemies of the faith—that is, *Glaubensfeinde*. This text documents both the inwardness of Jesus' ideal and its general unattainableness, not merely for the average but for the 'natural man.'[32] Aspiring to this ideal means violation of our human dignity and denial of our offended love for the *Vaterland*. At any rate, it would be a forced persuasion, and love of one's enemy can be genuine only when it is the expression of one's deepest inner disposition.[33]

Jesus' commentary on economics (Matthew 6:19-34) appears no less problematic from the perspective of contemporary culture, for he declines to place any importance on earthly things and consequently discountenances any concern for them by those for whom the heavenly world is the all-encompassing reality. Employer and employee, merchant and customer—all are confronted with the either/or of his total indifference to the realm of commerce and economics. ''Let us therefore not underestimate the difficulty of finding a compromise between the ethos of the *Bergpredigt* and the *Kultur der Gegenwart*.''[34] His ''do not lay up for yourselves treasures on earth'' simply means not to be capitalists, applicable both to the large-scale entrepreneur and the small investor. ''The model of early Christian communism in which no one claimed possession appears to be the only right interpretation of a single-minded life exclusively oriented to God and the heavenly realm.''[35] Jesus' words are not those of a moral reformer standing in the midst of worldly life but of a prophet who

---

[30]Ibid., 52.

[31]Ibid., 54.

[32]Ibid., 57.

[33]Ibid., 59.

[34]Ibid., 83.

[35]Ibid., 86.

has already foreclosed himself to this world in order to prepare for a higher order of things to come. Yet we who stand in the midst of our raw reality urge our fellow human beings to "take care" and not depend upon a higher hand.[36] Let it be known that no businessman, no statesman, no father of a family, and no one who seeks to better himself can live from hand to mouth in this manner. "In the maddening pace of our present world with its despairing struggle for individual and national existence, this song about carefreeness most certainly sounds like a melody from the lost paradise."[37]

Lastly, we are confronted with Jesus' injunction: "Ask, and it will be given you; seek, and you will find" (Matthew 7:7-8). If such petitioning is grounded upon the expectation of fulfillment within our lifetime, then we must call into question the discernment of Jesus. "Our experiences and our observations do not agree with this optimistic selective reading of life's experiences." In the days ahead the opposite will evidence itself a thousandfold. How many there will be seeking employment with their petitions ungranted! How many will seek a modest placement within the social order and not find it! And how much vain knocking is there on our own doors and on many doors as thousands go abroad to seek a living while the cripple with his barrel organ drags along the cold cobblestones!

> That was a sunny blissful land in which such claims could depend on general acceptance. And it was a sunny, blissful, good natured, sentimental person who here judges his whole environment from the perspective of his own being.[38]

Contemporary culture, however, compels one to quite different observations. Who, for example, after having survived this war can without reservation repeat this sentence about God's answering our every petition? Because Jesus said it, we conclude that it must be true. But must it really? Does not he exemplify the escapism of all estranged religious natures in selecting from life only those experiences which are favorable while humbly and thankfully repressing all unfavorable ones? Is it not characteristic

---

[36]"Deutsch sein heißt künftig mit beiden Beinen und mit aufgerafften Aermeln arbeiten und sorgen, damit die Not ferngehalten werde." Ibid., 90.

[37]Ibid., 91.

[38]Ibid., 96.

of all celebrated pious souls to blot out memory of misfortune and recall only a chain of blessed triumphs?

> Contemporary culture cannot respect such rosy optimism that represents a thousandfold illusion as worthy of aspiration and instead demands a strong, courageous realism that clearly reckons with the possible and indeed inevitable misfortunes. Above all, our experience of life demands a restriction of this happy confidence to the inner, personal life. We know that world events which intertwine us in their mighty mesh develop from cause to effect through iron fate and that, in between the individual links of this chain, prayer is efficacious only insofar as it tunes our inmost self to silent submission and joyful extinction in the will of God.[39]

Wherefore, Professor Baumgarten further counsels his students not to preach from this text nor to drill it into the minds of children in the catechism lest "it merely compel to perversion, intransigence, or that kind of truth-twisting and reinterpretation that has become most fatal for our contemporaries and that certainly does not lead to realizable expectations."[40]

Baumgarten attributes all misuse of the *Bergpredigt* and the resulting secularization of Christianity to the mistaken assumption that it is God's highest design for human life.[41] We are to remember that Jesus spoke to Palestinians and that his words about caring, asking, and earthly things presuppose the economy of the Orient with its characteristic absence of all desire for honor and justice and its absence of all national, judicial, and social ideals. These words apply to a people that had ceased to be a nation because the moral fiber of its social and cultural aspiration had been broken by Roman occupation. If these culturally-bound words of Jesus are exalted as the universal ethical norm for all times and climes, then, either great damage to cultural life will be the effect or else a miserable compromise will have to be negotiated. Roman Catholic interpretation since Thomas Aquinas provides the solution of a dual ethic, but for a Protestant ethic the Sermon on the Mount is much more difficult because it confines one to estrangement from the world while being committed to the world. Those seeking an either/or solution to this dilemma, such as the free church mystics, the silent Friends of God, and the enthusiasts, Denck, Hätzer,

---

[39]Ibid., 97.

[40]Ibid.

[41]Ibid., 110.

Müntzer and his associates, are, in this respect, all inwardly related. Endeavoring to be serious Christians, they withdraw from the sinful mass church to become the silent in the land and to cultivate in enmity against its culture their pious inwardness according to the temperament of Tersteegen, Tolstoy, and Kierkegaard. The Sermon on the Mount is indeed the finest unmatched expression of such religious sentimentality, reflecting a purely unspoiled inwardness and sensitivity of feeling.

But wherein lies the Sermon's abiding significance? It consists in constituting, in effect, the spiritual biography of Jesus' inner life. One must concede that the content of his life-style is unexcelled. However, one should not expand it beyond its intended sphere:[42]

> Jesus was essentially concerned with the relation of the soul to its God.
> . . .There has never been greater one-sidedness of religious interest. God
> the Father, his Kingdom and his kingship, constitute the all-fulfilling pathos of his soul, even when it observes the birds of the heavens and the
> lilies of the field.[43]

We have reviewed Baumgarten's treatise extensively not just because it deserves to be heard but because it indeed has been heard widely and credulously despite the fact that its inadequacies are so obvious that it appears neither necessary nor interesting to point them out. Perhaps it suffices to observe that in his *Weltanschauung* Baumgarten represents the *Kulturverherrlichung* (''glorification of culture'') of pre-war Liberalism.

Baumgarten's significance for our historical survey lies in the erudition and fanatical consistency with which he articulates the understanding of the *Bergpredigt* as Jesus' autobiographical self-expression of an unexcelled socially and culturally irresponsible religious individualism. Baumgarten's interpretation amounts to a solution of embarrassment (*Verlegenheitslösung*), for it implicitly concedes that the meaning of history lies not with *Kulturchristentum* but with the fulfillment of Jesus' intentions within those mystic and eccentric traditions that share Jesus' *Weltanschauung* and endeavor to walk in his steps. Baumgarten's despairing pessimism stems from the realization that sectarian escapism is no option for him as *Kulturmensch*.

---

[42]Ibid., 117.

[43]Ibid., 118.

Baumgarten's indebtedness to Wilhelm Herrmann's *Gesinnungsethik* is explicit, but he differs markedly from his mentor in not attempting to stretch the ethical intentions of Jesus to cover the demands of contemporary culture. Yet, in refusing to modernize Jesus, he has also failed to indicate what significance the Sermon on the Mount has for our times. Implicitly, Baumgarten accepted the conclusions of Naumann and, wherever expedient, incorporated into the logic of his argument the findings of Johannes Weiss. Baumgarten passionately and pathetically depicts the estrangement of Jesus from the culture of his time which, in turn, establishes his complete irrelevance for the cultural identity of modern man. Unlike Schweitzer, Baumgarten failed to indicate how Jesus' distance from us is meant to become fruitful or what significance, if any, his teaching has for us today.

Charles Gore, honorary chaplain to her majesty the Queen, undertook "A Practical Exposition" of *The Sermon on the Mount* (London: John Murray, 1900) which he understood to be "a law not only for individual consciences but for society—a law which . . . is to be applied in order to establish a new social order" (3). He associated "the hard demand of the letter" "with the promise of the Spirit" (4). Yet, he speaks of it not in terms of practicability but as "the letter which killeth, and, because it is so much more searching and thorough than the Ten Commandments, therefore does it kill all the more effectively" (4). We are also told that it does not teach "by literal enactments" (8). It is a new law which stands in direct continuity with what had gone before and yet completely supersedes the incomplete (51). The book is filled with compromising inconsistencies, such as Gore's argument that Jesus' revision of the Old Law obliges Christians to swear oaths (78) and to serve their duty in defense of society and its moral order (86) and never to practice "indiscriminate charity" (96).

H. Shears in his *Christ or Bentham? A Criticism of Dr. Gore's Work on the Sermon on the Mount* (London: Williams and Norgate, Ltd., 1927) particularly exposed this latter ambiguity which he ascribes to Gore's having been influenced by the social philosophy of utilitarianism. Shears rightly discerns that "indiscriminateness" is of the very essence of Jesus' demands (cf. 18). Satisfied in restoring to Jesus' words their intended harshness, he then compromises this emphasis by insisting that they are "counsels of perfection to which few ordinary Christians can attain" (22) and which "do not and cannot apply to the whole of life" (83). He accuses Gore of eliminating the Cross from his gospel by confusing it with a social ideal (101) which Shears eliminates by limiting the demands of the Gospel to a select few. Shears objects to Gore's counsel to retranslate our Lord's teaching into social action "according to the wisdom of the time or the wisdom of man or the wisdom of the church" on the assumption that such a cryptic process can at best result in a change of fashion rather than a transformation of character (108-109) and concludes that, "if Christians can do no better for society than this, they had better leave society alone" (108), rather than meddle in the hopeless attempt of applying the principles of Jesus to politics or of re-translating it into a social law (109). Rather than obliterate the contrast between Church and world, the Church would do well, thinks Shears, ''to leave the world to that Providence which has never ruled it and never will rule it with the law of meekness'' (111) and concern herself ''not with the political and social conditions of the fleeting world but with the help and guidance of the eternal individuals who are perpetually passing through it and beyond'' (112).

In his study of *The Sermon on the Mount and Its Application* (London: Geoffrey Bles, 1963) James Wood noted ''there is simply no one key to unlock its meaning'' (13). While this observation may appear as a compliment to the richness and vitality of its content so that no one answer can exhaust its meaning, it may, on the other hand, serve as an under-handed rationale for evading the demands of hermeneutical consistency in establishing the sense of the matter as it applies to us by giving priority to unchallenged assumptions on the grounds that they are self-evident to us though they have no place within the self-evidence of Jesus. Thus Wood concludes Jesus himself limited the application of his idealistic teach-ing to ''what was practicable under the circumstances,'' allowing himself to be appre-hended in Gethsemane ''only at the last moment, when resistance was beyond him and his disciples'' (104). Since Wood finds ''no one clear simple, unambiguous principle lying ready at hand, just waiting to be applied,'' he concludes that Jesus' word, ''Resist not,'' really means that we are to probe into the circumstances and resist whenever it seems prac-tical to do so. Jesus' words are not clear to Wood. What is clear to him is that whenever doing what Jesus says would endanger anyone it is a Christian's duty to do the opposite (cf. 109). Wood finds the idea of nuclear holocaust distasteful but holds that any appeal to total disarmament would be ''a misuse of the absolute demands of Christianity,'' (113) for ''men are not free to act according to the dictates of wisdom, and it is just a waste of time to present the claims of truth and wisdom in the language of absolute ideals and absolute Christian demands'' (114).

KARL BORNHÄUSER:
A HISTORICIST VIEW
OF THE SERMON'S RELEVANCE

These words are taught in order that they might be obeyed—and immediately at that—under the prevailing circumstances of the time.[1]

The opportunity of undertaking their fulfillment is directly given.[2]

Everything that Jesus says the Pharisaic scribes have also said. The great difference between Jesus and the scribes lies not in What they demand but for Whom they allow these demands to apply.[3]

The impossibilities which are to invalidate these demands of Jesus disappear immediately when one understands them in their historic contemporaneity.[4]

The fulfillment of this demand is expected only from Jesus' disciples.[5]

The nominally Christian assembly in our Volkskirchen *is overtaxed if one indiscriminately applies these demands to all their members. For the citizen of the state these demands are altogether impossible. . . . Therefore every generalized application of these demands beyond the disciple-group is unwarranted.*[6]

---

[1]Karl Bornhäuser, *Die Bergpredigt. Versuch einer zeitgenössischen Auslegung; Beiträge zur Förderung christlicher Theologie*; Zweite Reihe: Sammlung wissenschaftlicher Monographien (Gütersloh: Druck und Verlag von C. Bertelsmann, 1923) 60.

[2]Ibid., 111.

[3]Ibid., 93.

[4]Ibid., 99, 100.

[5]Ibid., 90.

[6]Ibid., 112.

Professor Karl Bornhäuser[7] of Marburg attempted to provide "a contemporary interpretation" of the *Bergpredigt*. He did not sanction the moratorium of the Sermon on the Mount that was generally in effect during the Great War, nor did he stand with the prophets of pacifism; instead, Bornhäuser undertook the arduous task of formulating a third alternative, one now commonly labeled "the modern historical approach."

Bornhäuser's fundamental premise stipulates that, "To understand Jesus' *Bergpredigt*, one must attempt reading it or, preferably, hearing it as would a Jew of his day."[8] For no text of the New Testament, declares Bornhäuser, is the danger of forgetting this obvious truth as great or as disastrous as it is for the Sermon on the Mount. Just as a good translation of the text presupposes a mastery of the original Greek, so an adequate understanding of its original meaning presupposes the capacity to hear it as would a Jewish contemporary of Jesus. The incapacity to understand the text as a contemporary of Jesus accounts, in Bornhäuser's opinion, for such universally disastrous misunderstandings as Tolstoy's "total misconception" of Matthew 5:38ff. To prevent such error, Biblical scholarship must make its decisive contribution to Christianity by opening the door to a correct understanding of the *Bergpredigt*—indeed, the exact proposal of Bornhäuser's weighty treatise. Its strength lies in its imaginative and exhaustive exegesis and above all in its careful attention to textual detail. Bornhäuser makes no apology for his conservative scholarship but proudly shares the reputation for what is now commonly known as "Biblical realism" with such notable predecessors as Bengel, Oetinger, Tobias Beck, Hermann Cremer, Martin Kähler, and Adolf Schlatter.

As an introduction Bornhäuser informs us that the text under consideration should never have been designated by the later tradition as a "Sermon" but rather as the "Teaching on the Mount" (*Berglehre*), for its content is not the εὐαγγέλιον of the κῆρυξ but the διδαχή of the διδάσκαλος. Jesus teaches *halacha* in the haggadic tradition (exemplified by his sitting posture), stating what is to be done and giving instructions for the way (ὁδός) to live as he previously had done in the synagogues.

---

[7]Karl Bernhard Bornhäuser (born 1868) was pastor at Sinsheim (1890-94) and Karlsruhe (1894-1902) and taught Systematic Theology at Greifswald before being appointed Professor of Systematic and Practical Theology at Marburg in 1907. He also published *Vergottungslehre des Athanasius und Joh. Damascus* (Gütersloh, 1903).

[8]*Die Bergpredigt*, 2.

Apart from the Beatitudes and the concluding parable, the body of this teaching is *halachot*, guides for living (*Lebensregeln*) and words (λόγοι) to be enacted immediately. How preposterous to assume that Jesus was expounding a *Gesinnungsethik*! There is simply no way of evading his forthright insistence on *praxis*.[9]

Despite mention of the crowds at the beginning and conclusion of the Teaching on the Mount, Bornhäuser is convinced that these rules of life were directed specifically to the Twelve rather than the masses in general. It is they, and not the masses, who stand out in contradistinction to those Pharisaic scribes Jesus castigates as hypocrites, and it is from the twelve disciples that Jesus demands a higher righteousness.[10]

The Beatitudes, says Bornhäuser, are not to be spiritualized. They apply to a particular historical condition. In blessing the poor (Matthew 5:3) Jesus takes issue with the hard bargaining of ruthless Galileans at their early morning Lake Gennesaret fishmarkets in order to defy the corrupt business enterprise of secularized Jews as well as the oppressive tax structures of their overlords. His first beatitude, as his later temple cleansing, attacks the religious sanction of economically exploiting the poor within the flourishing business of temple sacrifices. His blessing on the poor undermines the economic foundation of a religion whose manipulators find their security in the wealth of the temple treasury, that national Jewish central bank whose holdings are secured against deflation by the very presence of the divine glory within it. That the Kingdom also includes the poor might have been known to the Jews from Isaiah 61:1, but that it is only for the poor implies a revolutionary transvaluation of values. The Pharisees taught two ways of redemption: through merit or by grace. Jesus allows the way of poverty and repentance alone. From his blessing on those who hunger and thirst after righteousness the economically successful and the morally self-righteous are excluded. While the first three beatitudes parallel the first three petitions of the Lord's prayer, the blessing on the peacemakers anticipates the disciples' vocation as salt and light of the world and indicates their plan of action (*Arbeitsprogramm*).[11]

---

[9]Ibid., 8-10.

[10]Ibid., 8, 17.

[11]Ibid., 18-37.

Jesus' pedantic insistence on fulfilling the letter of the law (Matthew 5:18-19) has been a stumbling block to commentators, but Bornhäuser admits that Jesus meant exactly what he said and that every Jew knew what his reference to the whole law meant. The "extraordinary" righteousness Jesus demands of his disciples (περισσόν of Matthew 5:20) is no Pauline insight of righteousness through faith recovered by Luther. Jesus demands a new approach to living (*Lebensführung*). He demands a new life, not just a new attitude; he inspires a new commitment, not just a new insight. To characterize Jesus' Antitheses (Matthew 5:21-48) as *Gesinnungsethik* or *Interimsethik* is altogether misinterpreting the central point. "These words are taught in order that they might be obeyed—and immediately at that— under the prevailing circumstances. . . . "[12] In rabbinic teaching thought and deed are inseparable.

From a careful study of the context of Jesus' first antithesis (Matthew 5:21-26), Bornhäuser concludes this pericope is no universal prohibition of anger but rather Jesus' instruction for the interrelation of his disciples. As James admonished the brethren not to be haughty (James 1:19,20) and the Pauline tradition insisted that a bishop must not be quick-tempered (Titus 1:7), so Jesus endorsed the mild temperament of Hillel over against the haughty one of Shammai as becoming an apostle. Whereas the Pharisees took carnal delight in their personal disputes which not infrequently led to mutual excommunications, Jesus admonishes the Twelve, who are to be teachers of his new community, to conduct their mutual relations in a harmonious and forbearing manner.[13]

Similarly, the contrast with respect to adultery (Matthew 5:27-30) is not that the Pharisees judge sinful deeds while Jesus condemns sinful intention. Such interpretation would altogether misrepresent the teaching of the rabbis who vigorously denounced coveteousness of another man's wife as sin. Furthermore, it is gross misrepresentation of Jesus' teaching to assume he was concerned only with intention. Jesus' counsel concerns the relations of his disciples to their wives and to other unmarried women disciples. Rabbis were advised to speak only infrequently with women and to avoid temptation by not looking at them. Consequently, the faithful shut

---

[12]Ibid., 60.

[13]"Er bannt das Bannen, auch das der leichtesten Form, aus ihrem Kreise, um ihnen das recht eindrücklich zu machen, sagt er: solch ein Bann fällt auch unter die große Kategorie des Mordes (im weitesten Sinne)." Ibid., 67.

their eyes upon meeting a woman publicly so as to retain their pure intentions and not neglect the Torah. Jesus, on the contrary, did not presume woman to be an evil object of sexual desire and therefore insisted that his followers exercise a higher spiritual and personal interrelationship. Under no circumstances should relationship deteriorate to coveteousness. This is the better righteousness—not just a better intention—that applies to the manner of living exemplified by Jesus' disciples.[14] If Jesus' prohibition of remarriage for divorcees (Matthew 5:31-32) seems unrealistically hard, Bornhäuser reminds us that it was addressed specifically to the twelve disciples and not the entire nation.[15] The injunction to "Swear not at all" was also expected to be fulfilled only by the disciples.[16]

Bornhäuser then explores Jesus' fifth antithesis against the Pharisees (Matthew 5:38-42) concerning retaliation. No Jew of Jesus' day insisted on taking the formula "an eye for an eye" in the brutal, literal sense but instead claimed an equivalent financial indemnity as our insurance policies still prescribe for loss of eye or limb. It was this civil legal system of financial reimbursement for personal damages suffered to which Jesus here takes issue. The established civil practice of indemnification for personal injuries as later codified in the Mishnah which applied to the scribes was not allowed by Jesus for the disciples. Relationships between Jesus' disciples were, in contrast to those of the scribes, not to be governed by equity norms of civil jurisprudence. This text, Bornhäuser assures us, deals only with the contrast between apostles and scribes in their relation to civil jurisprudence, and any generalization expanding its relevance beyond this immediate context does violence to the text:[17]

What tremendous implications developed from the naïvely uninformed interpretation of the word, "Resist not evil," by the Russian Count Tolstoy, who went to battle against war in the name of Jesus. How much foolishness has been contrived about the impossibility of fulfilling the demands of Jesus because one did not know its specific civil-juridical context! . . . Furthermore, it is a bitter injustice against the Pharisees to claim they taught, "resist, go to court, retaliate" . . . everything that Jesus says the Pharisaic scribes have also said. The great difference between Jesus

---

[14]Ibid., 70-78.

[15]Ibid., 79, 85.

[16]Ibid., 90.

[17]Ibid., 92.

and the scribes lies not in What they demand but for Whom they allow these demands to apply.[18]

Matthew 5:39 is to be translated: "You (my apostle) shall not go to court with the evil one." All other translations rendering "Resist not evil" only block the path to true understanding.

Everyone in Israel who suffered personal injury could claim indemnification as provided by civil law. The Pharisees counseled restraint in pursuing one's rights particularly when the injury or insult was effected by a colleague but not necessarily if he were an "evil" neighbor (πονηρός) as the unschooled commoner (am ha-aretz) was frequently designated. The magnanimity of foregoing one's rightful claim to legal justice, which the Pharisees contemplated as a possibility under certain circumstances, Jesus demanded of his disciples as a necessity even when the offense were precipitated by an intentional "evildoer." In 1 Corinthians 6, Paul endorsed this church rule requiring that grievances be resolved without resorting to secular courts and without defending one's right or honor against insult or libel. The precedent for this attitude of forbearance in the church (cf. Romans 12:19-20, 1 Peter 3:9) was Isaiah's (especially 50:6, 7) "suffering servant" image of Jesus:

> The righteous have pity on the poor because God demands it, even though money is lost for the sake of brother or friend. That is the point at which Jesus differed from the Pharisaic scribes. He admonishes his disciples to loan to the good and the bad if they need it (and you are able).[19]

The final antithesis (Matthew 5:43-48) must also be understood entirely within the context of contemporary Judaism, according to Bornhäuser. For generations it had been deeply ingrained in the mentality of every Pharisaic scribe to despise the uncultured semi-pagan am ha-aretz who was ignorant of the Law and therefore did not fulfill its requirements, who was consequently considered "accursed," and, in turn, who despised those religious experts whose ground of being consisted in meticulous observance of the legal letter. This enmity between Pharisees and the am ha-aretz— comparable to that which developed between Pharisees and Messianists which led to the martyrdom of Stephen—was essentially nothing personal.

---

[18]Ibid., 92, 93.
[19]Ibid., 104.

It was the "perfect hatred" of "them that hate Thee" (Psalm 139:21), exemplified not least in the zeal of Saul. This is the situation to which Jesus addressed himself. In contrast to the practice of the Pharisees, he teaches his disciples, "Love your enemies and pray for those who persecute you (Matthew 5:44) for my sake" (Matthew 5:11).[20]

As Bornhäuser sums up the Sermon on the Mount, (1) Jesus demands good works (καλὰ ἔργα; Matthew 5:16) from his disciples as sons of God. (2) The Teaching on the Mount is neither *Gesinnungsethik* nor *Interimsethik* but concrete instruction regarding the conduct of the disciples in life situations. Its demands are neither idealistic, impossible, nor impracticable but were meant to be obeyed immediately. (3) The question is not whether one can seriously make such demands but whether God enables man to fulfill them. To project God as the one who demands over against man as the one who performs is to revert to the pharisaism Jesus sought to overcome. The relation of the disciples to God is that of sons to a Father who enables them to will and to do his good pleasure (Philippians 2:13). (4) Every generalization of these demands beyond the circle of disciples to whom they were originally addressed is unwarranted. (5) The *Sitz-im-Leben* of the Teaching on the Mount is genuinely Jewish as is evident in the terminology, the views expressed, and the situations presupposed. This teaching must therefore be understood from the perspective of a Jewish contemporary of Jesus.

These principles of interpretation are further applied in Bornhäuser's captivating treatise on the apostles' stance regarding possessions and work. By instructing his disciples not to lay up treasures on earth (Matthew 6:19-20), Jesus wishes to exempt them entirely from the necessity of earning a living and the encumbrance of possessions in their ministry.[21] Securing possessions and plying a trade was then a much debated question for a teacher. Jesus was not the first to declare, "You received without pay, give without pay" (Matthew 10:8), for the rabbis were also forbidden to make profit by the Torah even though it was common knowledge that some scribes "devour widows' houses" (Mark 12:40, Luke 20:47) in return for their services. Jesus categorically releases his disciples from the material responsibility of acquiring possessions and earning a living. In fact, he

---

[20]Ibid., 105-110.

[21]Ibid., 145.

commands them to sell what they now have, give the proceeds to the poor (Luke 12:33), and follow his example of accumulating treasures only in heaven. The disciples are to be like birds and lilies (Matthew 6:25ff.) not because these do not worry but because they do not work! With philological ingenuity, Bornhäuser establishes that the crucial term μεριμνάω (usually translated "to worry" or "to be anxious") really means "to labor" as does its synonym "to toil" in verse 28. In Exodus 5:9 (LXX) the same term refers to the "tedious labor" required of the Israelites by Pharaoh in making bricks without straw. And in Luke 10:41 Jesus reprimands Martha not for "worrying" but for "working." Accordingly in Matthew 6:27 Jesus does not ask, "who of you by 'worrying' can prolong his life or accomplish anything worth while?" but rather, "who of you by endless 'tedious labor' can guarantee a single day in advance?" The exegesis is involved, but Bornhäuser's intention is clear: Matthew 6:25-26 does not demand that all Christians stop worrying but that twelve disciples stop working; for, as Paul discerns, the Lord commanded those who proclaim the gospel shall live from it (1 Corinthians 9:14).[22]

As a historical scholar, Bornhäuser comprehended enough of the Jewishness of Jesus' Teaching on the Mount to reject Herrmann's *Gesinnungsethik* as a modern philosophical imposition altogether foreign to the context and therefore quite irrelevant for interpretation of the text. He disdains the mentality of systematic theologians who speculate about the meaning of history and force what limited data is at their disposal into the service of their dogmatic structures without bothering about authentic historical exegesis to substantiate their theological conclusions borrowed from some tradition extraneous to the text. Bornhäuser's approach contrasts even more with that of Ragaz, who was so captivated by the cultural implications of the *Bergpredigt* as the Magna Charta of Christian Socialism that he wasted no effort trying to understand its original context in relation to his modern cause. Although his methodology is historical, Bornhäuser—in contrast to Weiss and Schweitzer—never developed a philosophy of history to indicate the interrelation and interdependence of ideas in the development of consciousness. Bornhäuser never built a bridge of meaning between the past and the present as Schweitzer, via the mysticism of Paul, attempted in order to make the historical particulars of Jesus universally relevant.

---

[22]Ibid., 145-161.

Unlike Wünsch, Bornhäuser feels no need to acknowledge or defend his indebtedness to Luther for the presuppositions governing his own reading of history. In contrast to Naumann and Baumgarten, Bornhäuser appears oblivious to the agony of the modern uneasy conscience of Christendom caught in the dilemma of attempting to reconcile the claims of Jesus with the demands of culture.

Of all the positions examined thus far, Bornhäuser stands nearest the one he respects least. With Tolstoy he concurs that the obedience Jesus demanded of his disciples was entirely possible and altogether practicable. Indeed, he went deeper than Tolstoy in articulating the original context in which this obedience was to be realized by illuminating its character with rabbinic parallels. But it is precisely in this historical method that his difference from Tolstoy becomes evident. Bornhäuser approached the text with personal detachment and forced every historical insight into the service of justifying that detachment. Tolstoy, on the other hand, understood himself to be personally addressed by every word of Jesus, as though he were a contemporary. Because of Jesus' word to a rich young ruler, Tolstoy endeavored to sell all. Together with Jesus' original twelve disciples, he resolved to conform the circumstances of his living to the demands of the Kingdom Jesus proclaimed. Bornhäuser suggests none of this. With aloof detachment he maintains the *Berglehre* applies only to the twelve disciples addressed and that all hermeneutical problems disappear once we understand Jesus' teaching *zeitgeschichtlich*—within its historical context. Unlike Naumann, he does not first have to undergo the trauma of feeling existentially threatened by the harsh demands of an Oriental Jesus and then make his reasoned peace with the Kaiser's *Realpolitik* as the best of possible worlds. Historical methodology itself provides its own enlightenment; that, as Herrmann said, is the benefit of historical criticism, since it frees us from the pain of having no word from Jesus for our modern value structures. Indeed, it implies that we really do not need any. The significance of Bornhäuser's *Beiträge zur Förderung christlicher Theologie* ("Contribution to the Furtherance of Christian Theology," the subtitle of his monograph) is his realization that by consistent application of the historical method all ethical problems disappear. Bornhäuser assures us that Jesus' Teaching on the Mount was not intended for us and therefore has nothing to say to us. Those who are still looking for the Galilean Way should realize that Bornhäuser's learned treatise will not help them find it.

GEORG WÜNSCH:
CREATION ETHIC
VERSUS JESUS' ETHIC

The great practical difficulty of the Sermon on the Mount lies in certain material demands which are by no means to be applied to the contemporary situation and consequently could today be bypassed or thrust aside. That applies particularly to the section, Matthew 5:38-44. . . . Insofar as God has created and maintains the world and us, insofar as he has established the values immanent in the world . . . he also expects us to maintain ourselves, our families, our economic existence, and our people. So there is a correction of the Sermon on the Mount morality through the creator morality [Schöpfermoral], which Jesus positively acknowledged. . . . The morality of the Sermon on the Mount, insofar as it proclaims nonviolence and nonresistance of evil, must then be restricted by the creation morality [Schöpfungsmoral]. . . . Luther's escape from the difficulty of the demands of the Sermon on the Mount was based on this thought of creation in a purely religious way. Since God created the world, he cannot therefore in the Sermon on the Mount intend that it perish. From that perspective he [Luther] gains appreciation for the violence of government as divine service.[1]

Georg Wünsch's[2] captivation with the ethical problem of the Sermon on the Mount was inspired by Ernst Troeltsch's *Social Teachings*; there he found the conceptual tools to develop a trilogy of theological, economic, and political ethics. His undertaking reflected considerable discernment and insight, and it critically established for all time the influence of Martin Lu-

---

[1]Georg Wünsch, *Evangelische Wirtschaftsethik* (Tübingen: JCB Mohr [Paul Siebeck], 1927) 222, 226.

[2]Georg Wünsch (1887-1962) was professor of Systematic Theology and Social Ethics at the University of Marburg after 1922.

ther for a comprehensive understanding of what it ethically means to be "evangelisch."

Wünsch defines the ethical problem as a conflict of interests between terrestrial goals and celestial ideals, between the secular and the sacred, the worldly and the otherworldly. Until the 15th century, the Christian *Weltanschauung* had remained fairly intact. With the Renaissance and especially after the 18th century, the domains of politics, science, art, and economics progressively established their autonomy compelling the Church to yield its territory and restrict its influence over the lives of human beings. As a result, Christianity has been misinterpreted as a debilitating influence upon the human capacity for inner-worldly tasks, while the world has been misconceived as a barrier to eternal life. Wünsch argues that the ethical problems posed by these two worlds in collision cannot be resolved by mutual exclusion of either claim. For, alongside the eternal Christian ideals, the values of life in this world must also be affirmed and furthered. And the moral guidance that leads on towards this ideal, is, says Wünsch, essentially contained in the Sermon on the Mount.[3]

Yet the Sermon on the Mount constitutes the central problem of Christian ethics, for

> its demands are superhuman. To apply it literally to all aspects of life would endanger not only one's life but also that of one's family, of the state, and the economy. It would essentially jeopardize existence altogether. The Sermon on the Mount is unconcerned with the vital desires and realistic needs of the practical world. It establishes its claims irrespective of the unavoidable requirements in terms of nourishment, clothing, possessions, and honor of our human *Dasein*. The world and man would have to be created differently than they are if the arduous fulfillment of the words of the Sermon on the Mount were to be possible, for it speaks against the nature of man, against his *Daseinsberechtigung*, that is, against the demands of life implicit in the establishment of the world. Demand appears to stand over against demand: the demand of Jesus over against the demand of existence (*Daseinsbehauptung*).[4]

Since Christianity understood itself obliged to meet both demands, it has variously attempted somehow to reconcile them. First, there was the

---

[3]Georg Wünsch, *Die Bergpredigt bei Luther. Eine Studie zum Verhältnis von Christentum und Welt* (Tübingen: JCB Mohr [Paul Siebeck], 1920) 3.

[4]*Wirtschaftsethik*, 213.

familiar dual ethic of the Middle Ages represented by Aquinas, who misinterpreted Jesus' demands as counsels of perfection addressed to a select few who would be Christian with all their hearts, rather than intended for all human beings. Even as the vocational ethic of monasticism these counsels proved to be a mock solution which re-established the Pharisaism Jesus sought to avoid, replacing obedience with legalism and voluntary poverty with collective security.

Luther sought to expose the self-deceit of this vicious circle by separating the two kingdoms, that of God and of the world, a distinction Wünsch evaluates as unsatisfactory. Wünsch succinctly presents Luther's system:

> The Christian lives, on the one hand, in the Kingdom of God where he is blessed, where love abounds, and where he is inwardly prepared to leave all. On the other hand, he in effect lives in a wicked, corrupt world in which he needs protection for himself, his family, and his property. This protection is provided by the office of government which is not bound by the commands of the Sermon on the Mount but which has the duty of bearing the sword. Its task is not to endure but to govern with all the might that stands at its disposal. And, when a Christian is an "official person" (*Amtsperson*), he is then not to conform to the Sermon on the Mount but to the requirements of his office (*Amt*), . . . in which case he follows the order of creation and the order of sin, not the order of the Kingdom of God as documented in the gospel.[5]

Now nearly everyone by nature of his vocation has an "office" or "station" (*Amt*) according to which he must assert and establish himself in the struggle for existence and as a result of which "thousands of necessities to sin against the Sermon on the Mount are given." Luther internalized the conflict between worldly morality and the Gospel by placing on the individual the burden of responsibility for his decision, but instead of resolving the problem he only intensified it. Yet in that intensification he awakened public consciousness. Still, the dilemma remains—for, according to Luther, the Christian still stands between the conflicting demands of the Gospel and the Order of Creation which is subject to the operations of sinful powers.[6]

Wünsch concedes that Luther's correlation of Jesus' ethic and worldly morality in effect constitutes a compromise, but he surmises that one per-

[5] Ibid., 215.
[6] Ibid.

haps cannot manage without compromise. He discerns in Luther's separation of personal and official morality the implicit danger of limiting
personal ethics in such a way that the Sermon on the Mount becomes irrelevant—a tendency Protestant ethics has not avoided. Luther had not intended official morality to stand in its own right unrelated to gospel
morality; he saw the connecting link in the oneness of the same person participating simultaneously in both worlds: the realm of God's Kingdom and
the orders of creation confused by sin. The person of the Christian governor was to provide assurance that violence stood in the service of love.
But the resulting schizophrenic depersonalization of Luther's view of office paved the way for an unscrupulous German *Realpolitik* that continued
to appeal to Luther for its divine sanction.

Wünsch reviews various approaches to recovering the genius of Protestant ethics, all of which—by the light of his own critique—fall short of
the mark. Kant's formal ethic had the advantage of consistency and universality but failed to give material direction. It needed to be supplemented
by an ethic of historical goals, as Schleiermacher and Richard Rothe attempted (but instead "only led us into a still deeper problematic").[7] For
the same reason, Wilhelm Herrmann's *Gesinnungsethik* is shown to be inadequate, for it is significant not only how one acts but also what is done.
Bultmann's existentialist emphasis on the authenticity of the concrete moment of decision is nothing more than the Kant-Herrmann formalism.[8] A
purely formal ethic fails to reveal the content of what the moral law consists—for surely it does not consist in formal conformity itself—and fails
to enlighten us regarding the origin, nature, content, and hence meaning
of the moral imperative. Within the philosophic realm, the imperative cannot be referred to an unknown God, for that would imply referring one unknown to an even deeper unknown which is not the way to knowledge.[9]
The need for material considerations calls for an ethic of values (*Wertethik*) in which intention (*Gesinnung*) takes the form of value judgment
(*Wertgesinnung*). But the obvious limitation of a *Wertethik* lies in its inability to oversee all objective values or to determine their order of priority

[7]Georg Wünsch, *Theologische Ethik*; Sammlung Göschen 900 (Berlin und Leipzig:
Walter de Gruyter, 1925) 47.

[8]*Wirtschaftsethik*, 218.

[9]*Theologische Ethik*, 47.

(*Rangordnung*) or to give reason why one value should be preferred to another. Furthermore, any action based on a *Wertethik* at best reflects only the limited scope of values comprising one's value judgment (*Werteinsicht*).[10]

By contrast, theological ethics is oriented to the spiritual values exemplified in the Sermon on the Mount. However, Wünsch also knows of various evangelical attempts to invalidate or weaken the Sermon's moral injunctions. Not infrequently the solution is sought in the manner of Naumann or Baumgarten. Then the Sermon on the Mount is restricted in its applicability to the sphere of private life but excluded from one's cultural responsibilities in society. The difficulty inherent in this approach lies in its failure to realize that the conflict between Christ and culture is just as acute within the sphere of one's private life. Wünsch therefore argues for an all-inclusive understanding of evangelical ethics comprising the nature of Christian commitment in all areas of life.

Wünsch sees that the modern historical approach of Protestant scholarship has defused the radicalism of the Sermon on the Mount by its insistence that its text can only be evaluated within the original context in which it arose and to which it was addressed. Or, where its universal moral applicability is defended, its effect is weakened by being impressed into the service of one or another theological system—as, for example, in the identification of the genius of Jesus with Ritschl's conception of Christian personality or with Bultmann's *Selbstverständnis*.

Wünsch begins his own analysis of the Sermon on the Mount by emphasizing the religious orientation of Jesus' moral views; they have their goal in supernatural values—in God. The presupposition of Jesus' proclamation is the Kingdom of God, and to prepare for it is the purpose of Jesus' moral demands. "To transform oneself inwardly so that one qualifies for this kingdom and to make oneself so clean, true, and authentic that one can withstand the all-penetrating eye of God is what Jesus intends."[11] These demands, says Wünsch, immediately focus on the individual life. That is their central emphasis and actual task. Jesus intends the sanctification of the person for the Kingdom of God, and all else (the fellowship of the believers and the coming Kingdom) will take care of itself. Seeing

---

[10]Ibid., 57.

[11]*Die Bergpredigt*, 10.

Jesus' ethical significance primarily in its social effects distorts this perspective by placing the effect before the cause. Jesus' counsels concerning one's relation to the world are a consequence of this inmost direction: "For Jesus is primarily concerned about the relation of the disciples to God, about the condition of their hearts, and then only about their relation to their environment."[12]

In his Beatitudes, Jesus directs his disciples to penetrate the hearts of men to discern their inner scale of values and not to evaluate them by their outward social status. Through suffering, poverty, and oppression they are to sustain hope until God will rule all the world, true value will be recognized, and all outer and inner needs satisfied.

When Jesus speaks of the birds for whom God cares and the flowers which God arrays, there is no trace of pessimism in his words: "with childlike, cheerful, and simple disposition Jesus observes growth and becoming and enjoys the life and design of nature. All that happens is for him evidence of the love and providence of God"—not that he was insensitive to the dark shadows of life. When he says that no sparrow falls without the Father (Matthew 10.29), he knows that sparrows perish but not without the Father's will. He will have known that some birds starve and that some plants freeze but also that the Father permits it: "Jesus knew both sides of nature's process but preferred to focus his eye upon the happy appearances as revelations of God's love. With him there is no disparagement of nature but childlike joy and harmless indulgence."[13]

Jesus demands goodness without limit or exception and forgiveness and mildness in our relation to others in a measure that, because of the wickedness of the world, can, Wünsch says, hardly be fulfilled. In Jesus' prohibition of retaliation (Matthew 5:38-48), "the goodness to be practiced on one's neighbor is strained to the breaking point and enormously burdened to such an extent that its realization in practical life hardly appears possible." These commands create the greatest difficulty so that interpreters have not only compromised them, observes Wünsch, but indeed rejected them altogether:

> This command is so opposed to the fundamentals and resources of secular life that the consequence of its literal fulfillment would be the destruc-

---

[12]Ibid.

[13]Ibid., 13.

tion and disintegration of the good by untamed forces—a demand which can be realized neither in social nor private morality. Yet, as a genuine prophet, Jesus is concerned not with its realization, not with practicability but with the idealistic-moral necessity of the command.[14]

Precisely in his tremendous demand to be perfect as the Father is perfect lies the nucleus of the Sermon on the Mount and its deepest moral motif out of which all other demands arise.[15]

As to whether it also applies to war, "little can be said and then only in uncertainty."[16] Being a Jew under Roman occupation, Jesus understandably appeared to exclude a positive evaluation of the state. One can more readily speak of his love for his own people whom he seeks to redeem and inwardly renew and over whom he mourns and weeps: "By and large Jesus leaves us in a dilemma here."[17]

One may similarly regard his word about oaths (Matthew 5:33-37). "The brief words of Jesus allow themselves to be read in various ways with equal right."[18] In addition, his words regarding earthly goods "allow for the most diverse possibilities of interpretation,"[19] especially as to whether Jesus' prohibition is directed against treasures themselves or against the desire to possess them. In regard to riches as with respect to sex "Jesus had no objection as such but cautioned their enjoyment with serious deliberation and suggested sacrifice altogether if necessary."[20]

In his "theological ethics" Wünsch notes that "the perfection Jesus demands manifests itself in acknowledging God as the absolute value who renders all others irrelevant." As for not gathering treasures, not caring, indifference toward family bonds, sexual life, and earthly circumstances, indifference toward one's own dignity in relinquishing honor, in not resisting evil, and turning the other cheek—

this list of demands is restricted by the acknowledgment of God as the mighty Creator, who has indeed created everything that is here despised

---

[14]Ibid., 14.

[15]Ibid., 18.

[16]Ibid.

[17]Ibid., 19.

[18]Ibid.

[19]Ibid., 21.

[20]Ibid., 22.

as immaterial and demands that it be maintained. To do justice to these two mutually exclusive demands is the task of social ethics.[21]

In his later reflections on this task, Wünsch reiterates:

> The greater practical difficulty of the Sermon on the Mount lies in certain material demands which are by no means to be applied to the contemporary situation and consequently could today be bypassed or thrust aside. This evasion applies particularly to the section, Matthew 5:38-44.[22]

Here the application of the goodness of God which the Sermon on the Mount demands encounters enormous practical difficulties:

> The ethic of resignation . . . in this world must lead to the suppression of personal freedom, the narrowing of the sphere of one's life, yea, the destruction of existence. Malice and worldly wisdom scorn the ethic of goodness and take advantage of it for one's own purpose. The result would be total debilitation and inefficacy of all practical elements derived from the Sermon on the Mount. . . . Surely we might personally in many moments of our lives hold fast to this faith, indeed many who find themselves in an appropriate situation may do so with respect to their whole life, but always to appeal to God's help in all matters against all apparent experience is denied by the constitution of the world. . . . It is simply a fact that God would not in all cases protect the one who suffers evil defenselessly.[23]

If that is so, then the problem exists within the Christian ethic itself. For insofar as God has created and maintains the world and us, insofar as he has established the values immanent in the world and thereby as world-creator demands their sustenance, he also expects us to maintain ourselves, our families, our economic existence, and our people. So there is a correction of the Sermon on the Mount morality through the creator morality [Schöpfermoral] which Jesus positively acknowledged. He never attacked this world creation faith [*Weltschöpfungsglauben*]; it was self-evident for him. But then the morality of the Sermon on the Mount, insofar as it proclaims nonviolence and nonresistance to evil, must be restricted by the creation morality [*Schöpfungsmoral*]. . . . Luther's escape from the difficulty of the demands of the Sermon on the Mount via vocational ethics [*Berufsmoral*] was based on this thought of creation in a purely religious way. Since God created the world, he cannot therefore in the Sermon on

---

[21]*Theologische Ethik*, 125-26.

[22]*Wirtschaftsethik*, 222.

[23]Ibid., 225.

the Mount intend that it perish. From that perspective, he [Luther] gains appreciation for the violence of government as divine service.[24]

In the last analysis, "the Sermon on the Mount does not contradict the intention of creation but only assists in its restoration. . . . " It opposes the distortion of the world by sin. The realization of divine goodness implies restoration of pure creation: "The history of Christian ethics was always on the right track when it identified the morality of the absolute or pure *lex naturae* with the morality of the Sermon on the Mount."[25]

One need not go beyond Luther (hardly beyond Wünsch's study of Luther) to discern the roots of what Wünsch identifies as "evangelical ethics." The indebtedness of Wünsch to Luther is explicit: "I believe, after all I have seen, that from the time of primitive Christianity until now Luther was the first to do justice to the content of the *Bergpredigt* and its reasoning."[26] To the extent that Wünsch has done for Luther what Luther did for the *Bergpredigt*, criticism of Wünsch is, in turn, criticism of Luther and vice versa.

Wünsch laid bare the elemental strands of Luther's thought, uncovered their mystic origins, and indicated their problematic interconnections. In his estimate, "Luther's prime merit consisted in . . . his internalization of the Christian religion,"[27] its transposition from the external to the internal, "from 'works' to 'faith,' from obedience to *Gesinnung*, and from a lifestyle to a psychic disposition." Taken as a commendation, this observation reveals equally much about Wünsch's own approach to ethics—despite his trenchant critique of Kant and Herrmann. For Luther, "outwardly considered there is no mark of distinction between pagans and Christians,"[28] for which reason he denounced the Pope for making fake distinctions (*concilia*) out of Jesus' hardest commands, disdained Mohammed for substituting the easier rule of the Koran, and condemned the Anabaptists for clinging to the *nova lex Christi*. It was largely this evangelical tendency to internalize the faith, replacing *Nachfolge Christi* with compulsive emphasis on the *fides orthodoxa* of a Platonic *ecclesia invisibilis*, that pre-

---

[24]Ibid., 226.

[25]Ibid., 228.

[26]*Die Bergpredigt*, 212.

[27]Ibid., 28.

[28]Ibid., 29.

cipitated the Anabaptist dissent. The sense in which Jesus intended *imitatio Dei* to be appropriated in the life of his followers is still probably the knottiest problem of Protestant ethics. The root of Wünsch's own ethical formalism possibly lies in Luther's aversion to the "Catholic" emphasis on works in the *Bergpredigt* as a result of which John and Paul were accorded a distinctly higher esteem than the Synoptics in the Reformer's canon. Wünsch plainly tells us "it is obvious" that Luther could not consider the Sermon on the Mount as part of the Gospel.[29]

Wünsch identifies the sum and substance of Luther's problematic *Zwei-Reiche-Lehre* in his claim that "so long as he lives on earth the Christian belongs to two kingdoms: to God's *Reich* with his soul and to the *Welt-reich* with his body."[30] Thus Luther argued that Jesus' prohibition of retaliation (Matthew 5:39, 40) "belongs only in *Christo Reich*,"[31] implying that it concerns only the soul, not the body. Luther knows there are eagles, lions, sheep, and wolves in the same barn and that only sheep would keep the peace.[32] This questionable analogy of the "worldly barn" has for centuries provided the evangelical rationale for why all Christians, contrary to Jesus' plain words, must invariably wage all the "just and necessary" wars of history to keep the peace between "eagles, lions, and wolves." For centuries the church has sought to justify its troubled conscience with Luther's immortal sophistry: "The hand which bears the sword and murders is then no longer the human hand but God's hand, for not man but God hangs, racks on the wheel, executes, strangles, and wars; it is all his work and just."[33] By the same rationale, Lutheran hangmen must consider their vocation a divine calling and ministry motivated by love to their poor neighbor and undertaken as love's strange work for his sake, for

> with his "person" the Christian follows the morality of goodness and forgiveness; in his "station" (*Amt*) other perspectives apply and there he practices violence. Killing is, to be sure, forbidden, but, when a judge permits execution and torment, it happens by right and command of God.[34]

---

[29]Ibid., 32.

[30]Ibid., 64.

[31]Ibid., 76.

[32]Luther, Weimar Ausgabe (hereinafter WA) 11:252, quoted in ibid., 97.

[33]WA 19:627; quoted in ibid., 133.

[34]Ibid., 111.

Especially in his later years, Luther progressively disassociated himself from the morality of the Sermon on the Mount in liberally endorsing the persecution of dissenters from the "true church."[35]

Luther had even fewer compunctions regarding "swearing." He conceded, "It is indeed forbidden," and hastened to add, "but, when it happens by command of God, it is right and good." Luther leaves no doubt that by "command of God" he meant command of the *Obrigkeit* ("government") thereby implying, "this is the reason why it is right to swear, namely, the necessity of taking an oath in obedience to authority."[36]

Questions of marriage and divorce Luther deferred to the worldly realm since "wife and child are external things."[37] He allowed divorce on grounds of unfaithfulness or sexual incompetence and advised in the latter case that secret bigamy be preferred to public separation.[38]

Luther expressed great respect for simplicity of life-style but despised voluntary poverty—as exemplified in monasticism and Anabaptism—arguing that a certain wealth belongs to the divine order, for without it the world could not exist. It is especially appropriate for a feudal lord or prince to "have all such things for his 'office' and station."[39]

Finally, it needs to be said that Luther's assumption of a kingdom in which God is at work otherwise than by the norms revealed in Jesus is theologically unfounded! If temporal power is subject to the authority of God, it ought also to be subject to the authority of his word. Wünsch saw that Luther's separation of the two kingdoms "despairs at the recreation of the world for divine purposes, isolates God from it, and lacks faith in the possibility of ethical permeation of the world."[40] He envisions as the hope of humanity a creative convergence of both realms "to bring God to clarity in the visible world" though he does not intimate how this is to happen.[41] As an ethicist, he has not clearly enough seen that, whatever it means

---

[35]Ibid., 118.

[36]WA 32:381ff. quoted in ibid., 137.

[37]Ibid., 149.

[38]WA 6:558ff. quoted in ibid., 149-50.

[39]WA 32:307-308.

[40]*Die Bergpredigt*, 227.

[41]Ibid., 227.

to rule the world like God, *Schöpfermoral* cannot be equated with the self-interest of secular stations.

Ethics begins not by conceding what is but by discerning what ought to be. *Lex naturae* assumes all stations on the basis of their *Dasein*. *Schöpfermoral* evaluates them on the grounds of their *Sosein*. This distinction is distorted in Luther and remains ambiguous in Wünsch. Much of the resulting confusion in the Lutheran *Zwei-Reiche-Lehre* relates to the dubious equation of *Gottesordnung* with *Gottesdienst* by which divine sanction is in effect ascribed to *Schöpfungsunordnung* under the autonomy of a *lex naturae* that never claimed to function as παιδαγωγὸς εἰς χριστόν. Lutheran apprehension that *participatio Christi* might degenerate into self-conscious *imitatio Christi* as the self-righteous work of man explains, but does not justify, repudiation of discipleship and internalization of the faith and the consequent disintegration of personhood by a theological schizophrenia that sanctions secularity as a law unto itself contrary to the Gospel. Since Luther and Wünsch claim that apart from natural law there is no uniquely Christian morality, it is a contradiction in terms to refer to their ethic as "evangelical."[42]

---

[42]"Sinnlichkeit und Natürlichkeit das sind die Wurzeln, aus denen Luthers Weltethik entsprossen: darin liegen auch die Keime der späteren Entwickelung zur neuprotestantischen zwischen Diesseits- und Jenseits schwankenden Kulturethik." Ibid., 101.

For a more comprehensive analysis and critique of Lutheran ethics, see my essays: "Luther and the Turks: An Interpretation of Christian Responsibility from Within the Two-Kingdoms Doctrine, Christus Victor 107 (Dec. 1959): 3-15; "The Theology of 'The Two Kingdoms': A Comparison of Luther and the Anabaptists," *Mennonite Quarterly Review* (January 1964): 37-49, 60; and my book, *Gewaltlosigkeit im Täufertum* (Leiden: Brill, 1968) 170-222, 268-315, 346-58.

According to Hans Asmussen (*Die Bergpredigt.* Göttingen: Vandenhoeck & Ruprecht, 1939), Jesus in the Sermon on the Mount proclaims the breaking-in of the Kingdom of God and therewith the dissolution of the Jewish theocratic state rooted in Mosaic Law (25). With his Beatitudes and Antitheses Jesus proclaimed the fulfillment of the Law through the Spirit, not the letter. That is how he lived and why he died. That is what he taught his disciples and what the Church should continue to proclaim. Jesus neither abrogated the Law nor replaced the national ethos with a higher ethic. He simply declared the end of the Old Testament identity of Church and state. In the new aeon, Mosaic Law can no longer serve as juridical basis as it did in Israelite theocracy, for in God's Kingdom men are ruled not by the Law but through the Spirit. What Jesus therefore attacks with his Antitheses is the juridical function of legalized religion within the Jewish nation-state. Jesus' word about reconciliation instead of litigation (Matthew 5:21-26) therefore does not mean, says Asmussen, that Christians should never plead their cause in court but only that they should do so in the light of the ultimate judgment. Likewise, Jesus' prohibition of all oaths does not mean that we should not swear them. "When he himself swears, when his apostles swear, when the Reformers teach us to swear the required oath, they exemplify how Christians during their lifetime continue to live in the Kingdom of God in this way" (25). Similarly, Matthew 5:44-45 does not imply that we should be pacifists but only "that no kinds of religious wars are permitted or commanded" (30). In each case "it invariably remains the Christian's task to resolve how both can be attested: the breaking-in of the Kingdom of God and the fact that we still live in the body of death" (26). Asmussen's underlying assumption is that Jesus advocates a Lutheran view of separation of Church and state but does not provide us a design for living in the new aeon.

By a somewhat similar logic A. D. Lindsay concludes that *The Moral Teaching of Jesus* (London, 1937) is not applicable to ordinary people. It seems clear to him that most of us "quite honestly don't think we ought to act like that" (20). He is certain the Sermon on the Mount was not meant to be a moral code because "all thought of reciprocity is given up" (25). "It does not lay down a standard up to which we ordinary people may reasonably be counted upon to live, and its standard cannot be modified to suit us and our circumstances because the standard set up is a standard of perfection" (37). "Jesus bids us look at an absolute standard in order to give us a new sense of direction in our lives" (98) which also applies to his "gospel of nonresistance." "But, when we have failed, to refuse to use force might be a sign of even greater failure" (112-13). Therefore, Lindsay advocates "pursuing the double policy of seeking to make force unnecessary but being determined in the meantime to see justice done even if force must be used for the purpose" (118).

CARL STANGE:
LUTHERAN PAULINIZING
OF JESUS' MESSAGE

The moral problem [with respect to the Sermon on the Mount] is not the ideal of action but the conversion of the will. . . . Transformation of will cannot be made the object of a demand which the will is to fulfill. No one can pull himself out of the slough by a braid of his hair like Baron Münchhausen.[1]

The teaching about the ideal . . . only serves to make plain the reprehensibility of the human condition. . . . The meaning of the moral demand is not that it gives us the power for the good but rather that it shows us our impotence for the good.[2]

Every idealistic interpretation of these words [Matthew 5:48: "You shall be perfect as your heavenly Father . . . "] is a terrible hypocrisy. No person can seriously think that through an act of his will he could become equal with God. And therefore Jesus also could not have meant this demand in this way.[3]

Fellowship with God is not achieved through ethical performance.[4]

From an ethical standpoint, it is a derogation of the idea of the good to seek its realization by imitating Jesus.[5]

The Christian distinguishes himself from the non-Christian not in being free from all sin but in acknowledging his sin.[6]

Only in the priority of consciousness of God over ethical consciousness does moral life come to its completion.[7]

---

[1]Carl Stange, "Zur Ethik der Bergpredigt," *Zeitschrift für systematische Theologie* (1924):58.

[2]Ibid., 59.

[3]Ibid., 61.

[4]Ibid., 71.

[5]Ibid., 72.

[6]Ibid., 73.

[7]Ibid., 74.

In developing his own approach to the ethics of the Sermon on the Mount, Carl Stange[8] begins by proposing that the ethical meaning of an external act depends on the integrity of the inner conscience as exemplified in Jesus, whose uniqueness consists in his being the first to recognize and express the universal truths of life. Apart from these rational ethical principles, everything else about Jesus appears incidental to Stange. Who Jesus was is irrelevant, says Stange, for his identity does not affect the content of these ideas.

For Jesus, it was not enough that we conform to marriage laws while our motives are impure (Matthew 5:27-28) or abstain from killing our enemies without reconciling our antipathy towards them (Matthew 5:38ff.) or claim mental reservation for our spoken word without the integrity of our inner life, that is, without a good conscience (Matthew 5:33ff.).[9] The "perfect good" of which Jesus speaks (Matthew 5:48) is not just an external accomplishment but an inner perfection by a "good will," the absolute value of a good intention.

The ethic of Jesus differs from that of the Pharisees in its understanding of will, according to Stange. Pharisaic religion is a matter of asserting one's will egoistically. Pharisaic piety is a purely prudential calculation of how best to accomplish one's ends, a pragmatic consideration cast in religious form but entirely governed by the reward motif. The Sermon on the Mount is unique in that the will it demands is not a means to an end but a higher level of consciousness. While pharisaic piety is but egoistic assertion of one's will, the ethic of Jesus exemplifies transformation of one's will. That contrast, says Stange, is the essential difference. By his emphasis on the "good will" (as in Kant) and by his focus on the "pure intention" (as in Herrmann), Jesus raised morality to the highest possible level of human consciousness.[10]

---

[8]Carl Stange, born in Hamburg in 1870, became *Privatdozent* in Halle in 1895 and professor in Königsberg in 1903; after 1904 he was professor at Greifswald. His publications include *Die christliche Ethik in ihrem Verhältnis zur modernen Ethik* (Göttingen, 1892); *Das Dogma und seine Beurteilung in der neueren Dogmengeschichte* (Berlin, 1898); *Einleitung in die Ethik*, 2 vols. (Leipzig, 1901-1902); *Das Frömmigkeitsideal der modernen Theologie* (1907).

[9]"Zur Ethik," 40.

[10]Ibid., 39-43.

Stange points out that neither Catholicism nor Tolstoy nor Liberal Protestantism comprehended this level of moral consciousness intended by the Sermon on the Mount. Catholicism recognized the impossibility of universalizing the demands of the Sermon on the Mount and thus restricted its applicability to those few who in becoming ''perfect'' sought to achieve special merit by exceptional morality. Luther rejected this merit system together with its mechanics of acquiring, storing, and transferring merits and sought to recover Jesus' emphasis on the good will.

Stange is particularly critical of Tolstoy. He claims Tolstoy's urgent question ''What then shall we do?'' was derived not from Jesus but from tax collectors and soldiers. Despite his uncompromising anti-Catholic insistence on the universal applicability of the Sermon on the Mount in all its rigor and literalness, Tolstoy's perspective, argues Stange, is limited to the mentality of the ascetic monastics. Like them, Tolstoy fled his cultural responsibilities and made no contribution towards reforming the social order. He advocates communal life but denies the very conditions upon which it depends. His nonresistance is the most obvious evidence of his lack of realism and complete absence of human understanding.[11] Tolstoy's error, according to Stange, is his misconception of Jesus' demands as practicable precepts. In considering them practicable for everyone he regressed to a position behind Catholicism, which claims this only as an exception.

This problem also characterizes liberal Protestant ethical idealism which, in the tradition of Kant, insists that man can do good because he ought. It is precisely the other way round, Stange argues. Our self-consciousness experiences the moral idea as an ''ought'' whenever our will is not in harmony with it. Since idea and will then are in direct conflict, there is no reasonable basis for the derivation of ability from demand. Ethical idealism, like Pharisaism, misconceives the moral idea as a sum of individual commands on the fulfillment of which man's moral value is held to depend. The various forms of ethical idealism vary only in the content of their moral demands whether expressed as absolute submission to a moral code, the subjection of passion to reason, or the perfection of personality. They have in common the false assumption that an act of will is demanded of man through which some particular ideal is to be realized.[12] Liberal

---

[11]Ibid., 53.

[12]Ibid., 57.

Protestantism fails to realize that Jesus in his criticism of pharisaic morality rejects all forms of ethical idealism.

It is true that Jesus came not to abrogate the Law but to fulfill it (Matthew 5:17ff.). The fulfillment he demands, however, is not realized by the
rigor of external acts. Jesus really intends, Stange claims, genuine authentic inwardness:

> All reforms of social life are meaningless if men do not become dif-
> ferent inwardly. The moral problem is not the ideal of action but the con-
> version of will. . . . Transformation of will cannot be made the object of
> a demand which the will is to fulfill. No one can pull himself out of the
> slough by a braid of his hair like Baron Münchhausen.[13]

Even Tolstoy would concede that we are not literally to pluck out our eyes
to realize the new moral society.[14] Jesus says the Law will continue una-
bridged until all is accomplished (Matthew 5:18). Stange puts the accent
on the last phrase to imply that this whole pharisaic mentality will remain
intact and perpetuate itself unimpaired until it is eventually overcome.

> The teaching about the ideal . . . only serves to make plain the repre-
> hensibility of the human condition. . . . The meaning of the moral demand
> is not that it gives us the power for the good but rather that it shows us our
> impotence for the good. . . . Good intentions cannot transform the will. .
> . . They cannot alter the condition of the heart.[15]

It is presumptuous to assume perfectionistic tendencies.

What then should be done with Jesus' final demand, ''You, therefore,
must be perfect, as your heavenly Father is perfect'' (Matthew 5:48)? In
response, Stange counters: ''Can one make it one's maxim to want to be
as perfect as God is perfect?'' Obviously one cannot:

> Every idealistic interpretation of these words is a terrible hypocrisy.
> No person can seriously think that through an act of his will he could be-
> come equal with God. And therefore Jesus also could not have meant this
> demand in this way.[16]

To all those who, like Tolstoy, presume to meet Jesus' demands uncon-

---

[13]Ibid., 58.

[14]Ibid., 59.

[15]Ibid., 59, 60.

[16]Ibid., 61.

ditionally and without limitation, Stange recommends that they begin with this demand of absolute perfection: "The optimism that is convinced of carrying out Jesus' demands will then very soon vanish."[17] How characteristic it was of Tolstoy to waste his moral pathos precisely on those demands in which it was possible to concentrate on only the external, as in the case of nonresistance and voluntary poverty, rather than on the command to "be perfect," in which case the externalization of a moral criterion is completely out of the question! "Through this demand it becomes perfectly clear that what is implied is a new life which we can never bring about through our will."[18] Conversion of the will is not the goal of ethical achievement but its presupposition.

Kant insisted: You can because you ought. To understand Jesus' ethic of the Sermon on the Mount is to realize: I ought, but I cannot. In this initial stage of ethical discernment, self-evaluation becomes self-condemnation. So long as the ethical takes the form of a categorical imperative, one reckons, as did Kant, with the possibility of a transition from evil to good. All it takes then is a little more will power to realize the ideal on the assumption that the difference between what we are and what we ought to be is only relative. Imperfection, it is believed, leads along the line of a natural continuum to perfection, and evil is considered to be merely ignorance and weakness. But the moment self-evaluation becomes self-condemnation, one has shifted from the ethic of Kant to that of Jesus. Then "the possibility of a transition from evil to good is excluded."[19] So long as one banks on the possibility of this transition on the assumption that the good is merely a development of natural life, self-evaluation can become an incentive toward the good. But, the instant one realizes that the difference between good and evil is an absolute qualitative distinction, confession of sin becomes our only ethical option. This explains, says Stange, why idealistic ethics always takes the form of humanistic ethics, while the Christian ethic consists in acknowledging our sinfulness. The moment ethical consciousness unites with religious consciousness, the distance between good and evil becomes absolute in the realization that God's life is different from our own. Accordingly, the intention or purpose of the Ser-

---

[17]Ibid.,

[18]Ibid., 62.

[19]Ibid.,

mon on the Mount is to awaken consciousness of our sinfulness, a self-awareness that compels to self-condemnation. Through this deepening of our self-consciousness, the ethic of Jesus leads from imperative to judgment, from ideal to repentance.[20]

This means first that morality is not a matter of right action on the part of an individual. When a rich young man asked what good works he still needed to perform in order to achieve the ultimate good, Jesus first rebuked the young man for casting him in the image of a "good" example to be imitated. Then, realizing that the commands he presumed to have kept all belong to the second, not the first, table of the Law, Jesus informed him that the way of perfection does not consist in doing all these things. Nor does it lie in the renunciation of riches, adds Stange. This constitutes only an interlude (*Zwischenakt*) to what really matters, namely, fellowship with Jesus and entry into the Kingdom of God.[21] Ethics is not a matter of discerning whether a given action conforms to a particular moral code. Since one can produce good and bad acts without intending to do so, the external act, as such, is no ethical criterion. Luther as an Augustinian monk forever wavered between exaltation and depression, but as a Reformer he was controlled by unwavering assurance. By then he had realized that accusation of conscience and security of salvation are not mutually exclusive opposites but belong together and deepen each other:

> When we say that we are sinners, we mean that we are fundamentally separated from the good and that no exertion of our will can overcome this condition.[22]
> The Christian distinguishes himself from the non-Christian not in being free of all sin but in acknowledging his sin.[23]

How then does the reality of God take effect?

> Where consciousness of sin is awakened, faith in God simultaneously comes to life. . . . When our ethical consciousness reaches its highest level, it becomes consciousness of God. The ethical process becomes experience of God.[24]

---

[20]Ibid., 63, 64.

[21]Ibid., 72.

[22]Ibid., 69.

[23]Ibid., 73.

[24]Ibid., 69.

While this consciousness of God is incapable of transforming our sinful natures, it does affect our attitude toward this nature in not allowing us to consider the basic drives of nature as final. In awakening consciousness of sin, Jesus intended to awaken consciousness of God. It is in this consciousness of God that Stange sees the advantage of Christian over humanistic ethics: "Only in the priority of consciousness of God over ethical consciousness does moral life come to its completion."[25] Therein, according to Stange, lies the dogmatic solution to the ethical problem raised by the Sermon on the Mount.

In reviewing this theological interpretation, one is inclined to concur with Stange that, when the implications of Jesus' demands are fully grasped, the effect can be shattering. Experience documents how attempts to realize them in everyday life can drive one to despair. If our filial relationship to God depended solely on our ethical performance record, we would have to understand our fate with those "many" of Matthew 7:13 who never achieved entry into the Kingdom via the narrow pass of good works. That mountain pathway is simply too hard, too rugged, and too steep. Consequently, Stange's logic is very appealing, for, if we cannot satisfy these imperatives in the literal Tolstoyan sense, we must seek another way of salvation. If it is sheer folly to be deluded by Münchhausen's idealism, we had better find another way of understanding Jesus' intentions. It only remains for us to discern whether Stange's solution is consistent with the intention of the Sermon itself.

Stange sees the Sermon on the Mount primarily as call to repentance (*Bußpredigt*), proclamation of impossible law designed to awaken our consciousness of sin, repudiate our self-justification, shatter our self-reliance, evoke self-condemnation, and educe consciousness of God, whose unmerited favor constitutes our salvation. Stange claims that the sole purpose of Jesus' imperatives is propaedeutic—to prepare men for the Gospel by confounding them with the Law.

There is an element of validity in Stange's approach in that it fully recognizes the rigor of Jesus' demands. But, since these are addressed not to recalcitrant scribes and Pharisees but to men who have left all to become his chosen disciples, it appears incredible that Jesus only intended his teaching to drive them to despair. From a few sayings such as Matthew

---

[25]Ibid., 74.

5:29-30 about dismembering the offending eye or hand, one might infer the impossibility of fulfillment, but surely Stange would not base his hypothesis upon a literal interpretation of this text.

Could it really have been the sole intention of Jesus to convince his disciples of their total inability to do what he demanded of them? Despite the subtleties of Stange's theological hermeneutic, it is simply impossible casuistically to evade the forthright impression that Jesus in such pericopes as Matthew 5:17-20 unambiguously and lucidly expressed his clear intention of reinforcing by word and deed the continuing validity of the Torah in order to bring to completion by word and deed through his life and work the plan of the Creator for his people. There is no evidence for Stange's assumption that Matthew meant to convey Jesus' rejection of the nomistic point of view. Standing as they do within the Old Testament framework, it is obvious that the demands enunciated by Jesus were, like the Decalogue itself, meant to be observed without condition or qualification. What else could Jesus have intended with his concluding parables on "hearing and doing"? Just as in the Old Testament, so the Sermon on the Mount takes the practicability of its demands for granted as is evident both in the question of the rich young ruler and in Jesus' reply. Jesus nowhere speaks of man's inability to do God's will. Jesus expected his disciples to do what he demanded. His teaching is not merely a scheme to ensure their failure. It is no impossible ideal; it is real. Our intelligence demands that we admit this before we criticize it.

Stange appeared especially repulsed by Jesus' demand to "be perfect as your heavenly Father is perfect" (Matthew 5:48), which he depicts as an exorbitant, rigorous, and presumptuous Christian impossibility. The Rabbis of Israel, however, took for granted that the commandment to "walk after the Lord your God" (Deuteronomy 13:4) meant to imitate his character and good works. Why should it be such an offense to the theological mentality of Stange to accept Matthew 5:48 in the same way a pious Israelite would understand the command, "You shall be holy, for I the Lord your God am holy" (Leviticus 19:2)? Stange deprecated Tolstoy's conviction that literal fulfillment is possible as "a step backwards in comparison with Catholic ethics." We are not convinced that Stange's way of evading this step brings us nearer to the original intent and meaning of Jesus' words.

The *Bergpredigt* does not bear the stamp of a *Bußpredigt*. It does not pronounce condemnation but proclaims a living faith. It is not pessimistic but realistic and hopeful. The promise of the Kingdom and with it divine consolation, blessing, righteousness, mercy, theophany, fellowship, and sonship precede Jesus' demands. These are not an impossible ideal but the basis for a new life. The Sermon on the Mount knows nothing of Stange's distinction between an all-important God-consciousness and an unimportant ethical consciousness but conveys only the most intimate synthesis of both as unequivocally attested in Jesus' reproach, ''Why do you call me 'Lord, Lord,' and not do what I tell you?'' (Luke 6:46). The problem which Stange addresses does not exist for the Sermon on the Mount itself.

Stange's central axiom is derived not from Jesus but from Paul and reflects not the content of the Sermon on the Mount but the influence of Reformation dogma. Since the Sermon is evidently pre-Reformation, why superimpose upon it the Lutheran exegesis of Romans 7 and recast its context into the mold of Protestant anti-Catholic polemic? Stange made claims about the Sermon on the Mount which its content does not validate. He read into it theories and experiences foreign to its sphere. Stange's misinterpretation of the Sermon on the Mount exemplifies the characteristically Lutheran hermeneutical incongruity of superimposing upon the teaching of Jesus the theology of Paul.

The book by Arnold Schabert, *Die Bergpredigt. Auslegung und Verkündigung* (München: Claudius Verlag, 1966), exemplifies contemporary Lutheran exposition and proclamation in its traumatic *Anfechtung,* and the usual indictment of the ''Schwärmer'' for their heretical presumption of trying to follow Jesus. The function of such preaching is to disturb the conscience of the congregation by confrontation with Jesus' impossible ideal and then to administer the sacrament of forgiveness.

The dissertation by Karlmann Beyschlag, *Die Bergpredigt und Franz von Assisi* (Gütersloh: C. Bertelsmann Verlag, 1955), is a respectable source analysis of the Franciscan literary tradition and a commendable attempt to transcend Lutheran presuppositions in evaluating St. Francis's *imitatio Christi.*

GERHARD KITTEL:
THE SERMON ON THE MOUNT
AS PRAEPARATIO EVANGELICA

Not a single one of Jesus' ethical demands is absolutely unique.[1]

This means that the uniqueness of Christianity, as a religious and spiritual historical phenomenon, does not lie in any particular one of Jesus' ethical demands, be it ever so high.[2]

The meaning of the Sermon on the Mount in view of the absoluteness of its demands does not, in fact, lie in its practicability.[3]

The demands of Jesus, exaggerated to the point of paradox and nonsense. . .intend only to tear open and lay bare the great moral need of empirical humanity.[4]

Gerhard Kittel, in a definitive essay on "The Sermon on the Mount and the Ethics of Judaism" (1925), developed a theological position comparable to that of Carl Stange by exploring the uniqueness of Christianity as exemplified by Jesus' demands from within the perspective of Talmudic Judaism. Kittel maintains that Judaism differs from the religions of antiquity in that its center of gravity is ethical rather than mystical. In contrast to Judaism, the morality of antiquity was rooted not in faith in God but in philosophical systems. This is exemplified in Stoicism, the proponents of which (Epictetus, Cicero, Seneca, Marcus Aurelius) were not primarily

---

[1]Gerhard Kittel, "Die Bergpredigt und die Ethik des Judentums," *Zeitschrift für systematische Theologie* 2 (1925):560; cf. 577.

[2]Ibid., 577.

[3]Ibid., 583.

[4]Ibid., 584, 590.

saints but philosophers and moralists. The same principle pertains to ancient Chinese heroes: Lao-tze was lost in his mysticism, and the ethic of Confucius was only very remotely related to religion.[5]

In Judaism, however, ethics and religion became inseparably intertwined, for its ethical demands are entirely rooted in faith in God. Herein lies the tremendous impact of Old Testament prophetic religion exemplified in the demands of Isaiah, Amos, and Jeremiah, among others. Characteristic of this Old Testament religion is the preface of its Decalogue: "I am the Lord, your God." However, the tragedy of later Judaism, according to Kittel, lay in its inability to maintain this essential oneness of religion and ethics. The morality of the prophets either evaporated in moral philosophy (as in Stoicism and Confucianism) or crystallized into the ritualistic sophistry of the Talmud.[6]

Jesus came to take up the ethical demand of Jewish prophetic religion and with his call to μετάνοια ("repentance") once again to correlate the religious and the ethical: The *Shema Israel* of Deuteronomy 6:4 ("The Lord our God is one") and the commandment of Leviticus 19:18 ("Love your neighbor as yourself"). Thus he founded a new movement that transcended Judaism. How are we to explain that fact? Why did Jesus cease to be a Jew, Kittel inquires. What was new, special, unique, or simply different about his message? Kittel cautions against any comparison motivated by Jewish or Christian apologetic bent on proving the ethic of Jesus to be either inferior or superior to that of Judaism. It would be wrong and meaningless to establish such a claim by comparing sayings of Jesus with their literal equivalents from the Talmud. The Talmud, for Kittel, is an immense repository of tradition and a colorful confusion of thousands of individual comments and opinions on every imaginable ethical and nonethical theme.[7] Since none of these various interpretations of Torah are representative of Judaism as such, it would be worthless to assume any particular one as normative or to calculate consensus. Kittel argues that for purposes of comparison one must rather discern the great general ethical maxims that guided Jewish tradition throughout its history. Still, it is noteworthy that

---

[5]Ibid., 555.

[6]Ibid., 556.

[7]Ibid., 559.

for every one of Jesus' demands there is, Kittel claims, an equivalent in Jewish tradition.[8]

Kittel proceeds to illustrate this claim, with respect to Jesus' so-called Antitheses in Matthew 5, beginning with the demand, "Do not swear at all" (Matthew 5:33-37). There was, says Kittel, in the Judaism of Jesus' time much swearing by God, heaven, temple, altar, covenant, Torah, Moses, and even by one's own life or the life of one's children as assertion of the truthfulness of one's speech. To counteract this development, there were solemn warnings against unnecessary swearing, and sometimes heavy penalties were imposed for lighthearted and false confirmations. Quite frequently in statements identical in form and content to this saying of Jesus, the oath was spoken of as factually unnecessary since "the Yes of the righteous is a Yes and their No a No."[9]

Jesus demanded unconditional moral purity ("Every one who looks at a woman lustfully has already committed adultery with her in his heart," Matthew 5:28) while the Talmud allowed questionable laxness, claiming that God overlooks the evil intentions of Israelites and implying that adultery with non-Israelites is not subject to the prescribed penalty. On the other hand, there are Jewish sayings which are just as radical as those of Jesus which denounce an adulterous eye as well as body.[10]

Through absolute prohibition of divorce, Jesus confronted the laxity with which issues pertaining to divorce were often decided in his time. The school of Hillel allowed divorce on grounds of minor misdemeanor, personal indiscretion, or deficiency on the part of the wife (from spoiling the dinner to bad breath), while Rabbi Akiba allowed it without identifiable reason upon the whim and fancy of the husband who had developed an attachment to another woman. No wonder Jesus took issue with the moral license condoned and endorsed by Israel's religious leaders. Yet there were others, like Rabbi Eleazer, who considered divorce a great tragedy over which even the altar of God weeps, and there were those in Israel who held to Malachi 2:16, "I hate divorce, says the Lord," and who with Rabbi Jochanan pronounced the one who divorces to be accursed.

---

[8]Ibid., 559-560.

[9]Ibid., 562.

[10]Ibid.

Jesus outspokenly decried the hypocrisy of ostentatiously parading one's practice of charity, prayer, and fasting (cf. Matthew 6). According to a popular Jewish witticism characterizing various lands and cities, of the ten measures of lasciviousness in the world nine were in Alexandria, and of the ten measures of hypocrisy in the world nine were in Jerusalem. Various rabbis indicated that students of Torah were by no means beyond the farce of hypocrisy. Kittel cites numerous admonitions of rabbis who taught that alms and works of charity ought to be practiced only in secret and who condemned the hypocrisy of students and teachers of the Law as harshly as did Jesus.

Jesus warned against the danger of wealth corrupting one's heart. In Israel it was common to respect wealth and fear poverty as the hardest form of suffering in the world. The presence of God was said to rest upon the wise, strong, wealthy, and shapely man. But there were also teachers in Israel who noted that the wealthiest people in the world were the Sodomites, who trusted not in the providence of the Creator but only in their great riches which tended to drive out from their possessors the fear of God. Rabbi Abbuha was purported to have told his people to sell everything they owned and become proselytes, and Rabbi Jochanan was said to have exchanged all his vineyards and olive fields which God had made in six days for the Torah which God prepared in forty days.[11]

No one would doubt the occurrence in Judaism of the demand for love and concession, although there is a Talmudic saying which advises to kill first the one intending murder. In Judaism, as elsewhere, it was considered expedient to kill the murderer before he kills you.[12] But Judaism also wrestled with the ethical problem of loving one's enemy even though it never found doing so easy or self-evident. Perhaps it is characteristic of rabbinical interpreters to have had very little to say about the Biblical demand, "If your enemy hungers, feed him." There were, however, Judaic sayings emphasizing, "He who repays evil with evil, from his house evil will not depart," and he is the strongest of the strong who can make of his enemy a friend.[13] Still another Talmudic statement demands the injured to plead

---

[11]Ibid., 565-566.

[12]Ibid., 570.

[13]Ibid., 575.

mercy on behalf of the offender even though he has not requested forgiveness.[14]

These comparisons sufficiently document Kittel's claim that thorough search of Jewish tradition could produce a literal equivalent for each of Jesus' Sermon on the Mount sayings. Kittel concludes that the uniqueness of Christianity as a religious phenomenon lies not in Jesus' demands as such—be they ever so high—but in something altogether different. Kittel discredits any attempt to explain the lofty character of the Sermon on the Mount by Jesus' dependence on rabbinism. The rabbinic sayings in question were written down much later, some of them centuries later, although they are based on earlier traditions.[15] It would seem more likely that the rabbis were influenced by Jesus: but, in view of the sharp contrasts and conflicts between Judaism and Christianity since the middle of the second century, such an interdependence was not likely nor is there any evidence to support it.[16]

What Judaism and Christianity have in common derives from their common root: the piety of the Old Testament. The difference then is one of emphasis: Jesus' whole interest concentrates on the highest religious-moral aspirations of the Old Testament. Within this focus, all ritualism and dialectic disappear, and ethics is disassociated from nationalism.[17] The context of ethics is entirely religious: the demands of Jesus are the demands of God. Rabbinism understood Jewish tradition as a precious heritage to be perpetuated. In Jesus, Law and Prophets are fulfilled as the demands of God come to life with absolute intensity. He demands not little or much but all. He leaves no place for compromise with the empirical structures of life. He does not consider what is practically possible. His ethic is removed from all reflection concerning practicability by its rarified absoluteness.[18] And this, says Kittel, constitutes the basic difference between the demands of Jesus, on the one hand, and the ethic of the Old Testament and of Judaism, on the other.

---

[14]Ibid., 576.

[15]Ibid., 577.

[16]Ibid., 578.

[17]Ibid., 580.

[18]Ibid., 582.

As a case in point, Jesus absolutely and unequivocally prohibits all divorce. There is no question and no debate about that. Alongside this demand stands the concession of Moses, "on account of the hardness of men's hearts," implying accomodation to the empirical actuality of human weakness and sinfulness. He would be a poor and merciless lawmaker who refused to take this reality into account, says Kittel. But Jesus makes no concessions, and, therefore, the problem of the Sermon on the Mount consists in the paradox of its demands which are elevated to a rigorous and radical absoluteness.[19] That is the problem before which Tolstoy and all his following stand perplexed, for an absolute demand cannot be applied as an empirical law in everyday life. Instead of attempting the impossible, Dostoevsky resolved the problem by developing from the absoluteness of Jesus' demands a whole metaphysic of poverty and suffering. But every Jew knew that the absolutized rigor of Jesus was not applicable to actual life and at best leads again to an isolation of morality from life. The Jews rightly realized, according to Kittel, that commandments requiring perfection are not and cannot be fulfilled by people within this sinful world,[20] a realization which also explains why these radicalisms compiled into one unit comprising Matthew 5 were prefaced by blessings, not upon those who would proudly fulfill these demands, but upon the "poor" who hunger and thirst after righteousness.

"But how does Jesus arrive at these demands exaggerated to the point of paradox and nonsense?" asks Kittel.[21] The absoluteness of Jesus' moral demands can only be comprehended, he answers, from one psychological point: the realization that in Jesus' self-consciousness the Kingdom is identical with his own presence. In turn, this means that his demands are the demands of the Kingdom, the new aeon which, as such, tolerates no compromise with the empirical this-sidedness of the old aeon. In the Kingdom of God there is no divorce because there is no hardness of heart. At the point where Jesus claims this fulfillment in his person, he ceases to be a Jew, according to Kittel. This difference between the two religions Kittel sees exemplified in their respective understanding of sinfulness and forgiveness. The Judaism which remained rooted in the Old Testament has

---

[19]Ibid.

[20]Ibid., 583.

[21]Ibid., 584.

always known what it means to ask for forgiveness of sins and transgressions as expressed in the prayer of eighteen petitions: ''Forgive us, our Father, for we have sinned before Thee.''[22] But the consciousness of sin in Christian piety is something altogether different, according to Kittel, for it is not a relative but an absolute consciousness of sin as a corollary to the absoluteness of Jesus' demands.[23]

What is new and different about early Christianity, Kittel wrote, is not the teaching of Jesus but his Person: the consciousness of divine mission, sonship, and forgiveness present in his Person for the sinner.[24] The essential and unavoidable conflict between Christianity and Judaism is not over Jesus' teaching but over his authority, which consists not in what he said but in the unheard-of nature of his Antitheses. The uniqueness of Christianity lies in the Person of Christ himself rather than in any particular moral proposition or teaching:

> There remains for him who reduces Christianity to the ethical maxims of the Sermon on the Mount (if he lets stand the absoluteness of the Sermon's demands) either a paradox which is necessarily meaningless and hopeless because its key has been lost or (as in the popular way of enlightenment represented also by our schools) the dilemma of holding the Sermon on the Mount to be a collection of ethical maxims the individual demands of which one proceeds to trim and compromise until they appear to accomodate everyday morality, not realizing that the resulting moral catechism is as far removed from the demands of Jesus as is the earth from heaven.[25]

What is useful in this endeavor can be identified with Judaism but not what has been artificially abstracted from the problematic of life.

The Sermon on the Mount remains essentially unfulfillable demand, Kittel concludes. The Torah, the law of the Jews, intends as any other human law and order to be fulfilled and to build up the world: ''But the meaning of the Sermon on the Mount is to tear down. It can only destroy. In the last analysis, its singular meaning lies in tearing down and laying bare the

[22]Ibid., 585.
[23]Ibid., 586.
[24]Ibid., 587.
[25]Ibid., 589.

great moral need of empirical humanity.''[26] In its meaning and goal the Sermon on the Mount is really nothing else than paradox: a hopeless way of allowing the poor to become guilty except in so far as it points to the Cross of Jesus as the corollary to the demands of Jesus, that is, as the reality and presence of forgiveness answering to the need and sinfulness that has been exposed. In the final analysis, the Sermon on the Mount serves as *praeparatio evangelica* pointing to its fulfillment in the Cross for all who "hunger and thirst after righteousness." A Christless Christianity—that no longer focuses on that crucified one who breaks mankind with his absolute demands and leaves nothing but sinful transgressors healed by forgiveness and grace proclaimed through his death—has become a Jewish sect. For the rest it remains as Paul (for whom, after he was confounded by Jesus' demands, Christ became the end of the law) said: "For I do not claim to know anything but Jesus Christ and him crucified."[27]

Kittel identified the genius of prophetic Judaism as integration of religion and ethics and characterized the offense of radical Christianity as artificial abstraction of ethical absolutes from empirical reality. Jesus is at once credited with the former and blamed for the latter: on the one hand, he restored to later Judaism its former oneness of faith and life, on the other hand, his absolute demands, "exaggerated to the point of nonsense," isolate morality from life. Essentially the problem is that Jesus intended his demands to be fulfilled, but we do not fulfill them. To this moral problem Kittel applies a dogmatic solution that provides the framework for affirming Christianity without being embarrassed by Jesus' teaching. Kittel dissolves the moral problem of our deficiency into a Christological affirmation of Jesus' uniqueness. No longer do Jesus' absolutistic demands need to be radically obeyed; they need only to be theologically understood, and that, after all, is the function of dogmatics. It enables us to comprehend why it was necessary for Jesus to make "nonsensical" demands, namely, because he identified himself with the Kingdom of God. Since the claims of his otherworldly kingdom are impracticable for our this-worldly empiricism, we need not feel morally guilty for not doing what Jesus said when he was speaking out of context. What Jesus said applies to us not actually but tangentially, not literally but dialectically, not single-mindedly but

---

[26]Ibid., 590.

[27]Ibid., 591.

paradoxically. That is how Christianity differs from Judaism. Everything is absolutized: absolute demands make for absolute sinfulness; absolute destruction prepares for absolute redemption by the absolute sacrifice. All this becomes theologically intelligible only in the Cross, that absolute paradox for which the Sermon on the Mount is the *praeparatio evangelica*.

Nevertheless, Jesus, precisely in his radicalism, stands centrally within Old Testament prophetic religion, for what distinguishes his way from moral philosophy is the "rigorous element" of unconditional confrontation with the holy will of God, who does not accommodate himself to the empirical sinfulness of men. The function of Jesus' radical teaching is, however, not to throw men into the abyss of utter despair by nonsensical absolutes but to instruct them in the better righteousness and to enable them to walk in the light. The way of the Sermon on the Mount is the way of the lived Torah: it is the way of life. That way invariably leads to the Cross, not as a symbol of dogma but as a reality of life. Except for his teaching, Jesus would never have been brought to the Cross. By exalting Christ's person while debasing his teaching, Kittel—in contrast to Jesus—defines Christianity as a dogma rather than a way. Kittel has been commended for "bringing the conception of Lutheranism to its clearest expression,"[28] but in the process he reduced the Sermon on the Mount to its meanest depiction as ethical "nonsense."

---

[28]Johannes Schneider, *Der Sinn der Bergpredigt* (Berlin: Furche Verlag, 1936) 13.

The dialectic of Law and Gospel is also the thematic framework of Helmut Thielicke's postwar sermons entitled *Life Can Begin Again* (Philadelphia: Fortress Press, 1963 [German original: *Ich aber sage euch . . . Auslegung der Bergpredigt*, Stuttgart, 1946-1948]). Thielicke feels our interpretation of the Sermon on the Mount "should consider less the piercing radicality of its directions" and emphasize more "the definite purpose" Christ had in view "when he speaks in these radical terms" (xiii). Thielicke explains this "definite purpose" of Jesus' demands as follows: "At the very beginning and as a kind of introduction to discipleship Christ makes us feel the implacable severity of the law and thus leads us to death" (40). He does this to impress upon our consciousness the indelible realization that our battle with sin is not a battle with something alien to ourselves. "*I myself* am the antagonist," says Thielicke, quoting Romans 7. "*That's* why the law must remain in all its severity! It must remain like gauze in the deep wound in our heart to keep it from healing too easily and forming an invisible scar that would fool us into thinking that we are not wounded and sick at all and that we do not need anyone to die for us and to forgive and heal us as a Savior" (44). "Jesus breaks open our deepest wound and stuffs it with gauze, however severely it may hurt. Suddenly the Crucified is facing us here; and before we hear his cheering, redeeming words, 'This I have done for you,' *we* must daily be heard saying, 'This have I done against thee.' *Only then* will we comprehend the Cross of Calvary. Otherwise, it becomes so innocuous that ladies dare to use it to ornament an evening dress'' (45). In other words, first, God is my accuser and my heart is my defender. Then, as I lose my case, my heart becomes my accuser and God becomes my defender (46). ''In letting God defend me, I know there is something within me *against* which he must defend me. And that preserves me from pride and carelessness'' (47).

Though Thielicke cautioned against depreciating this Lutheran understanding of the law's function as ''morbid legalism,'' he hesitated to press the dogmatic logic of the *primus usus legis* as far as did Stange or Kittel. His parishioners were haunted by the ongoing denazification trials. The whole world seemed once again to stand in judgment of the Germans for having fought under the wrong flag, and the national consciousness was depressed by the awareness of collective guilt for the world catastrophe. The situation resembled that Greek tragedy in which the presence of the Sphinx haunted the city with the awareness that a terrible crime had been committed and which demanded atonement. Under these circumstances, Thielicke preached that ''life can begin again'' on the foundation of God's Word (Matthew 7:24-25) and emphasized that ''it is not the Word of God as such that becomes this rock foundation for us but only the Word of God that we *do,* the Word that we take seriously in our life.'' He explains that to ''do'' the Word means to ''live'' with it, ''to dare to be obedient'' (212), ''to anchor, fasten, and moor the Word of God in every situation of my life'' (213). Thielicke's appeal to his refugee parishioners to rebuild their broken lives is, however, confused by his unresolved ambivalence in neither denying with Luther that man is capable of any good will or deed nor affirming with Kant that man could do the good if he would and therefore should.

RUDOLF BULTMANN:
THE SERMON ON THE MOUNT
IN EXISTENTIALIST PERSPECTIVE

The ethic of Jesus, exactly like the Jewish, is an ethic of obedience, and the single though fundamental difference is that Jesus has conceived radically the idea of obedience.[1]

The obedience for which Jesus asks is easy because it frees a man from dependence on a formal authority and therefore frees him from the judgment of the men whose profession it is to explain this authority. . . . To the weak man it is a relief to have the judgment of good and evil and all responsibility *taken away from him. And* this *burden is just what Jesus puts on men; he teaches men to see themselves as called to* decision—*decision between good and evil, decision for God's will or for their own will.*[2]

Jesus teaches no ethics at all *in the sense of an intelligible theory valid for all men concerning what should be done and left undone.*[3]

This moment of decision contains all that is necessary for the decision.[4]

Whoever appealing to a word of Jesus refuses to dissolve an unendurable marriage or whoever offers the other cheek to one who strikes him because *Jesus said so would not understand Jesus. For he would have missed exactly the obedience which Jesus desires. . . . All these sayings are meant to make clear by extreme examples that it is not a question of satisfying an outward authority but of being completely* obedient.[5]

---

[1]Rudolf Bultmann, *Jesus and the Word*, ET Louise P. Smith and Erminie H. Lantero (London and Glasgow: Collins, 1958 [*Jesus,* Göttingen, 1926]) 58.

[2]Ibid., 65.

[3]Ibid., 66.

[4]Ibid., 67.

[5]Ibid., 71.

What a man must do in order to love his neighbor or his enemy is not stated. It is assumed that everyone can know that. . . .[6]

In 1926 Rudolf Bultmann,[7] one of the great New Testament scholars of our time, published a treatise which is said to contain the kernel of his thought. This book, *Jesus*, was intended to free the teaching of Jesus from modern accretions and interpretations so that one could understand it within the context of its original setting. Bultmann sought the meaning of Jesus not in his person or personality—about which, he claims, we can know almost nothing—but in his work or purpose as comprehended only in his teaching.[8] But, since Jesus taught in Aramaic, "everything in the Synoptics, which for reason of language or content can have originated only in Hellenistic Christianity, must be excluded as a source for the teaching of Jesus." Even if by critical analysis we can discern within the self-understanding of the first Christian community the oldest layer of tradition that inspired it, we would still "have no absolute assurance," Bultmann says, "that the exact words of this oldest layer were really spoken by Jesus."[9] That fact is depressing only for those "whose interest is in the personality of Jesus," not for those prepared to encounter the tradition associated with his teaching.

Jesus' ministry and message has its roots in the self-understanding of Israel as the chosen people whose life is determined by law and promise and whose meaning is defined as obedience and hope.[10] This is the context of his messianism and proclamation of the Kingdom of God, "that escha-

---

[6]Ibid., 84.

[7]Rudolf Bultmann (1884-1973), taught at Marburg after 1912 with an intermission at Breslau and Gießen (1916-1920). His numerous scholarly publications, many of which are now available in English, include *Die Geschichte der synoptischen Tradition* (1921), *Jesus* (1926), *Das Evangelium Johannes* (Meyer Komm, II, 1941), *Theologie des Neuen Testaments* (1953), *Glauben und Verstehen* I (1933), II (1953), III (1960), *Geschichte und Eschatologie* (1958), *Jesus Christus und die Mythologie* (1958), *Das Verhältnis der urchristlichen Christusbotschaft zum historischen Jesus (1960)*.

[8]*Jesus and the Word*, 15.

[9]Ibid., 17; cf. *The History of the Synoptic Tradition*, which documents the methodology and results of Bultmann's form criticism.

[10]Ibid., 21.

tological deliverance, which ends everything earthly.''[11] Bultmann shared Schweitzer's belief that Jesus understood the Kingdom to be wholly supernatural and therefore ''superhistorical,'' culminating in a tremendous eschatological drama. Its significance does not, however, lie in the dramatic apocalyptic events attending its appearance but in the fact that through them humanity is confronted with an ultimate Either/Or decision by that ''power which, although entirely future, wholly determines the present.''[12]

Jesus lived and taught as a Jewish rabbi, wherefore many of his sayings—including those on cares (Matthew 6:25-34), on judging (Matthew 7:1-5), on God's answering of prayer (Matthew 7:7-11), and on authenticity (Matthew 7:24-27)—resemble sayings that have come down to us from the Rabbis. Jesus did not question the authority of the Law nor attack religious practices customary for pious Jews, such as almsgiving, prayer, and fasting. He protested only their misuse and the undiscerning mingling in Jewish practice of pedantic ceremonial rules and fundamental moral precepts.

Bultmann tells us that ''the ethic of Jesus, exactly like the Jewish, is an ethic of obedience, and the single though fundamental difference is that Jesus has conceived radically the idea of obedience,''[13] not as external conformity and not as that which a pious man self-evidently does in the cultic ritual but as that which a man obediently *is* as he stands unconditionally before God. In striking resemblance to the expression of Wilhelm Herrmann, Bultmann contends: ''Radical obedience exists only when a man inwardly assents to what is required of him, when the thing commanded is seen as intrinsically God's command, when the whole man stands behind what he does, or better, when the whole man is *in* what he does, when he is not *doing something obediently* but *is* essentially obedient.''[14] In making men directly responsible to God, Jesus frees them from dependence on those whose profession it was to interpret and administer authority. His radical obedience ethic freed men from all humanistic ethic of self-realization, from all idealistic ethic of doing good for its own sake, and from all value ethic

---

[11]Ibid., 33.

[12]Ibid., 44.

[13]Ibid., 58.

[14]Ibid., 61.

of achieving ends through means.[15] In fact, says Bultmann, "Jesus teaches no ethics at all,"[16] no universal standards, no theory of value, no measure of action, not even a self-conscious, self-reflective ethic of intention—only unconditional obedience.

But how can a person perceive *what* God demands without recourse to formal authority? Bultmann replies that "the moment of decision is all that is necessary for the decision."[17] One does not need to compare or reflect on past or universal standards to know what is momentarily right: "The crisis of decision is the situation in which all observation is excluded, for which *Now* alone has meaning." Furthermore, there is no basis or reason for formulating

> general ideas about the highest good, about virtues and values, for every such theory originates from the spectator's point of view. In the view of Jesus there can be no such ethic, and therefore it is fundamentally a mistake to look to him for concrete ethical requirements or for his attitude to concrete ethical problems.[18]

What did Jesus understand then by obedience to the will of God? To answer this question Bultmann examines the demands of Jesus as formulated in the six Antitheses of the Sermon on the Mount according to Matthew 5:21-48. He notes that all these passages emphasize the same decisive requirement: that the good be done completely and unreservedly.

> He who indeed refrains from murder but does not master anger has not understood that he must decide completely. He who indeed avoids adultery but keeps lust in his heart has not understood the prohibition of adultery, which requires of him complete purity. He who divorces his wife has not understood that marriage requires of him a complete decision but thinks of it as a relative action which can be annulled. He who takes revenge for injustice does not realize that by so doing he himself upholds injustice; to reject injustice completely means not to retaliate. He who is kind only to friends does not know what love means, for complete love includes love of enemies.[19]

---

[15]Ibid., 65.

[16]Ibid., 66.

[17]Ibid., 67.

[18]Ibid., 68.

[19]Ibid., 70.

The claim of the Law upon a person is limited to that conduct which can be bound by formulated precepts. The radical obedience which Jesus demands goes beyond this formal obedience in that it claims not only specific acts but the whole man and allows no latitude to self-will. This is how and why Jesus distinguished obedience from legalism:

> It would obviously be a complete misunderstanding to take these "But I tell you" passages as formal legal precepts of an external authority, which can be fulfilled by outward behavior. Whoever appeals to a word of Jesus and refuses to dissolve an unendurable marriage, or whoever offers the other cheek to one who strikes him *because* Jesus said so would not understand Jesus. For he would have missed exactly the obedience Jesus desires; he would imagine that he could achieve and present an act of obedience when obedience is not really present as the determining factor of his life. All these sayings are meant to make clear by extreme examples that it is not a question of satisfying an outward authority but of being completely obedient. It is wholly impossible to regard Jesus' teaching as universally valid ethical precepts by which a man can once for all order his life.[20]

Nor do the requirements of the Sermon on the Mount present an ethical idealism. They "bring to light the absolute character of the demands of God."[21] For Bultmann, "the command of love explains nothing concerning the content of love."[22] Jesus assumed a person who knows *that* he must love also knows *how*. Jesus did not and could not spell out the content of love.

> The responsibility is put on man; he must answer for his own actions; they are regarded as the expression of his being, and by them he is judged. This is the meaning of the words: "Can men gather grapes from thorns or figs from thistles? Every tree is known by its fruit. A good tree cannot bear bad fruit." (Matthew 7:16,18 or Luke 6:43,44).[23]

In order to impress upon people's consciousness the absolute character of the divine command without any regard for personal interests, Jesus appropriated

an old Oriental proverb. . .to make clear to the hearer the Either/Or: "No

---

[20]Ibid., 71.

[21]Ibid., 71.

[22]Ibid., 72.

[23]Ibid., 73.

man can serve two masters. Either he must hate one and love the other, or he must hold to one and despise the other. You cannot serve God and Mammon.'' (Matthew 6:24).[24]

Similarly, Jesus' attack on wealth

must not be misunderstood as meaning that he made the general demand that everyone should give away his property, that he preached the ideal of poverty and demanded asceticism. . . .not *poverty* but *surrender* is demanded.[25]
Jesus speaks of *property* only as he does of *wealth*, that it becomes a fetter to man. . . .Everyone has to decide for himself whether his own property is of this character, and no economic theory about the productive value of property relieves him from the responsibility for his decision.[26]
Jesus desires no asceticism; he requires only the strength for the sacrifice. As little as he repudiates property does he reject marriage or demand sexual asceticism.[27]
Neither marriage nor celibacy is in itself good; either can be demanded of a man. How each individual must decide he will know if he seeks not his own interests but the will of God.[28]

Jesus also did not require fasting although

he recognized it as an allowable religious practice if it comes from the heart (Matthew 6:16-18). . . .Man does not have to achieve for himself particular qualities, either an especial virtue or an especial saintliness.[29]
Jesus does not ascetically renounce the world and its institutions nor measure it critically by the standards of a social ideal, neither does he give positive worth to the duties which grow out of life in this world. No program for world reformation is derived from the will of God.[30]

Jesus simply did not see his task ''as the founding of an ideal human society.''[31]

[24]Ibid., 75.
[25]Ibid., 75.
[26]Ibid., 79.
[27]Ibid., 76.
[28]Ibid., 79.
[29]Ibid., 76, 77.
[30]Ibid., 79.
[31]Ibid., 80.

On this point, according to Bultmann, Tolstoy completely misunderstood Jesus. Jesus took no interest in the construction of a better social order, not merely in view of the imminent expectation of the Kingdom of God but simply because "the hope of Jesus never included these elements." His sole purpose was "to make known the position of man before God." What possibilities and responsibilities of social, political, or economic action may arise from this the individual must himself decide. "The will of God is then for Jesus as little a social or political program as it is either an ethical system which proceeds from an ideal of man and humanity or an ethic of value."[32]

Jesus' requirement of conduct towards others is epitomized in the commandment to love God, one's neighbors, and one's enemies as an expression of God's will. Jesus' basis for the demand to love differs from that of Stoic philosophers in that it is

> not the conception of strength of character and personal worth but the concept of obedience, of renunciation of one's own claim. . . . Jesus does not support his demand for love by referring to other men as human beings, and love of enemies is not the high point of universal love of humanity but the high point of overcoming of self, the surrender of one's own claim. Jesus thought of love neither as a virtue which belongs to the perfection of man nor as an aid to the well-being of society but as an overcoming of self-will in the concrete situation of life in which a man encounters other men. . . . *What* a man must do in order to love his neighbor or his enemy is not stated. It is assumed that everyone can know that.[33]

One requirement of such love is the readiness to forgive which demands a definite attitude and indicates that what is demanded is not an affection or emotion but an act of will. Finally, Jesus demanded: "Be perfect, as your heavenly Father is perfect" (Matthew 5:48). The perfection, Bultmann explains, is not the Greek idea of the highest possible ideal of conduct attained by gradual improvement but the Semitic conception of being whole, undivided, integral, or authentic.[34]

According to Bultmann, the demands of the Sermon on the Mount do not constitute an Interim Ethic inspired by the imminent end of the world,

---

[32]Ibid., 81.

[33]Ibid., 83, 84.

[34]Ibid., 88-89.

as Schweitzer claimed. The coming of God's Kingdom and the proclamation of God's will are related but not as cause and effect. "The eschatological message and the preaching of the will of God are to be comprehended as a unity"[35] in that they both point to the present moment as the hour of decision, for the necessity of man's radical decision constitutes the possibility of his real future.[36]

In Greek thought God is the ruling law and form-giving power of the universe. In Jewish thought God is primarily creative and redemptive will. No distinction is made between the physical and spiritual nature of man, and in the Jewish idea of God there is no metaphysical dualism:

> God and the world do not stand over against each other as two hostile natures or substances. . . .And, though God and man are sharply contrasted as Creator and creature, as the Holy One and the sinner, still, this difference is never regarded as a difference between two natures nor is the redemption of man conceived as deliverance from a lower and endowment with a higher nature.[37]

God transcends the world but directs the world. Often the past and present age are associated with God's remoteness, and the future age, when his glory will appear, is identified with his nearness. To the extent that human beings lose the sense of God's providential presence now, they fear his future presence as judge. This constitutes the tension between present and future, hope and fear in Jewish thought. But for Jesus "the distant God is at the same time *the God near at hand.*"[38] This closed the chasm between future and present, hope and providence, judgment and grace in the realization of the petitions, "Thy Kingdom come, Thy will be done." Jesus did not speak of faith as a *Weltanschauung*, but he was convinced of the presence and power of God which enables obedience.[39]

Finally, the meaning of Jesus lies in his word, that is, in his teaching that God forgives man's disobedience and thus 'saves' him, redeems him, and prepares him for the future. This act of forgiveness is real only in relation to a particular man; it cannot be objectified as the event of Christ's

---

[35]Ibid., 95.

[36]Ibid., 96.

[37]Ibid., 100.

[38]Ibid., 110.

[39]Ibid., 136.

death and resurrection. Jesus, Bultmann writes, did not understand his death as a cosmic redemptive act affecting mankind in general; "Moreover, Jesus did not speak of his death and resurrection and their redemptive significance."[40] Sayings to the effect that he came "to give his life a ransom for many" (Mark 10:45) or that his blood was "shed for many" (Mark 14:22-24) Bultmann ascribes to Hellenistic Christianity.

> Jesus does not point to any way which can be universally recognized in which a man becomes conscious of the forgiveness of God—he simply proclaims this forgiveness. The event is nothing else than *his word* as it confronts the hearer.[41]

This is the eschatological message of the Kingdom of God relevant to every age—including our own. Nor did the primitive Christian community

> ascribe to him a particular metaphysical nature which gave his words authority. On the contrary, it was on the ground of the authority of his words that the Church confessed that God had made him the Lord of the Church. Greek Christianity soon represented Jesus as Son of God in the sense of ascribing a divine "nature" to him and thus introduced a view of his person as far removed as possible from his own.[42]

Jesus' understanding himself as one sent by God as bearer and proclaimer of God's forgiveness[43] constituted his *Selbstverständnis* and *Gottesverständnis*. And blessed is the one who when compelled to decision by confrontation with his word finds no cause of offense in him.[44]

Bultmann's insights, however fruitful, pose certain problems. On the one hand, Jesus' teaching is depicted as an ethic of obedience "exactly like the Jewish" only more radical. Then, almost in the same breath, we are told, "Jesus teaches no ethics at all." How can this be? That Jesus' ethic is Jewish means that it is a response to God, not a reflection about ends and means. Jewish ethics differ from humanist ethics in that glory is ascribed only to God, not to human beings. Jewish ethic lacks reflection on the moral idea and knows no catalogue of heroic virtues. In contrast to the

---

[40]Ibid., 150.

[41]Ibid., 151.

[42]Ibid., 152.

[43]Ibid., 152-53.

[44]Ibid., 154.

Greek value structure culminating in the ideal city state, Jewish ethics has no human ideal towards the realization of which man must discipline himself to strive. The Jewish ethic differs from a value-ethic in that no value is ascribed to or realized by the act of obedience as such. Obedience is not a performance to be judiciously evaluated either as an end in itself or as a means toward an end. Confronted by God himself, man in Jewish self-understanding has no recourse to such deliberations. He has no reflective options but to obey or disobey God's command. We therefore agree with Bultmann that Jesus' ethic was a Jewish ethic of obedience.

What we challenge is Bultmann's assumption that Jesus' demands are purely formal and void of material content, as implied in his premise that "Jesus teaches no ethics at all." Bultmann precisely identified the issue in claiming that by comparison to Judaism Jesus' demands are more radical. What is not clear is why they must therefore be less concrete. Why must radicalness be inversely proportional to concreteness to imply that complete obedience is completely void of content? Why should Jesus' demands not be as concrete as their Jewish parallels? And why should a moral precept such as the Golden Rule (Matthew 7:12) not have general validity and universal sanction? Bultmann's formal category of radical obedience fails to respect the material content of Jesus' teaching. Jesus' demands are not just a call to decision *in vacuo* but to a way of life informed by his word. To imply that the situation itself furnished the necessary insight for right conduct is to ignore the revelatory character of God's will through the teaching of Jesus. The demands of Jesus cannot simply be derived from the awareness that God claims man totally. The Torah was more explicit, and so was Jesus. If, as Bultmann contends, "it would obviously be a complete misunderstanding" to apply Jesus' demands to "outward behavior," then what is required is not *obedience*. And, if doing what Jesus says "*because* he says so" is to miss the point completely, then what is required is not obedience to *Jesus*. It is not clear why what remains is so "radical" when its form is disassociated from behavior and its reason is disassociated from Jesus.

The subjective character of Bultmann's existentialist ethic follows from the premise that we have no recourse to the original words or the actual person of Jesus behind the kerygmatic tradition of the Church. Since we cannot recover the Jesus of history behind the Christ of faith, the nearest we can get to the original Sermon on the Mount is the sermons of its interpreters. While they believed what Jesus believed, they did not preach what he preached. Instead of preaching like Jesus, they preached about him. Since the meaning of their preaching, as all preaching, is *Existenzerhellung* (''illumination of existence''), the Jesus message in the light of Easter faith is understood by Bultmann as a call to authentic self-understanding as exemplified by Jesus, the prime eschatological paradigm.

Realizing that the authenticity of the message presupposes the historicity of the text, Bultmann's critics seek to recover the *ipsissima verba* of the real Jesus within the kerygmatic tradition, hoping thereby to close Bultmann's docetic credibility gap and to restore respect for the Gospels as historical documents rather than as psychological case material extrapolated from primitive self-understandings. Whatever the future of this development, it suffices for our purpose to have noted that, while Bultmann's existentialist emphasis raised the level of consciousness of all concerned, it proved too frail a framework to communicate the genius of Yeshua's mountain teaching. Bultmann's thought demonstrated the effectiveness of Heidegger's philosophy as gadfly to activate Christian faith claims on contemporary terms. But, inasmuch as the resulting consciousness is abstracted from Jesus' words, there is no reason for identifying it as Christian.

HANS WINDISCH:
HISTORICAL EXEGESIS VERSUS
THEOLOGICAL INTERPRETATION

The radicalisms of the Sermon on the Mount are fed from two streams: eschato-logical proclamation and wisdom teaching, "but in the main they issue from the religious wisdom of Jesus."[1]

From the standpoint of Paul, Luther, and Calvin the soteriology of the Sermon on the Mount is hopelessly heretical.[2]

It is quite unPauline, in that it assumes the fulfillment of the commandments as something obvious, and it confirms our thesis that the doctrine of salvation in the Sermon on the Mount stands in sharpest contradiction to that of Paul, in any case, to the doctrine that is contained in Romans chapters 3 to 8. There is a gulf here between Jesus and Paul which no art of theological exegesis can bridge.[3]

If that teaching is to be correctly understood, the doctrine that Paul develops in Romans chapters 3 to 8 must be left entirely out of consideration.[4]

The imposing doctrine of the cancellation of God's curse by the blood of Christ . . . involves too great a depreciation of the Sermon on the Mount and, for that matter, the entire gospel of Jesus.[5]

The Sermon on the Mount stands wholly within the framework of Israelitish-Jew-ish religion.[6]

---

[1]Hans Windisch, *The Meaning of the Sermon on the Mount: A Contribution to the Historical Understanding of the Gospels and to the Problem of Their True Exegesis*, ET S. MacLean Gilmour (Philadelphia: Westminster Press, 1951) 40.

[2]Ibid., 6.

[3]Ibid., 107.

[4]Ibid., 121-122.

[5]Ibid., 174.

[6]Ibid., 144.

Jesus renewed the proclamation of salvation preached by the prophets and confirms the hope of salvation sung by the devout Psalmists.[7]

Thus our thesis that the message of salvation in the Sermon on the Mount is based wholly upon the experience of salvation under the old covenant receives renewed confirmation.[8]

The Sermon on the Mount contains commands, just as the Torah does, that must be obeyed if one desires to enter into "life." Its teaching is characterized by an ethic of obedience.[9]

We must honestly admit that we do not fulfill the Sermon on the Mount in many respects.[10]

It is sometimes said that Jesus' teaching is a criticism of contemporary culture, not contemporary culture a criticism of Jesus. Such an antithesis does not do justice to the facts, for each must be criticized by the other. Every evaluation of the Sermon on the Mount that concludes that Jesus' sayings cannot be fulfilled literally is actually a criticism of Jesus. We all criticize the Sermon on the Mount, although we do not all admit it.[11]

In his substantial treatise, *Der Sinn der Bergpredigt*, Hans Windisch[12] undertakes to "reconstruct the fundamental historical viewpoint" of the Sermon and from that perspective seeks to achieve "a theological validation" of its content. Throughout this monograph he emphatically insists upon strict differentiation between historical exegesis and theological interpretation. Authentic biblical scholarship may not jump to theological conclusions without traversing the difficult road via history to theology. The science of historical exegesis, of validating every insight within its original context, must precede any attempt at theologizing and at dogmat-

---

[7]Ibid., 175.

[8]Ibid., 177.

[9]Ibid., 72.

[10]Ibid., 194.

[11]Ibid., 197.

[12]Hans Ludwig Windisch (1881-1935) began his career as Privatdozent in New Testament at Leipzig; he served as Professor for 15 years at Leiden and 6 years at Kiel, and succeeded Ernst von Dobschütz at Halle-Wittenberg in 1935. His books include *Der Barnabasbrief* (2d ed., 1931), *2. Korintherbrief* (1920), *Der Hebräerbrief* (2d ed., 1931), *De tegenwoordige stand van het Christusprobleem* (2d ed., 1925), *Johannes und die Synoptiker* (1926).

ics. Windisch laments that confusion of these two approaches characterizes not only dogmaticians and expositors who seek to convey the edification of the text but also those who expound the original meanings of biblical texts.

In his own historical exegesis, Windisch contends against two fronts, the idealizing and the Paulinizing tendencies, both of which "represent violent reinterpretations of the biblical source materials." The categories with which idealistic exegesis operates—

> attitude, ethos, ethic, redemption from the law, morality. ethical idealism—have little or no relation to the Sermon on the Mount. Whoever makes use of them ought to be aware that, in so doing, he is translating biblical ideas out of one framework of thought into another.

Dogmatic exegesis makes its appeal to a right view of humankind. But the systematic theologian must realize that this idea of humanity is hardly represented in the Sermon on the Mount itself: "From the standpoint of Paul, Luther, and Calvin, the soteriology of the Sermon on the Mount is hopelessly heretical." Catholic theology could more easily come to terms with it. Nevertheless, Windisch proposes to show that there is a way from the Sermon on the Mount to what for Paul, Luther and Calvin is the basis of Christian belief, namely, justification by faith—"as little as the 'correct' conceptualization of this doctrine can be achieved from the Sermon on the Mount itself."[13] Windisch endeavors, therefore, first to give "an exclusively historical interpretation" of the text and then attempts "to understand the theological content of the Sermon on the Mount and its relevance to our time" by taking "historical exegesis and its results as our point of departure."[14]

Weiss and Schweitzer had first opened modern eyes to the eschatological character of the Sermon on the Mount. They convinced a generation of scholars that the Sermon on the Mount was irrelevant for modern civilization, an interim ethic that tore the hearer loose from all his natural moorings to prepare him for an imminent otherworldly Kingdom. Windisch concedes that the Sermon on the Mount as a whole is conditioned by such eschatological expectation but on exegetical grounds challenges the assumption that eschatology is really the heart of the matter. He notes its

---

[13]*The Meaning of the Sermon on the Mount*, 6.
[14]Ibid., 19.

dominant influence primarily in the Beatitudes, the thematic sayings regarding the Kingdom and higher righteousness (Matthew 5;19, 20), possibly the word on urgency of reconciliation (Matthew 5:25-26), the saying about the offending eye or hand (Matthew 5:29, 30), the Lord's Prayer, the logion about the two ways (Matthew 7:13-14) and about the final judgment (Matthew 7:21, 23), and the concluding parables. These are the passages that confront the individual with the two awesome eschatological possibilities—the terrors of Gehenna or the surpassing splendor of the Kingdom of Heaven: "Most of them fall into eschatological conditions of admittance."[15] According to Deuteronomy 4:1 and 16:20, obedience to the statutes of Yahweh was the condition for inheriting Canaan. Similarly, the commands of Jesus, the New Moses, become—according to Matthew— the eschatological conditions for inheriting the Kingdom.

To make his case, Matthew, argues Windisch, "has forced a great deal of material into the service of his point of view that originally was entirely unaffected by eschatological beliefs."[16] Windisch finds that such essentially noneschatological sayings include the similies of salt and light, the logion about the sacrifice (Matthew 5:23-24), the sayings about adultery, divorce, oaths, and revenge, the command to love one's enemy, the sayings about the eye, the two masters, about judging, concerning God's answering of prayer, and the Golden Rule.[17] Since none of these pericopes and logia expresses the nearness of the judgment and the eschatological rule, Windisch concludes that the Sermon on the Mount as a whole is no "interim ethic" or "exceptional legislation":

> the radicalness of the Sermon on the Mount is not dependent on the imminence of the final revelation or on the accidental brevity of the interim but on the essential circumstance that the event for which one must be prepared is the rule of God; that the summons comes from God who now, by the mouth of Jesus, demands something utter and absolute.[18]

Furthermore, Windisch identifies a third group of sayings

in which the eschatological motive is expressly stated but is not by any

---

[15]Ibid., 38.

[16]Ibid., 26.

[17]Ibid., 30.

[18]Ibid., 29.

means dominant. To these belong the antithesis to the sixth commandment, the didactic poem about the three acts of piety, and the passage that deals with anxiety.[19]

As a case in point, Windisch notes that the pericope on anxiety (Matthew 6:25-34) is not eschatologically oriented except for the mention of the Kingdom in verse 33: "Apart from this one verse, the whole poem is based on an attitude towards history . . . that is permeated by a vigorous religious optimism, a life- and world-affirming piety."[20] Though eschatological expectation of judgment and salvation is fundamental to the Sermon on the Mount as a whole, it contains groups of sayings "in which the eschatological situation is either not involved or is present only as a secondary factor."[21] The radicalisms of the Sermon on the Mount are fed from two streams, eschatological proclamation and wisdom teaching, "but in the main they issue from the religious wisdom of Jesus,"[22] which is characterized by its "understanding of all relationships of life, its appeal to reason and to judgment, its emphasis on the useful and the pragmatic, and its requirement of a judicious and intelligent way of living."[23]

Next, Windisch attacks modern interpretations of the Sermon which reject the practicability of Jesus' imperatives on other than eschatological grounds. He faults Herrmann's alleged assumption that "Jesus of Nazareth must have meant his commands to be taken exactly as the modern student of ethics who has read Kant, Tolstoy, Naumann, and others interprets them." His criticism of Dibelius and Bultmann is that

> they demonstrate wonderfully and at times convincingly how we can manipulate the often provocative and incomprehensible sayings of Jesus. Whether in so doing they have also explained what Jesus meant by them, remains a moot issue.[24]

He accuses them of confusing historical exegesis and theological interpretation by assuming that

---

[19]Ibid., 34.

[20]Ibid., 36.

[21]Ibid., 39.

[22]Ibid., 40.

[23]Ibid., 41.

[24]Ibid., 46.

>Jesus cannot have taught something that is no longer understood or accepted at Heidelberg or Marburg. . . . The whole approach is determined throughout by dogmatic and apologetic considerations. It seeks to establish the authority of the Sermon on the Mount and of Jesus for all time, including our own, by rejecting it as external authority.[25]

Because we cannot carry out Jesus' commands, they must convince us that doing so would be altogether too absurd, impossible, extravagant, Jewish, or simply ridiculous. That leaves two options: either to conclude that we have outgrown the Sermon on the Mount and need to get on with the "Kultur der Gegenwart," as Naumann and Baumgarten had argued, or to resort to a purely theological solution in the Pauline doctrine of the Cross, as Stange and Kittel had decided.

Instead, Windisch scrutinizes the text itself to discern the character of Jesus' imperatives. On the basis of examining the content and context of (1) the saying addressed to the disciples in Matthew 5:16, (2) the general sayings about the Law in 5:17-20 and 7:12, (3) the Antitheses of 5:21-48, and (4) the eschatological sayings and final parables, Windisch concludes:

>There can be no doubt whatever that the Evangelist has introduced the Sermon on the Mount into his Gospel as a collection of commands—an explication of the will of God as it applies to us.[26]
>
>The Sermon on the Mount contains commands, just as the Torah does, that must be obeyed if one desires to enter into "life." Its teaching is characterized by an ethic of obedience.[27]

The antithesis between understanding Jesus' imperatives either as commandments or as attitudes (as held by Herrmann and his following) Windisch rejects as false, for "by such individual commandments Jesus shows how the new attitude is to be manifested, and from such commandments the nature of the new attitude itself is to be deduced."[28] According to Windisch, the radical, vigorous form of Jesus' demands is characteristic of wisdom teaching. These injunctions cease to appear paradoxical and become immediately self-evident at the moment one realizes that the good to be done is God's command. Windisch emphatically asserts that the ques-

---

[25]Ibid., 56.

[26]Ibid., 65.

[27]Ibid., 72.

[28]Ibid., 85-86.

tion concerning the practicability or feasibility of Jesus' commands cannot be treated only in the light of our own contemporary situation, as modern theologians tend to do:

> The answer must be wrested from the source material, from its content and its presuppositions. From what is said it is clear that neither the Evangelist nor Jesus considered feasibility any problem. Since the demands are obvious deduction from the very essence of religious wisdom, every pious man must and can recognize and fulfill them. The idea of impracticability appears absolutely senseless within the framework of a correct understanding of the Sermon on the Mount. Jesus gives new commandments, principles, and examples for the true expression of piety, not only to convince men of the correctness of his prescriptions but also to bring about full obedience among men to God. To leave them undone would be just as foolish as to refuse to recognize their validity. It is taken for granted that everyone who hears and reads the demands will also obey them. Fulfillment is the natural and normal response. . . . Because the commands are "sensible," they are also practicable; because they are true commands, they are also capable of fulfillment. The teaching of the Sermon on the Mount is based on this line of reasoning, however strange it may appear to us. The one who hears and reads it may be startled, but, if he has understood it correctly, he has learned what he must do to be saved. The question of whether he is able to fulfill the commandments or not, as it emerged in Pauline and early orthodox theology and as it received its solution in the doctrine of the incapability of man and of the saving grace of God, is just as unfamiliar to the Sermon on the Mount as it is to the Law. Because the commandment is laid down and because one's share in the Kingdom of Heaven depends on its fulfillment, it is obvious that it is "feasible."[29]

Windisch is convinced that for the Sermon on the Mount the problem of fulfillment does not exist—except for one passage: the reference to the "many" and the "few" (Matthew 7:13-14), a saying in which he detects a pessimistic eschatological perspective quite out of harmony with the rational and optimistic spirit of religious wisdom. Nevertheless, even in this saying "it is taken for granted that what is commanded by no means exceeds the powers of the 'few.' "[30] That the "many" do not find Jesus' demands practicable is assumed to be their own fault.

Windisch contrasts Jesus with Paul, observing that:

---

[29]Ibid., 97.

[30]Ibid., 100.

the doctrine of salvation in the Sermon on the Mount stands in sharpest contradiction to that of Paul, in any case, to the doctrine that is contained in Romans chapters 3 to 8. There is a gulf here between Jesus and Paul that no art of theological exegesis can bridge. In . . . the Sermon on the Mount the typical disciple in the eyes of Jesus is not the poor sinner who cries for redemption but the servant of God who is wholly obedient to his Lord.[31]

Windisch notes, however, that this duality between Jesus and Paul is already evident in the teaching of Jesus itself, for, on the one hand, "Jesus endeavors to present the relevance and reasonableness of his demands as clearly as possible in order thereby to induce everyone to fulfill them" while, on the other hand,

he himself draws his hearers' attention to the fact that he is requiring something very, very difficult. In the former instance, it is manifest that he joyously expects that large numbers of men will be able to do the will of God if they are but urged to do so and if its individual demands are placed before them. In the latter instance, the preacher is free of all illusions and seeks to make his hearers also aware of the seriousness of the situation.[32]

Windisch locates the root of this duality both in the nature of the message and in the personality of Jesus—in Jesus as both a teacher of wisdom and an eschatological preacher of repentance. When the masses did not respond to his call, Jesus concentrated on the formation of a small group of disciples upon whom he impressed the urgency of the situation which put his own ability to fulfill the divine command to the supreme test in Gethsemane.[33] The assumed impracticability of the Sermon on the Mount that is so obvious to theologians like Stange, Kittel, and Bultmann never occurred to Matthew, Jesus, or his disciples: "Jesus takes it for granted that we will make no recourse to legal procedure and likewise that we will keep far from us 'anger, lustful passion, and hate.' " The situation of a human being before God is seen differently by Jesus than by Paul:

Our inability (apart from the Spirit) to fulfill the command, to which Paul gives so great a place in preaching and teaching, is not discussed in

---

[31]Ibid., 107.

[32]Ibid., 108.

[33]Ibid., 110.

Jesus' sayings, is not presupposed, and is only hinted at occasionally and under special circumstances.[34]

The teaching of Jesus, like that of the prophets, was . . . the declaration of an ethic of obedience. If that teaching is to be correctly understood, the doctrine that Paul develops in Romans 3 to 8 must be left entirely out of consideration.[35]

"In view of the necessity of interpreting the commands literally," Windisch argues that the Sermon on the Mount "has no political reference whatever. It is related to a man's neighbor, brother, enemy, and judge but not to his fellow countryman, fellow citizen, superior, employer, or governor. It is individualistic."[36] Social and national considerations are beyond its horizon.

In exploring "Christ and his attitude towards Judaism in the Sermon on the Mount," Windisch observes that "Matthew and his Christ pursue two diverse ends. They seek, on the one hand, to supersede Judaism, and, on the other hand, to fulfill it."[37] Windisch argues that in Judaism such radical sayings as those of Jesus "are essentially foreign while in the Christian gospel they are all that remain of Judaism."[38] But he appears to disqualify this assertion by pointing out that "even the most conservative Christian theologian has to admit that every word of the Sermon has some parallel in the Talmud and that this fact cannot be explained by postulating the influence of the former on the latter.[39]

Windisch notes that

the teaching matter in the Sermon on the Mount . . . lacks any radical impregnation with Christology. Fellowship with God and experience of salvation are not mediated by the person of Christ. The idea of Christ does not include his function as redeemer. There is no promise of the reception of the Spirit of God. . . . [However] the Messianic idea in the Sermon on the Mount includes Jesus' authority as a teacher, his authority as prophet,

---

[34]Ibid., 117.

[35]Ibid., 121.

[36]Ibid., 122.

[37]Ibid., 131.

[38]Ibid., 132.

[39]Ibid., 137.

and his prospective authority as world judge. This in itself possessed the power to inspire the formation of the Church.[40]

"The Sermon on the Mount," Windisch adds, "belongs wholly within the framework of Israelitish-Jewish religion." Nevertheless, Jewish rabbinism is not congenial to the Sermon; if it were, the opposition of rabbis to Jesus would be inexplicable. They took offense at Jesus' ethic of obedience and at the self-conscious personal relationship he assumed with respect to his teaching.[41] Although Jesus stands wholly within the Jewish tradition, he became alienated from rabbinical Judaism: "The Sermon on the Mount contains much that is Jewish, but as a whole it is anti-Jewish. In the Talmud there is much to be found that is 'Christian,' but as a whole it is anti-Christian."[42]

Finally, Windisch addresses himself to the task of theological exegesis to discern the meaning of the Sermon on the Mount for our time. At this point, Windisch is confronted with an important decision—whether "to regard the Sermon on the Mount as a binding authority" or to assume the freedom to employ it as one wishes. In the former instance, one "must either regard the Law, the doctrine of obedience, the assumption that the commands are capable of fulfillment, and the postulate that obedience is the condition of salvation as authoritative elements of the universal Christian gospel" or admit that one "no longer considers the ethic and the doctrine of salvation of the Sermon on the Mount in their original form as normative."[43] Windisch decides that

> since Jesus completed his work in Jerusalem, since the Passion, since Easter and Pentecost, we can accept only certain parts of the Sermon on the Mount as the divine proclamation to us of the Lord of the Church. Another foundation for its demands and promises has to be laid.[44]

Windisch identifies two objections to be raised against the literal interpretation of the Sermon—that is, against "its true and original meaning": (1) "the principle by which the Sermon incorporates ethics into a procla-

---

[40]Ibid., 139.

[41]Ibid., 144.

[42]Ibid., 151.

[43]Ibid., 171.

[44]Ibid., 172.

mation of judgment'' and (2) ''the particular formulation of individual demands.''[45] The former objection ''in principle'' is based on the realization that ''the requisite attitude and action, upon which our salvation and life are made dependent, is highly problematic'' without ''any promise of help from above'' or ''any indication of a way of escape from the terrible peril into which the Sermon on the Mount has cast us.''[46] The literal interpretation literally drives us to despair:

> If Christ's words really have to be ''done,'' our filial relationship to God becomes a doubtful possession, and for us the door to God's Kingdom will remain shut. . . . Our fate is the fate of the ''many'' (Matthew 7:13); it is definitive destruction! If any way of escape is open, that way is unknown to the Sermon on the Mount. . . . Where are we to seek comfort, encouragement, help?[47]

The familiar pattern is to find this consolation in the Pauline gospel with its two propositions: (1) that Christ by his blood redeemed us from the curse of disobedience and (2) the required attitudes and virtues are produced in us as the fruit of the Spirit. However, for Windisch,

> the imposing doctrine of the cancellation of God's curse by the blood of Christ . . . is not altogether acceptable. . . . [for] it involves too great a depreciation of the Sermon on the Mount and for that matter the entire gospel of Jesus.[48]

Since ''Jesus' gospel recognizes a fellowship of the saved that is not predicated on eschatological revelation and whose realization is by no means only a result of the death of Christ,'' Windisch proceeds to explore the alternative of taking ''theological hints from the Sermon itself as to how we are saved and helped out of the peril into which it has cast us.'' He concedes that ''there is an element of free interpretation in this'' but reasons that ''it is less arbitrary than its Pauline alternative.'' To begin, the first four beatitudes stand ''in contrast to the rigorous demands,'' for in them ''Jesus renews the proclamation of salvation preached by the prophets and confirms the hope of salvation sung by the devout psalmists.'' The poor,

---

[45]Ibid.

[46]Ibid., 172-73.

[47]Ibid., 173.

[48]Ibid., 174.

the mourners, the hungry and thirsty whose full reward is in the age to come may feel themselves "blessed" even now "if they are filled with the passionate longing for holiness, for fellowship with God."[49] "There are therefore many ways to God, and the person who is conscious of his spiritual poverty in God's sight is at least moving in the right direction." The second set of four beatitudes requires the attitude or will expressed in "a merciful character, purity of heart, active concern for peace, and patient perseverence when we are persecuted because of the righteousness we serve."[50] Once we have grasped God's outstretched hand of mercy he creates in us the will to show mercy and to make peace and to do so with spontaneous joy:

> Unwittingly, we become organs of the divine will to peace for men. The glorious prospect is ours of becoming children of God, children who belong to the Father because they are learning to do as the Father does, because in what they do they are allowed to function as instruments of God. . . . Thus our thesis that the message of salvation in the Sermon on the Mount is based wholly upon the experience of salvation under the old covenant receives renewed confirmation.[51]

Jesus authorizes us to pray for forgiveness as we pray for bread:

> If we at least forgive our enemies, we can petition the Father in full confidence for the forgiveness of our sins. . . . This faith in forgiveness is the way we are saved out of the spiritual distress into which the attempt to "carry out" the Sermon on the Mount casts us. While the word declares that the angry emotion, the lustful passion, the revengeful desire, and all care and anxiety in religious living are sinful, it also tells us that there is forgiveness, that our sins do not cut us off entirely from God, and that God is ready at all times to renew his fellowship with us.
> This consolation is expressed beautifully and clearly in the verse about God's hearing of our prayer (Matthew 7:11).[52]

The Sermon, Windisch reasons, presupposes "the work of the Spirit":

> Apart from the Spirit it is impossible to serve God wholeheartedly, to love one's fellow man and even one's enemy as oneself, to seek the King-

---

[49]Ibid., 175.

[50]Ibid., 176.

[51]Ibid., 177.

[52]Ibid., 181-82.

dom with complete abandon, to keep the heart pure of all passion, and to pray to God in utter trust. While this thought never occurred to Matthew, it does to us. . . . The God who demands perfection and who passes judgment on imperfection is also the God who bestows forgiveness and grants the Spirit.[53]

The Sermon's exclusive orientation to the idea of judgment Windisch holds to be a defect due in part to the Evangelist's eschatological frame of reference, for, upon examining the Sermon's content, "we discover a sphere of the grace of God and of the fellowship with God to which its imperatives can be organically related."[54]

Windisch identifies two reasons why we do not meet Jesus' anticipation: (1) our efforts are too feeble to accomplish what he demanded and (2) "we are disinclined, in actual everyday life, to cut ourselves loose from those ethical and religious responsibilities whose claims upon us we admit." Consequently, Windisch does not regard the demands of the Sermon on the Mount "as imperatives or prescripts that we are to fulfill literally," but rather

as expressions . . . of a religious attitude that, under other circumstances, may have to be phrased in other ways. When someone strikes us, insults us, or plunders our possessions, we will make use of the existing legal machinery to prevent a repetition of the incident, endeavoring at the same time to combat in ourselves every feeling of revenge or desire to retaliate. We will not say that in so doing we are fulfilling the command as Jesus intended it to be fulfilled, for what Jesus intended was literal fulfillment; but we shall be able to say that we do express by such conduct and are seeking to express by it the attitude he had in view.

In other instances our behavior can only be described as a compromise. We will continue to "lay up treasures" when opportunity affords, whether it be for ourselves and our families or for the social grouping to which we belong, and therefore are subject to the criticism of Jesus.

Although we recognize Jesus' logic in principle, we consider it to be valid for us only when "associated with intelligent reflection on the ways by which our natural existence can be maintained." We must perform our duty within our

organized social group without forgetting the struggle for the Kingdom and

---

[53]Ibid., 184-85.

[54]Ibid., 188.

the power and the glory of God. We combine two activities that Jesus strictly differentiated in the belief that the God who made the world, who ordained that we should work with our own hands, and the God who will bring his Kingdom and who has a heaven prepared for us, are one and the same.[55]

We admit the existence of a conflict between the demands of Jesus and the conditions of life:

> Jesus does not ignore the created order; he only views it from a different angle. He seeks to inspire us with enthusiastic faith that the created order itself makes all temporal anxieties unnecessary: that it provides for the maintenance of daily life. A different understanding of the actual conditions of creation compels us to correct Jesus' assumptions. We interpret the duty of laboring and making timely provision for economic and social necessities as a part of God's created order.

Thus, we paraphrase Jesus' word about the example of the lilies and the birds (Matthew 6:26, 28) to read:

> How much more will God clothe and nourish us, who sow and reap and gather into barns in obedience to his created order or who share in the bread of other men's labor in exchange for the contributions we make to the service of the social group in which he has placed us![56]

Windisch finds it ''more difficult to discover a clue in the Sermon on the Mount'' to the right attitude towards an enemy in the case of war. He maintains that,

> in approving a war and taking part in it, we are aware that we are serving our nation and our constitutional leaders but at the same time transgressing a commandment of Jesus that might be applicable. We can take refuge in the knowledge that the conflict is really one between the command to love one's neighbor and the command to love one's enemy; that in deciding against the command to love our enemies, we are nevertheless remaining obedient to another of Jesus' sayings.

Windisch concedes

> that the better part would have been to create a situation in which this fateful and dangerous conflict could not have arisen. The holy task of those who have the strength and the ability for it remains that of laboring to-

---

[55]Ibid., 189-90.
[56]Ibid., 191.

gether as true *pacifici* to change a situation that repeatedly throws us into a fearful and, in the long run, intolerable conflict.[57]

Jesus acknowledged that waging war is the natural expression of every worldly power. But the concepts ''love of Fatherland'' and ''defense of Fatherland'' are foreign to Jesus' horizon. One can only justify them if one ascribes to the nation an ethical character which is not conceded in the gospel of Jesus.[58]

In summary, Windisch finds that:

the Sermon on the Mount is not hostile to the world or to civilization. . . . Nevertheless, it fails to recognize any duties or responsibilities imposed upon us by virtue of participation in such an order. This indifference is explained in part by its eschatological perspective, . . . in part by the radically individualistic articulation of its ethic . . . and in part by its ''social teaching.''

That teaching, as in Jewish pietism, sanctions only the most necessary means of livelihood and provides that any excess shall be used only for alms, a way of life which ''Jesus himself demonstrated and prescribed for his disciples.''[59] Windisch holds such an attitude to be impracticable, for

even the religious anarchist can never completely dissociate his life from the economic and national organization that he repudiates. . . . We must honestly admit that we do not fulfill the Sermon on the Mount in many respects. We are satisfied to find a relative rather than an absolute disparagement of ''earthly things'' and to struggle against the worldly temptations that assail our attitude of faith.[60]

Windisch proposes supplementing the Gospel by those ''true and tested rules of conduct taken from the Old Testament'' that accord with the spirit of the Gospel. On this basis ''we attempt to outline a Christian morality for society and for state, to develop a Christian social and political ethic.''[61]

The final assessment of the Sermon on the Mount by Windisch approximates that of Herrmann and Dibelius with the significant difference that, in contrast to them, he does not identify his understanding of the Sermon with its original meaning:

---

[57]Ibid., 192.

[58]My ET from the second German edition (Leipzig: J. C. Hinrichs Verlag, 1937) 166.

[59]Ibid., 193.

[60]Ibid., 194.

[61]Ibid., 195.

It is we who do not regard Jesus' sayings as rules and regulations that require literal fulfillment. It is we who interpret them as general principles and as illustrations of the way these principles work themselves out in concrete historical situations. It is we who hold that as illustrations they are not mandatory upon us. It is we who, from suggestions in individual sayings, have put together the portrait of a child of God, of a disciple of Jesus, of a man who belongs to God's Kingdom and his righteousness, sins, and still remains the object of God's grace. It is we who see in the Sermon an ethos that is never static and that cannot possibly be defined as the sum of separate commandments, an attitude that in its becoming and its being feels itself bound to the gospel revealed in Jesus but that can also hear the voice of God in the call of the hour.[62]

If the best theory is a long string that ties all conflicting propositions together in one bundle, then Windisch is to be commended for having by all indications somehow accomplished this feat. He fully agrees with Tolstoy that Jesus said exactly what he meant and expected his hearers to do exactly as he said. But, at the same time, Windisch concurs with Stange that a literal understanding of Jesus' demands invariably drives one to despair. Consequently, Windisch endorses Naumann's conclusion that modern man cannot, need not, and—to the extent that he is enlightened—should not do what Jesus commanded because he is "disinclined" to cut himself loose from what Baumgarten has depicted as cultural responsibility. Together with Wünsch, Windisch considers himself obliged to "correct Jesus' assumptions" about the "created order" on the basis of his own superior understanding of the Creator's will, so as to enable us to combine the duty of maintaining the world—a duty which Jesus is said to have sadly neglected—with the task of proclaiming the Kingdom. And so Windisch must rewrite Jesus' text about 'cares' (Matthew 6:26-28) in order to imply the opposite of what it now says.

But to find even "a clue in the Sermon on the Mount to the right attitude we are to assume towards an enemy in the case of war" is for Windisch much "more difficult to discover," since " 'love of country' and 'defense of country' are foreign to Jesus' horizon." Jesus' horizon is unfortunately so limited that Windisch, in agreement with Baumgarten, concludes that Jesus' teaching is only "individualistic" and has "no political reference whatever." Quite like Schweitzer, Windisch nevertheless un-

---

[62]Ibid., 196.

dertakes to build a bridge to the estranged otherness of Jesus' antiquated world- and life-view by employing Paul's doctrine of the Spirit, on the assumption that his own kind of "theological exegesis can legitimately do this" for the same reasons that the "Paulinizing exegesis" of Stange and Kittel may not.

Bultmann rightly sensed that the decisive question to be put to Windisch is "whether the demands in point of fact are fulfilled."[63] Why, despite his emphatic defense of the practicability of Jesus' demands, does Windisch not assume that either he or anyone else actually fulfills them? Windisch counters by repeating that "the impracticability of the Sermon on the Mount that is so obvious to us never occurred to them"—neither to Jesus nor to his followers. But Windisch does not provide a criterion for evaluating or perpetuating what is "obvious" to us over against its non-occurrence to Jesus and his disciples.

Because of this inadequacy—not in Jesus but in Windisch—the ethical import of the latter's interpretation of "The Meaning of the Sermon on the Mount" does not go beyond the conclusion of Bornhäuser that contemporary application to Jesus' demands beyond the original disciple group is unwarranted. In his own words, Windisch considers his evaluation of the Sermon on the Mount to "approach very close to that of Herrmann and Dibelius," both of whom he derided for modernizing Jesus. He purports to differ from them not in his theological interpretation but only in the established basis for it: the difference is that what Herrmann and Dibelius ascribe to Jesus, Windisch assumes for himself—the responsibility and the reasons for limiting the contemporary applicability of the Sermon on the Mount. The essential difference as Windisch sees it lies not in criticizing Jesus for his irrelevance but in admitting that we do so.

Precisely in this admission, Windisch stands nearest of all to Naumann, except that Naumann not only conceded that the Sermon on the Mount cannot be fulfilled by us but resolutely proceeded to work out the pragmatic implications of this hard 'truth' that the Sermon is no longer authoritative for us. But Windisch leaves with us the theological and moral disillusionment that "our behavior can only be described as a compromise." Stange and Kittel at least provided a theological frame of reference within which to validate our failure in the providence of God as an evil

---

[63]Ibid., 117.

means towards a good end, but Windisch imparts an uncanny misgiving that there must be something spurious about theological enlightenment if it allows us to objectify our disobedience to Jesus without feeling any particular need to do anything about it.

Schweitzer revealed, not by his thought but through his life, how one can hold to Jesus despite criticizing his self-understanding to the point of rejection. Windisch forces upon us the question of integrity within the theologizing process itself. To what extent can one pursue historical exegesis without becoming captivated by what Jesus felt and wanted? And to what extent can one undertake theological interpretation as a modern reflection about a biblical text without existential openness to the Spirit that inspired it? At what point in the separation of these two disciplines does historical understanding become theological commitment?

In the final analysis, it is Windisch, who, by the objectivity of historical exegesis, has shown—far more convincingly than did Bornhäuser—that the Sermon on the Mount stands entirely within the context of the Old Testament and of Judaism. Therein lies, all criticism aside, the real merit of his work. It remains for others to develop the theological and ethical implications of this fact.

In 1936 Professor Johannes Schneider inquired into the meaning of the Sermon on the Mount as the basis for Christian living (*Der Sinn der Bergpredigt. Von Der Grundordnung christlichen Lebens*. Berlin: Furche Verlag, 1936 [Band 12 der Sammlung: "Aus der Welt der Bibel"]). For him the frame of reference for understanding the Sermon on the Mount is the Kingdom of God as proclaimed by Jesus especially in the Beatitudes. In these blessings Jesus assures the Kingdom to those "who in their inner and outer situation are called" (20). As Schweitzer, Schneider understands the Kingdom to be an eschatological otherworldly entity that God himself will bring about in his time. When it appears, everything will be new, and history as we now know it will end. At one point in history this new reality became visible: in Jesus the Messiah, in his words and deeds. To win people for this Kingdom Jesus proclaims a fundamental change of mind (*Sinnesänderung*), a reorientation of one's whole life which comes about through repentance and forgiveness of sin (21). Those who believe his message recognize, confess, and follow him as their Messiah, forming the Church of the elect who are members of this Kingdom and who will enter it when it comes.

But in the meantime, how shall these disciples who no longer belong to the old aeon continue to live in it during the interim before the Kingdom comes? It is to this question, says Schneider, that the Sermon on the Mount provides the answer. Its purpose is to instruct the disciples about their living as people of the new aeon within the old aeon (23). The Sermon on the Mount is not about presuppositions for entering the Kingdom but about its consequences for disciples during this interim in which they are to manifest in their actual living the "better righteousness." In the Sermon on the Mount Jesus shows how this new Kingdom-order of living based on love of God and neighbor applies to the human relations of Kingdom-of-God people. They are endowed with a new holy life-force and in the midst of this world constitute unique centers of strength (31). Within the world these disciples remain strangers, and, because they cannot without reservation affirm the world as it is, their estrangement may lead to hatred and persecution.

These Kingdom-of-God people, however, often fail to measure up to what they profess to be. Though not dominated by the powers of this world, they are, paradoxically, still subject to its temptations. Apart from God's mercy the resulting tension would be unbearable, consequently, Jesus taught them to pray, "Forgive us our guilt" and "Deliver us from evil." Jesus intended his disciples to fulfill the demands of the Sermon on the Mount, "but, given the actual conditions to which the disciples are subject on this earth, it factually cannot be fulfilled in its radical form. Therefore, the disciples constantly require renewed forgiveness" (36).

In all this it should be remembered, says Schneider, that the world itself is in no way obligated by the new order of God's Kingdom. "It has its own autonomy (*Eigengesetzlichkeit*) which determines its actual being (*Sosein*) regulating all conditions, relations, and associations." What is required of Jesus' disciples is not required of people who belong wholly to this world. The Sermon on the Mount will never apply to the lives of those who do not belong to the Kingdom (37). "The Sermon on the Mount is the Kingdom-of-God ethic of radical disciple-obedience. It reveals the divine order which will some day be unlimitedly valid." In the interval between the proclamation of the Kingdom and its realization, the Sermon on the Mount is generally valid as ground rules (*Grundordnung*) for the life of the elect minority of Jesus' disciples who walk the narrow way and enter the narrow gate as representatives of the new humanity. The Sermon on the Mount is Jesus' model for his Church (39).

What does the Sermon on the Mount then mean for us today? The disciples were part of Jewish national and religious society as a special group within Judaism. We Gentile-Christians have been freed from the curse of the law. "The particularities of the law . . . have no more meaning for us." The will of God expressed through the law applies to us, but we have been freed from the letter of the law and are personally bound to Christ. "Since we live after Easter and Pentecost and after the apostles, we must consider the whole gospel" (41). "Not only the Sermon on the Mount but also the Word of the Cross and of the living Christ has been entrusted to us" (42). In contrast to the disciples, we are citizens of two worlds. "We have our responsibilities and commitments from which we cannot withdraw, for they lie within the domain of our natural life to which God has directed us" (43). Perhaps we can bring both realms into harmony, but our peculiar situation puts us under great tension. This tension is unresolvable so long as both aeons make their claims upon us. Sometimes, "for the sake of our neighbor and our nation it is impossible for us to act as we are commanded in the Sermon on the Mount." All that then remains for us to do is to pray for the forgiveness of our guilt without which we could not live with ourselves (45). "The strength for new obedience in the tension in which our Christian existence places us comes only through forgiveness. Only as people who stand under this forgiveness and who in their personal experience know about God's forgiving love can we even risk to fulfill the disciple-call with which we have been charged'' (46).

According to Schneider, the Sermon on the Mount is essentially Interim Ethic. But unlike Schweitzer, Schneider does not press the eschatological assumptions to their logical conclusion. Therein lies his weakness and perhaps also his strength. He never makes explicit, as Bornhäuser did, that the relevance of the Sermon on the Mount is expressly limited to the historic disciples. Schneider's assumption that God himself will bring about his Kingdom in his time does, however, argue against understanding the Sermon on the Mount as the Church's mandate to participate in its realization. Similarly, his understanding of election tends to neutralize the existentiality of Jesus' call to discipleship as far as we are concerned. Schneider's treatise lacks the incisive delineation of Windisch in specifying the distinction between historical considerations and present implications. We are left with the underlying ambiguity as to whether, and if so to what extent, the Sermon on the Mount actually applies to us now as it did to Jesus' disciples then. On the one hand, it is assumed that we as Christians are included with the original disciples in an indefinitely expanded interim since we share their tension. On the other hand, it is clearly stated that we are excused from their obligations since (1) we are citizens of both worlds whereas they as members of God's Kingdom were pilgrims and strangers on earth and (2) because we as Gentiles are freed from the law by virtue of our personal attachment to Christ while they were bound to Jesus' radical obedience ethic in a Jewish way. This is Schneider's existential and theological rationalization of the double standard. For the small elect minority—whoever they may be—there is only the narrow way of the Sermon on the Mount ethic, but for all the rest of us there is worldly autonomy to accomodate our responsibilities and commitments which conflict with the teachings of Christ. Schneider assumes (1) that ''God has directed us'' to these commitments of natural life and that (2) God therefore tolerates and perpetually forgives the contradictions we indulge in ''for the sake of our neighbor and our nation.'' It appears, therefore, that according to Schneider Jesus' ''Grundordnung christlichen Lebens'' is neither the basis (Grund-) nor pattern (Ordnung) of our own lives. Consequently, what we today have most in common with those disciples is not their radical radiant obedience but that debilitating, despairing Anfechtung which perpetually drives us to plead for mercy and forgiveness lest we perish in our sins and their consequences. Whatever the real Sinn or meaning of the Sermon on the Mount, Schneider's understanding of it reiterates Luther's emphasis on the consolation of grace more than its triumph.

MARTIN DIBELIUS:
THE SERMON ON THE MOUNT
AS ESCHATOLOGICAL STIMULUS

The Sermon on the Mount . . . is a collection of radical, absolute commands and sayings. . . . The man who uttered them did not consider the circumstances of our life and the conditions of this world. He looks only to the coming world, to the Kingdom of Heaven.[1]

The Sermon on the Mount makes demands too exacting to be fulfilled in life on this earth, even in the life of the Saviour himself, for his life was bound by earthly circumstances too. . . . We are not allowed to interpret the Sermon on the Mount according to any incidents or circumstances in the life of Jesus, as is often done.[2]

The sayings of the Sermon on the Mount were originally meant in an absolute sense, but as a law for the coming Kingdom rather than as a law governing life in this world. Their practicability for the workaday world was therefore originally restricted. The Christians undertook to alter and adapt them in order to make them directly applicable to the circumstances of this life.[3]

[These] words of Jesus were Signs of the Kingdom of God, nothing more and nothing less. Nothing more, for they do not introduce the Kingdom of Heaven on earth; and nothing less, for they are far more than advice and prescriptions for life during this age. . . . The radicalness of the Sermon on the Mount is our judgment, its announcement of another world is our hope.[4]

The heroic ideal of doing the radical will of God . . . can assert itself only in combination with an eschatological outlook. Today, this eschatological outlook is lost. . . . Consequently, the ideal of full obedience to God's will seems impracticable.

---

[1]Martin Dibelius, *The Sermon on the Mount* (New York: Charles Scribner's Sons, 1940) 65.

[2]Ibid., 87.

[3]Ibid., 94-95.

[4]Ibid., 101-102.

The commandments of the Sermon on the Mount have no validity for the workaday life.[5]

The Sermon on the Mount is not an ideal but an eschatological stimulus *intended to make men well-acquainted with the pure will of God. It does not speak of human or worldly conditions but only of God's eternal will. We would misunderstand the radicalism of this will, if we were to believe that the Sermon on the Mount had been pronounced as a body of instruction for this life or as a program of reform for this world.*[6]

Martin Dibelius[7] of Heidelberg applied his insights from form criticism to the problem of the Sermon on the Mount in the hope of articulating the sense in which the sermon is still valid for us today. He observed that many contemporaries have lost confidence in the Christian religion because those who profess it have failed to prevent war and failed to provide solutions for the social problems of mankind. Consequently, a generation of concerned people not associated with the established church demands to know "whether the Christian message may still be regarded, as it formerly was, as a rule of conduct for mankind . . . and, if not, where the man of today can find such a rule." Dibelius agrees that it is not adequate for the elite to have a certain philosophical standard for their private lives. "An authoritative message for family life, for commercial life, for political life" is needed, "a message which is applicable to the requirements

---

[5]Ibid., 110.

[6]Ibid., 135-36.

[7]Martin Dibelius (1883-1947) was born in Dresden, where his father Franz Wilhelm Dibelius was court theologian; he became Professor of New Testament at Berlin in 1910 and joined the faculty of Heidelberg in 1915. He is known for his form-critical and exegetical studies of the New Testament, and for his attempt to determine the abiding validity of New Testament ethics in the context of eschatology. In addition to numerous essays, his major works include *Die Geisterwelt im Glauben des Paulus* (1909), *I, II Thess., Phil.* (HNT 11, 1911), *Die urchristliche Überlieferung von Johannes der Täufer* (FRLANT, 1911), *Kol., Eph., Phlm.* (HNT 12, 1912), *I, II Tim., Tit.* (HNT 13, 1913), *Die Formgeschichte des Evangeliums* (1919), *Der Brief des Jakobus*, 7th ed. (Meyer Komm. XV, 1921), *Der Hirt des Hermas* (HNT Erg. Bd. Teil IV, 1923), *Geschichtliche und übergeschichtliche Religion im Christentum* (1925), *Evangelium und Welt* (1925, 1929), *Geschichte der urchristlichen Literatur* I, II (1926), *Die Unbedingtheit des Evangeliums und die Bedingtheit der Ethik* (1926), *Das soziale Motiv im Neuen Testament* (1934), *Die Botschaft von Jesus Christus* (1935), *Jesus* (1939), *The Sermon on the Mount* (1940). See W. G. Kümmel, "Martin Dibelius als Theologe," *Theologische Literaturzeitung* 74 (1949):129-40.

of this troubled time" and which gives moral guidance to the man on the street, the governor of a state, the manager of a factory, and the scholar in his study. Dibelius did not seek an ideal blueprint for individual and social life, but rather "a dominant voice in the struggle for life, a powerful commanding force motivating our actions, and a star illuminating our way."[8]

Until the rationalism of the seventeenth century, the Gospel had continued to function as a norm for the Christian segment of humankind. But, observes Dibelius, since the secularization and mechanization of modern life, new values have overshadowed all supernatural obligations: "Thus, we are faced not only by a crisis in the Christian religion but rather by a crisis in all the standards of human life." Though "guidance for humanity as a whole is entirely lacking," Dibelius is convinced "in spite of everything, the Christian message actually has redeeming force and significance for mankind" but that it "has not been fully interpreted."[9] Further enlightenment requires discernment of the world of thought at the time of the Sermon on the Mount prior to approaching the problem of its relevance for today. First, we need to know which sayings are authentic words of Jesus and what they meant in their original context. Since we have the Sermon on the Mount as the content of preaching, we now need to understand the intentions of the evangelist who wrote this document and how the first Christian readers (for whom Jesus was not only teacher but also Saviour) interpreted it: "They understood Jesus' sermon not as wisdom . . . but as revelation, not as the address of a Rabbi but as a message from God."[10]

Apart from discerning how the first readers understood this document, we must of necessity inquire, "Are we still in a position to understand and to carry out the Sermon on the Mount as a message from God?" Is the ideal of this Sermon still practicable for us? If it is, "why is our life so far from this ideal?" If it is not, "what shall we say about our claim to be Christians?"[11] Those rejecting Christianity point to the discrepancy between the teaching of Jesus and the practice of Christians and generally share the counsel of Nietzsche, who in his *Zarathustra* suggested: "They should sing better hymns, then I would believe in their Redeemer; his disciples should

---

[8]*The Sermon on the Mount*, 3.

[9]Ibid., 4.

[10]Ibid., 10.

[11]Ibid., 11.

look more like redeemed people.'' Apparently, we ourselves stand judged by our interpretation of the Sermon on the Mount:

> If its efficacy is not recognizable in the world, we have to choose between two explanations. Either its time has gone and the Sermon on the Mount is a document of the past—and nothing more. Or . . . its time will come and we are not yet in the right position to be true Christians.

For Dibelius, this crucial choice constitutes "the greatest problem which the interpretation of the Sermon on the Mount puts before us."[12]

Following these introductory reflections on the urgency of discerning what the Sermon on the Mount meant then and what it might mean now, Dibelius proceeds to explain the character of the text. We are told that Matthew 5-7 is a composition of sayings which Jesus delivered at various occasions. Matthew arranged this material in a systematic rather than chronological way: "By so arranging his material, he made the Sermon on the Mount an ordinance governing the communities of his own age."[13] In addition to disregarding the historical order of events and sayings of Jesus, Matthew (or the community he represented and for whom he wrote) made certain textual alterations:

> The best known of them is the exception which Matthew grants to the prohibition of divorce (5:32). In the case of unchastity divorce is allowed, but, in the original wording of the sentence as preserved in Mark, divorce is absolutely forbidden: "What God has joined, then, man must not separate" (10:9).[14]

Dibelius ascribes these modifications

> to the tendency to make possible the impossible. In their original wording, some of the sayings of Jesus were not rules fitted for the common life. . . . They seem too paradoxical to be carried out; they were impracticable. When they were connected with other sayings which were really practicable

---

[12]Ibid., 12.

[13]Ibid., 18.

[14]"In trying to understand the reason for the change, we may imagine a situation where a pagan wife of a Christian has a lover," and it consequently becomes impossible for the Christian husband and for the Christian community to tolerate this situation. This, or some situation like it, may be what determined the Matthean wording of the saying and required the exception which it makes in the case of unchastity. This situation was possible only at an advanced period in the life of the Church when the Christian communities included men and women of the well-to-do classes." Ibid., 18, 19.

commands, the more or less paradoxical words were transformed in the direction of a practical and living realism. In this way the paradoxical sayings became practicable, and the whole mass of sayings in the Sermon on the Mount became a Christian law.[15]

In compiling these sayings in this way, Matthew

> wanted to incite the Christians of his own generation to live their lives according to these rules, and he endeavored to present a program of Christian ethics for all generations of the Church.[16]

> Are these rules and counsels practicable, and, if so, is their fulfillment desirable? In other words, is the Sermon on the Mount a law, a message, a vision, or a fancy?[17]

We are urged to investigate the *original* meaning of Jesus' sayings prior to their interpretation by the Early Church. Taking, for example, the group of sayings against 'cares' (Matthew 6:25-34), Dibelius ventures two form-critical judgments. First, "Be not anxious for tomorrow . . . " (Matthew 6:34) is a popular Jewish maxim inserted by the Evangelist "as a commentary on the words of our Lord" and, as such, is "obviously out of place after the heroic command of the preceding verse, 'Seek ye first his Kingdom.' "[18] Second, the query, "Who can by anxious care add one cubit to his height?" (Matthew 6:27), "should also be regarded in all probability as an independent saying, inserted here . . . out of harmony with the context, and should be omitted from our section." The remainder comprises Jesus' twofold warning, "Be not anxious for food . . . or for clothing." "Did he mean," Dibelius asks,

> that the disciples should live without cares and provision for the future? Did he really mean to recommend imprudence? Or are his words to be interpreted as a serious and therefore purposely exaggerated warning against greed for gain?[19]

At the outset, Dibelius would have us understand the eschatological nature of this pericope; it assumes "the hearers will live to see the end of

---

[15]Ibid., 19.

[16]Ibid., 21.

[17]Ibid., 44.

[18]Ibid., 46.

[19]Ibid., 47.

the world. They are not obliged to provide for their livelihood in a distant future, for there will be no distant future at all."[20] Once this has become clear, we need to realize that Jesus' command to improvidence "does not refer to a more natural form of conduct, illlustrated by ravens and lilies . . . but to a form of existence that would be free from all cares and worldly anxieties."[21] This is the divine will and therefore it applies not only when the Kingdom comes but before its actual coming, for

> the pure will of God does not suffer any restriction. . . . Jesus proclaims in an absolute way the pure will of God. This will is not confined to an interim and is thus not valid only for the period till the end of the world; it is God's actual demand upon men at all times and for all time. But it will attain its full validity only in the Kingdom of God. It is the sign of this passing age that the fulfillment of God's will is hampered and embarrassed by the conditions of our worldly existence. In the face of the coming end, Jesus proclaims God's demand without regard to any such considerations. God's will does not depend upon the eschatological hope and expectation: it is eternal, like God. The eschatological expectation, however, gives the occasion for the proclamation of the divine will, without regard to the circumstances of everyday existence. The eschatological expectation makes men free from all conditions of this world, free to understand what is the pure, unconditional will of God. Therefore . . . the passage is to be taken *in an absolute sense because it is eschatological*. . . . The warning against anxieties is the expression of a religious radicalism, not a rigid radicalism, but an eschatological one.[22]

This solution also applies to the other absolute commands and prohibitions constituting the nucleus of the Sermon on the Mount. We turn to the best known of all passages, the sayings about retaliation: "Whoever smites you on the right cheek, turn to him the other also" and "Love your

---

[20]"'Seek the Kingdom of God and all these things shall be added unto you!' . . . is not an oracle applying to this world; it would be quite out of harmony with the spirit of the Gospel to have Jesus promise such worldly things to those who accept the Gospel for their life here and now. Apparently the meaning of the sentence is: you must seek the Kingdom of God and nothing else! And when the Kingdom comes then all your needs will be fulfilled." Ibid., 49-50.

[21]Ibid., 50.

[22]Ibid., 51-52.

enemies'' (Matthew 5:39, 43). According to Dibelius, Jesus was thinking not of national enemies[23] but of private enemies:

> enemies who hail one before a judge, bad neighbors, etc. This is the real meaning of the word enemy for his listeners. So understood the command is much more difficult to fulfill than if we give it a limited political sense. It is the private enemy whom the simple farmer or workman really hates with all the fervor of his heart. Hatred of a national enemy is less intense and harder to develop. Hatred of the enemy is not familiar in the trenches; the real national hate is the work of stay-at-homes, not of soldiers. The most common and intense hatred is that directed against one's private enemy, e.g., the unfriendly neighbor, the competitor in labor, the malicious superior or ruler. And this hatred Jesus forbids, i.e., he forbids a natural psychological reaction against injustice and hostile deeds. He forbids it because hatred is opposed to the will of God. . . . Jesus not only forbids any hostile reaction but demands actions of love towards the enemy. His commandment is opposed to all the natural feeling of the human heart . . . so strangely contrary to all those reactions which men view as legitimately human. We may grant that the form of the command . . . is hyperbolic, in the Oriental manner. . . . But the word really holds good not only for the case in question but for all expressions of hatred. Hence, this formal observation must not be permitted to weaken in any way the seriousness of the command given. What Jesus proclaims here is again the pure will of God; and God demands that man should forego retaliation and hatred completely. He demands that man should be friendly and well-disposed even to his most violent and vehement antagonists. It is not a matter of legal defense, of legitimate anger, of resistance against power unjustly applied. . . . What we have before us are radical commands, an expression of the pure will of God, in no way weakened by the consideration of human necessities. This radicalism is an eschatological one. *Because* Jesus considers the Kingdom of God alone, he finds it possible to leave all worldly affairs, all human requirements, all the circumstances of human life out of consideration.[24]

---

[23]"The national enemy would need to be the Roman, and we would thus find Jesus meddling in the political problem which, as we know from another passage, from his word about paying tribute to Caesar, he wanted to leave unsolved. Moreover, it may well be questioned whether the ancient Orient had a conception of nationality, such as could produce the idea of a national enemy." Ibid., 54-55.

[24]Ibid., 55-57.

Dibelius interprets Jesus' prohibition of judging (Matthew 7:1) and his exhortation not to lay up treasures (Matthew 6:19) in much the same manner:

> Jesus refers here to practices in human life that are common and sometimes quite legitimate, but from the point of view of the coming Kingdom they are forbidden. They are significant for the condition of the old world: in a new world they will be superfluous, and the followers of Jesus must be representatives of this new world within the old age.[25]

Similar application is made of Jesus' words against oaths and divorce:

> Divorce provides the possibility of escape from this false kind of marriage. Oaths protect men from unreliable assurances. Therefore, oaths and divorce seem necessary to us as sinful men, but they are dependent upon the imperfect conditions under which we live and therefore must be abandoned even now by those who would fulfill the absolute will of God.[26]

In each instance Jesus ascribes the paradoxical nature of his commands to God Himself, who allows His sun rise on the wicked and the good and lets rain fall on the just and the unjust. On account of this paradoxical kindness—not of nature, but of God—we are to love our enemies. Likewise, the prohibition of oaths refers to God: "Man cannot swear without interfering with the rights of God, for in swearing he disposes of God as the witness of his oath."[27] As for divorce, "What God has joined together, let not man put asunder," for such dereliction destroys what God has done. And the prohibition against cares is rooted in God's sovereign will that we seek first his Kingdom.

The foundation of all Jesus' words and deeds is his eschatological concern:

> The reason why the words were spoken and why the deeds were done is the coming of the new world. The sayings of the Sermon on the Mount were uttered by Jesus in order to prepare men for the Kingdom. It was his purpose in these sayings to proclaim the will of God in all its severity, the absolute divine will, unconditioned by the circumstances of this world order. This will is, of course, the law of the Kingdom of God, but under the conditions provided by our earthly life this will in its paradox is a stum-

---

[25]Ibid., 58-59.

[26]Ibid., 59.

[27]Ibid., 60.

bling block for men. We should not mitigate or weaken this fact. We must rather emphasize the paradoxical radicalism of the commands proclaimed by Jesus in the face of the coming Kingdom.[28]

The possibility of Jesus' actually bringing "all incidents of his life into harmony with the law of the Kingdom" or of his turning the other cheek or taking an oath is, for Dibelius, a "not very fruitful" deliberation because "the conditions of the life of Jesus are not the conditions of the Kingdom of God":[29] "The Sermon on the Mount makes demands too exacting to be fulfilled in life on this earth, even in the life of the Saviour himself, for his life was bound by earthly circumstances too." From this consideration Dibelius concludes, "we are not allowed to interpret the Sermon on the Mount according to any incidents or circumstances of the life of Jesus, as is often done."

Before Easter, Jesus "was for his followers the personal embodiment of the coming Kingdom; he proclaimed its law by words, he gave a foretaste of its power by his healings, he inaugurated the new age."[30] After Easter,

> the Christians are waiting for the coming of their Lord. Consequently, all commandments of Jesus handed down to the communities assume the character of a testament. The Christians feel that Christ has instructed them to live in accordance with these sayings. They are not any longer proclamations of the will of God in all its radicalness; they become rules of conduct within the communities and are adapted to the condition of this life. They are . . . codified to form systems of ordinances like the new law laid down in the Sermon on the Mount.[31]

> The sayings of the Sermon on the Mount were originally meant in an absolute sense but as a law for the coming Kingdom rather than as a law governing life in this world. Their practicability for the workaday life was therefore originally restricted. The Christians undertook to alter and adapt them in order to make them more directly applicable to the circumstances of this life.[32]

---

[28]Ibid., 63-64.

[29]Ibid., 86.

[30]Ibid., 87.

[31]Ibid., 88.

[32]Ibid., 94-95.

Dibelius concluded that the Early Christians freely adapted the Lord's sayings to their own situation:

> If a man understood the will of God better than others before him, so that he was able to adapt this expression to the requirements of a workaday life, then with God's help by the Holy Spirit it was permitted him to do anything which might make the saying useful for a better understanding of God's will. . . . The Christians of those days expected the end of the world in the near future, . . . such alterations as they undertook had only a limited validity. The end of the world would soon come, and then in the new world the will of God alone will be of value. Whatever has been altered for the short span of life will be forgotten. Hence, it is not a sin to adapt the words of Jesus to the circumstances of the present day. The shortness of the time limits the validity of the change, and the word is thus made subject to the conditions which determine the life of the Christian in this world generally.[33]

Dibelius succinctly summarizes the theological character of the Sermon on the Mount. First, it reveals the "pure will of God and, therefore, must be fulfilled." Except for the hyperbole, "the sayings are to be regarded as practicable." Their application, however, "is limited so far as the present age is concerned. The performance of the pure will of God is in the present world consequently hindered. The real fulfillment of this great Christian law is possible only in the Kingdom of God."[34] Second, "the sayings of the Sermon on the Mount have an eschatological significance. They are the law of the Kingdom." They were not given for the interim but for eternity,

> because they represent the will of God. . . . Their standard is the existence of the coming world, not our human life within earthly circumstances. . . . Thus, the eschatological supposition enables the preacher of the Sermon on the Mount to speak as he does without any consideration for the conditions of this age.

Third, "full obedience here and now is impossible. We ought to be honest enough to confess our inability in this matter."[35] Yet we may not "overestimate the eschatological character of the Sermon on the Mount as to suppose that the fulfillment of its commandments must be postponed until

---

[33]Ibid., 96.

[34]Ibid., 97.

[35]Ibid., 98.

the coming age,'' for Jesus spoke these sayings to awaken, thrill, stimulate, and offend the listeners of his own age. Nor should we exaggerate the
hyperbolic character of Jesus' Oriental style so as to limit the validity of
his words or moderate their ideal: "The method of interpretation to which
we must give preference is that which will grieve and offend our natural
feelings."[36]

The Sermon on the Mount was not meant to be a system of ethics nor
was it Jesus' purpose, Dibelius contends, to give "a revolutionary law, the
fulfillment of which would throw the whole world into turmoil." Jesus'
words "were *signs of the Kingdom of God*, nothing more and nothing less.
Nothing more, for they do not introduce the Kingdom of Heaven on earth;
and nothing less, for they are far more than advice and prescriptions for
life during this age." Interpreting Jesus' sayings as "signs" allows us to
take them seriously as expressions of the divine will "even in this world"
while realizing that they "cannot be fully performed in this age. . . . The
radicalism of the Sermon on the Mount is our judgment; its announcement
of another world is our hope." Jesus intended his sayings as signs of hope.
After Easter, they became laws of conduct.[37]

Having explained the original meaning of Jesus' sayings as prophetic
signs proclaiming the Kingdom of Heaven and the post-Easter interpretation of these words as rules for Christian life on earth, Dibelius approaches
the final problem: "What shall we do as Christians today, if we want to be
obedient to the Sermon on the Mount?"[38]

Since A.D. 300, the Church has lived under circumstances entirely different from those presupposed in the Sermon on the Mount: "It soon became evident (to some extent even in the time of the ancient Church) that
there is a gap between this ideal of Christian conduct and real life." The
primary reason for this breach in credibility is the change in eschatological
outlook:

> The Church, after several decades of defeated hope, came to the in-
> sight that it was its duty to cope with an enduring world and to provide for
> centuries of existence. This was a radically different outlook which com-

---

[36]Ibid., 99.

[37]Ibid., 100-103.

[38]Ibid., 103.

pelled the Christian communities to revise their ethics . . . [and] to pose
the problem of a life "in Christ" within this world and its conditions.[39]

Once rich and powerful men in high office became Christians, the Church
automatically ceased to be an isolated sect and began to assume responsibility for the world, to penetrate humanity, and to replace the Roman
Empire. As a consequence of its secularization, the Church resigned its old
pretensions to sinlessness, realizing that "the heroic ideal of doing the radical will of God . . . can assert itself only in combination with an eschatological outlook."[40] Since today this eschatological outlook is practically
lost, Dibelius reasons that "the ideal of full obedience to God's will seems
to be impracticable. The commandments of the Sermon on the Mount have
no validity for the workaday life"—except for monastics. For the rest "only
small circles within the churches tried to live a Christian life. . . . The
mighty leaders of mankind were Christians by name, perhaps Christians in
faith, but pagans in conduct, at least if we take the Sermon on the Mount
as our standard."[41] Since the rise of Rationalism and the progressive development of Secularism, increasing evidence points to power and money
as the governing forces in politics, not the transcendent ideals of supernatural religion. Meanwhile, the process of industrial mechanization and
the resulting conflict between the individual and his competitor all but
abolished the relevance of Jesus' ideals for the everyday *Klassenkampf* of
human existence. Throughout these developments, Christianity proved not
so much to be a revolutionary as a conservative influence, supporting rather
than criticizing the existing social order. Consequently, radical movements arose to proclaim the gospel of social reform in opposition to the
established church, which served as the bodyguard of despotism and capitalism.[42]

Dibelius notes that "there were only a few solitary thinkers, whose
knowledge of the Gospel was deeper." Perhaps the first to fully realize the
discrepancy between the Gospel and "Christian" civilization was Søren
Kierkegaard. Dibelius lauds Kierkegaard for knowing "that sometimes it

---

[39]Ibid., 106.

[40]Ibid., 110.

[41]Ibid., 112.

[42]Ibid., 114.

is better to be a Christian than to do so-called Christian deeds.'' But Dibelius discounts Kierkegaard's revival of Christian radicalism because

> it does not lead to the solution of the problem of a Christian life in the existing world. . . . Kierkegaard does not see that the background of the primitive Christian radicalism is an eschatological one. He does not realize that . . . it is the loss of eschatology which prevents him from becoming a Christian leader or a prophet and makes him an antagonist of existing Christianity.[43]

Leo Tolstoy was overwhelmed by the uncompromising radicalism of the Sermon on the Mount "and the revolutionary force of its rules.'' But, according to Dibelius, Tolstoy

> does not see their relation to the Kingdom of God in an eschatological sense. Consequently, he puts the rules of the Sermon on the Mount in a wrong context, that is, in the life of this age. He attempts to change the whole course of this life, at least of his own life, in the direction of a static ideal formulated in accordance with the Sermon on the Mount. He does not see that Jesus himself referred to another world, to the Kingdom of God.[44]

It was the genius of Fyodor Dostoevsky, contends Dibelius, to comprehend the radicalism of the Gospel within an apocalyptic framework: "He recognizes the great alternatives of this life: either man wants to be free and must suffer or man prefers happiness—then he cannot be free. . . . Christ is the way to a new freedom, but freedom is not of this world.''[45]

As a final example, most revealing of his own sympathies, Dibelius cites Caspar René Gregory, professor of theology and military officer, a great scholar and devoted soldier, who in life and death exemplified

> the spirit of Christian love [or] we may say, the spirit of the Sermon on the Mount. . . . The military service of Professor Gregory and his death by a shell hitting his quarters in France were indeed an illustration of the word, "Greater love has no man than this, that a man lay down his life for his friends.'' It was neither youthful enthusiasm which led him nor national hate; he wanted to be faithful unto death.[46]

This example may appear slightly inappropriate, but not to Dibelius. His

---

[43]Ibid., 117-18.

[44]Ibid., 119.

[45]Ibid., 122.

[46]Ibid., 124-25.

point is that Professor Gregory, although exempt by profession and age from military duty, enlisted voluntarily rather than claim for himself an exemption from the service demanded of his fellow countrymen. Such devotion earned Dibelius's deep respect.

As a theologian, Gregory would know Jesus' command to love is subject to no restriction but that, for the man on the street, Jesus' command to love one's enemies is an absurdity. He would know that one must love his countrymen, his fellow workmen, and his family, but he cannot understand why one should be asked to love one's enemies:

> Confronted with the prohibition of cares, he would probably take it for granted that this commandment applies only to the wealthy classes, for the life of the poor consists, and must consist, of cares. We must realize that the man on the street (and perhaps some others) have a similar reply for every line of the Sermon on the Mount.[47]

These people realize that our whole modern way of life with all its economic, social, and political implications is in strict opposition to the ideals of the Sermon on the Mount. Hence, they want to be released from these commandments which seem so impracticable and inapplicable, but they do not know how.

"The worst thing is," Dibelius wrote, "that Christian people also have no clear answer to this condemnation of Christianity. Most of them are conscious of the difficulties; many of them are trying to avoid the difficulties by adapting and interpreting the commandments (as did the Church from the very beginning)," but the severity of the Gospel will not allow it. Some theologians admit these demands surmount all human capacities and seek their consolation in the Pauline assumption that the *nova lex Christi* was meant to compel knowledge of man's incapacity and sinfulness as the *conditio sine qua non* of experiencing forgiveness and grace. Dibelius does not agree. The only solution he allows is understanding Jesus' words and deeds as *signs of God's Kingdom*. "Jesus proclaims the pure will of God,"[48] but, Naumann to the contrary, "Jesus did not actually claim to improve the condition of this world."[49] "When he pronounced commandments and rules, his purpose was not to improve the world but to transform men" by

---

[47]Ibid., 128.

[48]Ibid., 131.

[49]Ibid., 133.

giving them "a conviction of the nearness of the Kingdom which stirred them and in this way transformed them spiritually." Before Easter, people were spiritually transformed by the anticipation of the imminent Kingdom, after Easter, by the anticipation of the imminent *parousia*. In both cases, it was the *eschatological stimulus* that created a new type of person:

> Whatever can we do with an eschatological admonition? We are not waiting for the end. We must needs be citizens of this world. We must provide for a life on the face of this earth. We have to live in the complicated circumstances of the modern age. . . . What, then, about this message of the Sermon on the Mount in our days; what about its eschatological presuppositions?[50]

Dibelius holds that we are still able to be transformed by the Sermon on the Mount even though we today do not think in eschatological terms and do not expect the end of the world in our lifetime. Despite this difference between our time and that of Jesus, Dibelius feels we must uphold "the standard of the Sermon on the Mount" as a symbolic expression of the perfect will of God,

> but we should not take it as a law in the Jewish sense, that is, we must not interpret it in a nomistic way and thus perform literally what is written and that alone, omitting what is not written. The Christian law does not demand that we *do something* but that we *be something*. In this way it creates the new type of man who knows the will of God in its ultimate eschatological aim and who wants to live here and now in accordance with his will. But he accepts the conditions of this world as the inescapable basis for all his actions and realizes that these conditions have completely changed since the days of our Lord. . . . The conditions of this world are not amenable to the Kingdom of God, and it is not our task to found this Kingdom. Rather, our task is to perform signs, not the signs described in the Bible but signs of our own time. . . . [51]

Our purpose, as that of Jesus, "is not to reform legislation or the exercise of justice on this earth but to illustrate the nature of God's will. For this reason, we should not seek in the Sermon on the Mount authoritative decisions concerning questions of today." Indeed, "it is meaningless to seek specific commandments concerning these matters in the Sermon on the

---

[50]Ibid., 134-35.

[51]Ibid., 137-38.

Mount.'' The Sermon on the Mount is the standard by which we are to solve such problems, but we have to make our own discernments and decisions

> as men who are responsible to God alone and who know the pure will of God from the Gospel. . . . This does not mean an application of any individual sayings to the world today. It means a continuous communication with God, whose will is recognized from the Sermon on the Mount.[52]

Dibelius ascribed widespread misconceptions of Christianity and of the world to those misunderstandings of the Sermon on the Mount that either (1) limit its relevance to the peculiar situation of Jesus' day (determined by eschatological presuppositions which no longer apply) or (2) continue to burden the church with the impossible obligation of fulfilling this new legislation today (as Tolstoy, who exemplified the nomistic intention of Matthew himself) or (3) interpret Jesus' teaching as divine law for the purpose of convicting us of our sinful incapacity to obey, thereby preparing us for atonement theology. Over against these interpretations, Dibelius proposes to expound the one which will do justice to the historical situation without invalidating the suprahistorical dimension of Jesus' words by modernizing or atomizing them.

Agreeing with Schweitzer, Dibelius maintains that Jesus assumed his hearers would see the end of the world and, therefore, intended his teaching to apply not to historical situations then or later but to an altogether otherworldly form of existence ''that would be free from all cares and worldly anxieties.''[53] Although Jesus was allegedly mistaken in his estimation and anticipation, Dibelius refrains from drawing the conclusions of consistent eschatology, insisting that Jesus' teaching is nevertheless valid ''at all times and for all time'' because the perfect will of God for man cannot be relegated to a hypothetical past interim which never materialized in the sense in which it was expected. Yet, Dibelius's claim that God's will for man ''will attain its full validity only in the Kingdom of God'' invariably implies that it is at best only partially valid now. Dibelius observes that ''the fulfillment of God's will is hampered and embarrassed by the conditions of our worldly existence,'' but he does not appear to challenge those conditions which oppose God's will. Though realizing that Jesus most certainly proclaimed God's will ''without regard for any such considera-

---

[52]Ibid., 138-41.
[53]Ibid., 50.

tions,"[54] Dibelius rests the case in contending "the conditions of this world are not amenable to the Kingdom of God" and pacifies our conscience with the consolation, "it is not our task to found the Kingdom."[55] That God's will "is not confined to an interim" because it is eternal means for Dibelius that it was valid for Jesus who lived for eternity but that it is therefore invalid for us who exist in time. By his category of the "eternal" he assumes to avoid Schweitzer's dilemma of limiting the relevance of Jesus' teaching to a past interim. It appears, however, that, according to Dibelius, the eternity Jesus anticipated is nevertheless a closed category which in effect does not differ from Schweitzer's mistaken interim. Because Dibelius cannot identify with Jesus' eschatology, he insists on relegating Jesus' intentions to an otherworldly eternity beyond all historical relevance. Since Jesus' teaching is allegedly exclusively unconditioned while our lives remain necessarily conditioned, virtually none of Jesus' sayings about cares, enemies, and so on applies. Consequently, we must remain conformed to this world while contemplating an "eschatological stimulus" few comprehend and none believe. The sophistry appears intellectually incredible and morally elusive.

As a case in point, Dibelius advises that Jesus' word about loving rather than hating one's enemies should not be applied to war or politics. How unlike Jesus of all people to be meddling in the political problem that "he wanted to leave unsolved." This assumption of Dibelius, so integral to his system, that Jesus' teaching had no political intentions or implications is disputed by other New Testament scholars. That Jesus must have meant only the private enemy is supported by Dibelius's doubt that the ancient Orient "could produce the idea of a national enemy," a doubt readily dispelled by a passing acquaintance with ancient history. Dibelius knows Jesus' word about loving enemies cannot apply to war because "hatred of the enemy is not familiar in the trenches"—an observation that might have eluded Jesus! Dibelius, therefore, limits Jesus' command to civilian life, where loving one's enemies "is much more difficult." However, since it is "opposed to all the natural feeling of the human heart," Dibelius presumes this command to be an Oriental hyperbole, hastily adding that this conjecture "must not be permitted to weaken. . .the seriousness of the

---

[54]Ibid., 51.
[55]Ibid., 137.

command," as if to ease somewhat the obvious implication that it would be foolish to take at face value an exaggerated rhetoric intended only to create a shocking effect. What criterion does Dibelius utilize for declaring which of Jesus' sayings are obviously hyperbole? Representing a proud military tradition, he knows this command of Jesus could not be meant literally because it is "so strangely contrary to all those reactions which [German] men view as legitimately human"! It appears too arbitrary to allow what Dibelius considers "legitimately human" to stand as a literary criterion for evaluating the intention of Jesus. The logic by which Dibelius defuses some of Jesus' Antitheses in designating them hyperbole contradicts his underlying "eschatological" assumption that Jesus came not to bless the status quo but to proclaim God's perfect will.[56]

As with Weiss and Schweitzer, the central concern of Dibelius is his contention that Jesus' radical demands are eschatologically conditioned in the sense that their fulfillment is possible only in the Kingdom which God has not established and which it is not our task to found. The Early Christians "believed Christ had instructed them to live in accordance with these sayings."[57] Now Dibelius reveals to us that Jesus never intended anyone to do what he said, Luke 6:46 to the contrary. Unfortunately, it was the error of the Early Christians not to have seen this hard truth. They mistook Jesus' "signs of hope" for laws of conduct, not realizing that by formulating his pithy paradoxical hyperbole he only meant to shock, stimulate, and offend his hearers. We now know, thanks to Dibelius, that we grossly misunderstand Jesus if we reduce his paradoxical intentions to the performance principle. Jesus, we are told, never intended anyone to do this or that. He anticipated a new state of being which would constitute the fulfillment of God's will for man. We should know better than to pervert the Christian uniqueness of Jesus by misunderstanding his demands in the nomistic Jewish way. But can we comprehend the commands of Jesus in any other way? Is it necessary or helpful to superimpose upon the Jewish consciousness of Jesus the modern philosophical distinctions between ethic and ethos, doing and being derived from Kant, Herrmann, or Dibelius? Is

---

[56]Ibid., 55-56. Jesus' saying about divorce also appeared "strangely contrary" to what Jewish men considered "legitimately human," namely, their practice of legitimizing their own lewdness by legal sanction while stoning adulteresses for transgressing God's perfect will.

[57]Ibid., 88.

this Protestant aversion to the Jewish nomistic understanding of Jesus' teaching theologically tenable? Has it actually been shown that Jesus' sayings were intended to be understood otherwise than as commands?

The Early Christians were captivated by the illusion of an imminent *parousia,* which, we are told, was the "eschatological stimulus" inspiring their obedience. But how shall we who "are not waiting for the end"[58] continue to be inspired by their mistaken "eschatological stimulus"? In their naïveté the Early Christians saw in Jesus' life the norm for their *Nachfolge.* But we "are not allowed to interpret the Sermon on the Mount according to any incidents or circumstances in the life of Jesus." If therefore Jesus is disqualified, to whom shall we turn in the hope and quest for the new humanity? If "the conditions of the life of Jesus are not the conditions of the Kingdom of God," how shall we ever know what the conditions of the Kingdom really are? And if Jesus' life has "no bearing on our problem," in what sense are we still Christian?[59]

Dibelius, nevertheless, urges us to "perform signs," not, however, signs of the Kingdom, for these, as we have seen, appear too "strangely contrary to all those reactions which men view as legitimately human." Instead, we are to perform "signs of our own time" without reference to those described in the Bible.[60] What can these secular signs mean? And what will they intend apart from everyone performing his own act in his own way?

Dibelius recognized the need of our age for moral guidance, for a message "applicable to the requirements of this troubled time," for an authoritarian voice that speaks to the struggles of life, for a star that illuminates our historical way.[61] He realized a utopian ideal for eternity is inadequate and that a vague Christian idealism is insufficient basis for the witness we must bear and encouraged us to retrace our convictions to the Bible. He raised our hope that, if correctly interpreted, the Sermon on the Mount would become a "redeeming force" for mankind, thereby validating our continuing claim to being Christian. He analyzed our need, but has he met it? He formulated the question, but has he answered it? He hopes the most

---

[58]Ibid., 135.

[59]Ibid., 86-87.

[60]Ibid., 138.

[61]Ibid., 3.

modern methods of critical New Testament scholarship "will help us understand what the Christian faith really is and what the standards are which we as Christians seek to uphold in these troubled times."[62] It is a generous hope, but is it realistic?

---

[62]Ibid., 143; cf. also "Die Unbedingtheit des Evangeliums und die Bedingtheit der Ethik," *Die Christliche Welt* 22 (1926):1107-1109, 1111; and "Das soziale Motiv im Neuen Testament," *Kirche, Bekenntnis, und Sozialethos* (Forschungsabteilung des ökumenischen Rates für praktisches Christentum, 1934) 9-32.

DIETRICH BONHOEFFER:
THE SERMON ON THE MOUNT
AND PARADOXICAL OBEDIENCE

The dividing line lies . . .with the Sermon on the Mount. And the time has come when the Sermon on the Mount must be brought to mind again.[1]

What did Jesus mean to say to us? What is his will for us today?[2] *If we answer the call to discipleship, where will it lead us?*[3]

We Lutherans have gathered like eagles around the carcase of cheap grace, and there we have drunk of the poison which has killed the life of following Christ.[4] *The word of cheap grace has been the ruin of more Christians than any commandment of works.*[5]

Humanly speaking, we could understand and interpret the Sermon on the Mount in a thousand different ways. Jesus knows only one possibility: simple surrender and obedience, not interpreting it or applying it, but doing and obeying it.[6]

The Christian is not a homo religiosus, *but a man, pure and simple, just as Jesus was a man . . . I believe Luther lived a this-worldly life in this sense. I remember talking to a young French pastor at A. thirteen years ago. We were discussing what our real purpose was in life. He said he would like to become a saint. . .At the time I was very much impressed, though I disagreed with him, and said I should prefer to have faith, or words to that effect. For a long time I did not realize how*

---

[1]Dietrich Bonhoeffer, letter to Reinhold Niebuhr, July 13, 1934; as found in Larry L. Rasmussen, *Dietrich Bonhoeffer: Reality and Resistance* (Nashville: Abingdon Press, 1972) 220.

[2]Dietrich Bonhoeffer, *The Cost of Discipleship*, ET R. H. Fuller (New York: Macmillan, 1961 [from the German *Nachfolge*, 1937]) 29.

[3]Ibid., 32.

[4]Ibid., 44.

[5]Ibid., 46.

[6]Ibid., 175.

*far we were apart. I thought I could acquire faith by trying to live a holy life, or
something like it. It was in this phase that I wrote* The Cost of Discipleship. *Today
I can see the dangers of this book, though I am prepared to stand by what I wrote.*

*Later I discovered and am still discovering up to this very moment that it is only
by living completely in this world that one learns to believe. . .This is what I mean
by worldliness—taking life in one's stride, with all its duties and problems, its
successes and failures, its experiences and helplessness.*[7]

Of all the commentaries on the Sermon on the Mount since Tolstoy,
none is more impressive than Dietrich Bonhoeffer's *Nachfolge.* In view of
the prevailing interest in the legacy of Bonhoeffer,[8] *The Cost of Discipleship* may prove to have been the most provocative and controversial treatise on the subject in our time. The book was written between 1935 and
1937 amid the crucial beginnings of the German *Kirchenkampf* against Nazi
totalitarianism and was inspired by the prophetic conviction that the dividing line between Hitler's Reich Church and Christ's Confessing Church
lay not with confessional orthodoxy as such but with the Sermon on the
Mount or, more precisely, "with a different understanding of the Sermon
than the Reformation's."[9] Bonhoeffer unequivocally confronts the Church

---

[7]Letter of July 21, 1944, in Dietrich Bonhoeffer, *Letters and Papers from Prison*, ET
R. H. Fuller (New York: Macmillan, 1961) 168.

[8]Dietrich Bonhoeffer (1906-1945) was born in Breslau into a large aristocratic family.
His father was a psychiatrist and professor in Berlin, and his mother was nourished in Mo-
ravian piety. After studying theology at Tübingen and Berlin, serving a vicariate in Barcelona, and spending a year at Union Theological Seminary in New York, he joined the
University of Berlin theological faculty and began lecturing in Systematic Theology in 1931.
When Hitler came to power two years later, Bonhoeffer abandoned his university career—
though he was not officially expelled until 1936—and pastored two German-speaking con-
gregations in London. From 1935 to 1937 he directed an underground seminary at Finken-
walde in Pomerania for ministerial candidates of the Confessing Church until the Gestapo
interfered. Meanwhile, he was very active in the ecumenical movement. After a brief return to America in 1939, he committed himself to the struggle of the Confessing Church in
Germany. In 1943 he was imprisoned and hanged two years later for his involvement in
the resistance movement. His most important translated works include *The Communion of
Saints* (1930), *Act and Being* (1931), *Christ the Center* [1933 lectures] (1960), *The Cost
of Discipleship* (1937), *Life Together* (1939), *Ethics* (1949) [written 1940-1943], and *Letters and Papers from Prison* [1943-1945] (1951).

[9]Letter of July 13, 1934, to Niebuhr, in Rasmussen, *Bonhoeffer*, 220.

with the imperative immediacy of uncompromising, unmitigated, single-minded obedience to Jesus Christ.

Alarmed at the realization that despite all the preaching and teaching of the gospel "the pure word of Jesus has been overlaid with so much human ballast," with so many hopelessly irrelevant man-made dogmas, Bonhoeffer directly focuses on what "behind all slogans and catchwords of ecclesiastical controversy" are the crucial questions. "What did Jesus mean to say to us? What is his will for us today? How can he help us to be good Christians in the modern world?" And what does Jesus Christ himself really want of us?[10] The book is an ardent and forthright confrontation with the Lutheran assumption that Jesus' demands are impracticable because we are unable to practice them. Only the person who leaves behind all theological casuistry to "follow the command of Jesus single-mindedly," says Bonhoeffer in his introduction,

> receives the power to persevere in the right way. The command of Jesus is unutterably hard for those who try to resist it. But for those who willingly submit, the yoke is easy and the burden is light. "His commandments are not grievous" (1 John 5:3). The commandment of Jesus is not a sort of spiritual shock treatment [as Stange and Kittel would have us believe]. His commandment never seeks to destroy life [as Luther himself feared if taken too literally] but to foster, strengthen, and heal it.[11]

But the fundamental question is what Jesus' call to discipleship really means for our actual life as workers, businessmen, squires, and soldiers in today's world. Will it imply an intolerable dichotomy between our being in Christ and our being in the world—between our sacred and our secular lives?

> If Christianity means following Christ, is it not a religion for a small minority, a spiritual élite? Does it not mean the repudiation of the great mass of society, and a hearty contempt for the weak and the poor?[12] And if we answer the call to discipleship, where will it lead us? What decisions and partings will it demand?[13]

---

[10]*Discipleship*, 29.

[11]Ibid., 31.

[12]Ibid., 31.

[13]Ibid., 32.

Bonhoeffer's book is an emphatic and outspoken protest against *cheap grace*, "the deadly enemy of our Church," the denial of discipleship and, in turn, of the Incarnation. "The essence of grace, we suppose, is that the account has been paid in advance; and, because it has been paid, everything can be had for nothing." The world finds in the Church a cheap covering for its sins. "Cheap grace means the justification of sin without justification of the sinner." Bonhoeffer cites Luther:

> We are still sinners "even in the best life," [so] let the Christian live like the rest of the world, let him model himself on the world's standards in every sphere of life and not presumptuously aspire to live a different life under grace from his old life under sin. That was the heresy of the enthusiasts, the Anabaptists, and their kind. Let the Christian . . .not attempt to erect a new religion of the letter by endeavoring to live a life of obedience to the commandments of Jesus Christ![14]

The Christian knows that the world has been justified by grace, so he justifies his living in conformity to the world so as not to strive against indispensable grace: "He must let grace be grace indeed, otherwise, he will destroy the world's faith in the free gift of grace."[15] Instead of following Christ, the Christian attempts to enjoy the consolations of cheap grace without discipleship, without the cross.

By contrast, *costly grace* implies commitment, demands *Nachfolge*. "It is costly because it costs a man his life . . . [as] it cost God the life of his son."[16] Ever since the Early Church became secularized, "realization of the costliness of grace gradually faded, the world was christianized, and grace became its common property"—except for its outer fringe where the Church made room for the monastic movement:

> Thus, monasticism became a living protest against the secularization of Christianity and the cheapening of grace. But the Church was wise enough to tolerate this protest and to prevent it from developing to its logical conclusion. It thus succeeded in relativizing it, even using it in order to justify the secularization of its own life.[17]

In the monastery, God showed Luther

---

[14]Ibid., 35-36.

[15]Ibid., 36.

[16]Ibid., 37.

[17]Ibid., 38.

that the following of Christ is not the achievement or merit of a select few but the divine command for all Christians without distinction. Monasticism had transformed the humble work of discipleship into the meritorious activity of the saints and the self-renunciation of discipleship into the flagrant spiritual self-assertion of the "religious."[18]

So Luther had to leave the monastery in order to follow Christ. Upon entering, "he had left behind everything except his pious self." Now even that had to go. "Luther had to leave the cloister and go back to the world, not because the world in itself was good and holy but because even the cloister was only a part of the world." Therefore, Luther concluded that "the only way to follow Jesus was by living in the world . . . in one's daily vocation of life"—"a duty laid on every Christian living in the world."[19]

> Luther had said that grace alone can save; his followers took up his doctrine and repeated it word for word. But they left out its invariable corollary, the obligation of discipleship . . . their orthodoxy spelled the end and destruction of the Reformation as the revelation on earth of the costly grace of God. The justification of the sinner in the world degenerated into the justification of sin and the world. Costly grace was turned into cheap grace without discipleship.[20]

Thus the fatal misunderstanding perpetuated itself in that

> the Christian life comes to mean nothing more than living in the world and as the world, in being no different from the world, in fact, in being prohibited from being different from the world for the sake of grace. The significance of it all is that my only duty as a Christian is to leave the world for an hour or so on Sunday morning and go to church to be assured that my sins are all forgiven. I need no longer try to follow Christ, for cheap grace, the bitterest foe of discipleship, which true discipleship must loathe and detest, has freed me from that.[21]

Bonhoeffer openly concedes: "We Lutherans have gathered like eagles around the carcase of cheap grace, and there we have drunk of the poison which has killed the life of following Christ."[22] "We justified the world

---

[18]Ibid., 39.

[19]Ibid., 40.

[20]Ibid., 41.

[21]Ibid., 42.

[22]Ibid., 44.

and condemned as heretics those who tried to follow Christ. The result was that a nation became Christian and Lutheran but at the cost of true discipleship. . . . We gave away the word and the sacraments wholesale, we baptized, we confirmed and absolved a whole nation unasked and without condition. . . . But the call to follow Jesus in the narrow way was hardly ever heard. . . . Was there ever a more terrible or disastrous instance of the Christianizing of the world than this?''[23] ''The only effect that such a word [of cheap grace] could have on us was. . .to seduce us to the mediocre level of the world, quenching the joy of discipleship by telling us that . . . we are spending our strength and disciplining ourselves in vain—all of which was not merely useless but extremely dangerous. After all, we were told, our salvation had already been accomplished by the grace of God. . . . Deceived and weakened, men felt that they were strong now that they were in possession of this cheap grace, whereas, they had in fact lost the power to live the life of discipleship and obedience. The word of cheap grace has been the ruin of more Christians than any commandment of works.''[24]

Bonhoeffer makes much of the immediacy of obedience through the mediation of the Word. Jesus summons Levi (Mark 2:14), and, because it is ''the absolute, direct, and unaccountable authority of Jesus'' who calls him, Levi follows at once. Jesus does not inform those whom he calls about the content of their discipleship, says Bonhoeffer: ''Follow me, run along behind me! That is all. To follow in his steps is something which is void of all content. It gives us no intelligible program for a way of life, no goal or ideal after which to strive.''[25] This emphasis on immediate, absolute obedience ''void of all content'' reflects the existentialism of Bultmann and, in turn, of Kierkegaard, though its roots lie in the Lutheran doctrine of vocation, interpolated from Paul. Bonhoeffer's point is, however, that he whom Jesus calls does not remain in the calling in which he was born but ''simply burns his boats and goes ahead. He is called out and has to forsake his old life in order that he may 'exist' in the strictest sense of the word.''[26] Had Levi remained at his desk and Peter at his nets, they could have—each in the vocation in which he was called—pursued ''their trade honestly and

---

[23]Ibid., 45.

[24]Ibid., 46.

[25]Ibid., 49.

[26]Ibid., 49.

dutifully, and they might both [have enjoyed] religious experiences, old and new. But if they [wanted] to believe in God, the only way [was] to follow his incarnate Son'' whose ''call frees them from all earthly ties and binds them to Jesus Christ alone. . . . Had Levi stayed at his post, Jesus might have been his present help in time of trouble but not the Lord of his whole life.'' And, ''if Peter had not taken the risk, he would never have learned the meaning of faith.''[27] A situation in which faith is possible is rendered possible only through faith. Stated in propositional form this means that ''only he who believes is obedient, and only he is obedient who believes'':[28]

> If the first half of the proposition stands alone, the believer is exposed to the danger of cheap grace, which is another word for damnation. If the second half stands alone, the believer is exposed to the danger of salvation through works, which is another word for damnation.[29]

In a chapter entitled ''Single-minded Obedience,'' we are introduced to the paradoxical complexity of Bonhoeffer's understanding of what it really means to discern the call to discipleship. When Jesus called Levi from the receipt of custom and Peter from his nets, it was clear that he expected of them single-minded, forthright obedience. But today, noted Bonhoeffer, we are accustomed to arguing ourselves out of such obedience. We admit that Jesus' demand is indeed definite, but then we remind ourselves

> that he never expects us to take his commands legalistically. What he really wants me to have is faith. But my faith is not necessarily tied up with riches or poverty or anything of the kind. We may be both poor and rich in the spirit. . . . Jesus may have said: ''Sell thy goods,'' but he meant: ''Do not let it be a matter of consequence to you that you have outward prosperity; rather keep your goods quietly, having them as if you had them not. Let not your heart be in your goods.''[30]

By the sophistry of this *Gesinnungsethik*, we exempt ourselves from single-minded obedience on the pretext of avoiding legalism: ''As Jesus realized, the trouble with the [rich] young man was that he was not capable

---

[27]Ibid., 53.

[28]Ibid., 54.

[29]Ibid., 58.

[30]Ibid., 69-70.

of such an inward detachment from riches.''[31] But we are capable, and we expect Jesus to respect our attitude in lieu of selling all. We know those whom Jesus called with ''absolute seriousness,'' but we understand true obedience to mean continuing in our present occupations, associations, and commitments, otherwise we would be shirking our responsibilities:

> Perhaps Jesus would say to us: ''Whosoever smiteth thee on the right cheek, turn to him the other also.'' We should then suppose him to mean: ''The way really to love your enemy is to fight him hard and hit him back.'' Jesus might say: ''Seek ye first the kingdom of God,'' and we should interpret it thus: ''Of course, we should have to seek all sorts of other things first; how could we otherwise exist? What he really means is the final preparedness to stake all on the kingdom of God.'' All along the line we are trying to evade the obligation of single-minded, literal obedience.[32]

We do the opposite of what Jesus says not only on the grounds that this is necessary but because we have been taught to believe that this is actually what he intends for us, despite all indications to the contrary. ''How,'' asks Bonhoeffer,

> is such absurdity possible? . . . When orders are issued in other spheres of life, there is no doubt whatever of their meaning. . . . Are we to treat the commandment of Jesus differently from other orders and exchange single-minded obedience for downright disobedience? How could that be possible![33]

''It is possible,'' Bonhoeffer replies, ''because there is an element of truth underlying all this sophistry.'' When Jesus invites someone into fellowship with himself, it matters not what that person *does*. What matters is only his faith in Jesus, irrespective of poverty or riches, marriage or celibacy: ''Everything depends on faith alone.''[34] ''It is possible to have wealth . . . and believe in Christ. But this,'' Bonhoeffer argues, ''is an *ultimate* possibility of the Christian life only within our capacity in so far as we await with earnest expectation the immediate return of Christ,'' (a qualification that reflects the emphasis of Dibelius). ''The paradoxical understanding of the commandments has its Christian justification,'' Bonhoeffer continues,

---

[31]Ibid., 70.

[32]Ibid., 71.

[33]Ibid., 71.

[34]Ibid., 71.

but it "is only possible and right for somebody who has already at some point or other in his life put into action his single-minded understanding."[35] A third restriction is added: "Anybody who does not feel that he would be much happier were he only permitted to understand and obey the commandments of Jesus in a straightforward literal way . . . has no right to this paradoxical interpretation of Jesus' words. We have to hold the two [that is, single-minded literal obedience and the paradoxical understanding] together all the time," counsels Bonhoeffer. We cannot eliminate single-minded obedience on principle, for that would constitute the worst kind of legalism which ignores the living Christ, in whom "the law is at once fulfilled and cancelled."[36] And yet, we "cannot identify ourselves *altogether* with those whom Jesus called, . . . [for] it would be a false exegesis if we tried to behave in our discipleship as though we were the immediate contemporaries of the men whom Jesus called."[37] The interrelation of both kinds of 'obedience' is such that Bonhoeffer concludes, "we must therefore maintain that the paradoxical interpretation of the commandments of Jesus always includes the literal interpretation," not because single-minded obedience is necessarily primary but "for the very reason that our aim is not to set up a law," be it some Christian or Franciscan ideal.[38]

Discipleship is not only a paradoxical experience, according to Bonhoeffer, but it is also a bitter and solitary one. "Discipleship means . . . submission to the law of Christ which is the law of the cross."[39] This cross is not a tragedy. It comes not as an accident of mortal life but as a necessity of the specifically Christian life. Following Jesus along the Via Dolorosa is also an invariably solitary experience. "Every man is called separately and must follow alone."[40] Finally,

> it is not for us to choose which way we shall follow. That depends on the will of Christ. But this at least is certain: in one way or the other we shall have to leave the immediacy of the world and become individuals, whether secretly or openly.[41]

---

[35]Ibid., 72.

[36]Ibid., 73.

[37]Ibid., 73.

[38]Ibid., 74.

[39]Ibid., 77.

[40]Ibid., 84.

[41]Ibid., 90.

Within this frame of reference, Bonhoeffer focuses on the Sermon on the Mount to discern in the Beatitudes, similes, and Antitheses of Matthew 5 the form of that "extraordinarily" visible obedience of the first disciples. Those who obeyed Jesus' call to follow him constituted the "little flock" that by its commitment stood out from the "great flock," though in the providence of God they constitute one people. They who for his sake lost all are literally "poor" (Matthew 5:3), for "in following him they lost even their own selves and everything that could make them rich. Now they are poor—so inexperienced, so stupid, that they have no other hope but him who called them" in contrast to "the representatives and preachers of the national religion who enjoy greatness and renown, whose feet are firmly planted on the earth, who are deeply rooted in the culture and piety of the people and molded by the spirit of the age."[42]

"With each beatitude," Bonhoeffer remarks, "the gulf is widened between the disciples and the people." They who "mourn for the world, for its guilt, its fate, and its fortune" become unwelcome guests, disturbers of the peace, and strangers to a society to whose standards they cannot accommodate themselves, and so the world rejects them.[43] They are the "meek" who "show by every word and gesture that they do not belong to this earth."[44] "Not only do the followers of Jesus renounce their rights, they renounce their own righteousness too," hungering and thirsting for the righteousness of God as did Jesus when he died "accursed on the cross with a desperate cry for righteousness on his lips." In their irresistible love for the downtrodden, the wretched, the wronged, and the outcast, the followers of Jesus "renounce their own dignity, for they are merciful."[45] They are "pure in heart" who are undefiled either by their own evil or their own virtues, who have a childlike simplicity, and whose "hearts are not ruled by their conscience but by the will of Jesus."[46] "They shall see God, whose hearts have become a reflection of the image of Jesus Christ."[47] These Je-

---

[42]Ibid., 97.

[43]Ibid., 98.

[44]Ibid., 99.

[45]Ibid., 100.

[46]Ibid., 101.

[47]Ibid., 102.

sus people "not only *have* peace but *make* it. . .they overcome evil with good and establish the peace of God in the midst of a world of war and hate." As partners of Christ's work, they are called "sons of God." Finally, blessing is upon those

> suffering in a just cause, suffering for their own just judgments and actions. For it is by these that those who renounce possessions, fortune, rights, righteousness, honor, and force for the sake of following Christ will be distinguished from the world.[48]

Those "summoned to follow the Crucified in a life of grace" are the "salt of the earth," whose imperishability guarantees "the permanence of the divine community."[49] Disciple community is visible community. Following Jesus "is as visible to the world as a light in the darkness or a mountain rising from a plain. Flight into the invisible is a denial of the call."[50] The "bushel" under which the light is hidden and extinguished "may be fear of men or perhaps deliberate conformity to the world . . . [or] it may be 'Reformation theology,' which boldly claims the name *theologia crucis* and pretends to prefer to Pharisaic ostentation a modest invisibility, which in practice means conformity to the world." Anticipating the objection, Bonhoeffer asks: "Ought not the Christian life to be as obscure as the cross itself?" And he answers, "it is wicked sophistry to justify the worldliness of the church by the cross of Jesus."[51] "If the good works were a galaxy of human virtues," Bonhoeffer concludes,

> we should then have to glorify the disciples, not God. But there is nothing for us to glorify in the disciple who bears the cross or in the community whose light so shines that it stands visibly on the hill. . . . It is by *seeing* the cross and the community beneath it that men come to believe in God. But that is the light of the Resurrection.[52]

In Matthew 5:17-20, Jesus informs his disciples that he came not to repeal the law but to vindicate its authority. It is the same law that the Pharisees also had. "It becomes a new law only because it is Christ who binds

---

[48]Ibid., 102.

[49]Ibid., 105.

[50]Ibid., 106.

[51]Ibid., 107.

[52]Ibid., 108.

his followers to it. . . . Every letter of it, every jot and tittle, must remain in force and be observed until the end of the world."[53] "He has, in fact, nothing to add to the commandments of God, except this, that he keeps them."[54] Israel tended to put the law in God's place, whereas the disciples were in danger of divorcing God from his law. But "there is no fulfillment of the law apart from communion with God and no communion with God apart from fulfillment of the law. To forget the first condition was the mistake of the Jews, and to forget the second the temptation of the disciples."[55] How does the righteousness of the disciples differ then from that of the Pharisees? The disciples' "doing of the law is in fact perfect." That, says Bonhoeffer, is the difference! How is this possible? It is the possibility of living in communion with Jesus, who embodies this "better righteousness" which submits to the cross because of what the law demands. The "perfect" righteousness of the disciples consists in their participation in the fulfillment of the law by Jesus.[56] "From henceforth they do the will of God and fulfill the law themselves."[57]

"The first law which Jesus commends to his disciples is the one which forbids murder and entrusts their brother's welfare to their keeping" (Matthew 5:21-26).[58] But on another matter, Bonhoeffer notes that the Church has been "strangely uncertain" about Jesus' teaching regarding the oath (Matthew 5:33-37). "In the early Church the most common interpretation was that 'perfect' Christians were forbidden to swear at all, but the weaker brethren were allowed to swear within certain limits." However, "in the Reformation Confessions it is expressly affirmed that there can be no question of Jesus prohibiting oaths exacted by the state in a court of law."[59] Although it is perfectly clear that Jesus' disciples "are forbidden to swear at all," for "they always speak the whole truth and nothing but the truth,"[60] Bonhoeffer contends that "no general rule can be laid down to enable us

---

[53]Ibid., 110.

[54]Ibid., 111.

[55]Ibid., 111.

[56]Ibid., 113.

[57]Ibid., 114.

[58]Ibid., 115.

[59]Ibid., 122.

[60]Ibid., 123.

to decide . . . where an oath is desirable precisely in the interests of the truth; each case must be decided on its own merits. The Churches of the Reformation were convinced that every oath demanded by the state was covered by this exception.'' Bonhoeffer questions this assumption as a general rule without, however, denying its possibility. He argues instead for narrowing the exception, allowing that "an oath can only be sworn where all its implications are first made clear beyond all doubt.'' Moreover, since a Christian "is never lord of his own future, he will always be extremely cautious about giving a pledge (e.g., an oath of allegiance), for he is aware how dangerous it is to do so. . . . For the sake of truth, therefore, and for the sake of his following of Christ, he cannot swear such an oath without the proviso, 'God willing,' [since], for the Christian, no earthly obligation is absolutely binding.''[61]

In a provocative manner, Bonhoeffer explores the implications of Jesus' antithesis to the law of revenge. (Matthew 5:38-42: "You have heard that it was said, 'An eye for an eye. . . . ' But I say to you, Do not resist one who is evil. . . . '') He explains that under the old covenant evil was requited so as to eradicate it from the body politic of the people of God, but "the right way to requite evil, according to Jesus, is not to resist it. This saying of Christ,'' says Bonhoeffer, "removes the Church from the sphere of politics and law. The Church is not to be a national community like the old Israel but a community of believers without political or national ties. The old Israel had been both—the chosen people of God *and* a national community—and it was therefore his will that they should meet force with force. But with the Church it is different: it has abandoned political and national status and therefore it must patiently endure aggression.'' Bonhoeffer elaborates on the Christian philosophy of nonviolence:

> The only way to overcome evil is to let it run itself to a standstill because it does not find the resistance it is looking for. Resistance merely creates further evil and adds fuel to the flames. But, when evil meets no opposition and encounters no obstacle but only patient endurance, its sting is drawn, and at last it meets an opponent which is more than its match. Of course, this can only happen when the last ounce of resistance is abandoned, and the renunciation of revenge is complete. Then evil cannot find its mark, it can breed no further evil and is left barren. . . . Evil becomes

---

[61]Ibid., 124.

a spent force when we put up no resistance. . . . Violence stands condemned by its failure to evoke counter-violence.[62]

By his willingly renouncing self-defence, the Christian affirms his absolute adherence to Jesus and his freedom from the tyranny of his own ego. The exclusiveness of this adherence is the only power which can overcome evil. . . . Suffering willingly endured is stronger than evil, it spells death to evil. . . . The worse the evil, the readier must the Christian be to suffer; he must let the evil person fall into Jesus' hands.[63]

The Reformers, Bonhoeffer notes, "distinguished between personal sufferings and those incurred by Christians in the performance of duty as bearers of an office ordained by God" and applied the precept of nonviolence only to the former but not to the latter on the assumption that, in a professional capacity (or *Amt*), "if we want to act in a genuine spirit of love, we must do the very opposite and meet force with force in order to check the assault of evil."[64] On this basis, the Reformers justified war and the capital punishment of dissenters. But, says Bonhoeffer, "this distinction between person and office is wholly alien to the teaching of Jesus. . . . He is the Lord of all life and demands undivided allegiance. Furthermore, when it comes to practice, this distinction raises insoluble difficulties."[65] "How then can the precept of Jesus be justified in the light of experience? It is obvious that weakness and defenselessness only invite aggression. Is then the demand of Jesus nothing but an impracticable ideal?" For Bonhoeffer, that conclusion does not necessarily follow, since "Jesus tells us that it is just *because* we live in the world and just *because* the world is evil that the precept of nonresistance must be put into practice."[66] To do so, however, does not mean to take the precept of nonresistance "as an ethical blueprint for general application." That would surely be "indulging in idealistic dreams," for "to make nonresistance a principle for secular life is to deny God by undermining his gracious ordinance for the preservation of the world"[67]—a somewhat surprising statement which, without further qualification, leaves open to question whether Bon-

[62]Ibid., 127.
[63]Ibid., 128.
[64]Ibid., 128.
[65]Ibid., 129.
[66]Ibid., 129.
[67]Ibid., 130.

hoeffer actually meant to challenge the validity of Luther's doctrine of ''The Two Kingdoms'' (and, if so, to what extent) or whether Bonhoeffer's so-called 'pacifist' sentiments still assume that traditional frame of reference intact.

Bonhoeffer aptly designates Jesus' teaching on loving one's enemies (Matthew 5:43-48) as ''the extraordinary'' which marks the distinctive quality of the specifically Christian life. He assures us that for the disciples of Jesus the 'enemy' was no mere abstraction. Apart from the political enemy of Rome, they had enough enemies and knew only too well those who hated, derided, insulted and persecuted them for Jesus' sake. Beyond this observation, Bonhoeffer appears peculiarly ambiguous as to what Jesus' reference to enmity actually refers. He says, ''Jesus is not talking of ordinary enmity but of that which exists between the People of God and the world.'' However, Bonhoeffer is quick to add that Jesus could not have condemned the 'holy wars' of Israel,

> for then he would have condemned the whole history of God's dealings with his people. . . . He is as concerned as the Old Testament with defeat of the enemy and the victory of the People of God. No, the real meaning of this saying is that Jesus is again releasing his disciples from the political associations of old Israel. From now on there can be no more wars of faith.

For the moment Bonhoeffer appears to leave unanswered the more relevant question as to whether disciples of Jesus today are also ''released'' from participation in nonreligious wars. But he adds: ''The only way to overcome our enemy is by loving him.''[68] To the natural man, this appears as an ''intolerable offense'' which contradicts his conception of good and evil and his understanding of God's law. Nevertheless, that is what Jesus demands. To be Christian means to love one's enemies. ''Be his enmity political or religious, he has nothing to expect from a follower of Jesus but unqualified love. In such love there is no inner discord between private person and official capacity. In both we are disciples of Christ or we are not Christians at all.''[69] ''The 'extraordinary'—and this is the supreme scandal—is something which followers of Jesus *do*. It must be *done* like

---

[68]Ibid., 132.
[69]Ibid., 133.

the better righteousness and done so that all men can see it." "In Christ crucified and in his people the 'extraordinary' becomes reality."[70]

For Bonhoeffer, the conclusion of the matter is this:

> Humanly speaking, we could understand and interpret the Sermon on the Mount a thousand different ways. Jesus knows only one possibility: simple surrender and obedience, not interpreting it or applying it, but doing and obeying it. . . . Jesus has spoken: his is the word, ours the obedience. . . . To deal with the word of Jesus otherwise than by doing it is to give him the lie. It is to deny the Sermon on the Mount and to say No to his word. If we start asking questions, posing problems and offering interpretations, we are not doing his word.[71]

Yet Bonhoeffer by his own involvement as German espionage agent and as conspirator in the assassination plots on Hitler's life has raised the most urgent questions, posed the most serious problems, and confronted us with the most paradoxical interpretations. In what sense was Bonhoeffer's clandestine activity a form of that single-minded 'doing,' an expression of that boundless Christian love for the enemy which he so highly commends? How are we to understand this book in the context of Bonhoeffer's own discipleship? Did Bonhoeffer rationalize tyrannicide as a form of the *Gestalt Christi*? Did he provide Christological criteria for sanctioning exceptions to the teaching of Jesus? Or did he really believe that assassinating the enemy is a Christian way of loving him? If so, what do words mean? If not, is there a 'shift' or 'break' somewhere in Bonhoeffer's thought and life? Are the 'Christian' and 'secular' spheres of his life somehow Christologically interconnected—as many interpreters claim? Or does his life and thought follow an unbroken course exemplifying the logical implications of Luther's doctrine of the two kingdoms? In the hope of resolving these perplexing ambiguities, we need to examine certain aspects of Bonhoeffer's thought and life before and after writing *The Cost of Discipleship*.

Six years prior to writing this book, Bonhoeffer, as a twenty-two-year-old Vicar serving in Barcelona, gave a lecture[72] on Christian ethics including a section on war in which he stated that "Christians, if they really want to be Christians, should have resolutely opposed military service, as

---

[70]Ibid., 138.

[71]Ibid., 175-76.

[72]Cited in Rasmussen. *Dietrich Bonhoeffer: Reality and Resistance*, 96-98.

has been done by a number of Christian sects." He documents his statement from Matthew 5:39ff., and he concludes:

> It stands clear and plain in the New Testament, and all the twisting of
> meanings possible doesn't help: "Do not resist one who is evil": "Thou
> shalt not kill." Does anyone still dare somehow or another justify war from
> a Christian point of view? . . . War is nothing other than murder. War is
> crime. No Christian can go to war. The argument appears perfectly clear
> and incisive.

But, in case anyone should therefore consider it convincing, Bonhoeffer
is quick to add that the argument

> is faulty at the most important point: It is not concrete and as a conse-
> quence does not take in the depth of Christian decision. It involves the
> commandment not to kill and thus thinks it thereby has the solution in hand.
> But the decisive dilemma is overlooked, the dilemma which becomes clear
> the instant my *Volk* is attacked, [the dilemma] that for me the love com-
> mandment extends at least as much to the protection of that which is mine
> as it does to the prohibition against killing the enemy. . . . If out of con-
> viction I do not go [to war], it means nothing else than abandoning my own
> in the very moment of their need.

Then the young Bonhoeffer gives emphatic expression to his overpowering *Volks*-consciousness and *Volks*-identity which were to become the
dominant factor in his later theological development and personal destiny.

> God has given me my mother, my *Volk*. What I have I have thanks to
> this *Volk*. What I am I am through my *Volk*. Thus, what I have should be-
> long to my *Volk*. This is a divine order, for God created the *Völker*. . . .
> Every *Volk* has a call of God within it to make history, a call to enter com-
> petitively into the life of *Völker*. . . . God calls the *Volk* to manliness, to
> battle and to victory. . . . for God himself is eternally young and strong
> and triumphant. . . . Should not such a *Volk* be allowed to follow this call,
> even when it disregards the life of other *Völker*?

Lest there be any Christian ethical reservation about these conclusions
in the light of the Sermon on the Mount, Bonhoeffer repeats the incredible
sophism of Augustine that the Christian kills his enemy as an act of love
and blessing, praying for his soul while surrendering up his body in the
realization that the enemy was likewise bound to defend his own *Volk*, the
implication being that both sides are mutually offering up each other as the
supreme sacrifice of mutual love! Without pausing to examine these premises, Bonhoeffer enthusiastically continues: "I will raise the weapon in the

awful knowledge of doing something atrocious but being unable to do anything else. . . . Yet love for my *Volk* will sanctify murder, will sanctify war." As for Christian pacifism, "its advocates make the commands of the New Testament into laws. They make themselves slaves of these laws when they should make their decisions in freedom. They act according to principles, not out of the extreme situation given me by God." It is evident that at this stage of his development Bonhoeffer's affirmation of the Christian call to participate in war is as emphatic as its basis is dubious, for it is filled with contradictions and inconsistencies that were to haunt the rest of his life and thought.

A year later, as a result of ecumenical experience while a student in America, a transition in Bonhoeffer's frame of reference from an organic *Volk*-identity to a transnational ecclesiological consciousness becomes apparent, as evidenced in an address delivered in New York in which he said: "It must never more happen that a Christian people fights against a Christian people, brother against brother, since both have one Father."[73] It appears he caught a vision of the brotherhood of mankind which, in turn, inspired in him a passion for peace which he never lost. His overtures to universal peace remained, however, highly tenuous and provisional. His own aversion to principles made conscientious objection to Christian participation in war unthinkable for him. This is evident from his 1932 ecumenical address in Czechoslovakia in which he argued that "the Church must not preach timeless principles forever valid but only commands which are valid today."[74] Though his goal was not pacifism but peace, the influence of Gandhi's nonviolence is evident in a speech Bonhoeffer gave at the ecumenical conference at Fanö, Denmark, in 1934, in which he conjectured, "Which of us can say he knows what it might mean for the world if one nation should meet the aggressor, not with weapons in hand, but praying, defenseless, and for that very reason protected by 'a bulwark never failing'?"[75] He planned to go to India "to see what Gandhi knows about these things."[76] But Bonhoeffer's superior, Bishop D. Heckel of the German *Landeskirche*, was not favorably impressed; about Bonhoeffer, he

---

[73]*Gesammelte Schriften*, ed. E. Bethge (München: Chr. Kaiser Verlag, 1958) 1:72-73.

[74]Ibid., 145.

[75]Ibid., 448.

[76]Rasmussen, *Dietrich Bonhoeffer*, 220.

recommended: "Because the reproach can be raised against him that he is a pacifist and an enemy of the State, it might be advisable . . . to take measures to assure that German theologians no longer be trained by him."[77]

In March 1939, two years after publishing *The Cost of Discipleship*, Bonhoeffer wrote George Bell, Anglican Bishop of Chichester and head of the Commission on Life and Work for ecumenical relations in Germany:

> I am thinking of leaving Germany some time. The main reason is the compulsory military service to which men of my age (1906) will be called up this year. It seems to me conscientiously impossible to join in a war under the present circumstances. . . . Perhaps the worst thing of all is the military oath I should have to swear. . . . I have not yet made up my mind what I should do under different circumstances.[78]

Under the circumstances, Bonhoeffer was objecting to participation in the Nazi war machine, but there is no indication that he would not have endorsed the oath of allegiance and military service under different circumstances. His opposition was not to war in particular but to Hitler.

Three months later, Bonhoeffer returned to America to escape the draft but remained only briefly. On June 22, 1939, he recorded in his diary that it is simply "unbearable" and "unthinkable" for a German to be here, for "we cannot part ourselves from our destiny, least of all here abroad." He confessed how difficult it was for him under the circumstances to identify with the Una Sancta Ecclesia, for his whole ground of being appears to have been wrapped up in the destiny of his own *Volk*. "It is not a matter of something pious, more like some vital urge."[79] He returned to Germany to join the resistance movement, for the alternative, as he then saw it, was between "Christian civilization" or Nazi Germany. He resolved to risk his own life for the former against the latter, a decision he never regretted.[80]

In his subsequent *Ethics* (written piecemeal between 1940 and 1943), Bonhoeffer denounced "arbitrary" killing as unlawful destruction of innocent life but maintained "the killing in war is not arbitrary killing" and therefore not unlawful. He even assumed as self-evident that there is noth-

---

[77]Ibid., 116.

[78]*Gesammelte Schriften*, 1:281.

[79]Ibid., 309.

[80]See the letter of April 11, 1944, in *Letters and Papers from Prison*, 119.

ing arbitrary about "the killing of civilians in war, so long as it is not directly intended but is only an unfortunate consequence of a measure which is necessary on military grounds."[81] Contemplating the possibility of being acquitted and released from prison, he hoped if he "had to join up," for the "wonderful" chance of joining Hitler's troop in Eberhard Bethge's regiment.[82]

Disappointed by the diffidence of the *Landeskirchen* and disillusioned by the lethargy of the *Bekenntniskirche*, Bonhoeffer had joined the political-military resistance as an accomplice in the conspiracy plotting Hitler's assassination and the overthrow of his regime. Here the advocate of nonresistance and nonviolence resorted to the very weapons of the enemy, deception and violence, and became entangled in a mesh of ambiguities and evil on the assumption that the end he sought justified the means he used. As a confidential informant (*Vertrauens-Mann*) in Hitler's counter-espionage, Bonhoeffer was able to render invaluable liaison between the resistance movement and the allies. The moral irony of the resistance lay in its guilt-power scenario: the higher the level of command and responsibility maintained by its members in the ongoing function of the Nazi war machine, the more power at their disposal to effect a military *Putsch*. It was not simply a matter of assassinating the Führer but of being reasonably sure the simultaneous take-over of all key government positions would not precipitate a blood bath. The moral scruples were all on the side of the resisters; none on the side of Hitler. Steeped in guilt for perpetuating the existing evils, the conspirators procrastinated indecisively, debating for years the legality and feasibility of overthrowing the Nazi regime by a coup d'état, and, in the end, they failed to bring it off. Had the coup not repeatedly failed for technical reasons, it still might not have succeeded for other reasons. The only power-structure capable of taking the necessary action to prevent a revolution was the army. Its generals were not conditioned to act with vigor and conviction except on orders from their superiors. They were ill-prepared to assume the initiative in an act at once of patriotism and treason, since their pragmatic goals were morally confused by the confluence of values and sanctions the Third Reich ideology shared with their own proud Prussian military tradition of loyalty and respect.

---

[81]Bonhoeffer, *Ethics*, 116.

[82]Letter of November 18, 1943, in *Letters*, 66.

Furthermore, the generals were prepared to end the war but not to lose it. Another Versailles was no option, and guarantees for a negotiable peace with honor were not forthcoming from the Allies. It was as Bonhoeffer apprehended: "The man of duty will in the end be forced to give the devil his due."[83]

In his *Ethics* and *Letters and Papers from Prison* Bonhoeffer relates the reality of God to the concrete center of life. He interprets the gospel 'nonreligiously,' that is, not within the context of the liturgy but as it really happened in the first place: in the wholeness, integrity, and freedom exemplified by the Hebrew patriarchs in general and by Jesus Christ in particular. Essentially, Bonhoeffer's ethic concerns itself with the manner in which "the form of Jesus Christ takes form in man."[84] It is an "ethic of formation" the task of which is to discern concretely "the way in which the form of Jesus Christ takes form in our world."[85]

Since Bonhoeffer disallows appeal to ethical principles and rejects *imitatio Christi* based on understanding the Sermon on the Mount as *nova lex Christi,* the critical question we must ask is not how tyrannicide can be deduced from the commandment of God, "Thou shalt not kill," or how it can be justified in the light of the demand of Jesus, "Love your enemy," but whether the act of tyrannicide as such conforms to the *Gestalt Christi* rather than the "form" of Judas.[86] While, by all indications of analogy and correspondence, conspiracy to assassinate appears a malformation rather than a conformation of "the way in which the form of Christ takes form in our world," could tyrannicide not, nevertheless, be considered the exceptional command of God for this particular *Grenzfall* ("borderline case")? As criterion for this discernment, we consider Bonhoeffer's statement: "If God's commandment is not clear, definite, and concrete to the last detail, then it is not God's commandment."[87] The procrastination, hesitation, and indecision of the resisters imply that they did not understand their clandestine venture as an unambiguously clear, indubitably

---

[83]"After Ten Years," in ibid., 15.

[84]*Ethics*, 20.

[85]Ibid., 25.

[86]"We used to find the figure of Judas an enigma, but now we know him only too well." *Letters*, 22.

[87]*Ethics*, 245.

definite, and unmistakably concrete commandment of God. Most of the conspirators did not even consider themselves confessing Christians, and those few who did were burdened with an overwhelming sense of guilt. In view of this predominant ambivalence characterizing the resistance movement, even Karl Barth was prompted to discredit publicly the claim that it was from God.[88] The only known operative guidelines Bonhoeffer established for justifying tyrannicide were not theological but purely pragmatic, adapted from the 'Just War' logic to ascertain the appropriateness of the means required to assure the end.[89] In fact, when Werner von Haeften, staff Lieutenant in the Army High Command, sought from Bonhoeffer, the pastor and theologian, divine permission to shoot Hitler during one of his military conferences, Bonhoeffer argued that tyrannicide was in the first instance not a question of conscience but of outcome.[90]

Bonhoeffer referred to deputyship (*Stellvertretung*) in acceptance of guilt (*Schuldübernahme*) as the *Gestalt Christi* in the world. He saw Jesus "as one who acts responsibly in the historical existence of men" and thereby "becomes guilty."[91] Generalizing from his own awareness of being "lost in guilt's dark maze,"[92] Bonhoeffer contended that "every man who acts responsibly becomes guilty."[93] He regarded Jesus as "my conscience," who "for the sake of God and men" became "a breaker of the law" by violating the Sabbath, forsaking his parents, and eating with sinners.[94] Thus, "He became guilty," and so, Bonhoeffer reasoned, "He sets conscience free even and especially when man enters into the fellowship of human guilt."[95] The inference appears to be that, in breaking the ceremonial law (by healing someone), Jesus freed Bonhoeffer's conscience

---

[88] "Ein klarer kategorischer Befehl Gottes zu jener Tat lag für sie nicht vor, sonst hätte sie jene Hemmung, die ja mit Ethik nichts zu tun hatte, bei ihnen überwinden müssen." Barth, *Kirchliche Dogmatik* III/4, 514.

[89] See Rasmussen, *Dietrich Bonhoeffer*, 145.

[90] Cf. ibid., 140-41.

[91] *Ethics*, 210.

[92] Bonhoeffer, "Prison," *Union Seminary Quarterly Review* (March 1946):6-8; quoted in Rasmussen, *Dietrich Bonhoeffer*, 127.

[93] *Ethics*, 210.

[94] Ibid., 213.

[95] Ibid., 213.

to break the moral law (by assassinating Hitler). Consequently, as Jesus remained innocent though he "became guilty," so for the conspirators "there is a kind of relative freedom from sin,"[96] for they, like Jesus, acted 'responsibly,' thereby demonstrating their "real innocence."[97] Thus, assumption of responsibility which required the proof of innocence becomes the evidence of innocence! The problem with this circular reasoning is that the analogy between tarrying in the temple, eating with peasants, and healing on the Sabbath, on the one hand, and conspiring to assassinate someone, on the other hand, is invalid for the purpose of inference, for it falsely equates violation of the moral law with transcendence of the ceremonial law, thereby confusing actual sin with forensic guilt. It is one matter to assume the guilt of others as one's own in Christ's image of the sinless one; it is another to be implicated in the sin of others by violating the divine law oneself. Even if one could rationalize the conspiracy to assassinate Hitler as a necessary exception to the teaching of Jesus, one may not justify that act by reference to the *Gestalt Christi*. What is contrary to the teaching of Jesus may not be justified as 'paradox' in the name of Jesus on the assumption that God can and will bring good out of evil.[98] In the absence of ethical criteria for adjudicating the exceptional case when paradoxical obedience claims priority over single-minded obedience, antinomistic sophistry becomes on principle the most arbitrary justification of pragmatism, for, if there is no way to measure what constitutes an exception, then, by the same token, there is no basis for limiting such cases to exceptions.

The difference between *Nachfolge* and *Ethics* is pronounced: the former emphasizes "our becoming 'like Christ' " who enables us "to model our lives on his" as "the only 'pattern' we must follow"[99] while the latter elucidates the structure of responsible life as holy worldliness. According to the former, "Christ removes the Church from the sphere of politics,"[100] "releasing his disciples from. . .political associations."[101] "Like a sealed train travelling through foreign territory, the Church goes on its way through

---

[96]Ibid., 213.

[97]Ibid., 210.

[98]*Letters*, 21.

[99]*Discipleship*, 274.

[100]Ibid., 127.

[101]Ibid., 132.

the world.''[102] The latter advocates sharing political responsibility and moral guilt with non-Christians in the military resistance. The former apprehends our "excusing ourselves from single-minded obedience to the word of Jesus on the pretext of legalism''[103] lest "in our effort to combat legalism we land ourselves in the worst kind of legalism.''[104] Later we are told that "the Church must not preach timeless truths forever valid but only commands which are valid today.''[105] "All other 'secure' possibilities which appear to give continuity to action are to be rejected,'' including "the Law, even in the form of the Sermon on the Mount.''[106] Before, it was "just *because* the world is evil that the precept of nonresistance must be put into practice.'' Afterwards, Bonhoeffer regards objection to military service as an illegitimate escape from responsibility—a private act of self-righteous pietism that would only bring suspicion upon his family and friends. According to the former, disciples "always speak the whole truth and nothing but the truth.'' Later, Bonhoeffer confesses to having "learnt the art of deception and equivocal speech''[107] to survive and accomplish his clandestine objective, for "if I refuse to tell a robust lie for the sake of my friend. . .then my action is in contradiction to my responsibility.''[108] Is this not evidence of a 'shift' or 'break'?

Bonhoeffer says of himself: "I am convinced that my life has followed a straight and even course.''[109] "I don't think I have changed very much.''[110] On July 21, 1944 he wrote: "Today I can see the dangers of this book [*The Cost of Discipleship*], though I am prepared to stand by what I wrote.''[111] In preparing his own defense from prison, he referred to this book as evidence of his loyalty to the state: "The appeal to submit to the

---

[102]Ibid., 251.

[103]Ibid., 70.

[104]Ibid., 73.

[105]*Gesammelte Schriften*, 1:145.

[106]Cited in Eberhard Bethge, *Dietrich Bonhoeffer, Theologe, Christ, Zeitgenosse* (München: Chr. Kaiser, 1967) 1075.

[107]*Letters* , 27.

[108]*Ethics*, 214.

[109]Letter of April 11, 1944, *Letters,* 119.

[110]Letter of April 22, 1944, ibid.

[111]Ibid., 168.

will and the demands of authority for the sake of Christian conscience has probably seldom been expressed more strongly than there. That is my personal position in this matter.''[112] To argue that under the circumstances Bonhoeffer's statement was intentionally equivocal is to overlook the point that he hoped to win his case; he knew that there is virtually nothing in this book to challenge that loyalty! Despite the fact that he lost, he still stood by what he said.

Pacifism and tyrannicide do not lie along the same path except in the very qualified way Bonhoeffer affirmed both within the Lutheran two-kingdoms stance. Whatever Bonhoeffer said about discipleship and resistance, this frame of reference remains intact. For the disciples, *Nachfolge* meant leaving all and ''going with Jesus.'' For us, according to Bonhoeffer, it means ''Word and Sacrament.''[113] ''All you have to do is to hear the sermon and receive the sacrament.''[114] The decisive ''visible act of obedience''[115] is infant baptism. Beyond that, the form of visible obedience is not indicated. It is assumed that each disciple who is called today will remain faithful in his 'calling' as a soldier, priest, hangman, Nazi agent, or whatever. Consequently, it is not necessary to posit a breach in Bonhoeffer's thought between discipleship and resistance.

As an example of ''a this-worldly life''[116] correlating holiness and worldliness, piety and responsibility, Bonhoeffer looked to Luther—whose controversial *Pecca fortiter, sed fortius fide et gaude in Christo* (''Sin boldly, but believe and rejoice in Christ more boldly still'') he recast in the best possible light ''as our comfort in tribulation and as a summons to discipleship''![117] Despite the ballast of theological interpretation applied to Bonhoeffer's 'stages,' the contiguous factor underlying his thought and life was something quite earthy: he loved his people. His decisive commitment was ''not something pious [but] more like some vital urge,''[118] and the

---

[112]Quoted from Rasmussen, *Dietrich Bonhoeffer*, 44-50.

[113]*The Cost of Discipleship*, 233.

[114]Ibid., 201.

[115]Ibid., 209.

[116]Letter of July 21, 1944, *Letters,* 168.

[117]*The Cost of Discipleship*, 43-44.

[118]*Gesammelte Schriften*, 1:309: ''Es ist gar nichts Frommes, sondern etwas fast Vitales.''

particular action for which Bonhoeffer—in contrast to Jesus—was martyred exemplifies the paradox of that commitment rather than the *Gestalt Christi*.

EDUARD THURNEYSEN:
CHRISTOLOGICAL
INTERPRETATION

The Sermon on the Mount must be interpreted in a way that is basically Christological. He who interprets it in other ways misses what it has to say. . . . The only possible understanding of the Sermon on the Mount is the Christological understanding.[1]

The preacher of the Sermon on the Mount is the Sermon on the Mount. . . . Jesus and he alone is . . . the whole content of the Sermon on the Mount.[2]

In no sense of the term does it have to do with a nova lex, *not even in the sense of a model that Jesus would place before our eyes for our imitation. . . . The Sermon on the Mount is no model for the moral and religious conduct of man. That would only defraud its real meaning and result in a futile legalistic attempt to fulfill its demands. . . . The Sermon on the Mount is gospel and nothing but gospel.*[3]

The Sermon on the Mount is then only understood aright when it is understood in terms of predestination. . . . It is not that we ourselves change our lives, undertaking perhaps to fulfill the law. The law is not fulfilled through us but for us by Jesus. . . . It is and remains the obedience of Jesus alone that speaks to us from the sayings of the Sermon on the Mount. It is not our obedience. . . . We are and remain sinners. . . . "The Christian life" can never and in no sense mean that the people addressed by Jesus were able to do or even merely invited to do what Jesus himself and he alone did.[4]

The Sermon on the Mount . . . must be read as basically a word of grace, that is, as . . . the fulfillment of Christ's law accomplished for us in Christ.[5]

---

[1]Eduard Thurneysen, *The Sermon on the Mount*, ET W.C. Robinson, Sr. with J.M. Robinson (Richmond: John Knox Press, 1963) 17.

[2]Ibid., 18.

[3]Ibid., 12, 14.

[4]Ibid., 64, 66, 67, 69, 70.

[5]Ibid., 27.

The Sermon on the Mount [must be] free of all moral and mystical contamination of its interpretation.[6]

While various interpreters of the Sermon on the Mount have recognized the message of grace, especially in the Beatitudes, no one more consistently and convincingly brought to light the basic Christological nature of the entire Sermon on the Mount than Eduard Thurneysen.[7] "He who interprets it in other ways misses what it has to say," he claimed.[8] Thurneysen was convinced, for example, that "in no sense of the term does it have to do with a *nova lex*, not even in the sense of a model that Jesus would place before our eyes for our imitation."[9] The subject and object of the entire Sermon on the Mount is the self-witness and self-realization of Jesus "the royal man": "All his sayings witness to him and have in him their goal."[10] It is his light that is put on a lampstand and that enlightens all who are in the house (Matthew 5:15). The Jesus of the Sermon on the Mount is no mere thinker or teacher; he himself is the doer:

> With his mighty, sovereign "But I say to you . . . " he reveals himself as the Messiah of Israel, the Christ of God. . . . In Jesus heaven triumphed on earth. The new world takes root in the old world. That is what the Sermon on the Mount is talking about. The Sermon is no model for the moral and religious conduct of man. That would only defraud its real meaning and result in a futile legalistic attempt to fulfill its demands. . . . The Sermon on the Mount is gospel and nothing but gospel.[11]

Not to contest this is not enough. Our whole interpretation of the Sermon on the Mount must, according to Thurneysen, be oriented around this singular fact in a methodological way.

---

[6]Ibid., 77.

[7]From 1927-1959 Thurneysen was pastor and professor of practical theology in Basel. His other books, apart from *The Sermon on the Mount* (which was first published in German in 1936), include: *Revolutionary Theology in the Making* (with Karl Barth), *Dostoevski*, and *A Theology of Pastoral Care*.

[8]*The Sermon on the Mount*, 17.

[9]Ibid., 12.

[10]Ibid., 13.

[11]Ibid., 14.

> If . . . Jesus himself and he alone is the whole content of the gospel, then this Jesus and he alone is also the whole content of the Sermon on the Mount, since it too is part of this gospel that revolves around Jesus. Then the preacher of the Sermon on the Mount *is* the Sermon on the Mount. The Sermon on the Mount only contains sayings that are . . . spoken about him.

These sayings may not be detached from him, for he himself is the true content of them all. The Sermon on the Mount is not a record of views or teachings of Jesus on a variety of independent themes, such as law, divorce, oaths, retaliation, possessions, and so on, which primarily concern disciples. Rather, his Antitheses (Matthew 5:21-48) are examples expressing and documenting "Jesus' own fulfillment of the law."[12]

Apart from Jesus, the subjects of discourse are not important in themselves. They are included in Matthew's Sermon on the Mount only because they point to Jesus. The Sermon on the Mount is a discussion concerning Jesus himself rather than problems of life on which he commented.

Thurneysen would not allow the Sermon on the Mount to be explained in terms of the history of those times, as Windisch and others attempted to do. The meaning of the Sermon does not lie, for example, in Jesus' historical opposition to certain Pharisaic scribes. The singularity of the Sermon on the Mount lies in Jesus, who presents himself rather than a better righteousness. In distinction from "the men of old," Jesus presents himself not merely as a new teacher of the law but as the messianic Lord of the whole law, as he is Lord of the Sabbath (Matthew 12:8): "The important thing is not the degree of distance between the teaching of the scribes and the teaching of Jesus. The important thing is only the christological meaning and reference in the statements of Jesus about the law."[13]

Those who, along with Weiss and Schweitzer, understand the Sermon on the Mount primarily in terms of the eschatology of its time also fail to validate the central Christological focus of the text. In Thurneysen's judgment, they fail to realize that eschatological texts in the New Testament are not ideological statements about the brevity of the age (or old aeon) as such but Christological affirmations of Jesus. He is not presented as some

---

[12]Ibid., 18-19.

[13]Ibid., 21-22.

Rabbi speculating about the nearness of the end but as the Lord Messiah who himself brings about that end.

Even Tolstoy, Ragaz, and all those "fanatics" who from earliest times until now take the Sermon on the Mount very seriously by applying it to contemporary situations have, according to Thurneysen, missed the point. They are wholly preoccupied with those problems of life raised by Jesus as, for example, the problem of nonresistance to evil. Not that Jesus has nothing to do with these problems, "but the point is that it is Jesus who has to do with them." The problem with Tolstoy and those like him is

> that when all is said and done he has not yet really sought and found Jesus, the Jesus of the Gospel whom he so earnestly sought. But for this reason he has not really found his path, wandering among the problems of modern life, but has perished in the maze, though accompanied by the Sermon on the Mount, although, of course, a Sermon on the Mount read by him in his way—and here it must surely be said—in a fanatical way![14]

Our ultimate concern lies other than in illuminating the historical situation as Schweitzer and Windisch attempted or in exploring the gospel's relevance for the human situation as did Tolstoy and Ragaz. Rather, we are to read the Sermon on the Mount with eyes "directed only to Jesus and not to all the problems of life as such."[15] Thurneysen adamantly insists that "absolutely everything" depends on such an approach. The Sermon on the Mount implicitly concerns Christ's completed and continuing action for us in distinction to our act. It is the genius of the Reformers—of Luther and especially of Calvin—to have grasped this conception. "Of them it can and must be said: They read the Sermon on the Mount christologically and only christologically." From them we comprehend the meaning of the Sermon on the Mount "as a word of grace" which is "the fulfillment of God's law accomplished for us in Christ" in contrast to something we ourselves must fulfill as Tolstoy and his disciples claim.[16]

"The Christology of the Sermon on the Mount," Thurneysen wrote, "presents Jesus as the bringer of the messianic kingdom with its new righteousness."[17] When the Messiah-King brings the Kingdom, he will over-

---

[14]Ibid., 27.

[15]Ibid., 26.

[16]Ibid., 27.

[17]Ibid., 29.

throw the powers of the world. That has not yet occurred except "at one place, namely, where Jesus cast out demons 'by the finger of God' " (Luke 11:20). All the rest "is only promise, promise of the real, the final end of these powers." Neither within nor without is the Kingdom already realized, therefore, the Beatitudes' reference to fulfillment in the present tense (Matthew 5:3, 10) must be understood, according to Thurneysen, in a futuristic sense: "So long as this world-time continues, it will never and nowhere be true that the meek already possess the earth."[18]

"The Sermon on the Mount is the sign of the coming world by portraying the conduct of the man of this coming world. . . . The man of the coming world is one man, the man of Jesus Christ and he alone." In the Sermon on the Mount we are "confronted with the portrayal of the new conduct of the new man, [a life that] has been lived once and only once, only in Jesus Christ."[19] Yet, Thurneysen continues,

> to the extent that this new man is Jesus Christ himself, this law is totally fulfilled in him. It is as this law fulfilled by himself that he proclaims it to us in the Sermon on the Mount. . . . The Sermon on the Mount does not deal with us primarily but rather with Jesus Christ alone.[20]

Since the fulfillment is his fulfillment, it cannot be our law. Therefore, all the 'thou shalts' and 'you shoulds' of the Sermon on the Mount are not to be taken as moral imperatives but as the future of promise ("you will be perfect," Matthew 5:48) in the realization of what we are in Christ who is our future. "He holds this new form of our life before our eyes in the Sermon on the Mount"[21] in quite another manner than the law of life understood by the "fanatical" sixteenth century Anabaptists and the later Tolstoy which produced such "profound upheaval." The life described in the Sermon on the Mount has, Thurneysen explains, never anywhere been "attained, begotten, or created by man, for we men do not fulfill the law of this life."[22] This new righteousness of Christ is ours by grace through faith; it is not something *we* ought to fulfill. If misunderstood in this way, "then

---

[18]Ibid., 32.

[19]Ibid., 38, 39.

[20]Ibid., 43.

[21]Ibid.

[22]Ibid., 46.

the Sermon on the Mount darkens the whole heaven above our lives. The Gospel is silent. The word of Jesus becomes the word of remorseless demand and judgment. Hell opens up before us. There remains only a curse or despair."[23] Jesus' repeated emphasis on "doing" (for example, Matthew 7:21, 24, 26) does not mean, insists Thurneysen, that we ourselves are to fulfill the law. Rather, it means that we are to place ourselves within Christ's fulfillment of the law (Matthew 5:17).[24]

In the Sermon on the Mount we are invited to place our whole lives into Christ's fulfillment as he portrays it. But we must understand that this identification is not a religiously motivated matter of general moral instruction through which we could, in appealing to Christ (Matthew 7:21), fulfill the law by our own power. Jesus held out little hope for the scribes and Pharisees who tried to erect their houses on the sands of their own resources. According to Thurneysen, the Sermon on the Mount has often been misinterpreted as a call to activism on the grounds that the so-called do-nothing disciples who only cry "Lord, Lord!" will be rejected "on that day" because they have no deeds to show forth (Matthew 7:22). Their lack "on that day" will not be deeds (of which they have many) but Christ, the true foundation. They have done "mighty deeds"—even in his name—but they lack a right confession, says Thurneysen:[25]

> In the messianic judgment one will recognize Jesus' true disciples by their fruit. But that means that here and now, in the world as it still stands, one cannot know them. . . . Here and now they remain ambiguous to our eyes. . . . There is always the temptation to wish to have it otherwise. . . . Whoever desires this is precisely the "evildoer" (Matthew 7:23b). . . . He makes the presumptuous attempt to come before the Judge with a deed this Judge cannot assail.[26]

Good works or fruits cannot be discerned by human beings, insists Thurneysen, until God "on that day" reveals what for the present ought to remain "in secret" (Matthew 6:2, 5, 18). He who manifests them now "has received his reward":

---

[23]Ibid., 47.

[24]Ibid., 49.

[25]Ibid., 52.

[26]Ibid., 55-56.

The Sermon on the Mount would be distorted in its whole meaning if our passage were taken to mean a direct knowing and showing of fruits and works. It would then become the preaching of a mere work righteousness, the preaching of religious morality. Jesus would become a mere sage who desires to direct us with God's help to do good. The Sermon on the Mount would then no longer be gospel but only law.[27]

Thurneysen argues that mercy is granted to us rather than law demanded of us. For that reason we are to "measure" our interhuman relations by the same grace (Matthew 7:2). Where Jesus' word of grace is misunderstood as law, the "holy" is cast before "dogs" (Matthew 7:6, according to Philippians 3:2 "dogs" are the legalistic advocates of circumcision) and irretrievably profaned. Concerning the "Golden Rule" (Matthew 7:12), Thurneysen contends that it "certainly does not affirm the platitude that we ought to do good to our neighbor in order to experience the same from him." To the contrary, it is "a word full of suppressed enthusiasm" for the witness to the grace of God by the recipients of grace who, in waiting for the Kingdom, long for "all" that the law and the prophets could promise.[28]

Especially in regard to the saying about the narrow and wide gates (Matthew 7:13-14) Thurneysen feels "the false, unmessianic, and legalistic understanding far overweighs the right christological understanding" in the history of interpretation. The saying does not mean, he insists, that the pious man who shuns the world enters the narrow gate. The content of the admonition is rather that we should not seek to work out our own salvation but rely upon the grace of God. "Those that find it are few" compared to the many who "prance along a religious and moral highway, parading a complete attainment." Those who travel this highway are no longer "poor in spirit," for "they fulfill the law themselves" and therefore "no longer need the fulfillment of Christ."[29] This parable and the latter two depicting the tree bearing good or bad fruit and the house built on rock or sand reveal the final mystery underlying the Sermon on the Mount— namely, election: "The Sermon on the Mount is then only understood aright when it is understood in terms of *predestination*."[30]

---

[27]Ibid., 57.

[28]Ibid., 59-60.

[29]Ibid., 61-62.

[30]Ibid., 64.

"Everyone" who really hears Jesus' word correctly (Matthew 7:24) perceives that it extends beyond commandment (*Gebot*) to offer (*Angebot*). All the commandments testify to grace because they all testify to Christ. The obedience demanded "is obedience on the basis of grace," for it is the "obedience of the disobedient, the sinful person. . . . It is not that we ourselves change our lives, undertaking perhaps to fulfill the law. The law is not fulfilled through us but for us by Jesus." The obedience of which the Sermon on the Mount speaks "is and remains the obedience of Jesus alone. . . . It is not our obedience."[31] But, as "the reflection testifies to the light," so do "fruits and works testify to the requisition of our life accomplished in Jesus. . . . We are and remain sinners, but we now become, in the coming of the law to us, sinners met and arrested by this law, that is, by the word of our God."[32] As a result, we become transformed persons because our disobedience is exposed: "This exposure, this conscientiousness is what is meant by the 'purity of heart' of the sixth beatitude (Matthew 5:8)." Yet, we are

in no sense . . . able to do or even merely invited to do what Jesus himself, and he alone did. His, the only absolute purity, truth, and love, fellowship and holiness remain quite conclusively unattainable and barred for us as our own work done by us. He who teaches otherwise, even if only in the smallest point, will not be called great in the eyes of Jesus (Matthew 5:19)."[33]

Jesus is not a model for our imitation, Thurneysen insists: "Following Jesus never means imitating Jesus." "False prophets" (Matthew 7:15) are those "confusing discipleship with imitation. Their fruits are rotten. Their house will fall!"[34]

Realizing that we cannot and should not fulfill the commandments as Jesus fulfilled them, what ought we to do? According to Thurneysen, we are to render "symbolic obedience" by turning the cheek, giving the cloak, going the second mile, granting the loan, and blessing the enemy. Our obedience fails entirely to approximate the complete obedience of Christ. It is merely a symbolic "demonstration." A demonstration, we are told,

[31]Ibid., 65-67.

[32]Ibid., 69.

[33]Ibid., 70.

[34]Ibid., 71.

is a witness to the obedience of Christ, not a repetition of it; yet, such demonstrations ought only to be undertaken "in complete hiddenness. We ought not to speak of them; we ought not to show them before men." Jesus' prohibitions of treasure gathering, anxiety, coveteousness, and hatefulness are so radical because, according to Thurneysen, they bear witness to his resurrection: "Only from there can they be understood and interpreted."[35]

The true church does not go out "to morally elevate the world by its own powers" but instead proclaims the love of God. Men are awakened through the Sermon on the Mount only if its interpretation is freed from all "moral and mystical contamination." The church that reads the Sermon on the Mount "as law that it attempts to fulfill. . . is no longer salt nor light nor a city on a hill. . . . This is why it has so little authority to forgive sins. On the contrary, with its mere Jesus-religion and Jesus-morality it drives man right into sin." In the view of Thurneysen all humanity pleads with the church: "No longer force us into sin! Do not cast us under the law. Give us, give us finally the gospel!" Therefore, it is the task of the true church, says Thurneysen, to cast off "the bonds of the Babylonian captivity in which it [lies] bound" and proclaim only "Jesus the Christ in his word."[36]

Any evaluation of Thurneysen's thesis must acknowledge the service he rendered the church in distinguishing the fundamental hermeneutical difference between focusing on Christ as the subject of one's gospel or on man as the object of one's problems. Thurneysen emphatically reminded historians and theologians that the sayings of Jesus ought not to be abstracted from Jesus because the essence of what is said in the Sermon on the Mount is inseparable from the fact that it was Jesus who said it. For, in the final analysis, the meaning of what he said is inseparable from his self-understanding as the Messiah and from our recognition and acknowledgment of that claim. Thurneysen is right to say that "the preacher of the Sermon on the Mount *is* the Sermon on the Mount" insofar as all speech is essentially the self-revelation of the speaker—indeed, *is* the event of the person speaking.

But does it not border on semantic misrepresentation to press the identity of "Preacher" with "Sermon" so that the subjectivity of the subject

---

[35]Ibid., 74-75.

[36]Ibid., 77-78.

demands the equation of the subject spoken with the subject speaking? Why should we exclude as a referent of that speech those to whom it was addressed? Why, of all speech, should the speech of Jesus be reduced to dialogue within himself? His Sermon on the Mount stands within a Jewish didactic tradition which cannot be forced into an existentialist or solipsistic mold. There is no more reason to assume that Jesus was speaking only about himself than there is to claim that he was speaking only to himself. Thurneysen implicitly presupposes the dialectical understanding of how God reveals himself as it is made explicit in Barth's dogmatics. Unless this hidden agenda is exposed and debated in its own right, it is merely confusing to say that "the preacher of the Sermon on the Mount *is* the Sermon on the Mount."

Jesus confronted people with the will of God, described in Matthew as the new righteousness or the new obedience of the people of God. Thurneysen insists that this new obedience cannot and ought not apply intrinsically to our lives. He forewarns us not to try to live by the Sermon lest the heavens above be darkened and all hell open up beneath us! Not only are we unable to do what Jesus said, but, according to Thurneysen, we are not even invited to do what Jesus did. For those who nevertheless seek to follow Jesus Thurneysen promises "only a curse or despair"! What matters is not our obedience but that of Christ who did everything "for" us. Thurneysen assumes that Jesus' gospel is the post-Easter Pauline theology of imputed righteousness superimposed upon the commandments of Jesus as fulfilled in his cross and resurrection. The interpretation of even apparently obvious texts, such as "Why do you call me 'Lord, Lord,' and do not what I tell you," is bent to imply that what Jesus demands is not "deeds" but only "the right confession," since whatever needed to be done Jesus did in his atoning work. Consequently, understanding the Sermon on the Mount as a guide for moral and religious conduct only "defrauds its real meaning" by a "futile" and "legalistic" distortion of the gospel of substitutionary atonement. Thurneysen excludes from this gospel any emphasis on *imitatio Christi*.

Jesus said, "Let your light so shine before men that they see your good works" (Matthew 5:16), but Thurneysen speculates that there may be no visible works as such, no actual obedience intrinsically considered on our part. He does concede some "symbolic" or token obedience, provided that it remain completely hidden as the invisible fruit of invisible members of the *ecclesia invisibilis*—all this invisibility based on the visibility of Jesus!

Why? Because the new humanity must remain invisible except for one man—Jesus. And his Kingdom must remain hidden except for one act— his exorcism of demons. For all the Christological emphasis, it appears that within Thurneysen's interpretation of the Sermon on the Mount there is no actual place for Christ's Church as the people of God living in the new aeon, walking in the light, participating in the perfections of God, obeying the commandments of God, and doing the works of God by the power of God for the glory of God. There is only the despairing actuality that "we are and remain sinnners" except for the mystery that lies behind everything: predestination.

Thurneysen's Christological interpretation of the Sermon on the Mount accentuates the fundamental truth that Christ together with his gospel stands at the decisive center of his teaching. But in so doing Thurneysen ignores the fact that Jesus was Jewish precisely in his teaching and that the Sermon on the Mount with its insistence on radical obedience stands wholly within the Jewish ethical tradition. Thurneysen says he learned his approach from Luther and Calvin, who, in turn, developed it as polemic to condemn at once the Jews, the Catholics, and the Anabaptists.[37] Even the loftiest defense of the gospel can in its overstatement become a form of its distortion.

---

[37]Hiltrud Stadland-Neumann (*Evangelische Radicalismen in der Sicht Calvins. Sein Verständnis der Bergpredigt und der Aussendungsrede* [diss.], in "Beiträge zur Geschichte und Lehre der Reformierten Kirche," Neukirchener Verlag des Erziehungsvereins Gmbh., 1966) documents how in reaction against the Anabaptist *imitatio Christi* emphasis Calvin's christocentrism led to a modification of Jesus' radicalisms.

Joh. Christoph Blumhardt the elder preached seven influential sermons at Bad Boll on the Sermon on the Mount in 1871 (*Die Bergpredigt [Mt. 5–7]*, Basler Missionsbuchhandlung, Basel [Druck von Karl Werner], 1944). In his foreword to the third reprint in 1944, Wilhelm Hensius surmises that of the many learned and edifying treatises the 19th century had produced on the subject Blumhardt's deserves to be included among those few that have lasting value, for "like the Reformers," he understood the Sermon on the Mount "really christologically, that is, with a view to the one who has fulfilled the divine law for us. . . . Blumhardt thereby evades every moralistic and enthusiastic [schwärmerisch] misunderstanding of the Sermon on the Mount." For, without this focus on the obedience Christ "completed and proclaims, the Sermon on the Mount becomes the law that kills us" (3).

Hensius's description is an adequate appraisal of the method and content of Blumhardt's sermons about the Sermon. A few samples will suffice to document it. When the Saviour proclaimed his manifold blessings through the Beatitudes—including "undisturbed possession of the earth" (5) and reward in heaven for disgrace and persecution suffered—his disciples inquired how all that might actually be realized. "Who indeed will and can do and effect this for us miserable sinners?" Whereupon it immediately occurs to them: " 'That is surely the man who not only says so but who will also accomplish it for us.' There he stood so entirely as the one . . . sent by the Father precisely in order to tell the people that he intends to do everything for them . . ." [sic] (6).

Then follows an elaboration of Jesus' blessing upon the poor which also becomes the definitive category for the sermon's relevance. "In order that we might understand it correctly the Lord says not just 'poor' but 'poor in spirit,' that means 'assumed to be spiritually poor' " irrespective of how rich one is by worldly assessments in terms of wealth, art, science, history, and so on! Whoever "feels poor and unhappy . . . he transposes into the blessed state." Later we are explicitly informed with respect to Matthew 6:19-34 that no critique of material acquisition or possession of wealth was intended by Jesus, for "the whole society would fall apart except for the many wealthy among it" (30-31). Abraham could not have maintained himself in Canaan had he not been so wealthy. Jacob " 'was rich beyond all measure' as indeed he needed to be having twelve sons," and Paul did not admonish the wealthy to give up their riches, only their pride. Jesus' prohibition of oaths is limited to those "not legally required" to avoid invoking this power for lesser causes. The absence of any interpretation of Matthew 5:38-48 is conspicuous.

Blumhardt's sermons conclude with an emphasis on "holiness and renewal" together with an admonition to take Jesus' commands seriously and strive to do them—not as a better righteousness through which one might inherit the Kingdom of God but as the fruit of imputed righteousness—"otherwise there is no repentance and without repentance no grace" (62).

This harmless series of edifying discourses representing the Reformers' tradition of "Christological interpretation" lacks theological articulation and ethical relevance and contains no discussion of the practicability or applicability of Jesus' teaching.

In his voluminous *Church Dogmatics* (Edinburgh: T. & T. Clark, 1936ff.) Karl Barth explored the meaning of the Sermon on the Mount from within the context of God's command and developed its basis, content, and form from the perspectives of election, creation, reconciliation, and redemption as God's sovereign, definite, and good decision for us. "As the doctrine of God's command, ethics interprets the Law as the form of the Gospel, i.e., as the sanctification which comes to man through the electing God." Accordingly, the function of ethics is "to bear primary witness to the grace of God in so far as this is the saving engagement and commitment of man" (II/2, 509). We experience God's Word, says Barth, as both Gospel and Law. "In its content it is Gospel; in its form and fashion it is Law. It is first Gospel and then Law. It is the Gospel which contains and encloses the Law as the ark of the covenant the tables of Sinai" (511). Barth understands ethics as the command of God issued to Jesus and fulfilled by Jesus which means that the question of ethics cannot be raised apart from the realization of the good in and through the Christ event. "We cannot act as if we had to ask and decide for ourselves what the good is and how we can achieve it, . . . [for] that general conception of ethics coincides exactly with the conception of sin" (518). In speaking of ethics we should therefore not try to evade the grace of God revealed and fulfilled in the Christ event, for ontically our obligation is grounded in the being of this event and noetically it is derived from it (532). "What ought we to do?

. . . In Him the obedience demanded of us men has already been rendered. In Him the realization of the good corresponding to divine election has already taken place—and so completely that we, for our part, have actually nothing to add, but only to endorse this event by our action'' (540).

Not unlike Thurneysen, Barth refers to the Sermon on the Mount as "the sphere where it is proclaimed and heard and authentic that the Kingdom of God has come because and as He, Jesus, has come'' (687). In the Christ-event the God of the covenant Himself completes and fulfills the conditions of the Sermon on the Mount. Though the Sermon on the Mount appears to be objectively concerned with the correct solution of certain problems such as "the maintenance of life and marriage, the question of swearing and justice, the problem of enemies" and other matters—this appearance, Barth assures us, "is incidental and only by way of illustration," for from these directions "it has always proved impossible to construct a picture of the Christian life." On the contrary, "the Sermon on the Mount is intended to draw our attention to the person of Jesus . . . [who] Himself is the kingdom of the new humanity" (688). In this way the Sermon on the Mount proclaims what was determined and promised but not given to Israel by indicating that Jesus Christ, the royal man, stands where, according to the Ten Commandments, man should stand. The Sermon on the Mount does not stand at the beginning of further fulfillment of the covenant in the history of the Church but stands rather "as a postscript of the completed covenant of grace and its concluded history" in the Christ event (688). "No human life is constructed as the Sermon on the Mount depicts it. Who can ever find himself achieving that higher righteousness (5:20) or really fulfilling the Ten Commandments and the rest of the Law as indicated in 5:21f. ? . . . Most certainly, we are not this. And in view of the notorious nonfulfillment of the Ten Commandments by the people of Israel, it would be sheer folly to interpret the imperatives of the Sermon on the Mount as if we should bestir ourselves to actualize these pictures. Yet the whole picture of the new man which seems to be there unfolded is not a fantasy but a reality. It has not been introduced as a reality by us but for us. We hear and do all this as the Word of Jesus" (689). The point of these imperatives is, according to Barth, that we allow the dark text of our lives to be illumined by the grace of God in Christ in whom "the kingdom, and with it the new man, has now appeared" (690). "This man is obviously the Israelite, the man of Jer. 31:33 of whom it was said that God implanted His Law in his inmost being, and wrote it on his heart" (691). "He has made true the whole prophecy of the Ten Commandments and the rest of the Law by its fulfillment in His own person. . . . Thus the righteousness which the Sermon on the Mount exacts is inseparable from the One who exacts it. It is His righteousness. . . . The righteousness of man required by the Sermon on the Mount consists objectively in the fact that Jesus recognizes him as His own, and subjectively in the fact that this righteous man belongs to Jesus. . . . What decides his [that is, man's] righteousness is not his life and work, nor his confession of Jesus, but Jesus' confession of him" (692). "That is why the Sermon begins with the blessing of the poor in Spirit (5:3). . . . The single eye which is the light of the whole body (6:22), the 'pure heart' which has the promise of seeing God (5:8), is the realism of those who accept the decision and Word of Jesus. . . . The arrogance which would seize the promise on its own initiative, the delusion which would aspire to fulfil the Law in human strength, the mischievous error of the sick who think they are whole and in no need of a physician, will always lead men past this narrow gate" (693).

Barth repeatedly emphasizes that Jesus alone fulfilled the Law and that it is only through Him that "those who in themselves are disobedient are claimed and absorbed by the act of His obedience" (694). In this sense they are by virtue of their divine election included in the reality of the new man, and thus the Sermon on the Mount is to them also "instruction and exhortation, the training and exercise of man," provided it is always fully understood that "every 'Thou shalt!' and 'Thou shalt not!' is seriously meant as an intensified indicative which has the force of an intensified imperative, [for] the man who is reached and affected and determined by these imperatives" is not man as such but Jesus. And, even though it is Jesus in *them,* it is still, as far as Barth is concerned, essentially *Jesus.* "The newness of the new creature is not, therefore, a goodness which he has achieved himself, or which has been imparted to him or infused into him, but simply the goodness promised and done to him. . . . " For Barth, the Golden Rule "has nothing whatever to do with Kant's categorical imperative, or with a recommendation to treat one's neighbour with an amiableness that one would like to receive from him" (694). The good works of the new man are the fruit of thankfulness, though this too is primarily and fundamentally the work of divine grace (695). "Left to himself he would certainly give that which is holy to the dogs [7:6] in favour of a system of law or lawlessness. His gratitude would immediately be turned into ingratitude" (696). The directions contained in the Sermon on the Mount are "as a whole so extraordinary" because "their aim is to call upon men to pray with Jesus, and therefore to enter with Him under the order of grace and never to leave it again." The Antitheses of Matthew 5:21-48 "are only examples" intended to make clear that the grace of God in Christ claims the whole man absolutely. "The only one who really fulfils the Law as understood in this way is Jesus Himself. All others are called to obedience only by the fact that Jesus is obedient for them." That "these sharpened requirements point—inevitably—to superhuman possibilities" does not mean for Barth that "any of them are inapplicable to us—even the plucking out of the eye or the cutting off of the hand (5:29)" (696), for surely the grace of God in Christ applies to us and through these sharpened requirements claims us as sinners, "as those for whom Jesus prays and whom He summons to pray with Him. . . . The limit of their capacity becomes irrelevant when that which Jesus the Lord accomplishes for them occupies the centre of the picture. . . . " (697).

Barth believes the Sermon on the Mount cannot be understood apart from God's commanding. The biblical commandments "are not empty forms which will be filled out only as they are applied to real life. In these texts [i.e., the Decalogue and the Bergpredigt] which consist predominantly of definite negations, the area is marked out in which the concrete divine commandments and prohibition take place. They show its bounds by telling what is impossible in this area. What . . . these men are to do in particular is told them neither in the Ten Commandments nor in the Sermon on the Mount, . . . [for] the command of God is in the Bible a historical reality, and not as understood by post-biblical Judaism and Christianity, a timeless truth in the sense of casuistic ethics" (III/4, 12-13). Fundamental to Barth's theological method is the conviction that Jesus does not give man an answer to his ethical questions apart from the fact that Christ Himself is God's answer to man's dilemma. By virtue of the sovereignty of God and through the triumph of his abounding grace, our predetermination is included within the determination of Jesus Christ so that God's will may be actualized in the self-determination of our sanctification within the context of our election in Christ. Through the work of the Holy Spirit who awakens us to faith, enlightens us to hope, and enables us to love, the command of God becomes the experience of our true freedom for God and for life in Christ who constitutes both the reality of our election and the actuality of our obedience.

The difficulty of reconciling Barth's theological method with a Jewish approach to ethics is indicated by Pinchas Lapide of Jerusalem, who begins his recent essay on "Die Bergpredigt—Theorie und Praxis" (*Zeitschrift für Evangelische Ethik*, 17. Jg., Heft 6 [Nov. 1973] as follows: "Karl Barth ist der Meinung, 'daß ein Bild christlichen Lebens aus diesen Anweisungen (der Bergpredigt) zusammenzusetzen sich noch immer als eine Unmöglichkeit erwiessen hat.' Kurz danach spricht er in seiner 'Kirchlichen Dogmatik' vom 'hellen Wahnsinn, die Imperative der Bergpredigt dahin zu verstehen, daß wir uns bemühen sollen, diese Bilder zu verwirklichen' (II/2, 706ff.). Als Jude finde ich diese Worte des großen evangelischen Theologen befremdend und, was das Judentum betrifft, zum Teil unrichtig. 'An ihren Früchten (nicht an ihrem Gefasel!) werdet ihr sie erkennen', sagte Jesus (Mt. 7:11) mit prophetischem Weitblick zu Ende seiner Bergpredigt, und für die Schwerhörigen fügte er noch hinzu: 'Nicht jeder, der zu mir sagt: Herr, Herr! wird in das Himmelreich eingehen, sondern wer den Willen meines Vaters tut, Der im Himmel ist' (Mt. 7:21). Diese Worte bezeugen nicht nur den gut jüdischen Pragmatismus des Galiläers, sondern liefern auch den verläßlichsten Maßstab, um die wahre 'Christentreue' der nachjesuanischen Welt zu messen. Nach diesem eindeutigen Wortsinn des Evangeliums gehören zu den ergebensten Jüngern Jesu nicht die, die ihn als 'Kyrios' auf Kreuz und Altar verherrlichen, sondern zahlreicher seiner Brüder 'nach dem Fleische', von denen viele verblüfft, wenn nicht empört wären, wenn man ihre Moralität als 'christlich' bezeichnen würde."

With respect to the practicability of the Bergpredigt, Emil Brunner declared: "Friedrich Naumann, too, was quite right when he said that he despaired of the usefulness of this ethic for the cultural life of our day. . . . We are accustomed to require an ethic to be practicable. If this is what we want, then we should turn to Aristotle! The ethic of the Gospel is not practicable because it is serious. To take morality seriously, leads to the despairing admission that it is impossible to do it. But the impossibility is no excuse. The phrase 'You ought and therefore you can' is a saying of the ancient serpent. It is the language of Pelagianism. It is impossible to do the Divine Will, because we are sinners, because this historical existence is sinful existence. Therefore the commandments of the Sermon on the Mount do not fit into it, however much they may be the standard which is the only one for us. Only the impossible is worthy to be obeyed. For only the impossible is the Will of God. That it *is* impossible is due to sin." (*The Mediator. A Study of the Central Doctrine of the Christian Faith*, ET O. Wyon [London: Lutterworth Press, 1937], pp. 418-19).

Walter Lüthi and Robert Brunner (*The Sermon on the Mount*. Edinburgh & London: Oliver & Boyd, 1963 [Translated from the original: *Der Heiland. Ein Gang durch die Bergpredigt*, 1936]) identify the source from which the Sermon on the Mount derives its strength as the cross and resurrection of Christ and seek to balance the realization that even our best efforts are in vain and we consequently live entirely by grace with the insight that "we must also work for the salvation of our own souls" (171).

JOACHIM JEREMIAS:
THE SERMON SEEN
AS GOSPEL, NOT LAW

Jesus was not a teacher of the law, or a preacher of wisdom, such as could be found among his contemporaries; his message burst the bounds of late Judaism.[1]

If the Sermon on the Mount is a catechism for baptismal candidates or newly baptized Christians, then it was preceded by something else. It was preceded by the proclamation of the gospel; and it was preceded by conversion, by a being overpowered by the Good News.[2]

Every word of the Sermon on the Mount was preceded by something else. It was preceded by the preaching of the Kingdom of God. It was preceded by the granting of sonship to the disciples (Matt. 5:16, 45, 48, etc.). It was preceded by Jesus' witness in word and deed.[3]

Only if we begin with the greatness of the gift of God can we really understand the heavy nature of the demands which Jesus makes.[4]

The Sermon on the Mount is not law, but gospel. . . . The law leaves man to rely upon his own strength and challenges him to do his utmost. The gospel, on the other hand, brings man before the gift of God and challenges him really to make the inexpressible gift of God the basis of his life.[5]

These sayings of Jesus delineate the lived faith.[6]

---

[1]Joachim Jeremias, *The Sermon on the Mount,* ET Norman Perrin (Philadelphia: Fortress Press, 1963) 6.

[2]Ibid., 23.

[3]Ibid., 30.

[4]Ibid., 32.

[5]Ibid., 34.

[6]Ibid., 35.

Joachim Jeremias[7] employed the techniques of literary and form criticism in his analysis of the Sermon on the Mount in order to answer the long debated question regarding its aim. Before presenting his own research, Jeremias exposed the inadequacies of the positions represented by Hans Windisch, Lutheran Orthodoxy, and Johannes Weiss.

With the approach of Windisch, which he inappropriately labels the "perfectionist conception," Jeremias concurs that "we may not lightly ignore the common ground between Jesus and the Judaism of his day" but then proceeds to indicate "great differences between the demands of Jesus and the ethic of late Judaism" which this position tends to minimize. Rejecting the assumption that Jesus also shared the "legalism" of late Judaism, Jeremias concludes "that Jesus was not a teacher of the law, or a preacher of wisdom, such as could be found among his contemporaries; his message burst the bounds of late Judaism."[8]

As for the Lutheran "theory of the impossible ideal" (represented in our analysis by Stange and Kittel), Jeremias finds an element of validity both in the apparent seriousness with which Jesus' demands are supposed to be taken in driving people to despair and thereby opening their eyes to the mercy of God and also in the humble realism of assessing one's own inadequacy to realize this impossible ideal. Jeremias is sympathetic to these Pauline insights, but he cannot find within the Sermon on the Mount itself any "clear statement which points unmistakably in this direction."[9]

With respect to the interim ethic of Weiss and Schweitzer, Jeremias holds that, while "the dynamic of eschatology lies behind every word of Jesus," the Sermon on the Mount "is not an ethic of the death-hour nor the utterance of a voice from a world on the brink of catastrophe."[10] Jeremias is quite certain Jesus was not an apocalypticist proclaiming an exceptional rule valid only for a short interim. Jeremias views these three positions, however divergent their perspectives, as having one thing in

---

[7]Joachim Jeremias served many years as Professor of New Testament at the University of Göttingen. He was born in Dresden in 1900 and spent much of his youth in Jerusalem. His special study was the first century background of the Gospels. Among his many books we may note *The Parables of Jesus* (1954), *The Eucharistic Words of Jesus* (1955), *Jerusalem in the Time of Jesus* (1969), and *New Testament Theology* (1971).

[8]*The Sermon on the Mount*, 4-6.

[9]Ibid., 8.

[10]Ibid., 11.

common—their conception of the Sermon on the Mount as law. Therein, he thinks, lies their common inadequacy.

Jeremias advances his own understanding of the meaning of the Sermon on the Mount based on an analysis of its compositional character. He claims the completed "edifice" of the Matthean and Lukan versions was built in several stages and that the "bricks" out of which the Sermon is constituted were originally isolated sayings of Jesus, possibly sermonettes or pieces of dialogue from the context of his teaching.[11] These sayings were collected by early Christians for the purpose of catechetical instruction of converts, as is evident from an analysis of the parallel accounts of the Lord's Prayer. The Matthean Jewish-Christian *didache* (Matthew 6:5-15) "is directed to men who come from a world in which people had learned to pray but in which there was the danger of a misuse of prayer,"[12] which accounts for the admonition not to pray like the hypocrites. According to Luke's version (11:1ff.), a disciple requests of Jesus, "Teach us to pray," whereupon he teaches the Lord's Prayer. Jeremias holds this to be instruction directed to Gentile Christian converts who had never learned to pray. If both versions of the Sermon take the form of pre- and post-baptismal instruction of Jewish- and Gentile-Christians, then, reasons Jeremias, this instruction (*didache*) must have been preceded by the proclamation of the Gospel (*kerygma*) which inspired their conversion.[13]

After further examining the individual sayings directed to the disciples, Jeremias concludes, "We can only rightly understand the individual saying when we presuppose in each case that *it was preceded by something else.*" Jeremias demonstrates his claim with five examples. " 'You are the light of the world' [Matthew 5:14], which compares the disciples to the sun, makes no sense when taken by itself" because their weakness and failures were not that illuminating. Therefore this saying presupposes "a previous, unexpressed sentence, 'I am the light of the world' (John 8:12)." "If you do not forgive men their trespasses, neither can your heavenly Father" (Matthew 6:15) would be misread "as if the law of reciprocity can be applied to the relationship between God and man, as in a commercial bargain," except for the awareness that this demand "was preceded by the

---

[11]Ibid., 17-18.

[12]Ibid., 21.

[13]Ibid., 23.

great debt cancellation of which the parable of the unmerciful servant speaks''[14]—the last line of that pericope (Matthew 18:35) is hinted at in the Lord's Prayer. Similarly, Jesus' rejection of divorce (Matthew 5:31-32) was preceded by his proclamation of the new aeon in which not Moses' concession but only the will of the Creator applies. Jesus' saying about turning the cheek (Matthew 5:38-39) was preceded by "the act of becoming a follower of Jesus and of publicly confessing allegiance to him" which brought the insulting blow on the cheek. Jesus' demand to love one's enemies (Matthew 5:44-45) is preceded, says Jeremias, by the message of God's impartial grace and unbounded goodness. In each case then "the gospel preceded the demand.''[15]

The Sermon on the Mount has therefore been designed as teaching for young believers who have been converted through the preaching to instruct them in the Christian way. For Jeremias, the difficulty of Jesus' original demands consequently presupposes that his disciples are already firmly grounded in the reality of the Kingdom of God "and radiate its nature." On this assumption, "bestowal (*Zuspruch*) of divine forgiveness includes God's claim (*Anspruch*) on the forgiven life. . . . Only if we begin with the greatness of the gift of God can we really understand the heavy nature of the demands which Jesus makes." Referring to the disciples' inability and weakness, Jesus spoke of a city set on a hill: "Its light, says Jesus, shines in the world. You belong to it. In the eschatological city there is no need for convulsive efforts; its light shines of itself.''[16]

In summary, Jeremias reasons that the Sermon on the Mount is not Law which "leaves man to rely upon his own strength and challenges him to do his utmost" but Gospel which "brings man before the gift of God and challenges him really to make the inexpressible gift of God the basis for his life." The Sermon on the Mount is "lived faith" (*gelebter Glaube*).[17] We do not do all this in order to be blessed in the so-called "perfectionist conception," and we do not do it as an exceptional Interim Ethic because the remaining time is so short. Nor are we confounded by an impossible ideal. "Rather," concludes Jeremias,

---

[14]Ibid., 26.

[15]Ibid., 29-30.

[16]Ibid., 32-33.

[17]Ibid., 34.

these sayings of Jesus delineate the lived faith. They say: You are for-given; you are the child of God; you belong to his kingdom. The sun of righteousness has risen over your life. You no longer belong to yourself; rather, you belong to the city of God, the light of which shines in the dark-ness. Now you may also experience it: out of the thankfulness of a re-deemed child of God a new life is growing. That is the meaning of the Sermon on the Mount.[18]

Jeremias' conclusions are beautiful and true, but not sufficiently ex-plicit. The underlying ambiguity pertains to his contention with Hans Win-disch over whether the Sermon on the Mount is an ethic of obedience. Jeremias rejects the term "ethic" as "inadequate and liable to misunder-standing" but goes further than Windisch in setting Jesus' teaching "over against that of the Torah" by showing that for Jesus' decisive sayings— the blessing upon the poor, the forbidding of divorce, the turning of the cheek, and the loving of one's enemies—"there are no parallels in the Tal-mud."[19] But does Jeremias concur with Windisch that Jesus intended his commands to be literally fulfilled? If so, why does he discredit this con-ception as perfectionistic misunderstanding? If not, why should the fact that Jesus' demands are more radical than those of the Torah imply that they are therefore to be taken less seriously *as demands*?

From the viewpoint of historical exegesis, Jeremias agrees with Win-disch that Jesus expected of his disciples "concrete, hard, and fast de-mands."[20] Windisch, as we have seen, insisted Jesus' demands were meant to be fulfilled but conceded that we do not fulfill them and therefore do not identify with the original meaning of the Sermon on the Mount. Where does Jeremias stand on this matter of its practicability today? He directs our at-tention to the "eschatological" city of God whose light "shines of it-self."[21] We question only whether the *gelebter Glaube* within this city is realized or futuristic eschatology.

Finally, there is the matter of Law and Gospel upon which Jeremias rests his case. He concludes that the Sermon on the Mount is "not Law, but Gospel" on the grounds that its early Christian use as *didache* presup-

---

[18]Ibid., 35.

[19]Ibid., 5.

[20]Ibid., 4.

[21]Ibid., 33.

posed the *kerygma*. Yet the crucial question is not how the Early Church used Jesus' sayings but whether he himself understood his message within these categories. Jeremias says that what preceded the demands of the Antitheses (Matthew 5:21-48) was often "unexpressed," "not specifically stated," or "ostensibly missing,"[22] but in Jesus' hardest saying, "Love your enemies," the so-called *kerygma* of the Father's impartial mercy *is* stated and does *not* precede but *follows* the demand. Even if that were not so, should loving one's enemies have Christian validity only because it is chronologically preceded by what Lutheran and Reformed theologians identify as "the gospel"—namely, "Your sins are forgiven"? Is not the sin itself hatred of others and the Gospel itself freedom to love all men as brothers under God? Is not the sole presupposition of Jesus' demands identical to that of the Decalogue: "I am the Lord your God"? We agree with Jeremias that Jesus proclaimed not just forgiveness of sin but simultaneous deliverance from both its guilt and its power. However, if that was God's intention through the Law, what is gained by redefining it as Gospel?

---

[22]Ibid., 26-31.

A. M. Hunter refers to the Sermon on the Mount as Christ's *Design for Life* (London: SCM [1953] 1965). He explains its style as proverbial teaching which "states truth in a vivid, extreme, hyperbolical way" and cautions: "We must, if we are to avoid the peril of a crude literalism in interpretation, always be seeking for the principle that underlies the proverb, the truth behind the paradox, ceaselessly resisting the temptation to water it down into a moral commonplace" (22). Noting how the interpretation of Jesus' moral imperatives (Mt. 5:21-48) has puzzled many, Hunter attests that light comes if we distinguish between *mandata* ("moral imperatives stating deep, broad principles") and *exempla* ("illustrations of these principles in action"). Thus, "Resist not evil" (Mt. 5:39) expresses, "the principle of nonvindictiveness in personal relations, not nonresistance to evil in any and every circumstance." As for turning the cheek and letting one's opponent have one's cloak, "to take these illustrations quite literally and erect them into principles of action is to land oneself in absurdity. Similarly, when Jesus says 'Swear not at all' (Mt. 5:34), he is calling for absolute sincerity in speech, not prohibiting oaths in all circumstances (e.g., in the law court)" (23).

Hunter considers Matthew 5:17-20 the "hardest" verses and feels they "can hardly be words of Christ," for "they read, rather, like some early Christian misapplication of some words of Jesus," characteristic of "Christian legalism such as may have arisen in ultra-conservative circles which were shocked by the attitude of Paul and his friends to the law" (47). Hunter objects to regarding Jesus' Antitheses to the Old Law as *nova lex Christi* as though "with a reasonable effort men may keep them." He is sure, however, that "this is how God means men to live" and realizes that "all who call themselves Christ's disciples must try to live according to this pattern'' but holds that no one in our fallen world actually can and does live that way. Therefore, "these verses at once declare the Christian moral ideal and convict us of our sin'' (49). In Matthew 5:31-32, "Jesus was not laying down a binding law about marriage but stating the divine ideal'' (54). Taking Matthew 5:33-37 "as an absolute prohibition of an oath under any circumstances, as the Anabaptists, the Quakers, and Tolstoy have done, is to confound the letter with the spirit,'' claims Hunter (56). For the same reason, Matthew 5:38-42 applies to nonretaliation only in cases of "personal'' wrong, but even in that case interpreting Jesus' "picturesque illustrations'' about personal assault, a suit at law, and so on would literally, in Hunter's view, "only result in violence, robbery, and anarchy'' (57). The sheer fact that a man, having lost his shirt, volunteered also his coat would consequently find himself practically nude is, says Hunter, "clear proof'' that Jesus did not intend this illustration to be taken literally. However, the "illustration'' about volunteering for a second mile of forced labor—though surely no less inconvenient—Hunter considers commendable (59). Similarly, Jesus' command to love our enemies (Mt. 5:43-48) is interpreted with considered ambivalence: "Complete catholicity in love—like God's—is the ideal Christ sets before his disciples.'' Nevertheless, "He does not mean that we should 'love' all and sundry in the same sense as we love our nearest and dearest'' (60).

Hunter argues that the Sermon on the Mount is best interpreted "as an ethic of grace'' according to Jeremias' view, which he finds "the truest and the best'' (104-105). Like Jeremias, he delineates the relation of the Sermon on the Mount as *didache* to the *kerygma* it presupposed in early Christian proclamation (107-111).

In summary, Hunter qualifies the Sermon on the Mount in four ways. (1) "It is a religious ethic . . . rooted and grounded in the 'Good News' of the Kingdom of God'' (114). (2) It is intended for the disciples, not for mankind at large, and primarily concerns committed Christians, though, cautions Hunter, "we must remember that we Christians to whom its terrifying challenges come are not invited to rise to these heights in our own strength'' (115-16). (3) It is a prophetic, not a legalistic ethic, for "to regard Jesus as a second Moses and his Sermon as a new code of laws is to lapse into that soul-destroying legalism which he condemned'' (118). Finally, (4) "the ethic of Jesus is an unattainable ethic which we, as his followers, are nevertheless challenged to attain'' (118).

Hunter takes a mediating position between those who experience the Sermon on the Mount only as condemnation unto despair to prepare us to accept Christ's saving work and "those who blandly argue for practicability of the Sermon.'' Hunter says, "We cannot accept the assumption that men can and do live according to the pattern shown them in the Sermon on the Mount'' (120). Nevertheless, he concedes that "Jesus meant his ethic to be a real design for living, not a blueprint for Utopia'' (121). Hunter knows of no happy resolution of this "tension between the ideal and the actual which must ever mark the life of Christ's disciples, now as then. For we have to live our lives at once as citizens of this world, with all its trials and temptations, and as citizens of the Kingdom of God'' (122). Hunter's final determinative statement designates the Sermon on the Mount as "Design for Life *in the Kingdom*'' (122, [italics mine]), which qualifies this tension eschatologically. The question remains whether (in the light of Mt. 5:17f. and Lk. 6:46) a compromise position is theologically and existentially tenable.

Thomas S. Kepler's devotional study, *Jesus' Design for Living* (New York: Abingdon, 1955), reflects Hunter's views on decisive issues. For Kepler, the Sermon on the Mount conveys ideals like stars which man can never touch but which guide him toward his destiny however dark the way (cf. 63).

Similar in emphasis to the interpretation of Dibelius and Hunter is that of Roger L. Shinn, who envisions *The Sermon on the Mount* (Philadelphia: United Church Press, [1954] 1962) as "the perfect ethic of God's Kingdom" while allowing Christians to use means "far from Christ's perfection" to avert greater evils (47).

WALTER STÄDELI:
THE CULTIC INTERPRETATION
OF THE SERMON ON THE MOUNT

The authentic Sermon on the Mount . . . may be described as the festal liturgy for the inauguration of the king of heaven.[1]

As yet another approach to understanding the teaching of Jesus, Walter Städeli proposed the "cultic interpretation" of the Sermon on the Mount on the assumption that its *Sitz-im-Leben* is "cultic poetry" analogous to the Psalms. For Städeli's thesis everything depends on the centrality of the temple cult as the frame of reference for understanding and applying these sayings of Jesus. Städeli's logic consists in establishing fantastic parallels between the cult of the mount and the Sermon on the Mount, implying that the latter presupposes the former and ought therefore to be appropriated within the liturgical context of the church.

That Jesus "went up on a mountain" (Matthew 5:1) assumes the connection between the Mount of the Sermon and Mount Zion (rather than Horeb) and marks the beginning of the "Way of the Lord" seen against the background of the festival cult commencing with the solemn procession of the Ark towards the temple-mount to the accompaniment of Psalm 95 and other hymns of ascent in commemoration of Yahweh's mighty salvation-acts. As part of the liturgy outlining the conditions for entering the temple gate, the Psalmist asks the question of eligibility: "Who shall ascend the hill of the Lord? And who shall stand in his holy place?" (Psalms 24:3f.). The answer re-echoes from the priests who serve as keepers of the

---

[1] Walter Städeli, *A Study of Christian Perfection in the Context of the Sermon on the Mount* (Ph.D. diss., University of Edinburgh, 1964), 401.

temple gate: "He who has clean hands and a pure heart, who does not lift up his soul to what is false, and does not swear deceitfully. He will receive blessing from the Lord, . . . " to which the procession about to enter the temple gate responds: "We have kept and fulfilled all this."[2] Supposedly, there were according to Psalm 15 ten entry conditions parallel to the ten commandments, one for each finger!—reason enough for Städeli to surmise that there were originally as many beatitudes in Jesus' Sermon—and these conditions were supposedly carved in limestone tablets at the temple entrance.

A parallel cultic setting is identified in Micah 6:6-8 where in answer to the question—"With what shall I come before the Lord?"—the priests guarding the "Gate of Righteousness," as the inmost temple gate was supposedly designated, reply: "He has shown you, O Man, what is good; and what does the Lord require of you but to do justice, and love kindness, and to walk humbly with your God?"[3] As the duly initiated and consecrated proceed through the temple gates, the antiphonal chorus resounds the affirmation of "blessing" upon these "righteous" children of Israel. In explaining the effectual character of the beatitude, "creating what it mentions," Städeli also refers to the Babylonian Marduk Temple, the twelve gates of which were named Gate of Grace, Gate of Blessing, Gate of Salvation, Gate of Life, and so on, assuring those entering the designated promise, by virtue of the "mana" power associated with each gate.[4]

Jesus' first condition for entry through "the narrow [temple-] gate. . . that leads to life" (Matthew 7:13-14) takes the form of blessing upon "the poor in spirit" (Matthew 5:3), a beatitude directed not towards the *am ha-aretz*, who are necessarily poor, but to Jesus' disciples who have become voluntarily poor and freed from the bondage of Mammon (Matthew 6:24). Städeli also knows that Jesus does not demand renunciation of all possessions—only of all attachments—since the parallel condition in the entrance-liturgy of Psalm 15:5 requires only that one "not put out his money at interest and does not take a bribe against the innocent."[5] Not finding a precedent in entrance-liturgy for Jesus' blessing upon "those who weep

---

[2]Ibid., 75-76.

[3]Ibid., 84.

[4]Ibid., 86.

[5]Ibid., 277.

now" (Luke 6:21), Städeli refers us to the "ritual weeping" of Ugaritic texts associated with the death of a deity. There are also no parallels for Jesus' "blessed are the meek" and "those who hunger and thirst for righteousness" (Matthew 5:5-6) except insofar as the latter alludes to the liturgy in expressing hunger for God Himself. Since the third promise, to "inherit the earth," means participation in the reign of God and the fourth refers to the "satisfaction" of victory, Städeli finds it fitting that the fifth blessing of mercy upon the merciful (Matthew 5:7) should imply renunciation of revenge upon the adversaries following the enthronement ceremony within the liturgy.[6] Then follows the promise that "the pure in heart . . . shall *see God.*" "Since the existence of a visible symbol on the Mount of the Sermon is not very probable, we have to look for another interpretation," reasons Städeli.[7] Invariably, he interprets this promise as a "cultic expression" for seeing the Ark of the Lord. As the blessing upon the "peacemakers" (Matthew 5:9) parallels the oracle of assurance delivered by the priest within the liturgy (as he supposes in Psalm 85:8f.), Städeli concludes "that all eight beatitudes were part of the initiation rite celebrated on the Mount." Upon receiving from Jesus the final blessing upon "the pangs of the Messiah," Städeli envisions the disciples responding with "Amen, Amen."[8] He also notes that similar initiation rites characterized the community at Qumran, where the priest blessed "all the men of God who walked perfectly in all his ways."[9] Furthermore, Jesus' blessings apply "now" (meaning within the liturgical contemporaneity)[10] as implied by the Greek present tense. The function of these Beatitudes is seen by Städeli as "the initiation of the disciples into the kingdom of heaven, which herewith to a certain extent already becomes a present reality."[11]

The cultic analogies to Jesus' similies of salt and light (Matthew 5:13-16) are equally noteworthy. The "salt" refers to seasoning the cultic meal[12]

---

[6]Ibid., 286-87.

[7]Ibid., 289.

[8]Ibid., 296.

[9]Ibid., 263.

[10]See Deuteronomy 5:2-3: "The Lord our God made a covenant with us in Horeb. Not with our fathers did the Lord make this covenant, but with us, who are all of us here alive this day."

[11]*A Study of Christian Perfection*, 266.

[12]See Leviticus 2:13, alluded to by Codex D in Mark 9:49.

and to the "covenant of salt"[13] associated with kingship. The "light of the world" reflects the light of the torch dance on the first night of the New Year's festival symbolizing life, happiness, and salvation and prefiguring the light of theophany as in all ancient light ceremonies.

Seen against their cultic background, Jesus' Antitheses (Matthew 5:21-48) "imply the eschatological renewal of the covenant."[14] Following the liturgy of initiation reflected in the Beatitudes, the disciples, Städeli explains, are adopted as "sons" (Matthew 5:9, 45)—not as subjects—of the heavenly king. Their entry into the Kingdom (Matthew 5:20) implies their "entering into filial relationship with God" as indicated by the Lord's Prayer, which, presupposing this adoption, equates realization of Fatherhood with realization of the Kingdom of Heaven.[15] "The vital point of the new cult inaugurated by Jesus is the individual initiation into the Temple || kingdom(-ship) of God."[16] This initiation and adoption Matthew identifies as perfection (Matthew 5:48), according to Städeli. He notes that in the Old Testament the religious term for "perfect" (*tamim*) stems from cultic terminology denoting the wholeness of the sacrificial animal, from which it was reapplied to the integrity of the worshiper. In this familiar cultic context, Matthew 5:48 meant: "You therefore must be wholly consecrated as your heavenly Father is wholly consecrated."[17] Städeli explains that according to Hebrews 2:10 God " 'perfects' the Son through suffering and the Son in turn 'perfects' the sons by his single offering of himself." Therefore, concludes Städeli, the "legalistic interpretation of perfection by the final redaction of Matthew, which makes man the subject of his perfection . . . [is] not in accordance with the teaching of Jesus."[18] For the same reason, Luke's reading of the Two Ways pericope urging that we "*strive* to enter by the narrow door" (13:24) is for Städeli an unacceptable reinterpretation of the "Way *of* Perfection" as a "Way *to* Perfection." "He did this once for all when he offered up himself," insists

---

[13]See 2 Chronicles 12:15.

[14]*A Study of Christian Perfection*, 401.

[15]Ibid., 269.

[16]Ibid., 271.

[17]Ibid., 403. Compare Leviticus 19:2: "You shall be holy, for I the Lord your God am holy."

[18]Ibid., 404. Städeli refers to Matthew 5:20: "Unless your righteousness exceeds . . ."

Städeli quoting Hebrews 7:27, wherefore there may be no *imitatio Christi*—no "question of an analogy in the life of Christians" to Christ's way of the cross.[19]

According to Städeli, "the authentic Sermon on the Mount, that is, roughly Matthew 5:3-10, 13-16, 21-24, 27-48; 7:2-27, may be described as the festal liturgy for the inauguration of the king of heaven."[20] These passages constitute for him the original liturgical context of Jesus' concept of perfection as initiation and adoption, a conception characteristic of Christianity ever since the Early Church substituted the initiation rite of baptism for the initiation in the Beatitudes. It is through baptism, explains Städeli, and not through ethics that one becomes a member of the new humanity, sharing in its blessing through God's work in Christ.

The merit of Städeli's cultic interpretation of the Sermon on the Mount consists in the light it sheds on the Jewishness of Jesus by showing us how deeply the roots of Jesus' sayings are anchored in the liturgical traditions of Old Testament piety. Yet, the evidence for Städeli's thesis appears incomplete and the deductions inconclusive. The case for cultic interpretation of the Sermon on the Mount is made most impressively for the Beatitudes, but even here the logic of analogy is strained to the point of incredulity when for half of the extant blessings—not to mention the woes—no analogies to liturgical initiation rites can be found except by reference to pagan cults. Citations from Hebrews are applied to cover the gaps left by the Psalter, to challenge Luke's understanding of Jesus' demands, and to discredit Matthew's interpretation of Jesus' way.

It is not at all clear why Städeli's hierocentric focus on the way of the Lord should minimize that obedience which constituted the central element of Israel's cultic reaffirmation of covenantal faithfulness. Matthew's gospel does not exactly create the impression that the Sermon on the Mount was authored by a Levitical priest who all his life had so deeply imbibed the sacred smoke of the Temple sacrifice curling towards the Kingdom of Heaven from Mount Zion that his absorbing passion was spent refining this cultic ritual on a mountain in Galilee. For very specific reasons Matthew's allusions are to another mountain called Horeb, and the evidence Städeli

---

[19]Ibid., 404-405.
[20]Ibid., 401.

presented to challenge the ethical implications of Matthew's association is not convincing.

One should not presume to understand the way of the Lord better than Matthew nor claim to interpret Jesus' demands more authentically than Luke—both of whom convey the priority of moral law over ceremonial rites in the teaching of Jesus. Nor should these moral demands be taken less seriously than intended within their cultic settings before Jesus radicalized them. To the extent that cultic analogies to Jesus' demands are indicated they are also acknowledged as practicable—otherwise no one in Israel could have participated in the cultic festivals.

Finally, one wonders why Städeli disparaged the mystic way whose purgative, illuminative, and unitive stages so closely parallel his cultic orientation. Whether the viewpoint is cultic or mystic, the extraordinary righteousness Jesus demanded referred to something more than baptism. The "way of the Lord" led from the festival to the Cross. With Städeli the church celebrates this way in lieu of following it. That is why Städeli—in contrast to Matthew and Luke—interprets the Sermon on the Mount cultically rather than ethically.

AFFIRMATIONS OF PRACTICABILITY

HECTOR WAYLEN

Hector Waylen's remarkable book, *Mountain Pathways*, reflects the buoyant spirit of Tolstoy. Waylen is convinced that the Sermon on the Mount contains the world's highest teaching on the meaning of life and that, if it were "carried out by mankind, the world would be a Paradise."[1] He attaches particular significance to the second century old Syriac versions of the text, noting that "Syriac is closely allied to Aramaic and that the original sayings of Jesus may therefore have been more exactly reproduced in them."[2] Like Tolstoy, Waylen observed that

> want of personal experience in the lives of professing Christians together with far too much reliance upon outward forms, church organizations, and clerical institutions has for many a long century produced a tendency to soften down and take the keen edge off many of the simplest sayings in the New Testament.[3]

Regarding Jesus' saying on marriage faithfulness, he finds that the Syrian reading translated, "But I say unto you that he that dismisseth his wife concerning whom adultery hath not been alleged—he causeth her to commit adultery, and he that taketh up a divorced woman doth indeed commit adultery" (Mt. 5:32), "probably expressed here the true meaning of the Greek by the word 'dismiss,' " which is generally "taken to mean

---

[1] Hector Waylen, *Mountain Pathways: A Study in the Ethics of the Sermon on the Mount* (London: Sherratt and Hughes, 1909) 13. [Cf. also Appendix in the 1922 ed. by Kegan Paul.]

[2] Ibid., 19.

[3] Ibid., 20.

'divorce' in an absolute sense.''[4] The implication is that Jesus, while conceding unchastity as the legitimate ground for separation, does not permit divorce, ''for in the sight of God the first marriage is still valid,'' otherwise the man who married the divorced wife would not thereby ''commit adultery.''[5] In support of his view Waylen notes that, according to the Shepherd of Hermas (about A.D. 100), ''it is the duty of the husband to put away an unfaithful wife, yet 'on account of her possible repentance' he is not to marry again. But he is not required to receive her back more than once.''[6]

Waylen is equally emphatic in endorsing Christian nonresistance, expressed most forthrightly in the Syriac *Evangelion Da-Mepharreshe* which reads for Matthew 5:39, ''do not stand up to the evil person,'' and implies that Jesus did not yield to anger when (according to the Syriac version of Mark 14:65) ''the guards were smiting him on the cheeks.'' As a fair example of those men who throughout the ages have exploited every Christian half-truth as an apology for war, Waylen cites Oliver Cromwell, who prepared for his trusty Ironsides ''The Soldier's Pocket Bible'' including ''most (if not all) of those places contained in the Holy Scriptures'' that fit a soldier ''to fight the Lord's battles.'' Thus a soldier is induced to swear allegiance to worldly powers, to ''resign his liberty to think and to act for himself,'' and instead go ''to the ends of the earth to slay men whom he has never seen in a quarrel the justice of which he has never had a chance to properly investigate. Such conditions,'' concludes Waylen, ''are incompatible with the Christian life.''[7]

Waylen advocates the higher spiritual way of the true soul that thrives on the purifying air of Jesus' lofty ''mountain pathways'' which constitute the Way of Life, a way that enables man to aspire to the highest and does not allow his faith to degenerate to mere assent to tradition nor his creative discernment to disintegrate into pessimism of life and lawlessness. He believes that if Christians would only live in conformity to Jesus' teaching

---

[4]Waylen refers to ἀπολύσῃ.

[5]*Mountain Pathways*, 27, 28, 81. Waylen translates the debated phrase, παρεκτὸς λόγου πορνείας in Matthew 5:32 ''independently of the question of [whether it be] fornication.''

[6]Ibid., 154. [The canon of Muratory dates *The Shepherd* at A.D. 140, cf. Kirsopp Lake, *Landmarks in the History of Early Christianity* (London: Macmillan, 1920) 108.]

[7]Ibid., 33-38.

they would be filled with the gifts of his Spirit. These teachings, he concedes, cannot be carried out

in the spirit of "enlightened self-interest." . . . It can be done only with perfect trust in God and by means of the help which He will give to all who commit their ways to his keeping. And if we fully trust God, it must lead us sooner or later to recognize in Yeshua the Nazarene, the Messiah and Saviour of the world.[8]

E. STANLEY JONES

"The greatest need of modern Christianity is the rediscovery of the Sermon on the Mount as the only practical way to live," E. Stanley Jones wrote in his inspiring book, *The Christ of the Mount*,[9] written at an Ashram in the Himalayas. India liberated Jones from the dogmatic accretions of the Church and taught him that "the main moral content in the word 'Christian' must be the Sermon on the Mount."[10] He laments that "the orthodoxy of the creed is looked on as more essential than the orthopraxy of the deed. We have saluted this ideal, but we have not taken it seriously. We have used it for polemic, but not for practice."[11] Jones deplores theologians considering Sermon on the Mount principles humanly unattainable foreign laws because it appears to turn everything upside down. But, the more he studied it, the more he concluded that it really turns everything right side up:

the first time you read it you feel that it is impossible; the second time you feel that nothing else is possible. The more I have pondered on this way of life, the more I am persuaded that instead of all the moral impossibilities lying in the Sermon on the Mount, as we often think, the fact is that all the moral possibilities lie here, and all the impossibilities lie outside.[12]

Jones regrets our having become so naturalized in all of life's impossibilities that the way of life God intended for us to walk seems foreign, unnatural, and impossible, at least in our worst moments. In our highest

---

[8]Ibid., 71.

[9]E. Stanley Jones, *The Christ of the Mount: A Working Philosophy of Life* (Toronto: McClelland and Stewart, 1931) 14.

[10]Ibid., 11.

[11]Ibid., 13.

[12]Ibid., 14-15.

moments we know better and realize that everything else is unbelievably impossible and absurd. The danger, says Jones, is not that we degrade the Sermon on the Mount by a "grotesque literalism" but that we do so by a "literaryism" that explains away its stark challenge by literary devices. He urges that we stop embalming the Sermon on the Mount and start embodying it—or else abdicate our claim to being Christian. In the East he observed that the real question is not whether we *can* apply it but whether we *will*. He concludes that "if the ethical side of our gospel is unworkable, then by that very fact the redemptive side is rendered worthless." If the Sermon on the Mount is unworkable, then there is no spiritual power, only spiritual "pow-wow" as we stand beside dead altars repeating dead creeds.[13]

It was thought "dangerous to send the Bible to India with its ideas on human equality without the safeguard of a commentary." Jones notes that it was dangerous indeed, not only "to the kind of society that existed in India, organized as it was on caste," but likewise "to the kind of empire that existed in Britain, organized as it was on the right of the white to rule."[14] But, as a result, both a new democratic India and a new self-respecting British Empire have come into being. "The Sermon on the Mount seems dangerous. It challenges the whole underlying conception on which modern society is built. It would replace it with a new conception, animate it with a new motive, and turn it towards a new goal. . . . This Sermon strikes at the whole selfish competitive idea underlying modern economic life and demands that men co-operate in love or perish in strife. . . . If we would take the whole of the Sermon on the Mount and apply it to the whole of life, it would renew our Christianity—it would renew our world."[15]

Jones finds Matthew 5-7 to be a portrait rather than a sermon. As Jesus "draws the lines of the picture of the Father and of the man-to-be, we find he is dipping his brush into the deeps of his own life and experience. . . . We have here not the lines of a code but the lineaments of a Character."[16] Furthermore, the Sermon on the Mount speaks of that which love impels rather than of that which duty compels. It is the charter of one's liberty

---

[13]Ibid., 16-18.

[14]Ibid., 18.

[15]Ibid., 19, 22.

[16]Ibid., 27.

rather than the chart of one's duty, "not a law but a lyre which we strike with the fingers of love in glad devotion."[17]

The entire Sermon on the Mount revolves about the goal of human living: to be perfect as the Father in heaven is perfect (Matthew 5:48). This, says Jones, is the theme of the New Testament which it elaborates in its texts and contexts. And this ideal of perfection prevailed in early Christian thought until the writing of Revelation, in which persecuted Christians grasped heaven as release. Ever since, heaven and hell rule supreme, for "men found it easier to take the framework of an outer heaven which is there depicted than the fact of an inner perfection of character which is the center of that heaven." Jones is convinced the New Testament emphasis must be restored if Christianity itself is to be restored to a way of life that commands the respect of thoughtful people. Christ's goal was moral and spiritual perfection, not just perfection in love, but in character and conduct as well, a goal that "goes beyond humanism in its affirmation of human values [and] puts dignity and meaning into human personality."[18]

In Matthew 5:3-47 Jesus identifies twenty-seven marks of the perfect life which consist as Jones understands them,

> in being poor in spirit, in mourning, in being meek, in hungering and thirsting after righteousness, in being merciful, pure in heart, in being a peacemaker, persecuted for righteousness' sake and yet rejoicing and being exceeding glad, in being the salt of the earth, the light of the world, having a righteousness that exceeds, in being devoid of anger with the brother, using no contemptuous words, allowing no one to hold anything against one, having the spirit of quick agreement, no inward lustful thinking, relentless against anything that offends against the highest, right relations in the home life, truth in speech and attitude, turning the other cheek, giving the cloak also, going the second mile, giving to those who ask and from those who would borrow turning not away, loving even one's enemies, and praying for those who persecute.[19]

Jesus demands that our righteousness exceed that of the scribes and Pharisees (Matthew 5:20); Jones laments that it has not usually done so: "The Crusaders sang, 'Fairest Lord Jesus, ruler of all nature' and then in his gentle name waded through blood in the streets of Jerusalem and praised

---

[17]Ibid., 33.

[18]Ibid., 41, 42.

[19]Ibid., 50-51.

him as they dashed out the brains of little children. . . . Sir John Bowring sits on a slave ship and writes the hymn, 'In the Cross of Christ I Glory,' while beneath him the hold of the ship was filled with manacled and wretched slaves. . . . When the lathi blows were falling on the unresisting heads of the satyagrahas in the streets of Bombay, a bishop, when asked why in the name of Christ and humanity he did not protest, replied, 'Men will never learn anything except through blows.' " It was the crucified Jesus, Jones added sardonically, "who learned through blows to be the Saviour even of the bishop."[20]

Jones interprets the new morality Jesus inspired as a new attitude of reverence for the socially inferior (Matthew 5:21-24), for the personality of woman (5:27-32), for truth (5:33-37), and for the personalities of our enemies (5:38-48). In each case he cites countless examples from his own experience and observation to illustrate how Jesus' teaching applies to various life situations.[21]

After placing before us perfection as the goal of human living, "Jesus puts his finger on the reasons why we do not reach that goal."[22] These reasons, says Jones, all pertain to "inward divisions in spiritual relations," such as the divided motive in our acts of charity (Matthew 6:1-4), in our praying (5-15), and in our fasting (16-18), the inward division regarding material things (19-34) and regarding our relationship to others (Matthew 7). Realizing this "inward division of motive and character," many concede: "perfection is beautiful but impossible; inward division is ugly but actual."[23] Jones offers release from this counsel of despair by "the inner reinforcement of our moral natures with immediate and saving contact with the Divine" through Jesus' offer of the Holy Spirit to them that ask (Luke 11:13; cf. Matthew 7:7-11).

After giving us the Golden Rule (Matthew 7:12) as "a comprehensive principle of guidance in regard to reverence for personality,"[24] Jesus in his call to life issues "a final plea for self-realization through self-renunciation" (Matthew 7:13-14: "Enter by the narrow gate . . . ") and "a final

---

[20]Ibid., 117-18.

[21]Ibid., 131-96.

[22]Ibid., 199.

[23]Ibid., 255.

[24]Ibid., 283.

warning against double-mindedness and spiritual unreality'' (Matthew 7:15-22).

Once the way of Jesus according to the Sermon on the Mount is put before us, there is, believes Jones, ''something within us that gives us the sense of this being the soul's homeland, that this is our native air, that we are made for this and for nothing else.'' He is convinced this philosophy of life which Jesus has given us ''works even under the most adverse conditions.'' ''The man who founds his life on this way is happy, for he is not dependent upon happenings—he is inwardly determined'' by a ''victorious vitality.''[25] ''There is not a single modern problem that could not be solved if we approached it in His spirit. . . . It is a working philosophy of life—the only one that will work. For the universe backs this way of life.''[26]

Jones hoped his book would be ''an unhesitating but not a too-light, easy 'Yes' to the question as to whether the Sermon on the Mount is practicable.'' Even if some of his exegesis appears a little forced, Jones fulfilled his commission as ''a divining rod'' by indicating ''where in the Sermon on the Mount I think water can be found.'' He urges us to dig and drink while leaving to the theologians ''the labeling of the wells and their more accurate description.''[27]

EMMET FOX

A refreshingly different emphasis from that of the theological treatises reviewed thus far is the 'metaphysical' study of the Sermon on the Mount by Emmet Fox. As the subtitle specifies, it proposes to be ''A General Introduction to Scientific Christianity.'' Within the Sermon on the Mount, Fox finds the ''spiritual key'' to spiritual development which enables an ''utterly new outlook on life and an absolutely fresh scale of values.''[28]

Fox expresses outspoken disdain for theological traditions. He says ''the plain fact is that Jesus taught no theology whatever,'' though all sorts of ''inconsistent legends'' and ''unutterably horrible doctrines'' are attributed to him, including the ''plan of salvation'' which ''is as completely

---

[25]Ibid., 314-17.

[26]Ibid., 321-22.

[27]Ibid., 22-23.

[28]Emmet Fox, *The Sermon on the Mount: A General Introduction to Scientific Christianity in the Form of a Spiritual Key to Matthew V, VI, and VII* (New York: Grosset and Dunlap, 1938) ix.

unknown to the Bible as it is to the Koran.'' Jesus insisted upon ''a certain spirit in one's conduct, and he was careful to teach *principles* only, knowing that when the spirit is right, details will take care of themselves.''[29] According to Fox, Tolstoy ''made a heroic but futile attempt to combine Christianity and materialism'' because he lacked the spiritual key to the mystery of the gospels. ''With this key one can afford to discard verbal inspiration and all superstitious literalism and yet understand that the Bible really is the most precious and most authentic of all man's possessions.'' This ''spiritual key'' rescues one from all the ''difficulties, dilemmas, and seeming inconsistencies'' of Ritualism, Evangelicalism, and Liberalism alike ''because it gives us the Truth.''[30] For some time the reader is kept in suspense as to what this ''spiritual key'' actually is. The first indication Fox gives is ''that all causation is mental,'' an insight which constitutes the focal point of the book.

The Beatitudes are seen as ''a spiritual synopsis'' which sums up in an Oriental mode (comparable to the eightfold path of Buddhism) the right mental states ensuring the growth of the soul to maturity. To be ''poor in spirit'' (Matthew 5:3) ''means to have emptied oneself of all desire to exercise personal self-will and . . . to have renounced all preconceived opinions in the whole-hearted search for God''[31] as well as all intellectual and spiritual pride, academic commitment, and social prestige:

> The poor in spirit suffer from none of these embarrassments. . . . They have got rid of the love of money and property, of fear of public opinion, and of the disapproval of relatives or friends . . . [and] they are ready to start again at the very beginning and learn life anew.[32]

Therefore, Jesus calls them blessed. His blessing upon the ''meek'' (Matthew 5:5) ''is among the half dozen most important verses of the Bible,'' according to Fox. It is ''the secret of overcoming any kind of difficulty. It is literally the Key to Life. It is the Jesus Christ message reduced to a single sentence.'' Fox goes on to explain that ''earth'' means the whole of our outer experience ''from our bodily health outwards to the farthest point in

---

[29]Ibid., 3-6.

[30]Ibid., 12-13.

[31]Ibid., 22.

[32]Ibid., 24.

our affairs. So this text tells us how we may possess or govern or be masters of our own lives and destinies.'' While ''to the modern reader 'meek' suggests a mean spirited creature, devoid alike of courage and self-respect . . . the true significance of the word 'meek' in the Bible is a mental attitude . . . which is the secret of 'prosperity' or success in prayer. It is the combination of open-mindedness, faith in God, and the realization that the Will of God for us is always something joyous and interesting and vital and much better than anything we could think of for ourselves.'' Moses ''was known pre-eminently for this quality,'' ''and no one, excepting our Saviour, has *inherited the earth* to a greater degree.''[33]

Jesus' blessing on the ''pure in heart'' (Matthew 5:8) is applied to the ''subconscious mind'' as a call to re-educate and integrate the subconscious by ''scientific prayer or the Practice of the Presence of God.''[34] The last beatitude upon those who are ''persecuted'' (Matthew 5:10) refers, says Fox, not to an outside persecutor but rather to our lower selves:

> Every spiritual treatment or scientific prayer involves a tussle with our lower self which wishes to indulge the old habit of thought and, in fact, persecutes and reviles us—if we like to put the thing dramatically in the Oriental way. All the great Prophets and Enlightened Ones of the race who eventually overcame did so by just such struggles with themselves when they were being persecuted by their lower natures or the Old Adam.[35]

Fox similarly spiritualizes the similes of ''salt'' and ''light'' (Matthew 5:13-16). In Jesus' reference to the city on a mountain (5:14),

> city always stands for consciousness, and the ''hill'' or ''mountain'' always means prayer or spiritual activity. . . . The soul that is built upon prayer cannot be hidden; it shines out brightly through the life that it lives. It speaks for itself but in utter silence and does much of its best work unconsciously. Its mere presence heals and blesses all around it without special effort.[36]

In Matthew 5:21-26 Jesus teaches that we must never let error take root in our life but immediately take steps to overcome it by positive thinking, for

---

[33]Ibid., 28-32.

[34]Ibid., 42-43.

[35]Ibid., 48-49.

[36]Ibid., 52.

if we are able to "come of age" spiritually, we have not merely to conform outwardly to outer rules but to change the inner man too. . . . The
Old Law said "Thou shalt not kill," . . . [but] spiritual demonstration demands that anger itself be overcome.[37]

With respect to marriage disharmony (Matthew 5:31-32), we must "let it
dissolve away of itself" as we permit our understanding to be illumined
and our action to be directed by Divine Wisdom.[38]

Fox applies Jesus' prohibition of the oath (Matthew 5:33-37) to the
church's ordination vow required of young ministers "to believe the doctrines of their particular sect" for the rest of their blessed lives which "is
what Jesus especially wished to prevent" so as to allow for daily enlightenment, Divine guidance, and spiritual growth.[39] The "yea" and the "nay"
(5:37) are to Fox the principle of Affirmation and Denial in "scientific
prayer" and mean we should not "outline" our own solutions to our problems. Instead of insisting on preconceived resolutions, we should pray ex-
pectantly for harmony and freedom.[40]

Fox holds belief in the justice of the old law—"an eye for an eye and
a tooth for a tooth" (Matthew 5:38)—to be "precisely the deadly fallacy
that lies at the root of all strife, public and private, in the world . . . and to
be the cause of much, if not most, of our ill health and our other difficulties." Instead of returning evil for evil, we are to forgive the one who in-
jures us and set him free, otherwise we

start a vicious circle to which there is no ending but the wearing out of [our]
own life and [our] brother's too. . . . This doctrine of "resist not evil" is
the greatest metaphysical secret. To the world—those who do not understand—it sounds like moral suicide, the feeblest surrender to aggression;
but in the light of the Jesus Christ revelation it is seen to be superb spiritual
strategy. Antagonize any situation, and you give it power against yourself;
offer mental nonresistance, and it crumbles away in front of you.[41]

---

[37]Ibid., 60.

[38]Ibid., 73.

[39]Ibid., 76.

[40]Ibid., 78.

[41]Ibid., 80-81.

The references to suing at law, to lending and borrowing, and to turning the other cheek are understood by Fox as symbolic states of mental consciousness. "This instruction about turning the other cheek refers to the changing of one's thought when faced by error, changing from the error to Truth"; that, Fox claims, as a rule works like magic.[42] Returning love for love is nothing out of the ordinary. Anyone would do as much. Jesus asks much more: "Get rid of all resentment and hostility. You must change your own state of mind until you are conscious only of harmony and peace within yourself and have a sense of positive good-will towards all." This is not only the best practical policy, says Fox, but physical health depends upon it:

> The secret of spiritual treatment is not to wrestle with the error which only gives it further life and power but to destroy it by withdrawing from it just that very energy of belief that gives it its body. The only existence it has is that which you give it by temporarily ensouling it with your thought. Withdraw this—and it fades into nothingness. You have thought the error into existence consciously, or, more often, unconsciously. Now unthink it. It is always your thinking that matters. As Shakespeare says, "There is nothing either good or bad but thinking makes it so."

By instructing us to "resist not evil" Jesus intends that we "refrain from resisting the trouble mentally," refusing "to feed our own soul-substance into it" and instead to "feel out mentally for the Presence of God. . . . This is the true spiritual method of loving your enemy. . . . Meeting hatred with love in the scientific way is the Royal Christ Road to Freedom."[43]

Jesus' command to be perfect "even as God Himself is perfect" (Matthew 5:48) is for Fox

> one of the most tremendous things in the whole Bible . . . and, as we know that Jesus will not command the impossible, he has here given his authority to the doctrine that this is possible for man to become Divinely perfect. . . . We see, therefore, from this that man cannot possibly be the miserable, hopeless, disinherited child of perdition that theology has too often represented him to be; but that he is even the very offspring of God—our Father which is in Heaven—and potentially Divine and perfect.[44]

---

[42]Ibid., 83.

[43]Ibid., 86-89.

[44]Ibid., 90-91.

Within this framework of "metaphysics," Fox has an ingenious explanation for everything including the mystery of the Kingdom. He explains that the Bible is essentially all about kings and kingdoms. These kings are either wise or foolish, wicked or righteous, victorious or defeated, and their kingdoms rise and fall "from every sort of cause." He tells us that each of these kings "is really Everyman, studied in various aspects of his mental outlook," and his respective "kingdom" "is nothing less than the world of his own life and experience." The New Testament develops these insights from a variety of perspectives: "Sometimes you are a king; sometimes you are a fisherman; sometimes a gardener, a weaver, a potter, a merchant, a High Priest, a Captain of Hosts, or a beggar." The uniqueness of the Sermon on the Mount consists in its considering you to be a king, "the absolute ruler" of your own kingdom, which means you are free to determine your own life: "You make your own conditions, and you unmake them. You make and unmake your own health. You attract to yourself certain kinds of people and certain conditions—and others you repel. You attract to yourself riches or poverty, and peace of mind or fear—entirely in accordance with the way in which you govern your kingdom."[45] Of this potential the world is unaware, assuming all along that the circumstances of life are determined either by fate or by other people when, in fact, they derive only from our own positive or negative thinking. Fox reads all of Jesus' sayings—whether these concern divorce, murder, oaths, prayer, or fasting—as though they were meant to convey the singular insight "that all causation is mental," thus implying that all tragedy and evil of life were meant to be overcome by the triumph of positive thinking.

One wonders why Jesus suffered such a terrible conflict and end in Gethsemane when he, from whom we have all this wonderful mind-science, should, of all people, have had all adverse circumstances completely under control by virtue of the supreme level of consciousness he attained. Fox resolves this paradox by pointing out that Jesus, in contrast to us, did not suffer on account of inadequacies of his own. Like Moses and Elijah he "could easily have gone away and transcended quietly, without any suffering. . . . But he deliberately chose to undertake this awful task in order to help mankind" and so become the Saviour of the World.[46]

---

[45]Ibid., 94.

[46]Ibid., 95.

Fox distinguished the voluntary suffering Christ endured for others from the unnecessary suffering we bring upon ourselves. However, he failed to establish a positive correlation between the rationale of his mind-science and the consciousness of Jesus at the precise point where Jesus differed from us but should be exemplary for us. It is in its failure to derive from our understanding of Jesus' tensions in life and his intentions in death the cues for our self-understanding and self-determination that the ''metaphysic'' of Fox falls short of the theology of the Church.

Fox's book is filled with wisdom regarding the purification of one's thoughts and the sanctification of the unconscious that nourishes the will. His simple and transcendent mind-science is a wholesome antidote to the complex and depressing pessimism of dogmatic theology. And yet one may not overlook Fox's lack of realism. Besides being fantastic and unrealistic, his mind-science borders on the illusory—not in overestimating the resources of grace but in failing to prepare people to cope with the phenomenon of failure. While it seems unfair to associate the metaphysic of Fox with the philosophy of Pangloss in Voltaire's *Candide*, they have in common that same naïve optimism which releases people from the fatalistic wheel of karma, wipes out all the consequences of past mistakes, and perpetually grants a new lease on life. ''Whoever has seen a field of poppies dancing and swaying in the breeze will appreciate the sense of relaxation and freedom and joy that Jesus had in mind as being our true birthright.''[47] While there is more happy truth in this naïve philosophy than most practicing Christians realize from their own somber theologies, the ''spiritual key'' it provides is incomplete and only tenuously associated with the real Jesus.

REINHOLD SEEBERG

According to Reinhold Seeberg in his *Zur Ethik der Bergpredigt*, Jesus preached repentance, and his Sermon on the Mount is an elaboration of what he meant by this change of mind or *Sinnesänderung*.[48] Jesus addressed himself to the lower classes because he sensed among the common people a greater openness toward God than among those schooled in the

[47]Ibid., 111.

[48]Reinhold Seeberg, *Zur Ethik der Bergpredigt*, Schriften des Instituts für Sozialethik und Wissenschaft der inneren Mission an der Universität Berlin, ed. Reinhold Seeberg (Leipzig: A. Deichertsche Verlagsbuchhandlung, 1934) 4:1.

nomistic tradition. It was to the attitude of the poor, not their outer circumstances, that he directed his appeal through seeking to establish a relationship of love rather than justice: "Through love man becomes like God and enters into a filial relationship with him. This love as the attitude and activity of pure morality raises man to a higher level of moral being."[49] The Sermon on the Mount was meant to be a "comprehensive reconstruction of the entire life-direction (*Lebensrichtung*)" of Jesus' followers. Meanwhile, they continued to be part of Jewish society and participated without objection in the Jewish cult. But a new spirit of brotherly fellowship and "an active ethic of love as they had learned it in association with Jesus" developed and directed their relations to others, including their oppressors. [50] In this spirit the new community abstained from litigation and condemnation.

The Q version of the Lukan Sermon served the Jerusalem congregation as a kind of moral catechism, Seeberg thought, while the longer Matthean version represents its later expansion, elaboration, and adaptation as a practical ethical code probably by leading persons in the early Christian community who no longer presupposed the continuity of the new movement with the Jewish religious society and its cult. Since many converts had come from the ranks of the rich, the Woes were dropped in the Matthean *Bergpredigt*, and the blessing upon the poor was spiritualized as the division was no longer an economic one but one between those who constituted the Kingdom and those who were of this world.[51]

In the self-understanding of the early Christian community the Sermon on the Mount constitutes a 'religious' ethic in contrast to Pharisaic legalism and, as such, is *Lebensethik* in contrast to the abstract formalism of Jewish ethics and, finally, is *Sozialethik* in contrast to the eudaemonistic individualism of the Pharisees. It is religious ethic because it is realized as a new relationship between human beings and God—the God who enables his people to keep and do his commandments here and now in our time. This religious dimension is exemplified in the Lord's prayer. It is a "life-ethic" in that it validates God's Law given through Moses as God's will for his people. And it is "social ethic" with positive implications for human brotherhood.[52]

---

[49]Ibid., 11-12.

[50]Ibid., 14-16.

[51]Ibid., 23, 29.

[52]Ibid., 60, 64-65.

Seeberg asserts with Windisch that the Sermon on the Mount should not be interpreted in the light of Pauline or Reformation presuppositions. Neither can cross and resurrection be utilized to explain the unique qualities of Jesus' commands—unless indeed one ascribes them not to Jesus but to the Early Church. How could Jesus' more radical commandments be regarded "easy" and "light" rather than burdensome? In the Hebrew Bible believers prayed for a pure heart, a new spirit, and for God's spirit not to be removed from them (Psalm 51:11-12). They trusted in the prophecy that God will pour out his spirit upon all people (Joel 3:1-2) and will write his law on their hearts and forgive their sins (Jeremiah 31:33). This promise, says Seeberg, was realized in Jesus' unique relationship to human beings. There was an inner connection between his healing miracles and his influence upon men's wills and decisions. Miracles happen as the will of Christ is united with the will of men who are moved by faith. When Jesus called disciples, they unconditionally left their vocations, obeyed him, learned from him, and believed in him. His whole being through his word and work created this faith and inspired this obedience in them. It is not an outwardly compelled obedience nor a calculated obedience but the obedience of children who easily and readily accept the will of their parents as their own.

> The essence of these commands is simply to be subject in faith to the rule of God manifest in the spirit of Jesus and to love and serve the brethren accordingly. Viewed in this way, the commandments of the Sermon on the Mount can be considered practicable. It is a matter of obedience to the spirit of God manifest in Jesus who effects that to which he obligates.

The Spirit of God through the word of Christ enables people to fulfill these commandments, but this effective spirit does not endow everyone with power because they resist the spirit (Matthew 12:32).[53]

CLARENCE JORDAN

Clarence Jordan's "cotton patch version"[54] of the Sermon on the Mount belongs to the finest of attempts at authentic communication in a style that is easy and earthy, imaginative and vivid. Dr. Jordan speaks from his ex-

---

[53]Ibid., 79-82.

[54]Clarence Jordan, *Sermon on the Mount* (Valley Forge PA: Judson Press, 1952). See also *The Cotton Patch Version of Matthew and John* (New York: Association Press, 1970) 22-31.

perience in applying the principles of the Sermon on the Mount on the Koi-
nonia Farms in Americus, Georgia, where he encountered considerable
difficulty and opposition. His forthright approach is exemplified in his
commentary on loving one's enemies according to Matthew 5:44-48. After
citing the familiar arguments of those who claim it is not practical and the
examples of those who believe it really works if given a chance, Jordan
concludes:

> The truth might be that in its initial stages unlimited love is very im-
> practical. Folks who are determined enough to hold on to it usually wind
> up on a cross, like Jesus. Their goods get plundered and they get slan-
> dered. Persecution is their lot. Surely nobody would be inclined to call this
> practical. Yet in its final stages, unlimited love seems to be the only thing
> that could possibly have made sense. Crucifixions have a way of being fol-
> lowed by resurrections. The end of love seems to be its beginning. Only
> he who is foolish enough to lose his life finds it. It's the grain of wheat that
> falls into the ground and *dies* that lives. But Jesus didn't tell his followers
> to love their enemies because it would or would not work. It probably never
> occurred to him to raise the question of whether or not it was practical. He
> told them that they should do it ''so that they might be sons of their spir-
> itual Father.'' . . . Of course, one does not *have* to be a son of God. It is
> purely a voluntary matter, though the choice is the difference between life
> and death. Yet if one does choose to become a son, then one of the con-
> ditions is that you ''love your enemies and pray for those who persecute
> you.''

Jordan discounts such irrelevant questions as ''Who is my enemy?'' since
they are usually followed by efforts ''to classify enemies as personal or
national, vicious or gentle, sane or insane, hopeless or redeemable,'' and
so on, in the hope of justifying our hatred of the worst of them. He advises
that ''until we know better, a safe guide for the Christian is to love all people.''[55]

Jordan inquires, ''Did Christ aim too high? Was he too idealistic?'' and
he replies:

> High aims and high ideals never handicap men. It certainly would not have
> helped us if Jesus had lowered the kingdom standards to the point where
> they would be within easy reach of the weakest person. If anything, this

---

[55]*Sermon on the Mount*, 63-65.

would have made us still more powerless. What we need is not a lowering of the goals but the strength to obtain them.[56]

This power, in Jordan's understanding, comes through faith and discipline. Pondering the "narrow way" (Matthew 7:13-14) of that discipline, he reflects: "At times it was sheer joy to travel it, for the flowers of accomplishment bloomed along the way. And the further one went, the less tired he became, and the more infrequent were his periods of depression."[57]

JEREMY INGALLS

In exploring what constitutes *The Galilean Way*,[58] Jeremy Ingalls first examines the pre-Christian wisdom that in the course of history had traversed those Galilean roads. She attempts to discern how the teaching of Jesus compares to the spiritual signposts that had been erected along those trading routes since the dawn of civilization by the peoples of the North and of the South meeting at that Galilean land bridge to exchange goods and gods.

By comparative analysis with Judaism, Ingalls finds that the Galilean Way of Jesus

> retains and clarifies one steadying factor in the Jewish view of the Way. This steadying factor is confidence in the dignity of human purposes according to the will of the creator of the Way. The Galilean Way preserves, as the Galilean himself emphasizes, the essential wisdom of Israel's law and Israel's prophets. But the Galilean Way also emphasizes a motive power which is not given equal emphasis in the traditional Jewish Way. This motive power is voluntary, individually responsible, inclusive love.

Ingalls claims that "this individual motivation supersedes traditional law and codified law as a method of maintaining balance—that is, justice—in the world neighborhood." She identifies this "open-world" view of the Way characteristic of Jesus as the highest level of consciousness in comparison to the more primitive evolutionary stages—the clan view, the heroic view, and the metropolitan view—all of which have their respective

---

[56]Ibid., 103.

[57]Ibid., 110.

[58]Jeremy Ingalls, *The Galilean Way* (New York: Longmans, Green, 1953).

parallels in the older pre-Christian religions. The Galilean Way differs from them in that

> Galilean love does not attack and does not pass judgment on other individuals. It is more feared because its essentials cannot be maneuvered into a battle of words or a quarrel over ceremonies. Individual voluntary acts of selflessness continue as a wordless criticism of every prejudice and every rationalization of "the good of the State," whether church-state or secular state, offered as a legal excuse for cruelty or disdain. The single law of the Galilean Way is: Love the Source of the Way and, as a necessary consequence, love your neighbor as yourself. Other answers offered as law still survive. An old Hindu answer is: Do your duty in the social condition in which you find yourself, maintaining proper distinctions among classes and castes. A Confucian answer is: Be kind to those who are kind to you, punish with equal justice those who are unjust, and do not trouble yourself with abstruse investigations. A classic Greek answer, significantly limited to one class, is: Be a gentleman among gentlemen, punish with equal justice those who are unjust, be patient with inferiors, cultivate your reasoning powers. A characteristic Buddhist answer is: Be kind but do not neglect concentration on your personal salvation by too deep involvement in kindness. Israel and Islam say: Be in awe of God who created all, lead others to share your awe, and be patient with the ignorance of strangers.
>
> To all these answers, with their facets of wisdom, there still attaches the false facet of special privilege, exclusiveness, or superiority. Only the Galilean answer cuts clear to a single, inclusive illumination. Galilean love will not discriminate among superiors, inferiors, or strangers. It accepts an equal value for ten talents or one talent so long as the talent is used, with love, in the service of others. Galilean love also includes "enemies," however unjust. Furthermore, the Galilean law reminds us that, as human beings, we are limited and repeatedly make errors. Therefore, Galilean Christians cannot assume the easy confidence of some priests and philosophers about infallibly judging, justly judging, neighbors.[59]

Ingalls also draws attention to the subtle simplicity of Jesus' speech and his extraordinary skill in transfiguring old values by imaginative use of highly charged symbols in the realization that "the human imagination is an essential part of our whole power to take hold of reality, to use the past toward shaping the future."[60] Ingalls herself stands in this imaginative tradition in drawing upon anthropology, history, and psychology to illumine the Galilean Way.

---

[59]Ibid., 84-85.
[60]Ibid., 161.

ERNEST M. LIGON

In a treatise on *The Psychology of Christian Personality*, Ernest M. Ligon interprets the Sermon on the Mount in terms of mental health and wholesome personality to illustrate that Jesus' teaching corresponds with the principles of psychology. Ligon's elemental supposition is "if God is good, mental health will be one of the results of obeying his laws," for God would not "so order the universe that godliness would produce unhappiness and mental disorder." The correctness of theological concepts is consequently measured by their psychological effects on personality development, since "mental health, powerful character, and attractive personality are at least a measure of spiritual law, if not identical with it." Too much "Thou shalt not" negative morality in religious education has produced repressed, warped, and pathetically ill personalities by manipulation of the sense of shame in social and religious taboo.[61] So Ligon examines the emotional attitudes implied in Jesus' teaching to indicate how they apply to the integration of personality.

"Loving your enemies" has been assumed impossible, yet, Ligon observes that if Jesus' teachings are to be applied to everyday life, "they must not be so far above the normal abilities of ordinary human beings." Ligon explains: "Jesus did not teach brotherly love; he taught fatherly love." And, for a father to love his enemy's son as David loved Jonathan is neither abnormal nor unnatural. "What parents do not pray fervently for their children 'who despitefully use them'?" Seen in this way, the great ethical principle of loving one's enemy and returning good for evil is perfectly normal behavior and not an otherworldly impossibility.[62]

The "poor in spirit" (Matthew 5:3) are those who are open to the experimentation of life while the "rich in spirit" uncritically defend their infallible opinions which they acquire without evidence. The personality of the "poor in spirit" is integrated about some worthy goal or purpose while the "rich in spirit" lack ambition and that happiness or blessing that comes through achievement. Their self-satisfaction leads to vanity that, if wounded, produces anger, conflict, and feelings of inferiority.[63]

---

[61]Ernest M. Ligon, *The Psychology of Christian Personality* (New York: Macmillan, 1961) 10-11.

[62]Ibid., 22-23.

[63]Ibid., 32-34.

"Meek" persons are those who pray "Thy will be done," expect the laws of nature to work with unfailing regularity, and do not ask God for miraculous exceptions to suit their needs.[64] Happiness of the meek depends on inner conditions of mental life rather than on outward circumstances. By their inner confidence, firmness, and steadfastness the meek stabilize society.[65] The "pure in heart" have singleness of purpose and always look for the best in others.[66] Their apocalyptic intuition foresees the coming Kingdom of God. They "see God" by their insight into spiritual laws. To "mourn" (Matthew 5:4) means to be sensitive to the sorrows and failures of others as Jesus mourned over Jerusalem.[67] Since "most mental illness is fundamentally self-centeredness," blessedness takes the form of mercifulness, kindness, and beneficence. "Do not swear at all" (Matthew 5:34) does not refer to oaths as evil, says Ligon, but to the type of personality that makes them necessary by fragmenting aspects of life into logic-tight compartments exempt from moral scrutiny.[68] "Murder, war, mobs, race prejudice, and narrow nationalism would be far less dangerous to civilization without the poison of anger," Ligon argues; Jesus sought to stop such evils by controlling the emotions that produce them through imbalance of the body chemistry (cf. Matthew 5:21-22).[69] Since war fails to overcome evil with evil and nonresistance only "engenders hate, suspicion, and anger on both sides of the quarrel," Jesus exemplified how to overcome evil with good (Matthew 5:40-42).[70]

Ligon explores methods of character development, reflects on the psychological value of prayer, and discusses the causes and cures of immature behavior patterns, inferiority complexes, and human fears, citing numerous case histories. He invariably relates everything to the text of the Sermon on the Mount. The book is filled with elemental psychological insights into the development and deformity of personality. Empirical and pragmatic in orientation, Ligon's study lacks the self-transcendence character-

----

[64]Ibid., 47.

[65]Ibid., 50.

[66]Ibid., 57.

[67]Ibid., 67.

[68]Ibid., 145.

[69]Ibid., 257.

[70]Ibid., 278.

istic of theological discourse and reduces the consciousness that inspired the Sermon on the Mount to the principles of mental health. By reinterpreting the principles of the Sermon on the Mount which brought Jesus to the Cross as the resources that bring us to abundant life, Ligon accomplishes the psychological function of neutralizing the tensions theology creates.

SWAMI PRABHAVANANDA

The Hindu Swami Prabhavananda[71] interprets The Sermon on the Mount with unusual clarity and beauty. In contrast to a far-off, scarcely attainable ideal, the teaching of Jesus is for him a practical program for daily living which enables the divine to unfold and manifest itself as the only real goal of human life. Every day of their contemplative lives the *sannyasin* of the Ramakrishna Order, to which Prabhavananda belongs, follow the way of perfection by clearing their minds of all sense of ego, hatred, resentment, fault-finding and criticism of others and by praying for love and sympathy toward all. Prabhavananda tells how his master Swami Brahmananda, who, although not a student of the Bible is said to have taught in the same way as Christ in almost identical words, one day beheld in a spiritual vision Christ "with his gaze fixed on him." Henceforth to this day Christ, the embodiment of love, "who poured out his heart's blood for the redemption of mankind," is worshipped "as a manifest expression of divinity" and revered "as one of the greatest of illumined teachers" in all monasteries of the Ramakrishna Order. As Swami Prabhavananda explains,

> Like Krishna and Buddha, Christ did not preach a mere ethical and social gospel but an uncompromising spiritual one. He declared that God can be seen, that divine perfection can be achieved. In order that men might attain this supreme goal of existence, he taught the renunciation of worldliness, the contemplation of God, and the purification of the heart through the love of God. These simple and profound truths, stated repeatedly in the Sermon on the Mount, constitute its underlying theme.[72]

The Sermon on the Mount, says the Swami, was intended for Jesus' disciples. As the elephant has two sets of teeth—tusks to defend himself

---

[71]Swami Prabhavananda, *The Sermon on the Mount According to Vedanta* (London: Allen and Unwin, 1964).

[72]Ibid., 13-16.

and teeth with which to eat—so every spiritual teacher has two sets of teachings. Jesus taught the multitude "who wanted less than the supreme truth" according to their capacity while reserving his highest teaching contained in the Sermon on the Mount to uplift the consciousness of his disciples, the ones who were spiritually ready.[73]

Prabhavananda interprets Jesus' first blessing upon "the poor in spirit" as the chief characteristic of fully committed disciples who humbly accept the wisdom of their illumined teacher. The "mourning" that he blessed arises from spiritual loneliness "in the imitation of Christ." Not until reaching the stage where nothing but a vision of God can give us peace does "comfort" come as God draws our mind near to himself. Only by sincerely giving up our ego to become "meek" do we gain anything and everything in this life. Upon practicing these spiritual disciplines, our desire "to realize him" becomes "a raging hunger and a burning thirst" after righteousness (Matthew 5:6).[74] By being "merciful" we raise a wave of thought that opposes universal weaknesses inborn in human beings, such as envy, jealousy, and hatred. The "vision of God" comes only to the "pure mind" (5:8): "Only the illumined soul has no ignorance, no sense of ego, no attachment, no aversion, and no fear of death." Regarding the way to holiness, the Swami writes: "God created us in his own image; purity and divinity are therefore basically our nature. If we cry all our lives that we are sinners, we only weaken ourselves" to become what we profess to be. Instead of repeating, "I am a sinner," "one should have such faith as to be able to say: 'I have chanted the holy name of God. How can there be any sin in me?' The more you move towards the light the further you will be from the darkness." Commenting on Jesus' blessing upon the "peacemakers," Prabhavananda says, "We cannot bring peace until we have realized our oneness with God and with all things."[75] With respect to the final blessing upon those persecuted "for God's sake," the Swami adds, "Only the illumined soul who sees God in all beings can maintain perfect patience, forbearance, and tranquillity in the midst of the conflicts and contradictions of life."[76] We all have the power to allow the divinity

[73]Ibid., 17.
[74]Ibid., 19-23.
[75]Ibid., 26-28.
[76]Ibid., 31.

latent within us to unfold itself, but the teacher who says, "You are the salt . . . You are the light," gives us the needed confidence "and actually illumines the hearts of his disciples and makes them the light of the world. . . . Only such illumined ones are fit to teach mankind; only they can carry on the message of a divine incarnation. . . . Only he who has seen God can receive his commission, his direct command to teach. Religion degenerates when taught by unillumined men." This illumination, Prabhavananda explains, does not come through college degrees in theology or through books, for they cannot give illumination. This lower knowledge must be distinguished from the higher knowledge of the immediate perception of God without which one cannot transform the lives of others. But, having experienced the vision of God, one does not need encyclopedic information because one teaches from inner experience: "A man who has seen God does not need academic knowledge in order to teach religion" nor does he need to go out looking for disciples. "When the lotus blossoms, the bees come from all around of their own accord to gather the honey."[77] This is the manner in which Jesus expects our light to shine before men (Matthew 5:16).

Jesus demands superior righteousness (Matthew 5:20) freed of pharisaic narrowness, intolerance, and dogmatism, declares Prabhavananda:

> The urge to live a truly ethical life and to practice spiritual disciplines comes to us only if we try to live the first commandment—if we learn to love God, and struggle to realize him. Without that ideal, morality degenerates into the external decorum of the scribes and Pharisees.

A man who achieves union with the absolute Good no longer discriminates consciously between right and wrong or practices self-mastery. "Holiness and purity become his very nature. He transcends relative righteousness and enters the kingdom of heaven." Jesus' word against anger (Matthew 5:21-24), maintains the Hindu Swami, can be realized only as we control our passions inwardly and subdue our ego, enabling divine love to grow in us toward our fellow human beings:

> But the love of God has to be won through self-discipline which we have neglected to practice. We have forgotten the aim of life—to realize and see God. That is our whole difficulty, and that is why, when Jesus asks us to

---

[77]Ibid., 36.

love our enemies, we are unable to obey him, even if we wish to do so. We do not know how.[78]

Prabhavananda acknowledges the near impossibility for most people to understand or practice nonresistance; they lack spiritual maturity and fail to cultivate the presence of God: "The high spiritual goal of life must be kept in view by all men. But, at the same time, different levels of being must be recognized so that everyone may be enabled, step by step, sooner or later, to attain to the supreme Good."[79] Prabhavananda explains how all this applies to life with a parable of a holy man who enroute to a village encountered a venomous snake that had killed many people. As the snake approached hissing and ready to strike, the sage charged it to give up the idea of biting and killing: "According to instructions, the snake, having received initiation into spiritual life with a sacred name of God, crawled off to its hole to pray and meditate; and the holy man proceeded on his way." Soon village boys exploiting the changed character of the snake attacked it with sticks and stones because it would never strike back. Upon hearing that the snake was nearly dead, the sage was greatly disturbed for concern that it die without attaining "the fruit of the holy word with which it was initiated." Upon hearing its teacher's voice, the crippled and emaciated snake, which had limited its food to only leaves and fruit, squirmed from its hole expecting to be praised for not resisting evil. But to its great surprise the holy man crossly cried: "How foolish you are! I told you not to bite. Did I tell you not to hiss?" For the "average householder" the Swami commends hissing "now and then" but without injecting venom. However, the monk must strive to practice nonviolence "in its higher form."[80]

"Be ye perfect as your heavenly Father is perfect" (Matthew 5:48) is "the whole purpose of man's life." "Seek perfection! [and] Realize God!" are the heart of all religion. In quoting Paul's assurance that "the spirit itself bears witness with our spirit that we are the children of God," Prabhavananda claims that "we have the right to aspire to that perfection, for it is our divine heritage. . . . To uncover this true being or divinity which

---

[78]Ibid., 44-45.

[79]Ibid., 54-56.

[80]Ibid., 60.

lies hidden within oneself is to become perfect.[81] The goal of all mystical experience is to remove the veil of ignorance that keeps us from comprehending the light and truth of God so that our whole being and our character may be transformed and transfigured into the highest state of consciousness which is the perfection of the spirit in mystical union with God. Prabhavananda testifies to his beloved master's experience in which his face was transfigured by the heavenly light and shone like that of Moses. The account resembles that of the transfiguration of Jesus and of the Christophanies in the New Testament record. The Swami regrets that most people only argue about whether God can be known or about what the Sermon on the Mount means instead of actually trying to live by it. What good, he asks, is it if, after coming to the mango garden, one only counts the leaves on the trees but does not eat of the fruit to satisfy one's hunger? "Christ taught his disciples how to know God, how to realize him while living in the world. He did not state that divine perfection can be attained only after the death of the body."[82] The fruits of true religion, the Swami concludes (commenting on Matthew 7:15-20), are "illumination, selfless love, and compassion for all,"[83] and the test of true religion is whether it teaches people to realize the love of God. Religion, he asserts, "must be neither egocentric nor altruistic but theocentric. We must center our whole mind upon God, and then, extending our arms to everyone, embrace all in the love of God."[84]

---

[81]Ibid., 62.

[82]Ibid., 65.

[83]Ibid., 105.

[84]Ibid., 108.

Cf. also: John W. Miller, *The Christian Way. A Guide to the Christian Life Based on the Sermon on the Mount* (Scottdale PA: Herald Press, 1969); Ulrich Luz, "Die Bergpredigt im Spiegel ihrer Wirkungsgeschichte" and Helmut Gollwitzer, "Bergpredigt und Zwei-Reiche-Lehre," in Jürgen Moltmann, Hrsg., *Nachfolge und Bergpredigt* (München: Chr. Kaiser, 1981, 1982) 37-72, 89-120; Volker Hochgrebe, Hrsg., *Provokation Bergpredigt* (Stuttgart: Kreuz Verlag, 1982).

CURRENT INQUIRY

GEORG EICHHOLZ

In his *Auslegung der Bergpredigt*[1] Georg Eichholz contributes to biblical studies the broad consensus of current exegetical research on historical and theological issues pertaining to the Sermon in general and to Matthew's role in shaping the Christian tradition in particular. The Sermon, Eichholz writes, is addressed to both the disciples and the people and emphasizes both eschatology and discipleship by proclaiming grace and demanding obedience. The Beatitudes apply to both present and future, are both indicative and imperative in nature, and encompass in their promises both the act of God and the response of human beings. With fine sensitivity Eichholz explores Matthew's Christological intention by reaffirming the Jewish-Christian emphasis on the abiding validity of the Torah over against the antinomian challenge.

On controversial issues Eichholz tends toward a mediating stance. He finds at least some "elasticity" in Matthew's divorce prohibition. The usual assumption that legal oaths are exempt from Jesus' prohibition of swearing he views as "problematic." The implications of the last two antitheses are not explored. The sum and fulfillment of the Torah is described as that divine love which overcomes all wrath, adultery, divorce, swearing, resistance, and enmity.[2] Reconciling the tension between Matthew and Paul, Eichholz explains that the expression, "Christ is the end of the law," means Christ "represents" the Torah, which is assumed in his Lordship so that the whole of the moral life is rooted "in Christ" in order that complete

---

[1]Georg Eichholz, *Auslegung der Bergpredigt*, Heft 46 der Schriftenreihe "Biblische Studien" (Neukirchner Verlag des Erziehungsvereins, 1965).

[2]Ibid., 103.

obedience might be free obedience.[3] Paul also knows of that love which fulfills the Torah. The emphases of Matthew and Paul are both Christologically based. The only difference is that Matthew reflects a time when the Church had not yet fully separated from Judaism, and therefore he sought via the Torah to establish a continuity between Israel and the new eschatological community. In the resulting tension between Matthew and Paul, Eichholz finds the stimulus to rethink the ground and meaning of Christian existence.[4]

ULRICH LUCK

In a treatise on *Die Vollkommenheitsforderung der Bergpredigt*[5] Ulrich Luck deliberates with considerable acumen a problem of standing perplexity for evangelical theology: How to reconcile Jesus' demand for perfection (Matthew 5:48) with justification *sola fide*.

Our definition of what it means to be a Christian ought, Luck thinks, to include the Sermon on the Mount. But by all indications it is very difficult to live with the Sermon. If our capitalist society is the source of the problem, then we should create a new society that conforms to Jesus' ideals. No social order could, however, meet those presuppositions. The Sermon itself, Luck reminds us, does not presuppose ideal conditions, otherwise it would have been addressed to the pillars of society rather than to poor people. Since Jesus' unconditional demands remain unfulfilled, it is assumed they are utopian and have no place in our world and life except to plague our conscience and make evident our need of salvation. The other option is to read the data positively and say with Thurneysen that everything has been fulfilled vicariously 'for' us by one person, Jesus Christ. That consolation, says Luck, fails to satisfy anyone who can read the Sermon on the Mount for himself, especially its concluding parable. And yet the church—and especially the Volkskirche—can make no peace with these demands.

Revolutionary change is no solution either, for then its message is soon captive to a radical ideology which has no place for either love of enemy

---

[3]Ibid., 163-64.

[4]Ibid., 165.

[5]Ulrich Luck, *Die Vollkommenheitsforderung der Bergpredigt,* Theologische Existenz Heute, 159 (München: Christian Kaiser Verlag, 1968).

or freedom from material cares, precepts which cannot be contained by any ideology or theology. The Sermon on the Mount perpetuates a permanent state of crisis, whereas the goal of every revolution is the establishment of a new order. And yet it ought to be possible Luck conjectures, to validate its message both for the time of Jesus and for our own. In the hope of doing this, Luck explores its place within the theology of Matthew, for whom the "better righteousness" Jesus demanded is identical with "perfection." Matthew seeks to establish a "symbiosis" between the Law and the proclamation of Jesus. Luck questions whether this is possible since Matthew reflects the context of a time for which the Law was valid whereas Jesus proclaimed the end of that world and time[6] and reflects the context of its transition (*Zeitwende*). Luck contends that "this exceptional state [to which Jesus addresses himself] is not attainable for people who live in time. Therefore we cannot hold to these demands because they cannot function in our world."[7] They applied only to the early Christians who still anticipated the imminent *parousia* of the Son of Man (Matthew 10:23) and hence adapted Jesus' Beatitudes to their own turbulent lives (Matthew 5:11-12) within the crisis "between the times." To be relevant to the ongoing process of history Jesus' demands must be adapted and "softened," argues Luck, by a process of modification the beginnings of which he discovers in the redaction of the text.[8]

For Luck, the fundamental problem is that Jesus addressed himself to Israel within the context of its Torah and that this frame of reference needs somehow to be enlarged to include the worldwide Church. That the world missionary movement was acutely aware of the difficulty of this transition is evident from the fact that it perpetuated the preaching of Paul rather than the teaching of Jesus.[9]

Matthew understands the way of perfection in the light of Jewish Wisdom according to which God's will is known and done.[10]

> The Law is the beginning of the way to perfection. It leads to knowledge, to wisdom, and to participation in the power and glory of God. In

---

[6]Ibid., 20.

[7]Ibid., 22-23.

[8]Ibid., 23-24.

[9]Ibid., 28.

[10]Ibid., 31.

this way the power of God itself is active in him who has studied the Law and leads to the keeping of the whole Law.[11]

Matthew sees the entire Jesus tradition in the context of Wisdom teaching. The yoke of heaven is the yoke of the Torah. As yoke of Wisdom it is a light yoke, for the truth enlightens every human being.

The key to understanding how this demanded perfection is to be accomplished Luck finds in Jesus' didactic triad on the hiddenness of the devout life according to which the secrecy of the deed (alms, prayer, and fasting) is reciprocated with the openness of the "reward." Luck argues that the text should read "fulfill" (rather than "reward")[12] to imply that God completes the work of human beings, thereby "revealing" what was "hidden": "He makes it public in the sense that he empowers the deed so that it achieves its goal,"[13] as the Psalmist says, "Commit your way to the Lord; trust in him and he will act" (37:5). From this premise Luck concludes that to act in "perfection" means to act in secret (that is, in *Verborgenheit*).

Luck's logic becomes problematic when he implies that what was meant to be hidden from the world is also hidden from the doer so that one has no way of knowing until the eschatological day of the Lord whether the fulfillment of his deed is indeed the fulfillment of the righteousness of God.[14] Here Luck finds the link between Jesus' apocalyptic frame of mind, according to which the world is rapidly approaching its end, and Matthew's Wisdom context, according to which all things remain within an appointed order that is to be learned and lived. The link between these so divergent *Weltanschauungen* consists in the "*Verborgenheit.*" Apocalyptic and Wisdom have in common the maxim that each deed has its consequences, from which follows the moral precept: abstain from unrighteousness and it will spare you. When that rule does not appear to apply and the righteous suffer while the sinners prosper, the consolation lies in the knowledge that God's righteousness is still hidden but will ultimately be revealed. In the context of this future hope, the lines between

---

[11]Ibid., 36.

[12]Luck cites the Hebrew equivalents for ἀποδώσει σοι in Matthew 6:4, 6, 18, and especially the thrust of the Piel of שׁלם in Proverbs 25:21-22; cf. ibid., 43-44.

[13]Ibid., 44.

[14]Ibid., 47-48.

Apocalyptic and Wisdom are fluid. Those who literally followed Jesus did so because they found their assurance of this promise of the Beatitudes in his word. After Easter, the hope of its realization became more remote except insofar as it was believed to have been fulfilled in the resurrected, glorified, and risen Lord Christ.

Luck's answer to whether Jesus' demands are practicable is haunted by the ambiguity of this *Verborgenheit,* according to which it is impossible for anyone to make any moral discernments regarding his own or another's deeds since humans are deprived of the capacity to understand fully God's will.[15] Total obedience is demanded but what is implied in that demand one cannot actually know[16] because the action of those who respond to Jesus' word cannot be measured by inner-worldly criteria[17] and because we cannot claim within our time the future that belongs alone to God.[18] Needless to say, Luck's "secret theology" is derived from a reading of the text which it is not necessary to superimpose upon either Matthew or Jesus.

HANS-THEO WREGE

Hans-Theo Wrege's thesis on *Die Überlieferungsgeschichte der Bergpredigt*[19] represents the culmination of recent form-critical investigation of the Sermon's literary history. Wrege challenges the assumption of a unified literary tradition referred to as "Q" and alleged to be the common source on the basis of which the parallels in Matthew's Sermon on the Mount and Luke's Sermon on the Plain could be explained. His redactional analysis establishes the literary independence of virtually every verse in Matthew's Sermon from its counterpart in Luke on the assumption that both traditions were shaped by different intentions and presuppositions and draw their materials from independent collections of unrelated sayings of diverse origins.

Wrege identifies what he considers to be a fundamental conflict between Matthew's Antitheses and his "Fulfillment-Christology" in that the

---

[15]Ibid., 57.

[16]Ibid., 58.

[17]Ibid., 58.

[18]Ibid., 59.

[19]Hans-Theo Wrege, *Die Überlieferungsgeschichte der Bergpredigt,* Wissenschaftliche Untersuchungen zum Neuen Testament, Band 9 (Tübingen: J. C. B. Mohr [Paul Siebeck], 1968).

radical form of antitheses 3 through 6 appears to negate what Matthew 5:17ff. so emphatically affirms. From this alleged discrepancy, Wrege concludes that Matthew's antithetical formulation is incompatible with his understanding of Jesus' messianic fulfillment and therefore reflects an independent literary tradition.[20] It appears, however, that Wrege's logic misrepresents Matthew's particular purpose in showing in what respects Jesus transcended rather than negated the Torah by fulfilling its original intention.

PETR POKORNÝ

Petr Pokorný of Prague applies the 'essence' or *Kern der Bergpredigt*[21] to the cultural and political determinants of the church and to its tendency towards institutional stagnation in metaphysical dogmatic abstractions and moralistic ethical conceptions.[22] Critical Protestant exegesis seeks a new understanding of existence free of such props, and Catholic theology endeavors to include the whole of history in its proclamation of hope. Pokorný, representing the tradition of the Czech Brethren, pursues a middle course engaging both alternatives in a complementary way. What he considers to be the literary "Kern" of the Sermon constitutes the "Q" tradition represented by Luke's Sermon on the Plain and comprises the first three Beatitudes, the sayings about loving enemies, judging, and fruit-bearing, and the concluding parable. Pokorný notes that in the Judaism of Jesus' day the "blessed poor"—as in the community at Qumran—were the ones proclaiming upon their enemies God's destructive wrath which, for tactical reasons, they abstained from implementing until the apocalyptic end-time.[23] It was over against this revengeful disposition that Jesus consistently taught love of one's enemies. While the message of Jesus was limited by its apocalyptic context, Pokorný nevertheless holds it to be relevant for us today. He observes that the deeper implications of Jesus' injunctions to "do good," "bless," and "pray for" one's enemies are explained by the prohibition of judging others. We are to work out the dis-

---

[20]Cf. ibid., 37-57.

[21]Petr Pokorný, *Der Kern der Bergpredigt: eine Auslegung* (Hamburg: Herbert Reich Evangelischer Verlag, 1969).

[22]Ibid., 10.

[23]Ibid., 24.

ruptive differences between people through the process of responsible interaction involving warning, admonition, and forgiveness in order to raise the effective level of human relations to that of the Good Samaritan in accordance with the Golden Rule.

The Christological element of this "new morality" does not consist in restricting its demands to Jesus as if they were meant to be fulfilled by him alone and as if no one else could repeat that fulfillment. On the contrary, Jesus pioneers the new way which we are to follow.[24] According to the old morality, the righteous are redeemed by doing good, through which activity they achieve perfection. Jesus demands that we do the good for its own sake. Fruitbearing is the goal of the moral life and the sole criterion of faith.[25] The Sermon on the Mount is a call to a converted life that envisions a fundamental transformation of the world, a hope that is not an evolutionary conception but an optimism of faith.

As Pokorný understands him, Jesus challenges all tradition, yet interpretation of his teaching demands historical perspective and continuity. His Sermon protests against the dualistic morality of Jewish apocalyptic and its speculative tendency, and yet apocalyptic is of its essence. Apocalyptic demands qualification of the meaning of the present in the light of the future and allows neither absolutization of the present nor indifference towards it.[26] Its openness toward the future inspires responsible action which may take widely differing forms ranging from martyrdom to science, from charity to social planning in order to bring about the 'perfection' Jesus demanded by the power of love, the realism of the Cross, and the belief in Resurrection. The history of Jesus is not a closed event but a means towards historical transformation which is not only Christian but also practicable.[27]

Pokorný, however, rejects a too naïve optimism regarding the triumph of the good. Nor can he endorse the "compulsive dogmatization" of the Christological interpretation which fails to acknowledge Jesus' call to a new life.[28] Neither does he allow Jesus' call to commitment to be institution-

---

[24]Ibid., 29.

[25]Ibid., 31.

[26]Ibid., 36.

[27]Ibid., 39.

[28]Ibid., 56.

alized in a sectarian way to exclude the ongoing challenge of dialogue and confrontation. He sees the Sermon as a call to responsible discipleship within the social context in accordance with the missionary mandate to "disciple all people."

The Sermon on the Mount applies the will of God to the historical process with the intention of transforming the world and not merely affirming an otherworldly Christ-revelation. To fulfill its historical intention in its political application it may sometimes be necessary, Pokorný reasons, to contradict its literal meaning. From experiences in World War II Pokorný concludes that absolute pacifism can, under circumstances, be responsible for the death of thousands, from which he infers there can be no "absolute" morality: "This means also that a revolution which has the prospect of saving life must, from the perspective of faith, be considered a possibility,"[29] though it would appear that in an atomic age nonviolence remains the only effective way. Nonviolence is better than violence, says Pokorný, not because it is a perfect moral principle but because it is more effective, and, by sparing the life of the opponent, allows for the possibility of further dialogue. The new direction indicated by Jesus is, according to Pokorný, no new law but a new responsibility that transcends the reign of vengeance and constitutes the new hope which the Christian tradition represents in the spirit of John Hus, Peter Chelcický, and Johannes A. Comenius.

---

[29]Ibid., 59.

Additional titles deserving special mention include: Ernst Lohmeyer, *Das Evangelium Matthäus* [Werner Schmauch, Hrsg.] (Göttingen: Vandenhoeck & Ruprecht, [1956] 1962); Harvey K. McArthur, *Understanding the Sermon on the Mount* (London: Epworth Press, 1961); W. D. Davies, *The Setting of the Sermon on the Mount* (Cambridge: University Press, 1964); Tal D. Bonham, *The Demands of Discipleship. The Relevance of the Sermon on the Mount* (Pine Bluff: Discipleship Book Company, 1967); Warren S. Kissinger, *The Sermon on the Mount. A History of Interpretation and Bibliography* (Metuchen NJ: Scarecrow Press, 1975); Fred L. Fisher, *The Sermon on the Mount* (Nashville: Broadman Press, 1976); D. A. Carson, *The Sermon on the Mount. An Evangelical Exposition of Matthew 5-7* (Grand Rapids: Baker Book House, 1978); J. Dwight Pentecost, *The Sermon on the Mount. Contemporary Insights for a Christian Lifestyle* (Portland: Multnomah Press, 1980); Robert A. Guelich, *The Sermon on the Mount. A Foundation for Understanding* (Waco TX: Word Books, 1982); Eduard Schweizer, *Die Bergpredigt* (Göttingen: Vandenhoeck & Ruprecht, 1982); Ursula Berner, *Die Bergpredigt. Rezeption und Auslegung im 20. Jahrhundert* (Göttingen: Vandenhoeck & Ruprecht, [1979] 1983).

Georg Strecker, *Die Bergpredigt, ein exegetischer Kommentar* (Göttingen: Vandenhoeck & Ruprecht, 1984) seeks within a form-critical perspective to discern the "Spannung" between Jesus' absolute demands and Matthew's theological interpretation and practical application in the hope that this "tension" might in some paradoxical way become ethically and politically relevant towards averting an impending "apocalyptic" nuclear crisis in our day. While Strecker doubts that the criteria for right interpretation can be definitively discerned (187), he hopes that the *Feindesliebe* Jesus demanded may be included in his Great Commission to "make disciples of all nations . . . teaching them to observe all that I have commanded you."

Modern Catholic interpretation of the Sermon on the Mount is still characterized by a predictable uniformity on almost all significant issues. In 1941 Thaddäus Soiron concluded his treatise on *Die Bergpredigt Jesu* (Freiburg i.B.: Herder) with the assertion that its demands express Jesus' irretractable commitment to an "Ordnung des Daseins" constituting the Kingdom of God and that mankind can partake of the blessing of this new life to the extent that it reciprocates Jesus' commitment to the new righteousness. As Jesus said of himself, so each individual and every human community must say of themselves, "I have come in order to fulfill" (Mt. 5:17) what Jesus proclaimed in the Sermon on the Mount (466). Despite this general affirmation of the Sermon's practicability, Soiron's exegesis fails to make explicit for whom Jesus' demands actually apply. This unresolved ambiguity surfaces at every decisive issue in Catholic interpretation of the Sermon. As a case in point, Soiron simply informs us that the Church requires the legal oath which Jesus prohibited because it must assure itself of the trustworthiness of its members. Having made his point, he then casually adds that the oath "is still less dispensable for the civil order than for the Church" (290, 292). With respect to Jesus' other demands (and especially Mt. 5:38ff.), Soiron repeats the tedious argument that, if they were to be unconditionally fulfilled, "they would effect an injustice that would be unbearable not only for the individual disciples of Jesus but also for the Church" (292). In much the same way Alois Stöger (*Ich aber sage euch. Die Bergpredigt lebendig gemacht.* München: Pfeifer, 1952) established the necessity of the oath on the authority of Augustine (58) and insists that Jesus' saying on nonresistance was not intended to affect the civil order (64).

According to Josef Staudinger (*Die Bergpredigt.* Wien: Herder Verlag, 1957), our interpretation of Jesus' sayings is determined by the cosmic conflict between God and Satan which requires the oath in order to preserve the truth from the lie (106-110). For the same reason Christ condemns neither self-defense nor the "Just War" of the state (120). "Specially elected souls" endowed with the fullness of the Holy Spirit are able to forego all compromises in faithful adherence to the teaching of Jesus. But, where "the fullness of the Holy Spirit does not compel thereto," God does not demand such neglect of natural laws (130), even as he does not demand of all men that they abstain from marriage in order to avoid sin (131). In Staudinger the traditional Catholic two-level ethic is still clearly intact.

In Rudolf Schnackenburg's estimation, the danger of Catholic interpretation of the Sermon lies not so much in limiting its hardest demands to the "state of perfection" as in "softening" them in the interests of a natural morality ("Bergpredigt," *Lexikon für Theologie und Kirche*, 1958, II, 226). Bernard Häring (*What Does Christ Want?* London: Geoffrey Chapman, 1968) exemplifies the Catholic assumption that there is no principal conflict between the Order of Creation and the Order of Redemption. He explains the oath as "essentially a way of revering God" (59) and is satisfied with updating the Just War conditions of Antiquity (200f.). Above all, Häring tells us, Christ wants our renewed commitment to the sacraments which he gave his Church.

In the context of Catholic interpretation, it is courageous of Wolfgang Knörzer to ex-press regret that Jesus' prohibition of the oath has been so little regarded by the practice of the Church. He indicates, however, that within the New Testament there is another tradi-tion (as reflected by Hebrews 6:16 and Romans 9:1) according to which the swearing of oaths is almost self-evident (*Die Bergpredigt. Modell einer neuen Welt*. Stuttgart: Verlag Katholisches Bibelwerk, 1970, p. 56). Knörzer does not seek to resolve the tension be-tween these two traditions nor does he explore the contemporary implications of Jesus' last two Antitheses except to say that they do not endorse the approach of nonviolence which by a superior tactic seeks to disarm one's enemy (58). Nevertheless, Knörzer would not have us discard "the experiment of the Sermon on the Mount" until we have actually tried it (61). "Only if one succeeds in applying the Sermon on the Mount concretely to all cir-cumstances of life can it serve as model of a new world" (99). Meanwhile we continue living in the tension between the Old Order and the New Aeon (101). Though the Sermon on the Mount is no "recipe" for solving our problems, it can serve the function of a com-pass pointing out the true course. Even though the obstacles we encounter along the way require us to navigate in other directions, the goal remains unchanged (105).

III
RETROSPECT
AND PROSPECT

RETROSPECT AND PROSPECT

Our history of interpretation began with Tolstoy because it was through him that the hermeneutical possibilities and liabilities of understanding or misunderstanding the Sermon on the Mount were most acutely focused within the developing modern historical consciousness of Western Christian thought. As every great prophet, Tolstoy also proved to be a great divider of men. Those who are captivated by the romantic pathos of his mighty Russian soul see behind his every weakness a hidden virtue while his many theological critics reject as heresy everything he stood for, often without bothering to tell us why.

Tolstoy's celebrated dissent and consequent excommunication from the Orthodox Church was precipitated by his disillusionment over those aspects of its teaching that failed to commend themselves either to reason or conscience, particularly the unconscionable sanction of mass murder perpetrated by Russia's "Christ-loving army" as acts establishing and confirming Christian faith. As Jesus, Tolstoy lost faith in a religious tradition that had deteriorated to superstition, lost its capacity for ethical discernment, and consequently no longer exercised a positive moral influence on life and human relations. The inconsistency of professing Christ in words of doctrinal affirmation while denying him in deed greatly perplexed Tolstoy. Witnessing a public execution in Paris and observing how the head of a man was officially separated from his body and hearing "the sound with which it fell separately into the box," Tolstoy suddenly understood, not with his reason but with his whole being, that, irrespective of how persuasively this act be rationalized as a necessary thing, it was essentially a bad thing. Henceforth Tolstoy was committed to the quest for a higher way and, after comparing the Chinese, Buddhist, Moslem, and Christian scriptures, he concluded that the clearest and best answers to life's aim and purpose are found in the Sermon on the Mount. Consequently, it became the singular passion of his life to explore the meaning of this teaching which alone makes life possible and worthwhile.

Tolstoy found the precepts of Jesus in the Sermon on the Mount to agree with experience of life and to be in accord with reason and conscience. Furthermore, he felt convinced they were not only perfectly easy to comprehend but also perfectly possible to live by. For this claim Tolstoy has become the subject of much criticism by theologians and the object of derision by the church. Virtually every commentator in the modern history of the Sermon's interpretation found reason to contest Tolstoy's view— reason enough to wonder what kernel of eternal truth it contained which could be exterminated neither by argument nor slander. Tolstoy was convinced Christ meant exactly what he said and intended his words to be taken in childlike trust and not allegorically or casuistically evaded. Jesus did not say his commandments were too hard for us to keep; he said his yoke is easy. But throughout the centuries the church insisted it is impossible for us to do what Jesus says and that consequently his "Antitheses" are impracticable unless accommodated to human weaknesses. Since men are too weak and Christ's commands too high, "Do not be angry" was limited to anger not "uncaused," adultery was recognized as a legitimate exception to marriage faithfulness, swearing allegiance "upon the gospel" was accepted in lieu of "Swear not at all," coercion by the powers that be was exempt from Jesus' command "Do not retaliate," wars waged by "Christ-loving" armies were sanctioned as just exceptions to loving one's enemies, and any social or juridical implication was excluded from Jesus' prohibition, "Do not condemn." Tolstoy's ethical question, "What then shall we do?" became an illegitimate question when all man can do is mourn over the death of Adam and rejoice in salvation through Christ while praying for that faith which the prayer of faith presupposes. Instead of living by the law of Christ in love, humility, and self-denial, we allow our life to be determined by that contrary law of our lower nature (Romans 7) which is so repugnant to our heart, our conscience, and our reason. Instead of striving after what is good, we may only hope in believing that Christ once for all redeemed us from all sin. Clearly, these are the issues over which not only Catholics and Protestants suffered a great division but which still constitute the great divide within Protestantism itself in terms of what Troeltsch identified as the absolutistic Sermon-on-the-Mount "sect" ethic over against the Paulinistic pragmatic "church" ethic.[1] Subsequently, it

---

[1]Cf. *Die Soziallehren der Kirchen und Gruppen*, (1911).

will be our aim to lay bare the theological roots of these differences within the respective hermeneutic traditions and to point towards the resolution of this polarization insofar as that is theologically possible.

At this stage, we must conclude that in Tolstoy the relation between Moses and Jesus, between Jesus and Paul, between dogma and ethics, between Law and Gospel remains unresolved—not to mention the implications for Jewish-Christian rapprochement which Tolstoy had no reason to envision or anticipate. Tolstoy was at heart a romantic captivated by the ideals of Rousseau which his primitivist mentality, yearning for the simplicity and rusticity of nature, tended to equate with those of Jesus. In reaction against the superficiality, conceit, and social injustice of the landed gentry, Tolstoy over-idealized the humble, natural simplicity of the peasants whose poverty of mind and matter enabled them to endure life without complaint and death without fear. As Rénan, he almost envisioned the Kingdom of God when he beheld the clear and mild eyes of these honest simple souls whose divinely enlightened consciousness contemplated the universe in its ideal source and whose purity of heart deserved one day to behold God.[2] Applied to biblical hermeneutics, this reductionist mentality demands that one extrapolate from the wealth of religious tradition that elemental essence (*Wesensschau*) which underlies all truth. This *Grundprinzip* Tolstoy conceived to be the apodictic precept of nonresistance, the holy barrier one may not transgress to destroy the life of his brother. In its formulation, "Resist not evil," this precept appears intrinsically negative. Perhaps that is how all moral consciousness develops. Even Socrates in his last dialogue following his unjust condemnation by the court of Athens confessed to Crito that the "voice" which since early childhood always told him what not to do convinced him "that it is never right to do a wrong or return a wrong to defend one's self against injury by retaliation."[3]

Tolstoy concluded that the whole force of Jesus' teaching somehow lay in this prohibition and that all the rest of the New Testament was but a commentary on the universal application of that great principle to all situations of life. Every moral ambiguity could now be clarified by reduction to an Either/Or with respect to this fundamental principle, an approach which characterizes the ingenious strength and implicit weakness of all un-

---

[2] Cf. Ernest Rénan, *The Life of Jesus* ([1863] London, 1908) 71.

[3] Plato, *Crito* (Chicago: The Great Books Foundation, 1968), Set One, I:50. Cf. *Apology,* ibid., 23.

compromising radicalism. Tolstoy's idealist penchant for utopias enabled him, like all prophets who envision the coming Kingdom, to live by the implicit belief in the triumph of good over evil. All the problems and possibilities of eschatology and ethics are somehow included in this hope together with the "anarchistic" vision of the eventual obsolescence of the coercive powers that be as these are replaced by the spontaneity of brotherly love without oaths of allegiance, legal proceedings, or war taxes to maintain military defenses. In his alleged anarchism, Tolstoy shared with the American poet-naturalist Henry David Thoreau the conviction, "that government is best which governs least . . . which governs not at all," but as a personal rather than a political philosophy, one developed from the perspective of the Sermon on the Mount. Unfortunately, many of Tolstoy's critics have misconstrued his vision as a subversive influence that fanned to flame the smoldering embers of proletarian discontent which eventually erupted in the violent revolution of October, 1905. While there is an implicit causal relation between the gospel of peace and the Cross to which the Gospel points and invariably leads—as current Jewish and Christian New Testament studies on the politics of Jesus have shown—it is slanderous to ascribe the evils of violence to the influences of those most committed to nonviolence. Though Tolstoy's deepest sympathies were with the peasants, his religious works were no grist for the revolutionary mill of Marxist ideology. As Lenin and Plekhanov indicated, Tolstoy's nonresistance pointed in a quite different direction.

Tolstoy's idealism has been rejected by most Christian theologians as an irrelevant legalism inspired by a perfectionist obsession. According to Tolstoy, the Sermon on the Mount seems to make life impossible only when people mistake the indication of an ideal for the laying down of a rule. Tolstoy clearly distinguished between the ideal towards which it is natural for all men to strive and that degree of attainment which men can even now reach by swimming against the stream. Tolstoy never wearied of encouraging all men everywhere to obey Christ "as far as possible." Theology is still debating what that means. Meanwhile Tolstoy's influence inspired, among others,[4] Leonhard Ragaz in Europe, Gandhi in India, and Shailer

---

[4]Note the similarity of emphasis in the *Thoughts* of Ellen G. White and especially in the *Mountain Pathways* of Hector Waylen.

Mathews[5] and Walter Rauschenbusch[6] in America to apply the precepts of the Sermon on the Mount to the social order.

Wilhelm Herrmann confronted us with the problem of modernizing Jesus by the inner logic of *Gesinnungsethik*. The contrast between Herrmann's ethic of inner disposition and Tolstoy's insistence upon external obedience could hardly be greater. According to Herrmann, the goal to which Tolstoy aspires is not only not within our reach; it is also not within Jesus' intention. Since it is impossible to apply the Sermon on the Mount to any situation of our contemporary life, it is futile and vain to strive to do so.

Luther too, says Herrmann, was still too much of a literalist to be able to see Jesus in proper historical perspective. Thanks to critical historical scholarship, we have now been freed from the painful guilt of an impossible *imitatio Christi* to live freely and responsibly within our own time and circumstances as Jesus did in his own day and way. By virtue of his apocalyptic *Weltanschauung,* Jesus freed himself from what continues to bind us: the cultural and social responsibilities guaranteeing the maintenance and furtherance of civilization. We, in turn, must therefore free ourselves from what bound him. Since Jesus was no social reformer, we are left without guidance from him. Consequently, we must fall back upon our own resources to cope with our very different world. Jesus was confronted with the end of the world, while we are confronted with endless responsibilities to perpetuate it. What was authentic for him would be self-deceit for us. Therefore, following Jesus is no option for us. Historical research has exposed the impossibility and hence impropriety of that monastic presumption. Tolstoy's literalism has proven nothing except the sickness of the erring conscience. Even if Tolstoy's naïve anarchism could be tolerated as an individualistic option within the primitive Russian social structure, it does not apply to Western Europe where the responsible exercise of political power has acquired moral dignity, argued Herrmann.

Apart from being an impotent game that violates the very spirit of Jesus, falling back upon the legalism of imitation also constitutes the most serious misunderstanding of Jesus' intention. Jesus does not demand that

---

[5]Cf. *The Social Teaching of Jesus* (New York: Macmillan, 1897) and *Jesus on Social Institutions* (New York: Macmillan, 1928).

[6]Cf. *A Theology of the Social Gospel* (New York: Macmillan, 1927).

we renounce our possession but rather that we employ God's good gifts in his service. Our relations to others, including our enemies, are not to be predetermined by outer prescriptions but rather inspired by inner motives. It would be sheer hypocrisy to love unless one were inwardly motivated. Those not compelled by their own volition nor convinced of their own resources to love others should not pretend to do so out of a sense of duty or a feeling of guilt. There are also times when nature compels us into conflict with others in order to prove ourselves, observes Herrmann. Thus, even violence can be exercised with good conscience within the context of one's calling quite independent of Jesus' *Gesinnung* because the final goal of responsible action today is the *Kulturstaat*, the defense of which demands that one wills war. Since war is necessary, it cannot, surmises Herrmann, be considered unchristian, for the state is not Christian but natural, and so is the promotion of national patriotism.

Instead of absolutizing the ethical counsels of Jesus as universal moral laws applicable to all the changing circumstances of life, we should, advises Herrmann, hold to the abiding person of Christ himself. Outwardly, we have been freed from his past, but inwardly we are all the more bound to the mystical wonder of his person and to his *Gesinnung*. Jesus' words are not cords that outwardly bind us to conformity but cues that inwardly direct us to freedom. What matters is not *what* we do but whether we do whatever we do freely and joyfully rather than fearfully or piously. Jesus' words are not addressed to us today in a literal historical way. We are to comprehend his inner life and power, not imitate his outward acts and deeds. Our faith is not dependent on and our life is not determined by the external facts of Jesus' historicity. Our faith and life rest not on the outer uncertainties of historical discernments but on the inner certainty of experiencing Christ's personal presence and power.

In superimposing his own *Weltanschauung* upon the *Sitz-im-Leben* of Jesus as the presupposition for responsible ethical discrimination, Herrmann exempted those modern philosophical and cultural determinants which comprised his own *Vorverständnis* from the critical analysis he applied to Jesus. Instead of simply identifying with the value judgments of Jesus, as Tolstoy assumed we should and could, every historical and exegetical insight derived from Jesus of Nazareth, if it is to acquire contemporary moral validity, must henceforth first pass through the filter of those unexamined modern assumptions comprising the current intellectual milieu of critics like Herrmann of Marburg. Since Martin Kähler had already repudiated the historiographical verifiability of the facticity of Jesus' words and deeds, all that presumably could pass the filter test of critical scientific judgments unscathed by such analyses were the vague sentiments of faith's inner attachments to the person of Christ. Indeed, critical research had freed modern man from an allegedly impossible imitation of Christ but without providing an alternative discriminatory structure to effectively challenge the subjective arbitrariness of Herrmann's own nationalistic priorities.

While much of the credit for distinguishing Christology from history goes to Kähler and a fair share of the fault for relegating Jesus' words and deeds to the "husk" from which an intangible, ineffable, inscrutable "kernel" of inner truth is to be somehow extrapolated goes to Harnack, it is nevertheless Herrmann and his *Gesinnungsethik* that subsequent interpreters of the Sermon on the Mount have to thank or blame for challenging biblical hermeneutics and theological ethics with an alternative to *imitatio Christi*.

Like Tolstoy, Leonhard Ragaz interpreted the whole Gospel and Christ himself from the perspective of the Sermon on the Mount, but, unlike Tolstoy, he sought with unflagging zeal to implement its ideals through the politics of Christian Socialism, which he understood to be its very subject and agenda. Ragaz was convinced that we can and shall do the good works demanded by Christ—"du kannst denn du sollst" (Kant)—in applying his Beatitudes to exploited factory workers here and now rather than much later in heaven. The promises of Jesus are to be fulfilled through a socialistic transvaluation of values, a political, economic, and social revolution that transforms the order of the world into the order of God according to the Sermon on the Mount, the Magna Charta of the Kingdom of God. Ragaz believed Jesus would free us from the natural necessity to hate and from all the mutually destructive tendencies implied in that necessity, provided we look to the deeds of Jesus as example and inspiration rather than to the creeds of Paul and the Reformers for consolation and justification of our weaknesses. Since organized religion lacks the spiritual resourcefulness to implement "die Sache Christi," the Sermon on the Mount leads us beyond its Christology, beyond its dogmatics, and beyond its ethics to an intuitive awareness of and an implicit captivation by the spirit and power of Jesus. Ragaz rejected both Herrmann's *Kulturprotestantismus* and Tolstoy's literalism and considered the Catholic duplicity of a two-level ethic (exemplified by St. Francis' *imitatio*) as invalid as the Lutheran *Zwei-Reiche-Lehre* dichotomy. Ragaz sought instead to correlate the political structure to the Kingdom of God by means of an inner-worldly *Nachfolge Christi* which neither makes peace with life's imperfections nor feels discouraged or threatened by them. Ragaz aspired to God's perfect goal for history while identifying with man's imperfect means of bringing it about. Rejecting the absolutistic Either/Or and the fanatic All-or-Nothing polarizations, he sought to reconcile the pacifist conscience with patriotic sentiment as a morally responsible citizen of both the *civitas dei* and the *civitas terrena*.

While the logic of his exegesis leaves much to be desired, Ragaz interpreted the Sermon on the Mount as the biblical hope for the world in a messianic sense to be implemented by men committed to the politics of Jesus. In the Sermon on the Mount Ragaz foresaw the implications of the messianic consciousness for the faith and life of Israel and the Church—the People of God in the world.

While the ideals of Tolstoy and Ragaz had been theologically challenged by Herrmann, they were existentially shattered by Naumann. In good faith Friedrich Naumann had pilgrimaged to the land of the lost grave of Jesus. There he lost the Jesus he sought. His European image of Jesus as social reformer was shattered on the bad roads of Palestine by the hard facts of history which exposed the Oriental Jesus, king of beggars as stranger to our ways and times. For a moment he wavered between Jesus and Bismarck. Then, he cast his lot with the Kaiser's *Realpolitik* and proceeded with persuasive eloquence to rationalize his decision theologically. Jesus said: "Care not." Our economy, however, requires planning. He said, "Sell all," but who wishes to relinquish his real estate? Jesus meant his words literally, but our way of life will not allow that option. We must conduct our economy by its own intrinsic competitive axioms without attempting to christianize it by the spirit of Jesus. That pertains also to our political responsibilities. Our modern conflicts have nothing to do with Jesus. Not the whole of our morality is rooted in the gospels. Without the claims of justice and power, society cannot exist. The hardest problems are not solved by yearning for purity and love. The ethic of Jesus may supplement but cannot replace the civil ethos. It is not a matter of either howling with the wolves or dying with the lambs. Life demands both: the clenched fist of Caesar and the outstretched arm of Jesus. That may seem hard, but it is true. Within the providence of God and the symbiosis of nature, raw paganism and universal love somehow complement each other. One should be as clear about the basic conditions of life as about the relation of one's soul to God. Christians must do their duty even if doing so breaks their tenderest emotions. In the last analysis, conflict is the principle of progress. Our civilization is not supported by the cedars of Lebanon but founded upon the building blocks of the Roman capitol. This Roman culture the religion of Jesus cannot displace. The more pure we proclaim the Gospel, the less useful it becomes, argued Naumann.

Naumann exemplified the trauma of Lutheran duplicity. With utter frankness he had exposed its uneasy conscience. We know, says he, that it is not enough to proclaim the Lamb of God that bears the sins of the world, but we do not know how to relate the preaching of the Cross to the teaching of the Way. Our religious piety has awakened feelings and ambitions which we cannot express ethically. The hoped-for resolution of this predicament through historical inquiry was shattered in disillusionment. Theology is in a dilemma if it cannot press on beyond the Christ of faith to the Jesus of history. Yet, the more one reaches out to Jesus, the more one realizes how impossible it becomes to grasp him historically.

Johannes Weiss provided the exegetical documentation for the irrelevance of Jesus' teaching for our time by his persuasive claim that Jesus understood the Kingdom of God exclusively as an otherworldly bliss without any analogies to this world. In his proleptic enthusiasm, Jesus dramatized the nearness of the Kingdom but without confusing its otherworldliness with our time. The Kingdom could not be coterminous with history because its coming implied the end of history. Consequently, for Jesus the Kingdom of God was not a subjective personal experience nor a present historical claim but a future otherworldly hope. Jesus was not interested in maintaining this world, only in preparing men for the world to come. Righteousness of God is not achieved through striving and the Kingdom of God is not realized through human effort. Those who receive the Kingdom will enter it like a child. Together with the Son of Man, the Kingdom of God will appear suddenly out of heaven by supernatural means as God's new creation, terminating and replacing the present historical order. As there is no overlapping of the two aeons, there is no conflicting of their loyalties. Though fully aware of the political oppression and economic exploitation of his people under Roman rule, Jesus was indifferent to the orders, concerns, and problems of this world. He blessed only the poor of earth whom God elected to inherit the Kingdom of Heaven. Those seeking legal arbitration in worldly courts he urged to settle their suit en route, leave their cloak as surety, and forego all legal rights before the imminent Kingdom would overtake them. Now, just before the final judgment of the world, was not the time to argue over legal personal claims. Now it was best to acquit the guilty of every wrong and to love all enemies. The moment had come for the elect to burn all bridges, hate Mammon, even hate one's parents or spouse if that is what is required to break all remaining ties with this world in anticipation of the next. The Sermon on the Mount reflects no social reference and no concern for long-range coexistence within the old aeon. It is an ethic of the last hour—like martial law—before everything will be finalized in blessed salvation for some and terrible damnation for others.

Since the Kingdom did not come during Jesus' life, his disciples expected it soon after his death, so Paul advised believers not to get involved in worldly affairs. However, in the light of Easter and Pentecost Paul eventually reinterpreted the postponement of the Kingdom as its realization in the life of the expanding Church. Weiss validated this Pauline shift in its own right provided it not be superimposed upon Jesus which, however, is exactly what happened, forever blurring the distinction between Jesus' unfulfilled hope and our realized faith. Nevertheless, to Weiss it was clear: the Kingdom Jesus expected never came, consequently, the Sermon on the Mount which presupposed its realization is invalidated. Since Jesus was mistaken, we who are not his contemporaries do not identify with his apocalyptic and therefore need not imitate his ways or comply with his demands. Since we cannot share his eschatology, we should not feel guilty about readapting his words to our situation. How ridiculous it would appear, says Weiss, to preach "Do not care for tomorrow" to unemployed factory workers today! How unreasonable it would be to prohibit divorce today when allowing it protects the sanctity of marriage!

Weiss tempered the disillusionment of realizing that Jesus' teaching is irrelevant for us by noting that even for the original disciples the decisive influence was not the Jesus of history but the Christ of faith experienced through Easter and Pentecost. By incorporating the concept of discipleship into the idea of the Kingdom as the expanding work of God in us, Weiss corrected Jesus' theological misunderstanding of the nature and coming of the Kingdom and absolved us of ethical embarrassment over the impossibility of *imitatio Christi*.

Albert Schweitzer was troubled by this unresolved antithesis between the claims of the historical Jesus and the Church's faith in the heavenly Christ. He perceived that, in sublimating the historical Jesus into the supramundane idea of the Kingdom of God, creedal formulations had cut off the possibility of returning to the historical Jesus. Schweitzer realized the Christology of Chalcedon would first have to be shattered before men could undertake *Leben-Jesu-Forschung* or even begin to grasp the thought of Jesus' historical existence. In quest of the relevance of Jesus' ethical teaching, Schweitzer pursued the insights of Weiss to their logical conclusion.

Schweitzer assumed Jesus understood the Kingdom to be a supernatural entity into which the elect dead would be resurrected and the elect living metamorphosed together with the Son of Man. Being supernatural, the Kingdom would also be supramoral—beyond the conflict of good and evil. Rather than being the realization of ethics, the Kingdom would be the end of ethics. Since the historical Jesus sees the Kingdom as a supra-ethical entity, he proclaims only Interim Ethics valid solely for the brief interval before the imminent appearance of the Kingdom. Seen in this context, the Sermon on the Mount is a profound, spiritual, inward-looking ethic required for entry into the Kingdom. It has, however, nothing to do with this world and its conditions.

Schweitzer rested his case for *konsequente Eschatologie* on the assumption that Jesus' apocalyptically determined *Weltanschauung* was consistently world- and life-negating. However, fifty years later, Schweitzer conceded a certain *in*consistency in Jesus inasmuch as Jesus rejected asceticism and advocated an ethic of active love. This inconsistency is not inconsequential. Positively, it salvaged a historical basis within the teaching of Jesus for life-affirmation upon which the future of civilization depends. Negatively, it raised serious questions about Jesus' ethical integrity with implications for our own. If Jesus' apocalyptic belief was inconsequential for his ethics, why should *our* faith determine *our* life? Since Jesus was mistaken about the basis of *his Weltanschauung,* where shall we find a basis for *ours*? Should we bypass Jesus and return to the early prophets? Or should we attempt to salvage from Jesus whatever can be modernized?

Rather than neutralize the conflict between the primordial apocalyptic character of Jesus' *Weltanschauung* and our own, we should, proposed Schweitzer, allow this tension to become fruitful in confronting us with the necessity of contending with Jesus every step of the way for our modern sense of values. Rather than tune his denial of the world to our acceptance of it—by ascribing the eschatology of Jesus to the redactionary influence of the Early Church—we in our individual spirit should allow general affirmation of the world to be christianized and transfigured by the personal rejection of the world proclaimed by Jesus. This happens, explains Schweitzer, as a result of personal life-negation through self-sacrifice in the life-affirmation of others. We ourselves, argues Schweitzer, must hold fast to world- and life-affirmation and seek to deepen it despite the realization that there is no evident meaning within the universe to give our life stability and direction. When disintegration of our *Weltanschauung* threatens to sink our life-affirmation, we also, like Jesus, must salvage the latter by severing its connection with the former. In that case the range and scope of our ethics which is now independent of our *Weltanschauung* would also be narrowed to an interim. The hope of Schweitzer's consistent eschatology lay in the inconsistency—not a German virtue—which he ascribed to Jesus whereby it became possible to indirectly relate his ethic to us despite the fact that his eschatology directly separated him from us.

Tolstoy and Ragaz had sought to recover the contemporary relevance of Jesus' teaching from the stony rocks of ecclesiastical dogma as Naumann had sought to do from the stony soil of Palestine. Then Weiss and Schweitzer concluded the Sermon on the Mount could not be wrenched loose from its eschatological soil to be transplanted into our *Kulturchristentum*. Naumann found it impossible to reach out to Jesus on account of the way he lived. To Schweitzer, Jesus remained a stranger and an enigma on account of what he believed. Naumann had rejected the Sermon on the Mount on cultural grounds: the Oriental life-style it presupposed was too incompatible. Schweitzer challenged its validity on theological grounds: the apocalyptic *Weltanschauung* it presupposed was too unacceptable. Naumann had argued we could not live the way Jesus lived. Schweitzer reasoned we could not believe what he believed. Both arrived at the same conclusion—Naumann for cultural reasons, Schweitzer on exegetical grounds—that Jesus remains historically inaccessible to us, and his Sermon on the Mount remains essentially irrelevant for us. Consequently, Jesus, who was about to enter our time, passed by and returned to his own.

For Schweitzer as for Weiss, the theology of Paul (which had been a stumbling block to Tolstoy and Ragaz) spanned the bridge of meaning from our modern *Weltanschauung* to the apocalyptic of the historical Jesus, who claims our faith even though he cannot claim our reason.

The Liberal quest of Jesus ended with Schweitzer's critique in 1906. The same year, Johannes Müller's bestseller appeared. It said what people wanted to hear, namely, that nothing good could come through critical historical-philological study because one can understand Jesus only "experientially.'' The genius of Jesus needed to be disassociated from the torturous morality of Tolstoy, the personal trauma of Naumann, the social context of Ragaz, and the theological dilemma of Weiss and Schweitzer. In order to comprehend the essence of Jesus' teaching with German feeling, its Jewishness first had to be exposed and discarded. Secondly, the abstracted kernel of abiding truth needed to be contemporized in order to purify it of all outdated historical irrelevancies. Thirdly, the remaining distilled impressions were to be subjectively internalized. Müller identified the end-product of this process as ''nature's laws of humanization'' by means of which he transposed the uniqueness of Jesus into the uniqueness of Aryanism. Though Müller avoided the dilemmas of historical and theological inquiry largely by evading the seriousness of these disciplines, it must be admitted that he exposed the limitation of assuming the understanding of Jesus' sayings to be a strictly historical-theological matter. To the dismay of theologians, it appeared of little consequence to Müller whether one be a Christian, Jew, atheist, materialist, spiritualist, or whatever so long as one shared the vision of the emergence of the new humanity. While he himself contributed little towards the articulation of that vision, Müller, reflecting the influence of Herrmann, appealed to the universal need for spiritual self-realization and self-authentication, concepts which later acquired theological respectability through the influence of Bultmann.

All the various strands of thought and impulse represented by the positions and dispositions reviewed thus far were intricately interwoven in the logic of Professor Baumgarten's eloquent and passionate deliberation on the irreconcilable conflict between the idealism of the *Bergpredigt* and the *Kultur der Gegenwart*. During the Great War, Baumgarten had fervently defended Bismarck's *Realpolitik*, though inwardly he had meanwhile become as convinced as Tolstoy about its incompatibility with the Sermon on the Mount. He sought somehow to extricate himself from this crisis of conscience without sacrificing his moral and intellectual integrity as professor of theology. In the process he persuaded himself and his theology students of the theological resources for resolving this tension. From Troeltsch he learned Jesus had addressed his teaching to only a few disciples whose impact upon the social order had been negligible. With Harnack he concurred that Jesus proclaimed only the inestimable value of the human soul and had no intention of involving himself or others in political, social, or cultural affairs. Herrmann convinced him Jesus wanted only *Ge-*

sinnungsethik. He discerned through Weiss that Jesus had turned his back upon this world in anticipation of an otherworldly Kingdom and agreed with Schweitzer that Jesus had proclaimed the elimination of the social order in expectation of the supernatural order. His view of Jesus as a sunny, blissful, sentimental, Oriental flower-child, who had somehow escaped the hardships of life and the conflicts of history, resembles the insights of Rénan. Somewhat like Müller, Baumgarten saw the Sermon on the Mount as a fine specimen of unspoiled religious sentiment reflecting the inner life of Jesus and exemplifying the eternal bliss of the soul's relation to God— like a perfect poem whose beauty and truth should not be forced out of context to provide pragmatic meanings. Baumgarten's sympathies lay with Nietzsche, for whom Jesus was the grand corrupter of mankind. For his claim that we must restrict Jesus' happy confidences to our inner life, he relied on Luther. Baumgarten realized, as had Naumann, that, while the rosy optimism of Jesus inspired a thousand beautiful Oriental illusions, our *Kultur* requires of us a courageous realism. In view of Jesus' cultural estrangement and irresponsible individualism, Baumgarten concluded we should reject his teaching and not allow the Sermon on the Mount to violate our human dignity, offend our sense of patriotic loyalty, or contradict our deepest dispositions. Baumgarten counseled his young theologues not to teach the hard sayings of Jesus in catechism so as not to confuse the tender minds of youth with the paradoxes of Jesus nor to preach from these texts in order to spare the people the spiritual torture induced by them.

The historical realism of Karl Bornhäuser presents a far more serious contribution and challenge to the interpretation of the Sermon on the Mount than do the ecclectic reflections of Baumgarten. Bornhäuser was the first to expose Herrmann's *Gesinnungsethik* as a preposterous and irrelevant modern imposition totally foreign to and altogether incompatible with the Jewishness of Jesus. Jesus, says Bornhäuser, taught *halacha* or *Lebensregeln*. These apply to the actual local conditions of life; they are not to be spiritualized or abstracted from the concrete context from which they derive and to which they refer. In Rabbinic teaching, thought and deed are inseparable. Teaching is for living. Jesus teaches what is to be done and there is nothing idealistic, unrealistic, irrelevant, impractical, or impossible about it. The only question to be asked is: To *whom* does Jesus' teaching apply? For Bornhäuser the answer is self-evident: the words apply to those originally addressed. According to Bornhäuser, all the problems of interpretation begin either by overlooking this simple historical fact (as in Müller) or by forcing it to yield universally valid moral precepts applicable to all people at all times. The fact of the matter is that Jesus taught twelve disciples. These he instructed not to be angry with one another. If disputes arose, they were to be settled privately rather than in the courts. They were to live pure lives and not divorce their wives. If accused of wrongdoing, they were not to resort to legal oaths or seek indemnification for personal injuries through civil jurisprudence. They were to practice charity without discrimination and without expecting reciprocation—they were even to love and intercede for their enemies and to condemn no one. Then he taught them how to pray. Finally, he told them not to teach for profit (as some Pharisees allegedly did) nor to lay up earthly treasures by plying their own trades but to trust God for the needs of life. This was how Jesus himself lived, and therefore, argues Bornhäuser, it was by no means too hard or unrealistic of Jesus to expect his chosen twelve to follow the example of his life-style. The whole interpretation of the Sermon on the Mount is obvious, concludes Bornhäuser, once we fully realize that it was meant for Jesus' disciples. Then we need not try to turn the world upside down by applying it to mankind en masse.

To his own satisfaction Bornhäuser, by the logic of historicism, eliminated the ethical question. Paradoxically, it was his dubious evasion of the contemporary relevance of the Sermon on the Mount that enabled him to make his decisive contribution to the modern quest for its meaning. His personal detachment freed him to objectively elucidate this text within its historical context as understood by Jewish contemporaries of Jesus. He was free to explore the Jewishness of Jesus because he avoided on principle the contemporary implications of historical insights. Bornhäuser enabled us to understand in a more Jewish way the historical meaning of the Sermon on the Mount. Though we must pursue our quest for its meaning beyond historical considerations, the integrity with which we do so depends largely on the correctness of historical insights.

Implicit in the logic of most preceding positions was an irreconcilable dichotomy. Herrmann gave priority to attitudes over against acts. Naumann, in affirming the *Realpolitik* of the German Kaiser, relinquished the gospel of the Oriental Jesus. Weiss identified with the realized eschatology of Paul rather than the mistaken apocalyptic of Jesus. Schweitzer preferred modern world-affirmation to Jesus' world-negation. Baumgarten abandoned the *Bergpredigt* in order to defend the *Kultur*. Bornhäuser severed the connection between history and ethics. In each case the tension between worldly and otherworldly claims and their respective value structures remains unresolved. Catholicism had institutionalized the ethical conflict by providing sanctuaries for the sinless monks, on the one hand, and spiritual consolations for the sinful laity, on the other hand. By his emphasis on faith over against works, *fides orthodoxa* rather than *Nachfolge Christi*, Luther internalized the problem, obviating all marks of distinction between pagans and Christians.

In the light of these developments, Georg Wünsch sought to reclaim the material content of ethics characteristically absent from the Kant-Herrmann ethical formalism. Wünsch recognized in Luther's Two-Kingdoms dichotomy the inherent tendency towards limiting the demands of Jesus to the sphere of personal ethics and, in turn, allowing *Realpolitik* its autonomy from the Gospel. Wünsch reproved Naumann and Baumgarten for excluding cultural responsibilities from the influence of the Gospel, challenging their assumption that the tension between Christ and culture is less acute within the private than the public sphere. Wünsch believed Jesus intended the sanctification of the whole person and the whole of life and that, accordingly, the Sermon on the Mount essentially expresses the will of the Creator. Seen in its best light, Luther's *Berufsmoral* was thus a form of *Schöpfungsmoral*. However, the distortion caused by sin precipitates the tension between Christ and creation. Under these circumstances, reasons Wünsch, God who created the world wills that we do what is necessary to maintain it. Since the means required to prevent its disintegration conflict with the teaching of Jesus, the Sermon on the Mount ethic must be corrected by the *Schöpfermoral* to allow for the use of violence in the restraint of evil. Luther not only allowed but sanctioned as *Gottesdienst* the means necessary for the maintenance of *Gottesordnung*. Therein, believes Wünsch, lies our only hope for ultimate convergence of *lex Christi* and *lex naturae*. Meanwhile, the conflict between the *opus alienum* and the *opus proprium* remains unresolved, hence Luther could not consider the Sermon on the Mount as part of the gospel and Wünsch could not allow the ideals of Jesus to claim priority over the laws of nature.

Carl Stange denounced every idealistic interpretation of the Sermon as terrible hypocrisy and insisted, more emphatically than Wünsch, that no man can satisfy the imperatives of Jesus in the literal Tolstoyan sense. For Stange, the *Bergpredigt* is *Bußpredigt*—proclamation of impossible law designed to expose the reprehensibility of the human condition and provoke self-condemnation through which comes consciousness of God as justifier of the unjust. The Sermon on the Mount tells us what we ought to do but cannot. It's sole purpose is propaedeutic: to confound us with the Law in the hope of preparing us for the Gospel. Seen in this way, the Sermon on the Mount is nothing but a scheme to ensure our failure. What is required of us is not right action but contrite confession—that is the substance of ethics, according to Stange. Our reservations about Stange's view need not be repeated here other than to note that the Sermon itself does not convey self-condemnation as its central blessing, thus, Stange found it expedient to superimpose upon the *Bergpredigt* his own despairing pessimism based on a misreading of Romans 7. Such prooftexting in the name of hermeneutics not only misrepresents Jesus but exploits Paul.

Observing that one can find in the Talmud a virtual equivalent for every saying of Jesus in the Sermon on the Mount, Gerhard Kittel concluded the difference between Christianity and Judaism must lie in the Person of Christ rather than in the teaching of Jesus. Nevertheless, Kittel identified one decisive difference: Moses and Judaism allowed concessions to accommodate the empirical structures of life. Jesus does not. Insisting on the unconditional command of God apart from all ritual and nationalism, Jesus isolates morality from life, making his absolute demands absolutely irrelevant. The Torah, says Kittel, intends to build up, but the Sermon on the Mount can only destroy. At the point where he insists on its fulfillment, Jesus ceases to be a Jew. Since his demands "are exaggerated to the point of paradox and nonsense," everything in the Christian faith is in turn absolutized: by making us absolute sinners deserving absolute condemnation, the absolute demands of Jesus prepare us for the absolute redemption of God through the absolute sacrifice of Christ—all of which constitutes the absolute paradox of atonement. To a Jew this absolutization is absolute nonsense. For Kittel it constitutes the uniqueness of Christianity without which it would be nothing but a Jewish sect! Kittel's conclusion raises the question as to whether the uniqueness ascribed to Jesus does not originate with attempts to evade his radical Jewish teaching by exalting his person and consequently redefining Christianity as a dogma rather than a way. As Weiss and Schweitzer challenged us to reconcile the hope of Jesus with the faith of Paul, so Kittel confronts us with the necessity of relating Christ's teaching to his person. Without their intending to do so, Stange and Kittel alert us to the need for reconsidering the Jewishness of Jesus.

Rudolf Bultmann acknowledged Jesus' ethic to be an ethic of obedience exactly like the Jewish only more so. That Jesus conceived the idea of obedience radically is, according to Bultmann, no reason for us to disregard his teaching in favor of an atonement theology—as Kittel had assumed. The meaning of Jesus, who lived and taught as a Jewish Rabbi, lies in his word rather than his person or his death. Jesus never spoke of the redemptive significance of his death and resurrection, says Bultmann. He proclaimed God's forgiveness through his word. Bultmann believes Jesus does not expect us to do something obediently. Rather, Jesus intends to free us from all outer acts of conformity and from all systems of ethics. We are to be directly responsible to God, intuitively aware of what he momentarily demands of us, and inwardly prepared to respond immediately and unreservedly. While the claims of law are limited by formulable precepts, the claims of God are unlimited and unconditional. That is why and how the radical obedience Jesus demands differs from legalism, says Bultmann. Obedience must be spontaneous and instantaneous, not an astutely deliberated and judiciously evaluated "ethical" performance. However, since Bultmann rejects on principle all precept for discerning what radical obedience means, it is impossible for us to know when it happens or what difference it makes. We are left, as in the case of Herrmann, with an indiscernable inwardness not subject to correction by the outer word. Consequently, Bultmann's concept of radical obedience is too abstract, intangible, and unreal to be considered Jewish. Kittel had dispensed with the relevance of Jesus' demands by absolutizing them. Bultmann obscured their Jewish concreteness by existentializing them. Nevertheless, in contrast to Weiss, Schweitzer, and Bornhäuser, who had discounted the contemporary relevance of Jesus' demands on eschatological and historical grounds, Bultmann, by reinterpreting Jesus' eschatology in existential terms, validated for our time the formal context of Jesus' ethic—albeit while evaporating its material content.

Hans Windisch censured Bultmann for rejecting the Sermon as external authority while affirming its relevance as internal authority. It is a contradiction, contends Windisch, to affirm its validity while rejecting its practicability. Historical exegesis demands our admitting that the Sermon on the Mount, just as the Torah, contains commands meant to be obeyed. From the sources, there is no evidence that the idea of impracticability— which seems so obvious to modern theologians—ever occurred to Matthew, Jesus, or his disciples. Moreover, the Sermon was not addressed to sinners crying for redemption but to disciples committed to obedience.

Windisch, however, admitted we do not comply with Jesus' intentions and, as his predecessors, proceeded to explain why. With Baumgarten he argued that Jesus' sayings were individualistic and lacked cultural or political reference partly in view of their eschatological perspective, as Weiss and Schweitzer had noted, and partly on account of the narrow horizon of Jesus' piety, as Bornhäuser had maintained. Windisch even supported Naumann's conclusion about our cultural responsibilities keeping us from obeying Jesus, yet he hoped with Wünsch that our struggle for self-realization could somehow be reconciled with the realization of God's Kingdom. Basically, Windisch concurred with Kittel (notwithstanding some statements to the contrary) in considering the emphasis of the Sermon anti-Jewish despite its Jewish content. He agreed with Tolstoy against Herrmann and Bultmann that Jesus intended his demands to be fulfilled literally while concurring with Herrmann and Bultmann against Tolstoy that we cannot fulfill them literally and should not try to do so lest, as Stange feared, we literally be driven to despair. Nevertheless, Windisch differed from his predecessors in exposing what they had concealed, namely, that the discrepancy between Jesus' demands and our performance is not a historical, universal, or philosophical problem but essentially a moral one which we should neither evade by ascribing it to a peculiarity of Jesus nor rationalize in terms of cultural progress. By candidly admitting that it is we who are to blame for not doing what Jesus says, Windisch challenges us to rethink the maze of ambiguity encompassing Christian ethics today.

His own contribution towards recovering the meaning of the Sermon on the Mount was prompted by reluctance to accept the imposing doctrine of substitutionary atonement because it bears no evident relation to the Sermon itself and too greatly depreciates the entire Gospel of Jesus. Reexamining the assumptions of Paulinizing exegesis, Windisch discovered that a considerable portion of the Sermon on the Mount consists of Wisdom literature rather than eschatological material. Contrary to the claims of Weiss and Schweitzer, Windisch found the vigorous form of Jesus' hardest demands permeated by a world- and life-affirming optimism unaffected by eschatological belief. Furthermore, the Sermon, far from being exclusively oriented to judgment, contains a way of salvation conveying the grace and fellowship of God. Its implicit soteriology is not predicated by eschatology and stands in sharpest contrast to the teaching of Paul in Romans 3 to 8. Jesus reaffirms with his blessings the promise of salvation preached by the early prophets and sung by the devout psalmists as he proclaims the grace, mercy, peace, and joy of the Lord upon all who seek his righteousness, holiness, and fellowship. Moreover, Jesus teaches us to petition our Father confidently for forgiveness provided we forgive our enemies. The inner processes described and presupposed throughout the Sermon on the Mount are, believes Windisch, the work of the Spirit. Independent of eschatology and legalism, Windisch recovered within the Sermon on the Mount a tradition of Jewish Wisdom to whose implicit prophetic soteriology the imperatives of Jesus organically relate.

Seeking a modus vivendi between those interpretations of the Sermon on the Mount which either burden us with impossible legislation or absolve us of all obligation, Martin Dibelius rejected the conclusions of most of his predecessors while seeking to salvage and integrate their insights. Dibelius felt the Sermon on the Mount should be valid for today but not in Tolstoy's perfectionist sense. He affirmed the eschatological context of the Sermon but not Schweitzer's implication that it was therefore limited to a past interim. He conceded the conviction of Bornhäuser and Windisch that the demands of the Sermon on the Mount, just as those of the Torah, were meant to be obeyed literally but rejected the implication that we should therefore interpret them in a Jewish sense and apply them in a nomistic way. He concurred with Stange and Kittel that Jesus' radical demands are unconditional but rejected their assumption that they constitute an impossible ideal intended only to prepare us for atonement theology. Of the positions identified in this survey Dibelius stands closest to Bultmann in endeavoring to validate a modern category of relevance with historical and theological integrity.

According to Dibelius, the original hearers who expected to see the end of the world understood Jesus' Sermon as the revelation of God's unconditional will for the coming Kingdom in which they would be free of all earthly cares and concerns. But, in view of the continuation of historical existence, Matthew, realizing that the pure will of God could attain its full validity only in the age to come, modified Jesus' demands to accommodate the conditions of this life. Jesus intended his sayings as signs of hope. After Easter they became laws of conduct. Radical commitment to God's will is possible, says Dibelius, only within an eschatological context. Before Easter the disciples anticipated the imminent Kingdom. After Easter the Church expected the imminent *parousia*. In both cases the eschatological stimulus created the new type of man. Since that hope has been lost, the ideal of full obedience seems impracticable. Because the severity of the Gospel does not allow further adaptation of its demands to our circumstances, Christians appear to have no clear answer for their condemnation of conscience apart from the consolation of atonement theology. Dibelius, however, feels that we who do not think in eschatological terms and do not expect the imminent end of the world can nevertheless be transformed by the Sermon on the Mount provided we uphold it as a symbolic expression of God's perfect will. Because God's pure will applies to the Kingdom which God has not established and which it is not our task to found, we must accept the conditions of this world as the inescapable basis for our actions. As representatives of the new world in an old age we are to perform signs, not those of the Kingdom described in the Sermon on the Mount but signs of our own time illustrating the nature of God's will. In this way Dibelius hoped the demands of Jesus which are too exacting to be fulfilled in this world may nevertheless become a symbolic factor in our struggle for life.

Over against all ethical ambiguity and casuistry, Dietrich Bonhoeffer argued the case for single-minded obedience as the ultimate possibility of the distinctively Christian life. He exposed the sophistry of *Gesinnungs-ethik* as a false pretext for avoiding the error of legalism and insisted there is no communion with God apart from fulfillment of his law. Rather than rationalize our disobedience by the paradox of the cross or justify it by the cheap grace of atonement theology, Bonhoeffer urged that we find in the *Gestalt Christi* the form and norm of our Christian discipleship without offering a thousand explanations why we could not or should not do God's will. Nevertheless, cautions Bonhoeffer, we ought not confuse discipleship with a Franciscan ideal. For Bonhoeffer, discipleship meant paradoxical commitment exemplified by his simultaneous involvement in the Nazi war machine and the resistance movement. While it is hard to believe Bonhoeffer's clandestine activity in Hitler's counter-espionage was governed by Christological rather than pragmatic criteria and impossible to sanction tyrannicide by reference to the *Gestalt Christi*, Bonhoeffer's martyrdom for his people exemplifies the paradox of ethics at the boundary of existence.

According to Eduard Thurneysen, all consideration of the Sermon on the Mount as ethical model defrauds its Christological meaning: that Christ did for us what we are neither able nor invited to do, a message which (contrary to Stange and Kittel) is alleged to be implicit in the Sermon itself. We are not expected to imitate Jesus by futile legalistic attempts to fulfill the Sermon's demands. Rather, we are invited to appropriate and attest the righteousness Jesus fulfilled for us, explains Thurneysen. The Sermon on the Mount must therefore be freed of all moral contamination (Tolstoy), mystical confusion (Müller), preoccupation with history (Bornhäuser, Windisch), with eschatology (Weiss, Schweitzer), and with the present situation (Ragaz) in order to recover its singular intention of proclaiming Christ in whom alone the Kingdom of God is realized. Though Thurneysen's interpretation of the Sermon on the Mount appears, from a Jewish perspective, to exemplify the genius of Christian dogmatic evasion of its moral meaning, his Christological emphasis demands consideration of the sense in which Christ's obedience constitutes the fundamental basis of our own.

In the considered opinion of Joachim Jeremias, those who interpret the Sermon on the Mount as moral imperative in the perfectionist sense (Tolstoy, Windisch), as impossible ideal in the Lutheran Orthodox sense (Stange, Kittel), or as Interim Ethic in the apocalyptic sense (Weiss, Schweitzer), for all their differences, have one thing in common: they all regard the Sermon as law rather than as gospel. Jeremias claims that in its original function as Christian catechism the Sermon on the Mount as a whole presupposed the *kerygma* through which the believers to be instructed in the Christian conduct of life had been converted by missionary preaching. Furthermore, the individual demands of Jesus are either explicitly preceded by the gospel of forgiveness or implicitly presuppose the reality of the Kingdom. This insight prompted Jeremias to interpret the Sermon on the Mount as gospel, hoping thereby to resolve its apocalyptic disillusionment, correct its legalistic distortion, and temper the claim of its impossibility. While Jeremias' reversal of the logic of Lutheran Orthodoxy (which had mistaken the Sermon to be propaedeutic law) by redefining Jesus' demands as gospel obscures the issue regarding their practicability, his emphasis on the gifts of God preceding his demands established a priority fundamental to ethical thought.

However, this priority of God's gifts over his demands is inadvertently qualified by Walter Städeli's research on the cultic context of the Sermon on the Mount within the temple liturgy inasmuch as the entrance requirements which Matthew associates with the Kingdom were originally enforced by the keepers of the temple gates whose responsibility it was to exclude from its precincts all who failed to meet its entrance requirements.

According to Hector Waylen, God actually enables man to meet the entrance conditions of the higher spiritual way that leads to sanctification and salvation. Likewise, E. Stanley Jones believes it necessary and possible to embody ''the ethical side of our gospel'' as the form and power of the uniquely Christian life. With Emmet Fox this possibility takes the form of a new 'metaphysical' disposition which transcends all pessimism and overcomes all difficulties. Reinhold Seeberg understands the new obedience as the influence of God's Spirit upon the wills and decisions of men who, in Clarence Jordan's terms, are committed to faith and discipline. Jeremy Ingalls identified this ''Galilean Way'' as essentially the Jewish way of Wisdom indicated by Israel's Law, exemplified by Israel's prophets, and fulfilled in the 'Galilean' law of love. Ernest M. Ligon demonstrates the soundness and profoundness of the spiritual principles of Jesus from a psychological point of view in their effect upon character development, while Swami Prabhavananda illumines the nature of spiritual transformation inspired by the vision of Christ through the Sermon on the Mount.

Georg Eichholz refocuses the differences between the Christological intentions of Matthew and Paul in historical perspective and hopes that the resulting Jewish-Christian tension may somehow activate our faith. Ulrich Luck identifies the unreconciled difference between Jesus' demand of perfection and Paul's understanding of justification as the fundamental ongoing perplexity of Evangelical theology. The underlying problem, as Luck sees it, is our inability as Christians to identify with Jesus' Jewish frame of reference and its Wisdom tradition. Our only hope, according to Luck, lies in the progressive ''softening'' of Jesus' demands as exemplified by the Christian *Redaktionsgeschichte* of the Sermon's text on the dubious exegetical assumption that the marks of the devout life embodying the perfection Jesus demanded were intended to remain an inscrutable mystery until God will reveal and fulfill his intentions in another age. Hans-Theo Wrege challenges the literary intactness of the Q tradition while Petr Pokorný defends it as the ''Kern'' of Jesus' proclamation which, from within its Jewish context, intends to inform our view of history and its social dynamics even though our action may contradict its literal meaning.

Three fundamental problems recur in various modes and interrelations throughout our entire historical analysis: (1) Jesus' understanding of the future and the extent to which contemporary theology can appropriate Jewish eschatology as the viable context of Christian hope, (2) Jesus' re-

lation to the Mosaic tradition and the meaning of Christian ethics as fulfillment of the intentions of the Torah, and (3) Jesus' expectation of his
followers and the sense in which the historical truth of his teaching is practicable and relevant for us today. It comes as no surprise that these problems to which we now address ourselves in systematic order constitute in
effect a Christian *Auseinandersetzung* with the Jewishness of Jesus.

IV
THE JEWISHNESS
OF JESUS

ESCHATOLOGY AND ETHICS

No serious analysis of Jesus' teaching can evade the disturbing realization that, although Jesus was a Jew, his followers are not Jews, and his own people are not Christians. Joseph Klausner reasoned:

> Had there not been in Jesus' teaching something contrary to the "world-outlook" of Israel, there could never have arisen out of it a new teaching so irreconcilable with the spirit of Judaism: *ex nihilo nihil fit*. Though Jesus' teaching may not have been deliberately directed against contemporary Judaism, it certainly had within it the germs from which there could and must develop in the course of time a non-Jewish and even anti-Jewish teaching.[1]

On the other hand, Julius Wellhausen claimed Jesus "did not proclaim a new faith but taught men to do the will of God."[2] Regarding Jewish-Christian understanding, Schalom Ben-Chorin concludes: "The belief of Jesus unites us—the belief about Jesus divides us."[3] It is therefore of paramount importance to discern (1) what Jesus believed and (2) whether we can believe what he believed. Since Jewish apocalyptic was the context of Jesus' thought, the immediate question is to what extent he must be judged by what he shared with his contemporaries rather than by the way he differed from them.

Wilhelm Herrmann's modernization of Jesus' teaching along individualistic and spiritual lines reflects the influence of Adolf Harnack, for whom Jesus' connection with Judaism appeared to be "only a loose one" and its

---

[1]Joseph Klausner, *Jesus of Nazareth: His Life, Times, and Teaching*, trans. from the Hebrew by H. Danby (London: Allen and Unwin, 1925) 9.

[2]Julius Wellhausen, *Einleitung in die drei ersten Evangelien* (Berlin: Georg Reimer, 1905) 113.

[3]Schalom Ben-Chorin, *Jesus im Judentum*, Schriftenreihe für christlich-jüdische Begegnung, Band 4 (Wuppertal: Theologischer Verlag Rolf Brockhaus, 1970) 51.

influence virtually "of no importance at all.'"[4] For Harnack, Judaism and its apocalyptic constitute the "husk" from which the kernel of Jesus' uniqueness must be extracted. In the process, Jesus, the historical Jew, disappears and his messianic features are abolished. "Gone, too, are all external hopes for the future." All that remains is "God and the soul, the soul and its God."[5] Though Jesus' flaming eschatological message was cast in the turbulent apocalyptic mood, its "essential" element purged of everything dramatic, external, historical, and futuristic is essentially restive and static in nature, a "timeless" repository of universal wisdom addressed to a "timeless" people. Extracted from his Jewish world and history, Jesus allegedly towered so far above Judaism as to remain untouched by it.

These theological presuppositions of Harnack were implicit in the political commitments of Friedrich Naumann and became explicit in the religious sentiments of Johannes Müller who de-judaized Harnack's de-eschatologized "essence" with German anti-Semitic zeal. Harnack, Herrmann, Müller, and everyone they influenced[6] considered Jewish apocalyptic an accidental and irrelevant factor in the milieu of Jesus. They believed that the essential elements of his religion could be preserved only as these are stripped of all association with Judaism, on the dubious assumption that divine sanction rests only on the noneschatological sayings of Jesus and that his personality and thought remained essentially untainted by late Jewish apocalyptic.

Johannes Weiss and Albert Schweitzer challenged this modern misunderstanding of Jesus as a meek, 'spiritual,' romantic, non-Jewish liberal by showing that Jewish apocalyptic constitutes the very substance or kernel of Jesus' teaching and that, consequently, eschatology is the key that explains everything Jesus ever said or did. According to Schweitzer, eschatology is not only the framework of Jesus' ethic but the sole basis of its validity, for, apart from his expectation of imminent world catastrophe,

---

[4]Adolf von Harnack, *What Is Christianity*, ET T. B. Saunders (London: Ernest Benn, 1958) 23.

[5]Ibid., 50.

[6]Gösta Lundström, *The Kingdom of God in the Teaching of Jesus, A History of Interpretation from the Last Decades of the Nineteenth Century to the Present Day*, ET Joan Bulman (Edinburgh: Oliver and Boyd, 1963) 14, claims that Dibelius "is palpably under the influence of Müller's thought." See also ibid., 170.

Jesus would never have proclaimed his interim ethic. Furthermore, Jesus' understanding of the Kingdom of God was not subjective, inward, and spiritual but objective, external, and revolutionary. He saw the Kingdom as a future, not a present, reality, to be effected by God, not man, maintained Schweitzer. Since the fundamental character of Jesus' teaching is held to be prophetic, the gift of salvation is seen as purely predictive, and the meaning of Jesus' life appears to be exhausted within his mistaken Jewish hope that, contrary to all expectation, was not realized within his experience. Consequently, Jesus throws himself upon the wheel of history which, over his mangled body, makes its last eschatological revolution— a reading of history that 'in turn' ends the modern Christian quest for the Jewish Jesus.[7]

"No one," writes Gösta Lundström, "had ever so completely denied that Jesus in any way diverged from the Jewish idea of the Kingdom of God as Albert Schweitzer."[8] But his error lay in assuming Jewish apocalyptic to be consistently transcendental in the sense of Daniel 7. Instead of reconciling within Jewish eschatology the twofold basis of messianic hope—one historical, the other suprahistorical—Schweitzer ascribed to Jesus only that otherworldliness which Reimarus had denied him,[9] thereby eliminating the historical realizability of Jesus' hope and equating his *Enderwartung* with the end of ethics. The major objection to Schweitzer's view is that, while the Gospel is framed in the context of Jewish hope, its central emphasis is not on a supernaturalistic age to come but on the healing and teaching ministry of Jesus among his people. Schweitzer pressed the 'presence sayings' about the Kingdom of God being realized in Jesus' word and deed into the service of a futuristic point of view, thereby forcing the false option of either "thoroughgoing" eschatology or the noneschatological skepticism of W. Wrede[10]—a false "either/or" which should be replaced

---

[7]Klausner (*Jesus of Nazareth*, 105-106) is undoubtedly correct in concluding that the nineteenth-century quest for the historical Jesus failed because the Christian scholars who undertook it could not find any other setting than Judaism as the *Sitz im Leben* for a Christian Jesus while maintaining their own opposition to and hatred of this same Judaism.

[8]Lundström, *The Kingdom of God*, 69.

[9]See Hermann Samuel Reimarus, *Fragments*, ET R. S. Fraser (Philadelphia: Fortress Press, 1970).

[10]Cf. Wilhelm Wrede, *Das Messiasgeheimnis in den Evangelien* (Göttingen: Vandenhoeck und Ruprecht, 1901) and Albert Schweitzer, *The Quest of the Historical Jesus*, 330ff.

by a "both-and." It appears that Schweitzer, unable to accept the realistic eschatology he ascribed to Jesus, unknowingly drove that position to its logical absurdity so as to justify discarding it in favor of modern optimistic world-affirmation. The logical 'consistency' of Schweitzer presupposed the moral incongruity of rejecting for himself on modern personal grounds what he established for Jesus on historical, exegetical grounds, namely, the indispensability of Jesus' *Enderwartung* as the essence of Christian religion. Unable to resolve theologically the problems he raised, Schweitzer turned to the mystic alternative of recovering "reverence for life" on a philosophical existential premise.

To avert the embarrassing conclusions of thoroughgoing eschatology, the origin of the apocalyptic vision Weiss and Schweitzer ascribed to Jesus was relocated in the *Gemeindetradition* reflecting the self-understanding of the Early Church. According to this view, Early Christians had, after the death of Jesus, attributed to him their own hopes and fears regarding the future.[11] It is, however, hard to account for the presence of apocalyptic influence in the oldest layers of tradition unless Jesus actually identified himself with it.

While Jewish apocalyptic may be considered the mother of all Christian theology,[12] its theological history appears to be one of progressive de-eschatologization. Harnack had argued that the Kingdom of God was realized primarily in the human heart. Herrmann equated the Kingdom with *Gesinnungsethik*. Müller referred to it as "the hidden force of the All that comes to life in man enabling his creative development."[13] By making Jewish apocalyptic unacceptable to the modern mind, Weiss and Schweitzer paradoxically furthered the de-eschatologization process. In turn, realizing that the problems of life are not resolved by the otherworldly outlook of the New Testament, Naumann and Baumgarten relinquished all transcendent claims of the Kingdom of God in order to fulfill themselves solely within the national cultural process, while Leonhard Ragaz, ignoring all

[11]Cf. Julius Wellhausen, *Israelitische und jüdische Geschichte* (Berlin: Georg Reimer, 1894) 383 and *Einleitung.*, 96.

[12]As Ernst Käsemann observes, in "Die Anfänge christlicher Theologie," *Exegetische Versuche und Besinnungen* (Göttingen: Vandenhoeck und Ruprecht, 1964) 2:100.

[13]Johannes Müller, *Die Bergpredigt, verdeutscht und vergegenwärtigt* 4. Aufl. (München: Oskar Beck, 1917) 31.

exegetical problems, sought the realization of eschatological promise within the social process in a manner commanding the respect of many Jews in Israel.

Dialectical 'crisis' theology appeared once more to restore eschatology to its pre-eminence. World War I had discredited de-eschatologized belief in man's evolution into the Kingdom of God. Too many victims of catastrophe were confronted with the imminent end of hope and meaning. The time was ripe for Barth's dialectic proclamation of the Kingdom of God confronting man with the unconditional claims of God—not at some future end of universal history but at the present end of his own resources.[14] The original eschatological tension of the coming aeon about to displace the existing aeon was replaced by the dialectical tension of experiencing eternity in time. The realization of eschatology was interpreted not as the future fulfillment of time at its τέλος but as existential fulfillment in its midst. Dialectical eschatology conceived the Kingdom of God in a supratemporal way at the neglect of its futuristic aspect.

According to Rudolf Bultmann, the coming of the Kingdom of God originally meant deliverance for the Jews, restoration of the Davidic dynasty in Jerusalem, return of the Diaspora, and overthrow of Roman rule. But, for Jesus, Bultmann assumed, eschatological deliverance had no historical content. He thought of it as a transcendent event confronting human beings with an "Either/Or" decision.[15] For Jesus, contends Bultmann, the Kingdom of God was not an event in time but a future power that wholly determines the present.[16] Jesus understood the Kingdom of God as the will of God which cannot simply be 'described' in terms of things in this world or another.[17] In Jesus, eschatology was realized in the momentary simultaneous contemporaneity of the eternal in the midst of time. The distant God was experienced as near at hand, an awareness closing the chasm between future and present, hope and providence, grace and judgment, thus

---

[14]Cf. Karl Barth, *The Epistle to the Romans*, ET E. C. Hoskyns (London: Oxford University Press, 1933) and Thomas F. Torrance, *Karl Barth: An Introduction to His Early Theology, 1910-1931* (London: SCM Press, 1962).

[15]See Rudolf Bultmann, *Jesus and the Word*, ET L. P. Smith and E. H. Lantero (London and Glasgow: Collins, 1958) 37ff.

[16]Ibid., 44.

[17]Ibid., 47.

fulfilling the prayer that God's Kingdom come and his will be done.[18] Bultmann does not believe Jesus subscribed to the central Jewish idea of restoration and therefore did not regard himself as the Messiah[19]—a factor of no consequence for Bultmann's existentialist eschatology. Bultmann renounced the futuristic orientation of Jewish hope as mythological and transposed the quality of the real future into a qualification of an existential present. Futuristic eschatology is demythologized and existentialized so that the ultimate future of universal history is relocated into the immediate future of personal historicity. In this way the meaning of an objective future end time is obliterated. Existentialist eschatology discounts as meaningless the Jewishness of Jesus' hope and, in turn, the content of his ethic.

Assuming Jesus was mistaken in his *Enderwartung*, Martin Dibelius sought to preserve the faith that inspired it apart from the eschatological form through which it expressed itself. Somewhat like Bultmann, Dibelius saw in the overwhelming nearness of God—understood in a dialectical sense—the motive and meaning of his teaching. Jesus' "End-belief" is viewed as the unconditional suprahistorical timeless reality of the Gospel which has eternal validity. Through his teaching and acts Jesus mediated signs of the Kingdom which indicated its nearness, as we ourselves are called upon to do. The signs to be performed will, however, invariably reflect the ambiguity of the *Enderwartung* they are meant to symbolize.

In contrast to Harnack, C. H. Dodd assumed with Schweitzer the centrality of eschatology for understanding Jesus while concurring with Harnack, in contrast to Schweitzer, that Jesus' understanding of the Kingdom differed from Jewish teaching. Whereas Weiss and Schweitzer held Jesus' eschatology to have been exclusively futuristic, Dodd maintained with equal persistence that

> the sayings which declare the Kingdom of God to have come are explicit and unequivocal. They are moreover the most characteristic and distinctive of the Gospel sayings on the subject. They have no parallel in Jewish teaching or prayers of the period. If therefore we are seeking the *differentia* of the teaching of Jesus upon the Kingdom of God, it is here that it must be found.[20]

---

[18]Cf. ibid., 110-11.

[19]Ibid., 15.

[20]C. H. Dodd, *The Parables of the Kingdom,* 3rd ed. (London, 1936) 49.

Dodd sidestepped Schweitzer's existential inability to believe what Jesus believed first by depicting all apocalyptic references[21] as poetic symbols not meant to be taken "with prosaic literalness"[22] and then by assuming that predictions regarding the future are not intended as "specifications of what is going to happen, like history written in reverse."[23] For Jesus, "the *eschaton* has moved from the future to the present, from the sphere of expectation into that of realized experience."[24] In substance the crisis of the coming Kingdom is realized in the ministry of Jesus: "The crisis began when he started his ministry; it was complete when he returned from death."[25] Therefore, "the Gospel of primitive Christianity is a Gospel of realized eschatology."[26] Nevertheless, the question remains "whether the Kingdom is *wholly* realized in Jesus' ministry, leaving the future as a kind of meaningless epilogue to the present."[27]

According to T. W. Manson, the Kingdom is for Jesus "primarily the living of a life of complete loyalty to God. . . here and now. . . . The essence of his preaching of the Kingdom is in the words 'Thy will be done': all the rest is commentary."[28] The apocalyptic is replaced by the commonplace and the supernatural by the natural[29] with the intent of inspiring loving service to one's fellow creatures. With Manson, Jesus' view of the Kingdom is subsumed in the context of *Heilsgeschichte* centering on the

---

[21]For example, references to the Son of Man descending on a cloud, then riding on a white horse; to the eclipse of the sun and moon; to the falling of stars; to earthquakes; and to the collapse of the material universe.

[22]C. H. Dodd, *A New Testament Triptych on Christ's Coming, His Gospel, His Passion* (Cincinnati: Forward Movement Publications, 1955) 9.

[23]Ibid., 8.

[24]Dodd, *Parables*, 50.

[25]Dodd, *New Testament Triptych*, 20.

[26]C. H. Dodd, *The Apostolic Preaching and Its Development* (New York: Harper and Brothers, 1954) 85.

[27]Carl E. Braaten, *History and Hermeneutics*, New Directions in Theology Today 2 (Philadelphia: Westminster Press, 1966) 164.

[28]T. W. Manson, *The Teaching of Jesus* (Cambridge: Cambridge University Press, 1959) 161.

[29]Ibid., 162: "He finds the tokens of God's rule over nature, not in the occasional and stupendous manifestations of power, but in the commonplace things of the field and the hedgerow which any man might pass by without a thought. The wild flowers in the field and the daily provision for the birds take the place of the earthquake and the storm."

"Servant" motif in Deutero-Isaiah. The righteous and saved "remnant" is said to constitute the "Son of Man" of the new humanity which Jesus "sets out to create in Israel." However, since few respond to his call and none follow him to the end, he travels that way alone "and at the cross he alone is the Son of Man, the incarnation of the Kingdom of God on earth." Then "the cross proves to be the key that opens the Kingdom of God to men," accomplishing "what his teaching could not."[30] In this way, the idea of the remnant descends through the prophets, psalmists, and apocalyptists to the teaching of Jesus and Paul, culminating in the faith and life of the Church. This line of interpretation eliminates the futuristic aspects of Jesus' *Enderwartung* and limits the eschatological consciousness of the many to the one by whose death many come to life.

Having reviewed the various alternatives proposed by liberal, social, form-critical, existentialist, realistic, and incarnationist eschatology to the 'consistent' eschatology of Schweitzer, we are still left with the challenge of validating Jesus' futuristic sayings in a manner commensurate with his Jewishness—without invalidating his ethic. This task is put into critical perspective by Hans Windisch, who distinguished within the Sermon on the Mount a body of Wisdom sayings which Matthew put into the context of his eschatological point of view but which originally had no eschatological connotations. Wisdom teaching is characterized by "its appeal to reason and judgment, its emphasis on the useful and the pragmatic, and its requirement of a judicious and intelligent way of living."[31] Pericopes that reflect these interests make no mention of the judgment or rule of God and are therefore isolated as noneschatological. They include the sayings about salt and light (Matthew 5:13-16), sacrifice (5:23-26), adultery (5:27-28), divorce (5:31-32), swearing, (5:33-37), retaliation (5:38-42), love of enemies (5:43-48), forgiveness (6:14-15), the sound eye (6:22-23), serving two masters (6:24), anxieties (6:25-34), the mote and the beam (7:3-5), God's answering of prayer (7:7-11), and the Golden Rule (7:12). Furthermore, the antithesis to the sixth commandment (5:21-26) and the didactic triad on almsgiving (6:1-4), prayer (6:5-8), and fasting (6:16-18) are also of the Wisdom tradition in their content, except for isolated additions which place them in an eschatological context in Matthew (as, for example, the addi-

---

[30]Ibid., 235.

[31]So Hans Windisch, *The Meaning of the Sermon on the Mount*, 41.

tion of "in heaven" in Matthew 5:19-20). Explicitly eschatological sayings which confront the individual with the Either/Or of final judgment or entrance into the Kingdom include, apart from the Beatitudes (5:3-12), only the sayings about the Kingdom of Heaven (5:19-20), about hindrances (5:29-30), treasures (6:19-21), judging (7:1-2), the two ways (7:13-14), and "saying Lord, Lord" (7:21-23).[32] This means that more than sixty percent of the Sermon on the Mount can be isolated as Wisdom teaching, an additional ten percent is Wisdom in content but eschatological in context, and less than twenty percent is predominantly eschatological. As Windisch concludes:

> In the Sermon on the Mount two great currents of the Synoptic proclamation of Jesus are brought together—purified and radicalized Wisdom teaching and prophetic-eschatological proclamation of salvation and judgment. They exhibit a twofold relationship. Sometimes they flow along side by side, unmixed, and sometimes they intermingle because they contain common motives. . . . It is characteristic of the Sermon on the Mount that its radicalisms are fed from both streams; but in the main they issue from the religious wisdom of Jesus. Both the wisdom and eschatology in Jesus' teaching are heightened to radical demand, and this fact is one of the most important in accounting for the combination of these two forms of proclamation that originally were essentially foreign to one another.[33]

Even though we may not concur in detail with the discernment of Windisch, it suffices to realize that, contrary to Schweitzer, the Sermon on the Mount need not be seen exclusively in an eschatological context. But, irrespective of what extent the demands of Jesus were originally eschatologically conditioned, their relevance for today may not be evaded by discounting the future aspect of Jewish hope. The relation of the future to the present in the eschatology of Jesus must be seen in the light of the origin and development of the messianic idea and ideal.

Jewish Messianism is the product of Israel's *Leidensgeschichte* beginning with bondage in Egypt and intensified through captivity in Babylon. These two landmarks account for the Mosaic prototype in the messianic ideal and the apocalyptic nature of the messianic idea. Jewish eschatology is Jewish faith in desperate quest for meaning and hope in exile and suf-

---

[32]See ibid., 30-43.

[33]Ibid., 40.

fering.[34] In the course of its development, Jewish messianic hope intertwined two inseparable conceptions: that of historical political deliverance and that of spiritual ethical commitment, both exemplified by Moses. "And so it is with the characteristics of the Messiah," wrote Joseph Klausner, "the ethico-spiritual characteristics are the principal ones, but the political characteristics are not lacking."[35]

Eschatological expectation is the heart of Hebrew religious *Selbstbewußtsein*. God's covenant via Abraham and Moses was to realize God's rule midst his people as a "kingdom of priests" (Exodus 19:5, 6). Israel's resistance to this theocratic ideal constitutes the eschatological tension between God and history, a tension embodied in Samuel, who endorsed the kingship, and documented by the successive failure of the anointed one to realize the anointing.[36] God promised that David's kingship would last forever (2 Samuel 7:12-16). Since history had taken another course, the glowing memory of the golden age of David became the ideal of messianic hope. Israel's frustration over the past gave rise to apocalyptic anticipations for the future. Despair over the nonrealization of the ideal in history inspired its projection into a nonhistorical otherworldly future.[37]

---

[34]"Das echte eschatologische Glaubensleben ist—in den großen Wehen der Geschichtserfahrungen—aus dem echten geschichtlichen Glaubensleben geboren; jeder andere Ableitungsversuch mißkennt sein Wesen." Martin Buber, "Königtum Gottes," *Werke* (München: Kösel-Verlag, 1964) 2:490.

[35]Joseph Klausner, *The Messianic Idea in Israel from Its Beginning to the Completion of the Mishnah*, ET W. F. Stinespring (London: Allen and Unwin, 1956) 17. "As Moses was brought up in the house of Pharaoh among the enemies of his people, so will Messiah dwell in the city of Rome among the destroyers of his land; just as Moses, after revealing himself to his brethren in Egypt and announcing to them that deliverance was near, was forced to go into hiding for a time, so will Messiah be forced to hide himself after the first revelations; just as Moses crossed from Midian to Egypt riding on an ass (Exod. 4:20), so also will Messiah come riding on an ass; just as Moses caused manna to rain from the sky, so will Messiah bring forth different kinds of food in a miraculous way; and just as Moses gave to the children of Israel wells and springs of water in the wilderness, so also will Messiah make streams of water to flow in the desert." Ibid., 17-18.

[36]"The history of the kings is the history of the anointed king's failure to fulfill the meaning of his anointing. From this source alone is Messianism, faith in an anointed one who shall fufill the meaning of his anointing, to be understood." Martin Buber, *Kampf um Israel* (Berlin, 1933) 101, as cited in Hans-Joachim Schoeps, *Paul: The Theology of the Apostle in the Light of Jewish Religious History*, ET H. Knight (Philadelphia: Westminster Press, 1961) 90.

[37]Schoeps, *Paul*, 91.

The eschatology of the prophets was thoroughly earthy and essentially political, envisioning the restoration of "the booth of David" (Amos 9:11) and the Kingdom from "the stump of Jesse" (Isaiah 9:6, 11:1) as "the Lord will become king over all the earth" (Zechariah 14:9), a hope that signifies not the end of earthly history but its fulfillment through the theocratic ideal. The messianic hope of the prophets has to do not with the inbreaking of a supernatural order but with the divine ordering of history through the succession and restoration of the Davidic kingship. But, since this theocratic Kingdom-of-God ideal remained unrealized in Israel's history, the prophets perpetuated the eschatological hope of its ultimate fulfillment while continuing to criticize the empirical reality in the light of this ideal. Once the gap between the ideal and the actual appeared too great to be corrected by a call to repentance and a program of reform, the prophets proclaimed "the terrible day of the Lord" of divine intervention "to make the earth a desolation and to destroy its sinners from it" and to redeem from the chaos of history "all who call upon the name of the Lord," an event associated with the darkening of the sun, moon, and stars, the trembling of the heavens and the shaking of the earth (Isaiah 13:9-13) with "blood and fire and columns of smoke" (Joel 2:31-32) and culminating in the creation of "a new heaven and a new earth" (Isaiah 65:17).

Following the actual disintegration of the nation, political and moral restoration was no longer conceivable. As the Jews in Babylonian captivity became estranged from their native soil, their messianic consciousness developed a nonpolitical strain associated with otherworldly dimensions of utopian futuristic hope. When, after returning from exile (520 B.C.) the Davidic ideal was not realized, the messianic image became blurred and embellished with Oriental fantasy, so that around the second century B.C. apocalyptic trends from apocryphal sources envisioned (as in the dream of Daniel and the Book of Enoch) a pre-existent heavenly being, "one like a son of man," coming "with the clouds of heaven"[38] to "expel [the un-

---

[38]Schoeps (*Paul*, 93-94) refers to R. Eisler's conjecture that the mysterious image of the *bar enash* (son of man) coming "with the clouds of heaven" (Daniel 7:13) may have originated in a transliteration of Anani (עֲנָנִי) cf. LXX ἐπὶ τῶν νεφελῶν) the last member of David's household (1 Chronicles 3:24), derived from עֲנָנְיָה ("God has answered"). In popular usage, according to Eisler, this term may have been confused with עָנָן ("cloud"). Klausner (*The Messianic Idea*, 230) insists that "one like a son of man" represents "the saints of the Most High" (Daniel 7:18), meaning Israel.

godly] kings from their thrones.''[39] The future historical hope through the Davidic dynasty is thus recast into the framework of a cosmic dualism. The prophetic tension between present and future is restructured as an apocalyptic polarization of *Diesseits* and *Jenseits*, replacing the horizontal prophetic perspective with the vertical apocalyptic vision. The ''coming day'' is no longer anticipated in time but is relegated to eternity, for he who comes to bring fulfillment is not a descendant of David but a pre-existent supernatural being descending from heaven to terminate history. Although eschatological hope in Israel ''is primarily always historical hope,''[40] in the prophetic vision and apocalyptic fantasy of Judaism—and hence also in the messianic consciousness of Jesus—both traditions, that of historical restoration and that of otherworldly intervention, were conjoined without sharp conceptual demarcation.

Validating the Jewishness of Jesus implies conceding that, given the oppression of Roman occupation (circumstances under which the messianic ideal appeared unrealizable), Jesus did not consider apocalyptic an altogether inappropriate popular medium for conveying the radical demands and boundless promises of God. But it would be as mistaken to depict Jesus' eschatology as essentially apocalyptic otherworldly escapism as it would be false to misinterpret the entire prophetic hope in that transhistorical context.[41] Underestimating the impending nature of Jesus' expectation of the Kingdom either on the grounds that Jesus had no conception of time or that the future must be explained away in favor of present concerns[42] or that temporal imminence must be seen as a function of spiritual imminence[43] amounts to an overreaction to Schweitzer's claim and to a distortion of the textual evidence. While the nearness of the Kingdom may be considered the effective dominant motive for Jesus' call to disci-

---

[39]Enoch 46 (a text that may have originated among the Essenes), as quoted in Klausner, *The Messianic Idea*, 291.

[40]Martin Buber, ''Königtum Gottes,'' 490: ''Denn die 'eschatologische' Hoffnung in Israel. . . ist zuvor immer Geschichtshoffnung: sie eschatologisiert sich erst durch die wachsende Geschichtsenttäuschung.''

[41]As Klausner (*Jesus of Nazareth*, 228 and elsewhere) depicts the message of Jesus primarily as the longing of the meek for otherworldly redemption.

[42]As exemplified by Bultmann and Dodd.

[43]Cf. Amos N. Wilder, *Eschatology and Ethics in the Teaching of Jesus* (New York: Harper and Brothers, 1950) 161.

pleship and teaching of the Sermon on the Mount, it is of paramount importance to realize that this eschatological sanction was essentially inspired not by the shortness of the remaining time but by the nature of God's loving-kindness to which his hardest demands make their explicit appeal (See especially Matthew 5:45, 48; 6:28-30). In the final analysis, all Jewish eschatology, including its apocalyptic, is the restless and therefore imminent hope that the holiness of God will be vindicated and that God's will will be done through the historical process by natural and supernatural means.

The inability of Gentile Christians to identify with the political and national aspects of Jewish eschatology accounts for the tendency in Christian interpretation to ascribe to Jesus only the ethical-spiritual dimensions of Jewish hope that can be more readily universalized in various ingenious ways. For the same reason that the politics of the Messiah have been spiritualized, their future aspects have been eliminated on the assumption that these were fully realized in the person and work of Christ. All references to the future not predicated of Jesus and not fulfilled in the experience of his disciples are thereby ignored as superfluous. Jesus' view of the Kingdom cannot, however, be interpreted as either only future or only present, as either only unfulfilled or altogether realized because Jewish eschatology embodies both the future hope and the present tension of *Heilsgeschichte* from the creation of the world to its consummation.[44] Truly the disciples experienced in Jesus the Kingdom of God in their midst,[45] and it was this present experience which constituted the basis for their future anticipation.

In the eschatological context of the Sermon on the Mount, the *eschaton* is uniquely linked to the present inasmuch as encounter with Jesus determines one's future.[46] The demands of Jesus are validated within the context of Jewish faith which confirms their present relevance without denying its future hope.[47] Jesus' demands express his faith in the fulfillment of the

---

[44]Norman Perrin's conjecture, in *Rediscovering the Teaching of Jesus* (London: SCM Press, 1967) 205, that "in the teaching of Jesus the emphasis is not upon a future for which men must prepare" has the appearance of an anti-Jewish interpolation.

[45]Cf. Mt. 11:5.

[46]That is implicit in the eschatological sayings of the Sermon on the Mount (for example, Matthew 7:13-14, 7:21-22); cf. Werner Georg Kümmel, *Promise and Fulfillment: The Eschatological Message of Jesus* (London: SCM Press, 1957) 46, 47, 142, 155.

[47]The astounding correlation between the Sermon on the Mount and the prophetic redemption program of Isaiah 61 has been demonstrated by William Manson, *Jesus the Messiah* (London: Hodder and Stoughton, 1943) 80.

theocratic ideal.[48] Jesus believed in the future and lived in anticipation of its realization—and so do we.[49] His correlation of present and future, of eschatology and ethics constitutes the meaning of our faith and life.[50]

---

[48]Martin Buber, "Königtum Gottes," 490-91: "Der messianische Glaube Israels ist . . . seinem zentralen Gehalt nach das Ausgerichtetsein auf die Erfüllung des Verhältnisses zwischen Gott und Welt in einer vollkommenen Königsherrschaft Gottes."

[49]Jews and Christians "are united in the common expectation that the decisive event is still to come, that event which will disclose the consummation of God's ways with men, already partially and differently manifested in His dealings with Israel and the church." Schoeps, *Paul*, 258.

[50]This refocusing of the reference point of *Heilsgeschichte* from the end of history to its decisive center characterizes the uniqueness of Jesus and, in turn, of the Christian point of view; cf. Oscar Cullmann, *Christ and Time*, ET Floyd G. Filson (London, 1951).

JESUS AND THE LAW

Christian interpretation of the Sermon on the Mount is fraught with ambiguity regarding Jesus' relation to Jewish law—caught in the tension between the Mosaic tradition, on the one hand, and the Pauline tradition, on the other.

According to Tolstoy, the Church neutralized the contrast between the demands of Jesus and the concessions of Moses by claiming equal inspiration for both Testaments and exchanged the law of Christ for the law of our lower natures (Romans 7) by equating Paul with Jesus. Herrmann contested Tolstoy's equation of Jesus' demands with Mosaic laws which were meant to be obeyed. Ragaz declared that Jesus abolished the legalistic misuse of the Law by his radicalized demands which lead to the moral heights of Sinai. Windisch understood the demands of Jesus within the Old Testament convenantal context in which their fulfillment was assumed as obvious—in sharp contrast to Paul in Romans 7. With Tolstoy and Ragaz, Windisch argued against recasting the demands of Jesus into the framework of Pauline soteriology. Naumann realized that Pauline preaching of the Cross only awakens pious feelings that have no ethical relevance, but he found no way of relating the demands of Jesus to our life. While his historical quest had challenged the creedal tradition from Paul to Chalcedon, Schweitzer, as had Weiss, identified with the redemption theology of Paul which had replaced the Kingdom ethic of Jesus.

Müller freed Jesus of all Mosaic associations, and Baumgarten found Jesus' clinging to iotas incompatible with an expansive and culturally responsible mentality. Bornhäuser and Bultmann confirmed the Jewishness of Jesus' demands, the former on the assumption that they apply to a different time than now, the latter on the condition that they be interpreted in a different way than then. While Herrmann, Müller, and Bultmann spiritualized the demands that Tolstoy, Ragaz, and Windisch had insisted Jesus came to radicalize, Stange and Kittel declared that Jesus not only confirmed the Mosaic Law but, indeed, absolutized its demands so as to make their fulfillment impossible. Jesus intended, they said, to prepare us for the gospel of Pauline atonement theology that allegedly constitutes the uniqueness of Christianity over against Judaism. This understanding of "Christ's strange work" (as it is referred to in the 1776 Formula of Concord)[1] is also evident in Bonhoeffer's belief that Jesus alone fulfilled the Law in his death and in Thurneysen's insistence that the Law is fulfilled not through us but for us by Jesus who did what we are neither able nor invited to do.

This evident diversity and polarization of positions regarding Jesus and the Law indicate that the following decisive questions demand further exploration: In what sense did Jesus both fulfill the Law and affirm its continuing validity? Did he neutralize, spiritualize, radicalize, or absolutize its demands? Are the demands of Jesus parallel or antithetical to those of Moses? In what way is Jesus' law new, better, or different from that of the Jews? Is the gospel to be understood as law so that the performance principle takes its place alongside the gift of righteousness? Or is the Law a form of the Gospel?

The pentateuchal motifs in Matthew present Jesus in a positive relation to Moses. The parallels in setting and content between the Sermon on the Mount and the Decalogue portray Jesus as the messianic fulfillment of the Mosaic prototype. The 'new Moses' is not opposed to his forerunner and his demands are not antithetical to the commandments from Sinai. This Mosaic typology is meant to confirm the mountain teaching of Jesus from the perspective of Sinai. Mosaic categories are transcended in that the Messianic Torah reflects the personal authority of the Lord Messiah (Matthew 7:24,28), whose call to faith is at once an invitation to *Nachfolge Christi* and whose instruction in righteousness is training in *imitatio Christi*. Consequently, to fulfill the commandments and "be perfect" means to follow Jesus (Matthew 19:21). Perfection consists in discipleship, and that means obedience to the Law as interpreted by Jesus.[2]

---

[1]Alec R. Vidler, *Christ's Strange Work. An Exposition of the Three Uses of God's Law* (London: SCM Press, 1963) 25-26.

[2]"Jesus took over from Moses, from the prophets, from the wisdom literature, and also from rabbinism, the idea that those who are children of God must live out that relationship according to the formulas of an ethic of obedience"; Windisch, *The Meaning of the Sermon*

Jesus is very explicit in declaring that he came not to abolish, destroy, abrogate, or annul the Law but rather to fulfill it (Matthew 5:17).[3] He came both to clarify its intention by setting forth its right meaning and to perform and actualize what it says. The "fulfillment" of the Law by Jesus does not refer to his 'sacrificial' obedience but to his teaching of the full meaning of the Law and the prophets. There is no reason to introduce Pauline doctrine into this text in order to make it intelligible.[4] The Law God intended for creation applies "till heaven and earth pass away" (5:18). Jesus insists on the abiding validity of the Law "until all is accomplished." It appears that the emphasis on the "all" (πάντα) refers to the Law (not to eschatological events) and exemplifies the manner in which Jesus understands his teaching and his whole life in the context of Law. Jesus' emphasis on the significance of the Law is underscored in Matthew's epilogue (Matthew 28:20) where the risen Christ commissions his disciples to teach the people "to observe (τηρεῖν) everything (πάντα)" which he had commanded. Accordingly, Jesus' insistence on the inviolability of the Law "until all is accomplished" (5:18) refers to the works of the disciples who are to continue the work of their Master.[5] Jesus demands that his followers

---

on the Mount, 144. "Es geht dem Evangelisten in aller Deutlichkeit um eine Jesusnachfolge in 'Tat und Wahrheit' "; Hans-Theo Wrege, Die Überlieferungsgeschichte der Bergpredigt, 56.

[3]If πληρῶσαι is translated "fulfill" as through action or "keep" (as in Matthew 3:15, Romans 8:4), then it appears to apply more directly to the Law than to the prophets. If it is translated "fulfill" in the sense of promises (as in Matthew 2:17,23), it applies more properly to the prophets than to the Law. If it is translated "confirm," "make valid," "bring into effect," that would appear to satisfy the dual subject in Matthew 5:17. But Joachim Jeremias, in his New Testament Theology: The Proclamation of Jesus (New York: Scribner's, 1971) 83, argues that such a translation would unduly strain the Aramaic equivalent that he sees underlying the Greek text. Jeremias translates: "I did not come to take away from the Law of Moses, rather, I came to add to the Law of Moses." Here everything depends on the Aramaic equivalent translated "rather," which expresses contrast and implies that Jesus came to bring something new. Jeremias prefers the alternative reading "neither" instead of "rather" which implies that Jesus left everything as it was. That would agree with the attitude expressed in Deuteronomy 4:2: "You shall not add to the word which I command you nor take from it; that you may keep the commandments of the Lord your God which I command you." This emphasis is repeated in Deuteronomy 12:32 and Revelation 22:18.

[4]Cf. Günther Bornkamm, Jesus of Nazareth (London: Hodder & Stoughton, 1960) 108.

[5]Cf. Eduard Schweizer, "Mt. 5:17-20," Theologische Literaturzeitung 77 (1952):479-84.

have to fulfill the Torah better if they wish to enter the Kingdom and to teach men to do the new righteousness without evasion or concession, without modification or relaxation (5:19,20).[6] This complete establishing of God's will through the Law is the intent of the entire Sermon.

It is commonly assumed that Matthew 5:17-20 reflects debate between "conservative" law-observing (Palestinian) and "liberal" law-free (Hellenistic) elements in the Early Church.[7] The antinomistic point of view, which Matthew possibly identified as "the false prophets" (Matthew 7:15-20) and "doers of lawlessness" (Matthew 7:23), would explain the inference in Luke 16:16 that the validity of the Law terminated with the appearance of the Baptist.[8] The origin of this antinomianism has at least indirectly been ascribed to the influence of the Apostle Paul, an association that, in turn, gives the entire Sermon on the Mount an anti-Pauline orientation and rationale. While the hypothesis that the Sermon on the Mount is inspired by Matthew's reaction against Paul is, to say the least, somewhat problematic—as making bricks without straw—it must be conceded that Paul's emphasis on *sola fide* is clearly different from the manner in which Jesus, according to Matthew, equates faith with obedience to the Law. Some things in Paul's teaching even Peter found hard to understand, wherefore he admonished fellow Christians not to be "carried away with the error of *lawless* men" (2 Peter 3:15-17). Paul taught that believers "are not under law but under grace" (Romans 6:10), for "Christ is the end of the law" (Romans 10:4). Consequently, Paul is accused of wresting and isolating the Law from the context of God's convenant with Israel and establishing out of the inseparable relation of Torah and Berith the false antithesis of Christ versus Law.[9] The center of interest for Paul was clearly not Jesus the teacher of righteousness as it was for Matthew but the cru-

---

[6]Sjef Van Tilborg, *The Jewish Leaders in Matthew* (Leiden: E. J. Brill, 1972) 126.

[7]Instead of simply assuming that Jesus in this text is countering the insinuation that he is an antinomian, it is interesting to note that conservative Christian commentators who are normally anxious to salvage from the 'ravages' of form-criticism as much as possible of the Sermon on the Mount are not nearly so keen about ascribing Matthew 5:17-18 to Jesus and appear relieved to entertain the possibility that the most difficult phrases of this text originate from the *Gemeindetradition*.

[8]Compare Matthew 11:13 where no such termination is implied.

[9]Hans-Joachim Schoeps, *Paul, the Theology of the Apostle in the Light of Jewish Religious History,* ET H. Knight (London: Lutterworth Press, 1961) 213.

cified Son of God raised from the dead. It has often been held against Paul that he showed no interest in the life of Jesus κατὰ σάρκα (2 Corinthians 5:16) and developed instead an elaborate atonement theology based on the death and resurrection.[10] In turn, this theology constituted the ideological superstructure for his understanding of freedom from the Law. As Klausner explains the Pauline emphasis,

> Paul consistently aimed at exalting the spiritual Jesus over the material Jesus, the Jesus who rose from the dead over the Jesus who lived a human life and performed human acts. He could not otherwise lay claim to the title of "Apostle"; he was not one of Jesus' disciples nor, apparently, had he ever seen him while he was on earth; in the latter event he must have been subservient to James the brother of Jesus, to Peter, and the other Apostles.
>
> Therefore, since Paul believed himself, and impressed the belief on others, that his own teaching was more important than that of James and Peter and that he had authority to set aside Jewish Law and its ceremonial ordinances and make Christianity entirely spiritual and a matter of personal piety—for this reason he was bound to make little of the earthly life of Jesus.[11]

According to Leo Baeck,

> Paul left Judaism when he preached *sola fide* (by faith alone) and thereby wound up with sacrament and dogma. . . . The Gospel—that old gospel which had not yet been adapted for use of the Church and made to oppose Judaism—was still wholly a part of Judaism and conformed to the Old Testament. . . . The boundary of Judaism was crossed by Paul at the

---

[10]This polemic against Paul is most outspoken in Nietzsche: "Paulus geht vom Mysterienbedürfnis der großen religiös erregten Menge aus: er sucht ein Opfer, eine blutige Phantasmagorie, die den Kampf aushält mit den Bildern der Geheimkulte: Gott am Kreuz, das Bluttrinken, die *unio mystica* mit dem 'Opfer'. —Er hat das *große Bedürfnis der heidnischen Welt* verstanden und aus den Tatsachen vom Leben und Tode Christi eine vollkommen willkürliche Auswahl gemacht, alles neu akzentuiert, überall das Schwergewicht verlegt . . . er hat prinzipiell das ursprüngliche Christentum annulliert." See Nietzsche, *Werke*, ed. K. Schlechta, III:655, cited from Schoeps, *Paulus,* 295 [ET, 276].

[11]Klausner, *Jesus of Nazareth,* 64. Soon after Paul's death, emphasis on his atonement theology was diminished in favor of his proclamation of the *nova lex Christi*. As Schoeps (*Paul,* 265) expresses it, "From Clement Romanus to Clement Alexandrinus the voices unanimously ring out: Jesus was the master teacher." Since they came from a gentile background, the leaders of the early church no longer understood negative associations of the Law that presented themselves to the mind of Paul, for they had not experienced his struggle to free himself from its bondage.

point where mystery wanted to prevail without commandment, and faith without law.[12]

As a result of his conversion, Paul understood his life in a new light. Formerly, being a devout Jew he was under the Law and confounded by its demands. Now, in the context of his new being 'in Christ'[13] he was freed from the Law and only under grace—though still subject to the paradox of being *simul iustus et peccator* in the context of Romans 7. But, since Paul also considered himself to be an imitator of the Lord (1 Corinthians 11:1, 1 Thessalonians 1:6), acknowledged being "within Christ's Law" (1 Corinthians 9:21), called upon converts to "fulfill the Law of Christ" (Galatians 6:2), and settled disputes citing the "commandment of the Lord" (1 Corinthians 7:10, 9:14, 14:37), it is just possible that he did not after all intend to repudiate Matthew's understanding of Christianity as a new law.[14] While a certain unbridged difference remains between the Sermon on the Mount and the presuppositions of Romans 1-8, in its atmosphere and emphasis Paul's ethic in Romans 12-15 parallels and indicates dependence on the teaching of Jesus.[15] In fact, "it has been estimated that at over a thousand points the words of Paul recall those of Jesus,"[16] an observation that should suffice to correct the indictment of anti-Paulinism in the Sermon on the Mount through the influence of the Christian community.[17]

---

[12]Leo Baeck, "Romantic Religion," *Judaism and Christianity*, ET Walter Kaufmann (Cleveland: Meridian Books, 1961) 177. To appreciate this paradox, one must realize that Paul was a citizen of two worlds—Judaism and Hellenism. His heart was in the former and his mind in the latter. His ideas are Jewish but his terminology is Hellenistic. His doctrines—election, salvation, sacraments, eschatology—are Jewish, but his metaphysic is Greek. See Albert Schweitzer, *Paul and His Interpreters* (New York: Macmillan, 1912).

[13]A formula recurring 164 times in Paul's letters.

[14]C. H. Dodd, *Gospel and Law: The Relation of Faith and Ethics in Early Christianity* (Cambridge: University Press, 1953) 66.

[15]Direct parallels to the Sermon on the Mount include Romans 12:14, 17-21. For additional parallels to Jesus' teaching cf. Romans 13:8-10, 14:10, 19, 1 Corinthians 13, Colossians 3, Galatians 5:13-6:10.

[16]W. D. Davies, *The Sermon on the Mount* (Cambridge University Press, 1966) 97.

[17]To the extent that the Sermon on the Mount originates with Jesus it obviously could not presuppose the Pauline atonement theology which could not have developed until after Good Friday.

If the Old Law is still in force[18] and the way of Christ does not differ in principle from the way of Judaism,[19] how are we to understand the six so-called *Anti*theses(Matthew 5:21-48)? In his life and thought Jesus was entirely absorbed with the written Torah of the Old Testament and frequently quoted from the Pentateuch, from the major and minor prophets, and from the Psalter. On the strength of this identity with the written Law, Jesus deepened its demands, thereby fulfilling its intention in a radical way. Jesus' prohibition of anger (Matthew 5:21-25) does not annul or contradict the Mosaic prohibition of murder. Realizing that anger leads to murder, Jesus demands reconciliation with one's brother so as to fulfill the covenantal intention implied in the mutual coexistence guaranteed by the prohibition of murder in the Law. In prohibiting lust (Matthew 5:27-30), Jesus does not violate the law against adultery. Nor does he abrogate the Law of God prohibiting divorce (Matthew 5:31-32); rather, he discounts the Mosaic concession to men's sinfulness and appeals to God's will "from the beginning" (Matthew 19:8) according to the written Law (Genesis 1:27, 2:24). Certainly his prohibition of the oath (Matthew 5:33-37) in view of its flagrant misuse is not a violation of the meaning of covenant but an endeavor to recover its integrity. In the last two antitheses (Matthew 5:38-42, 43-48), Jesus replaced the *ius talionis* of capital punishment and 'just war'—the prevailing exceptions to the sixth commandment ("You shall not kill")—with the unconditional 'new' commandment to "love your neighbor" and "love your enemy." In the final antithesis, it becomes perfectly clear that Jesus' conflict with the Rabbinate is not over the written Law of the Old Testament (which nowhere demands, "Hate your enemy") but over the misinterpretation and misappropriation of the Law within the oral tradition of the Rabbinate.[20] As W. D. Davies observed,

---

[18]"Weil diese Verwirklichung noch im Gange ist, und ihrer Vollendung harrt, muß das Gesetz als Kundgebung göttlichen Heilswillens unangetastet bleiben"; Günther Harder, "Jesus und das Gesetz (Matthäus 5, 17-20)," *Antijudaismus im Neuen Testament? Exegetische und systematische Beiträge.* Abhandlungen zum christlich-jüdischen Dialog, Band 2, Hrsg. Helmut Gollwitzer (München: Chr. Kaiser Verlag, 1967) 118.

[19]Günther Bornkamm, "The End-Expectation and the Church in Matthew," *Tradition and Interpretation in Matthew,* ed. Bornkamm, Gerhard Barth, and Heinz J. Held (London: SCM Press, 1963) 31.

[20]"Here if anywhere, does the Jewish critic put forward all his strength to show that the teaching, so far as it is good, is not new, and so far as it is new, is not good." C. G. Montefiore, *The Synoptic Gospels* (London: Macmillan, 1927) 2:77.

"in none of the antitheses is there an intention to annul the provisions of the Law but only to carry them to their ultimate meaning."[21] It is the Torah and scribal interpretation that are set over against each other.[22] Jesus does not call in question the authority of the scribes to represent Moses. In fact, "he deliberately inserts his understanding of the Law into the Jewish scribal tradition."[23] Attacked is the discrepancy between their teaching and their practice (Matthew 23:3ff.). From the formalities of legalized tradition with its sophistic elaborations and casuistic evasions of the Law Jesus recovers the unconditionally radical will of God for his people.

Jesus' function and ministry consist above all in interpreting the Law. It is this function that characterizes his Christology and in which he appears as the second Moses and which makes the Mount of Beatitudes appear analogous to Sinai. Jesus' relation to Moses is therefore not one of antithesis but of correspondence. His "but I say unto you" is itself rooted in the Law and constitutes its proper interpretation.[24] Jesus does not set himself and his authority over against the Law. Jesus was a Jew faithful to the Law who, unlike Paul, never had to adapt his Judaism to a Gentile environment and way of life. According to Matthew, the Law of Christ is the true interpretation that completes rather than annuls the Law of Moses. Neither does Jesus question the ceremonial law in principle. He much more assumes the validity of private sacrifice (Matthew 5:23-24), almsgiving, prayer, and fasting (Matthew 6:1-18), provided their practice is not hypocritically motivated.[25] The same understanding applies to Sabbath observance and purity rites. There is no incident in the synoptics of Jesus violating

[21]W. D. Davies, *The Setting of the Sermon on the Mount* (Cambridge: Cambridge University Press, 1964) 102.

[22]Jesus differed from the Rabbis in not ascribing to the Oral Torah or Rabbinic Halacha the same validity as to the Written Torah of the Mosaic tradition.

[23]Bornkamm, "The End-Expectation," 31.

[24]"In spite of the 'antitheses' of the Sermon, I do not believe that Jesus had any deliberate intention of teaching a new religion of a new 'righteousness.' He was well content with Micah's 'What does the Lord require of thee' and with the love of God and neighbor demanded by the Law" (Montefiore, *The Synoptic Gospels*, II:55).

[25]The indictment of hypocrisy (especially with regard to alms, prayers, and fasting) refers, according to the analysis of Sjef Van Tilborg, *The Jewish Leaders in Matthew* (Leiden: E. J. Brill, 1972), p. 166, to one "who depises the Law of God . . . who is intent on winning fame and praise . . . who allows the human forum to prevail over the divine forum."

the Law.[26] That Jesus' teaching is deeply rooted in the Mosaic tradition and that its aim and intention is not contrary to the written Torah is further evident from the many rabbinic parallels that prohibit anger,[27] denounce the lustful look, limit grounds for divorce, and counsel endurance rather than vengeance. These intensifications of the moral law within the rabbinical tradition in some measure parallel Jesus' own advance on the Mosaic tradition and fully establish the *Sitz-im-Leben* of the Sermon on the Mount within the framework of Judaism.

Israel hoped for a new day when God's Law would be understood in a new way. In the context of this hope, Jeremiah envisioned God's establishing with his people "a new covenant" and writing his Law "upon their hearts" so that everyone would "know the Lord" intuitively or pneumatically rather than didactically.[28] It does not appear, however, that the new covenant of the Messianic Age also implies a new Torah but rather new knowledge of and new obedience to the existing Torah, as this is internalized and spiritualized in the process of being radicalized and realized.[29] The

---

[26]The disciples, not Jesus, were accused of violating the Sabbath (Matthew 12:1ff.) by plucking grain, an indictment Jesus (according to 12:4) does not accept. As David Flusser (*Jesus*, trans. Ronald Walls [New York: Herder and Herder, 1969] 46) explains the situation, "The general opinion was that on the sabbath it was permissible to pick up fallen ears of grain and rub them between the fingers; but according to Rabbi Yehuda, also a Galilean, it was also permissible to rub them in one's hand. Some of the Pharisees, therefore, found fault with Jesus' disciples for behaving in accordance with their Galilean tradition." "The precept about washing hands before a meal [cf. Mt. 15:2ff.] was neither part of written nor of oral teaching. In Jesus' time the precept ran: 'Washing hands before a meal is a matter of choice, ablution after a meal is obligatory'. . . . Even the most bigoted village Pharisee of those days would have shaken his head uncomprehendingly had anyone asserted that, because Jesus' disciples did not always wash their hands before eating, Jesus had broken the law of Moses." Cf. 49-50 regarding Jesus' compliance with the current practice of Jewish law concerning healing on the sabbath.

[27]Regarding one who becomes angry Resh Laquish (about 250 CE) said: "If he is a scholar, his wisdom leaves him: if he is a prophet, his gift of prophecy leaves him"; quoted from Paul Fiebig, *Jesus Bergpredigt. Rabbinische Texte zum Verständnis der Bergpredigt* (Göttingen: Vandenhoeck & Ruprecht, 1924) 43. For numerous similar rabbinic parallels to Jesus' Antitheses cf. 32-97.

[28]Jeremiah 31:31-34: "No longer shall each man teach his neighbor and each his brother, saying, 'Know the Lord,' for they shall all know me, from the least of them to the greatest."

[29]Though the Torah was held to be immutable, certain modifications were envisioned for the Messianic Age inasmuch as sin offerings and purification rites would be irrelevant: cf. W. D. Davies, *The Setting of the Sermon on the Mount*, 158ff.

Messianic Torah of the Sermon on the Mount is the Mosaic Torah interpreted in a new way so as to illuminate and clarify God's will for human beings. Its interpretation by Jesus constitutes its newness. What is new is not with respect to Sinai but with regard to the Rabbinate.

What *was* 'new' in Jesus' message that had not already been expressed in Judaism? The Pharisees themselves, says Harnack, were in possession of it. He explains:

> With them it was weighted, darkened, distorted, rendered ineffective and deprived of its force. . . . They reduced everything to one dead level, wove everything into one fabric . . . the spring of holiness had, indeed, long been opened; but it was choked with sand and dirt, and its water was polluted. The rabbis and theologians who came in afterwards and tried to distil this water, even if successfully, made no difference. Now, however, the spring burst forth afresh, and broke a new way for itself through the rubbish—which priests and theologians had heaped up so as to smother the true element in religion. . . . They thought of God as a despot guarding the ceremonial observances in His household; he breathed in the presence of God. They saw Him only in His law, which they had converted into a labyrinth of dark defiles, blind alleys, and secret passages; he saw and felt Him everywhere. They were in possession of a thousand of His commandments, and thought, therefore, that they knew Him; he had one only, and that was why he knew Him. They had made this religion into an earthly trade, and there was nothing more detestable; he proclaimed the living God and the soul's nobility.[30]

Could the contrast be drawn more sharply? In the absence of Jewish-Christian dialogue it has been the tendency of Christians to argue that Judaism, inspired by fear and external reward, contents itself with that measure of legalistic conformity that the letter of the Law demands, whereas Jesus emphasized inner motive. Montefiore, representing Jewish sensitivity, protests this denunciation:

> It is false that Rabbinic ethics knows nothing but "actions." It is false that Jesus, in saying that God's Law has to do with *Gesinnung*, . . . was opposed to the whole spirit of Judaism. It is false that in Judaism religion was mere outward obedience; it is false that the relation of man to God was conceived only as one of action and reward and that character remains wholly out of account. It is false that the Law was an outward taskmaster,

---

[30]Adolf Harnack, *What is Christianity?* ET T. B. Saunders, 5th ed. (London: Ernest Benn, 1958) 44-46.

which evoked fear and not love. No one can understand the Rabbinic religion with these presuppositions. There is no such fundamental contrast between it and the religion of Jesus. The Law was not a mere external Law, fulfilled from fear of punishment and for hope of reward. It was the Law of the all-wise and all-righteous God, given to Israel as a sign of supremest grace. It was a token of divine affection, and in its fulfillment was the highest human joy.[31]

No less passionately Abraham Heschel reminds us that

> it is a distortion to say that Judaism consists exclusively of performing ritual or moral deeds, and to forget that the goal of all performing is in *transforming* the soul. Even before Israel was told in the ten commandments what *to do* it was told what *to be: a holy people.* To perform deeds of holiness is to absorb the holiness of deeds. . . . Judaism asks far more than works, far more than the *opus operatum.* The goal is not that of a ceremony to be *performed*; the goal is that man be transformed; to worship the Holy in order to be holy. The purpose to the mitzvot is to *sanctify* man. . . . . Judaism is not another word for legalism. The rules of observance are law in form and love in substance. The Torah contains both law and love. Law is what holds the world together; love is what brings the world forward.[32]

In Jewish understanding the Torah is inseparable from the meaning of life, for its aim is "earthly embodiment of the holy."[33] With the devout in Israel Jesus shared the conviction that the Torah expresses the way God wants us to live and that its mitzvot are signposts marking the way of holiness.[34] Jesus taught his disciples to follow him in this way of perfection

---

[31]C. G. Montefiore, *The Synoptic Gospels* 2:55.

[32]Abraham J. Heschel, *Between God and Man. An Interpretation of Judaism* (New York: The Free Press/London: Collier-Macmillan Ltd., 1959) 164, 170.

[33]Schoeps, *Paul*, 282.

[34]"What does the Lord require of you, but to fear the Lord your God, to walk in all his ways, to love him, to serve the Lord your God with all your heart and with all your soul, and to keep the commandments and statutes of the Lord . . . ." (Deuteronomy 1:12-13). God's Law constitutes the *Daseinsberechtigung* of God's people. "If this fixed order departs from me, says the Lord, then shall the descendants of Israel cease from being a nation before me forever." (Jeremiah 31:36). The hope and faith of Israel continues in the belief that "the gifts and the call of God are irrevocable" (Romans 11:29). "Christians give Sinai a strictly historical meaning, forgetting that the covenant of Sinai lives on within the Jewish people . . . But we are here! . . . we are alive and do not want to be by-passed . . . because we have a message to hand on. . . . " Schalom Ben-Chorin, "Possibilities and Limits of our Dialogue," *The Jews and Ourselves* ("Judaism and Christianity in the World Today," II:4 [Autumn 1964]) 131.

by taking upon themselves the yoke of the Kingdom. But Jesus also realized that meticulous compliance with the Law does not in itself constitute the true fulfillment, for through the sheer punctiliousness of its pedantic observance one may become oblivious to its purpose of inspiring sensitivity to the living Presence, especially when its interpretation is encumbered with hundreds of additional commandments and prohibitions as was the case in Jewish exegesis. While deeds may be the expression of the inner self, they are not the essence of the inner life. Unless the essential is interrelated with the specific and the universal is correlated with the concrete, the intention and meaning of the Law may be missed by either sheer atomization or generalization, and the revelation behind the commandment may within the labyrinth of custom and convention be a jewel that is lost in its setting. In order to teach people how to be one with what they do and so to resolve the tension between the regulation and fixation of the code, on the one hand, and the spontaneity and integrity of the person, on the other hand, Jesus assumed the prerogative of establishing within the *lex corpus* an order of priority giving preference to the written over the oral Torah and singling out from the latter what he considered to be of primary importance. In the process, his prophetic spirit established at various points the inadequacy of the tradition of the elders whose concessions and limitations he superseded by appealing to the validity of the original or higher principle as he interpreted or formulated it. Though he had in principle no quarrel with the cultic regulations, he estranged the Rabbinate by his exclusive emphasis on the moral and religious content of the Law and the prophets—to disregard of the ceremonial, cultic, and nationalistic elements of the tradition. His radicalization of the written Torah and his rejection of the oral Torah, insofar as the latter obscured and evaded the will of God by putting casuistry in the place of love,[35] stirred up the opposition within the Rabbinate.

Jesus gave priority to the principle of love as "the law within the law" that governs all human relations.[36] He gave supreme expression to the

---

[35]Cf. Jeremias, *New Testament Theology, 210.*

[36]"Inhalt dieser Tora (d.i. der neuen Tora des Messias) aber ist die Nächstenliebe, die Barmherzigkeit, die an die Stelle der Opfer tritt und ihre Geltung allein vor Gott, nicht im Großsein vor Menschen sucht. Eben das ist die 'bessere Gerechtigkeit,' die in den folgenden Versen verkündigt wird, und die in der Gemeinde Jesu 'geschieht.' So setzt sich das

principle of love as the law of life under the reign of God. The command to love in its twofold direction was for him the essence of the Law upon which everything 'hangs' or 'hinges.' Love of God and neighbor constituted the quintessence of Jewish ethics. Jesus went further. In extending the category of neighbor to include the national enemy Jesus transcended the national ethos and threatened the national identity. The Torah commanded, "Love your neighbor as yourself" (Leviticus 19:18). Again Jesus went further, declaring: "This is my commandment that you love one another *as I have loved you*" (John 15:12). The prophetic spirit and 'messianic' authority by which Jesus exalted the principle of love over the ethnocentric ethos appeared incomprehensible, strange, sinister, unlawful, and sacrilegious to the Rabbinate whose sense of cultural and national responsibility he did not appear to share.[37] Though he evidently had stood in a relation of special nearness to the Rabbinate, the question of his authority and their security[38] soon reached passionate intensity, culminating in his condemnation and their justification. Jesus had forced upon the Rabbinate the painful decision of either accepting his 'messianic' authority or defending their own in the name of the inviolability of the tradition—a confrontation which eventually brought him to the cross.[39]

Thus the entire Sermon on the Mount appears to bear a contradiction in that Jesus is apparently pursuing diverse ends: on the one hand, he fulfills the tradition of Judaism and, on the other hand, he supersedes it;[40] on

---

Gesetz und die Propheten zur Vollendung bringende Tun des Messias in seiner Gemeinde fort. Wo das geschieht, da wird kein einziges Gebot 'aufgelöst'—es findet ja hier seine 'Erfüllung'—und doch sind so radikalle Sätze möglich, wie sie in V. 21ff. stehen''; E. Schweizer, "Matth. 5, 17-20—Anmerkungen zum Gesetzesverständnis des Matthäus," TLZ (1952): 483-84.

[37]Cf. Windisch, *The Meaning of The Sermon on the Mount*, 149-50.

[38]"If we let him go on thus, everyone will believe in him, and the Romans will come and destroy both our holy place and our nation" (John 11:48). "These things always begin very innocently, being at first only internal religious matters, and they always end up with revolts against . . . Rome''; Sholem Asch, *The Nazarene* (New York: Pocket Books, 1956) 173.

[39]From the perspective of *Heilsgeschichte*, the decision of the Rabbinate was predictable. Jesus' teaching was rejected by the Rabbinate for the same reason that it is evaded by the Church. This rejection and this evasion of his Messianic Torah is what Jews and Christians have in common.

[40]According to Harvey K. McArthur, *Understanding the Sermon on the Mount* (Lon-

the one hand, he accentuates the Torah, and, on the other hand, he transcends it.[41] On the one hand, it is alleged that the Sermon on the Mount "contains nothing that is essentially antagonistic to Judaism."[42] On the other hand, it is maintained that "no Jewish writing exists that represents an approximation to the Sermon as a whole"[43] and that this fact by itself proves its transcendence over Judaism and, in turn, constitutes the ground for Jesus' conflict with Judaism. To determine the basis of this conflict apart from Jesus' teaching[44] appears evasive, and to establish the uniqueness of his teaching apart from Judaism is impossible.[45] Jesus' demand for the right and the better is made within the framework of Judaism and for that reason threatened the prevailing practice of Judaism. As one standing wholly within the Israelite-Jewish religion, Jesus superseded it and alienated himself from it by making love the principle of its fulfillment.

---

don: Epworth Press, 1961) 36ff. The Early Church generally regarded the Sermon on the Mount as an advance on the Mosaic tradition, whereas, the Reformers (Luther, Calvin, Zwingli) who looked to Christ as Redeemer rather than as Lawgiver held—in sharp contrast to the Roman Catholic position—that the Sermon on the Mount was nothing more than a recovery of the Mosaic order obscured by Judaism.

[41]For an analysis of the Antitheses with respect to whether they accentuate or transcend the Torah, see Jeremias, *New Testament Theology* 251ff.

[42]Montefiore, *The Synoptic Gospels*, 2:126.

[43]Windisch, *The Sermon on the Mount*, 150.

[44]Many theologians concur with William Manson (*Jesus the Messiah*, 51) that "the new thing in Christianity was not its ethic."

[45]Johannes Müller and Harnack to the contrary. Windisch (*The Meaning of the Sermon on the Mount*, 149) concludes: "If Judaism is to be understood as orthodox, Talmudic-rabbinical Judaism, then Jesus was intolerable to it. He shattered all its presuppositions by his use of the Torah, by his own interpretation of the divine command, and by his consciousness of 'authority' and of 'mission.' Jesus did not reform such Judaism. He destroyed it. This is true despite the fact that he had much in common with it. But if Judaism is to be understood as a whole religious movement dominated by the Old Testament and expressed in it, then Jesus certainly belongs within its sphere." T. W. Manson (*Ethics and the Gospel* [London: SCM Press, 1960] 295) understood this conflict within Judaism between Jesus and the Rabbis as a conflict "between the prophetic spirit and the legal, between two ways of approaching the problem of conduct . . . the prophetic is concerned with persons, the legal with acts."

PRACTICABILITY AND RELEVANCE

The fundamental problem of the Sermon on the Mount is, in the final analysis, its practicability. The question whether obedience to Jesus' demands is possible constitutes the great divide.

The *Gesinnungsethik* of Herrmann was meant to free Christendom from the guilt of an impossible and irresponsible *imitatio Christi*, but Herrmann's contrived antithesis between 'mind' and 'deed' led to evasion rather than resolution of the difficulties with which the demands of Jesus confront us. Naumann believed the precepts of Jesus were originally meant to be taken literally, but he concluded that it is impossible and unnecessary for us to make ethical deductions from the Gospel because Jesus was a product of Oriental culture, the influence of which is not determinative for us. According to Weiss and Schweitzer, Jesus' radical demands are invalid for those who have outlived and outgrown the apocalyptic disillusionment that inspired them. For Müller the Sermon on the Mount represents a torture rack upon which people needlessly torment themselves until its insane demands are humanized and its moral law is reduced to natural law. Baumgarten urged that the applicability of the Sermon on the Mount be radically and energetically limited lest its demands undermine the validity of contemporary culture. He cautioned against preaching and teaching the hard sayings of Jesus lest they confuse the mind of the people. Bornhäuser considered any contemporary application of Jesus' demands unwarranted, not only because they are altogether impossible for us but because they were intended only for the original disciples and therefore have nothing to say to us. In the thought of Wünsch the *lex Christi* is valid only insofar as it is identical with or corrected by the *lex naturae*. According to Stange and Kittel, Jesus intended his demands to be impracticable so that we would be convinced of and convicted by our inability to do what he says.

Bultmann found in the Sermon on the Mount no material guidance as to what one must do in order to be obedient. While insisting that the impracticability of the Sermon on the Mount, so obvious to us, never occurred to Jesus, Windisch nevertheless rationalized our noncompliance with its demands in view of our weakness (in being so feeble) and our strength (in being so responsible). His historical exegesis claims Jesus' demands are to be fulfilled while his theological exegesis disclaims our need to fulfill them. Dibelius considered the demands of Jesus possible only within an eschatological context apart from which they have no validity except for monastics. Since Jesus' eschatological outlook has been lost, his demands are restricted by our circumstances which make full obedience impracticable. For Thurneysen, considering the Sermon on the Mount normative for moral and religious conduct defrauds its meaning and results in futile legalistic attempts at doing what we are neither able nor invited to do. Bonhoeffer's call to discipleship was overshadowed by the paradox of his own understanding and commitment, according to which the possibility of single-mindedness remains the ultimate impracticability of the distinctively Christian life.

Those who defend the Sermon's practicability invariably reflect Tolstoy's conviction that Christ meant exactly what he said and that his precepts are clear and intelligible and commend themselves to everyone. Tolstoy believed the Sermon on the Mount expresses both Christ's ideal and that degree of its accomplishment which mankind can attain even now. Ragaz shared this vision in the implicit assumption that the demands of Christ are thoroughly realistic and practicable and constitute the hope of the social order. In comparison to the weighty authority of theological pessimists, the 'cloud of witnesses' attesting the optimistic persuasion of Tolstoy and Ragaz appears to be only the size of a man's hand (cf. 1 Kings 18:44), nevertheless their testimony has not gone unheard. Waylen believed it is possible for Christians to follow the mountain pathways of Jesus. Jones observed that our problem with the Sermon's practicability is essentially a Western one, for in the East the real question is not whether we *can* do it but whether we *will*. He defended the Sermon as the only philosophy of life that works—the only one backed by the universe.

According to Seeberg the practicability of the Sermon on the Mount is a matter of obedience to the Spirit who inspired it and who effects that to which he obligates. Fox discovered in the Sermon on the Mount the spiritual key to the meaning of life as understood within the framework of

Christian "mindscience," which overcomes the theology of despair and unlocks the mysteries of divine perfection. Jordan observed that in its initial stages the way of unlimited love is very impractical and usually ends on a cross. But, as resurrections follow crucifixions, the end of love becomes its beginning and Christ's way alone makes sense. The power to live that way comes, says Jordan, through faith and discipline. Ingalls characterized the "open world" view of the Galilean Way as the highest level of consciousness the motive power of which is voluntary, individually responsible, inclusive Galilean love that does not discriminate among superiors, inferiors, strangers, or enemies and therefore establishes confidence in the dignity of human purposes. Ligon discovered in the precepts of Jesus (including love of enemies) the outgoing emotional attitudes that make for mental health and therefore constitute normative behavior for enlightened beings rather than otherworldly impossibilities. In his own inimitable way Prabhavananda interpreted the Sermon on the Mount as the unfolding of the divine goal of life by a transformation of character that enables man to know God in this life and to experience illumination, selfless love, and compassion for all. John Miller sought to recover the original function of the Sermon on the Mount as catechetical instruction or training in discipleship for those committed to the Christian Way of becoming a community of peace, purity, integrity, and love.[1]

How are we to account for this fundamental difference in orientation between those who affirm the practicability of the Sermon on the Mount and those who deny it? How shall we explain that for some the Sermon on the Mount exemplifies the finest statement of normative Christian morality while the Church as a whole has viewed it as an utterly impossible ethic that either inspires an irresponsible otherworldly escapism or fixes upon us "the bondage of a salutary despair"?[2] According to Ernst Troeltsch, it is these respective attitudes towards the teaching and example of Christ that determine the identity of 'church' and 'sect.' Troeltsch observed that "the sects take the Sermon on the Mount as their ideal; they lay stress on the

---

[1]John W. Miller, *The Christian Way* (Scottdale PA: Herald Press, 1969).

[2]Alec R. Vidler, *Christ's Strange Work*, 57. In the view of D. M. Baillie (*God Was in Christ* [London: Faber & Faber, 1947] 116) "the main function of the impossible ethic is to drive us away from ourselves to God." For an attempt to resolve the conflict between Law and Gospel in Lutheran and Reformed theology, see Arnold T. Ohrn, *The Gospel and the Sermon on the Mount* (New York: Fleming H. Revell, 1948).

simple but radical opposition of the Kingdom of God to all secular interests and institutions . . . expressed in refusal to use the law, to swear in a court of justice, to own property, to exercise dominion over others, or to take part in war." In contrast, "the Church-type represents the longing for a universal all-embracing ideal, the desire to control great masses of men, and therefore the urge to dominate the world and civilization in general." Troeltsch identified the marks of the sect-type as

> lay Christianity, personal achievement in ethics and in religion, the radical fellowship of love, religious equality and brotherly love, indifference toward the authority of the State and the ruling classes, dislike of technical law and the oath, the separation of the religious life from the economic struggle by means of the ideal of poverty and frugality, or occasionally in charity which becomes communism, the directness of the personal religious relationship, criticism of official spiritual guides and theologians, the appeal to the New Testament and to the Primitive Church [and to moral demands that] are founded only upon the Law and the Example of Christ.

In all this, Troeltsch declares, "it must be admitted that they [the sectarians] are in direct contact with the Teaching of Jesus."[3]

Troeltsch concluded his evaluation of these contrasting mentalities with the observation that

> on the one hand, there is development and compromise, on the other, literal obedience and radicalism. . . . The sects gained on the side of intensity in Christian life, but they lost in the spirit of universalism. . . . On the side of personal Christian piety they score, and they are in closer touch with the radical individualism of the Gospel, . . . but they lose spiritual breadth and the power to be receptive. . . . The Church emphasizes the idea of Grace and makes it objective; the sect emphasizes and realizes the idea of subjective holiness. . . . The sect does not live on the miracles of the past, nor on the miraculous nature of the institution, but on the constantly renewed miracle of the Presence of Christ, and on the subjective reality of the individual mastery of life.[4]

Troeltsch ascribed the Church's dominating ambition to Paul's desire to conquer the world for Christ and his validation of the state "ordained and

---

[3]Ernst Troeltsch, *The Social Teaching of the Christian Churches* ET Olive Wyon (London: Allen & Unwin, 1931) 332, 334, 336.

[4]Ibid., 337, 341.

permitted by God'' as a means toward that end:[5] ''the Church can trace its descent from Paulinism, which contained the germ of the sacramental idea. . . . The sect, on the contrary, starts from the teaching and example of Jesus.''[6]

While there is much elemental wisdom in this typology of Troeltsch, all of his insights do not apply to our analysis. As a case in point, the vision of those who affirm the practicability of Jesus' demands is not for that reason any more restricted than that of the 'church' nor any less so than that of Jesus himself. Nor is ''the longing for a universal ideal'' the prerogative of only those who deny the practicability of the messianic ideal. Furthermore, our analysis has already shown that the great 'ecumenical' diversity of positions on almost every aspect of historical and theological interpretation cannot simply be reduced to such a single-phased polarization as that of 'church' and 'sect.' It should also be noted that the divine optimism of those who together with Jesus declare these precepts to be the Creator's will for the universe does not allow their validity to be restricted to an exclusive society of metamorphosed saints. There is general agreement that these demands were originally directed to Jesus' disciples and that they therefore apply in the first instance to the new community—provided one does not specify in what sense. Despite this common ground, there emerges a deep and serious cleavage that is both theological and practical. The assumption, on the one hand, that nonfulfillment of Jesus' demands establishes their impracticability contradicts the premise, on the other hand, that the meaning of these demands lies in their practicable fulfillment.

Not only theology but history itself appears divided over the issue of the Sermon's practicability. Friedrich Nietzsche thought it still possible any moment to be a Christian—just as it is possible to be a Buddhist—provided only that one follow the example of Christ. The practice of Christianity is no fantasy, Nietzsche contended. Jesus lived a real life, a life that truly confronts conventional life. To be a Christian means to identify with Christ's demands, but for that the Church lacks courage and will: ''Of what benefit is all scientific training, all critique and hermeneutic, when such a contradiction in biblical interpretation as that which the church maintains

---

[5]Ibid., 334.

[6]Ibid., 342.

does not make one red with shame?"[7] Similarly, Marx asked professing Christians, "Does not every minute of your ordinary life give the lie to your theories [in the Sermon on the Mount]?"[8] Freud, on the other hand, blamed the demands of Jesus in general and the Golden Rule in particular for civilization's discontent because "nothing else runs so strongly counter to the original nature of man." Human beings are so unhappy, Freud explains, because their aggressive erotic instincts are unduly restrained by the demand of the Christian superego to love one's neighbor. Since this command provides too little happiness and is too hard, Freud recommends that for therapeutic reasons one should oppose the superego by lowering its demands. Otherwise, if the demand exceeds the resource, a revolt or neurosis develops resulting in even greater unhappiness.[9] Dostoevsky claimed that

> Christlike love for men is a miracle impossible on earth. He was God. But we are not gods. . . . One can love one's neighbors in the abstract, or even at a distance, but at close quarters it's impossible. If it were on the stage, in the ballet, where if beggars come in, they wear silken rags and tattered lace and beg for alms dancing gracefully, then one might like looking at them. But even then one should not love them.[10]

Bertrand Russell spoke for many in surmising, "There is nothing to be said against [the Christian principle] except that it is too difficult for most of us to practice sincerely."[11]

---

[7]Friedrich Nietzsche, "Der Wille zur Macht. Versuch einer Umwertung aller Werte," *Nietzsches Werke* (Leipzig, 1901) 15:141. "Christen der allgemeinen Wehrpflicht, des parlamentarischen Stimmrechts, der Zeitungs-Cultur—und zwischen dem Allen von 'Sünde,' 'Erlösung,' 'Jenseits,' 'Tod am Kreuz' reden—: wie kann man in einer solchen Wirtschaft es aushalten!" Ibid., 157-58. "Wir sind keine Christen mehr: wir sind dem Christentum entwachsen, nicht weil wir ihm zu ferne, sondern weil wir ihm zu nahe gewohnt haben, mehr noch, weil wir aus ihm gewachsen sind, —es ist unsere strengere und verwöhntere Frömmigkeit selbst, die uns heute verbietet, noch Christen zu sein." Ibid., 318.

[8]As cited by Bornkamm, *Jesus of Nazareth*, 222.

[9]See Sigmund Freud, *Civilization and Its Discontents* (Chicago: Great Books Foundation, 1961) 61ff.

[10]Fyodor Dostoevsky, *The Brothers Karamazov*, ET C. Garnett (London: William Heinemann, 1913) 249.

[11]As cited by Roger L. Shinn, *The Sermon on the Mount*, 45.

The complexity of scientific biblical hermeneutics can create the false impression that the difficulty is in the realm of understanding, that it is epistemological rather than existential. On hearing people complain how hard it is to understand the Bible, Mark Twain is said to have confessed that he was bothered more by those parts he understood than by those he did not understand. The process of discernment lies not in the abstract sphere of rational speculation nor in the objective sphere of historical inquiry but consists in personal response to an incontestable concrete moral obligation. The difficulty of understanding Jesus is not unrelated to the difficulty of following him. One's understanding of his demands is invariably predetermined by one's stance with respect to *imitatio Christi*. According to Herrmann, *Nachfolge Christi* only ends in dishonesty and has nothing to do with the spirit of Jesus. Weiss warned that one should not allow piety to degenerate to *imitatio Christi* of the Franciscan type. Since the image of Jesus is no longer ethically normative, Weiss proposed that *imitatio Christi* is invalidated and should be replaced by attachment to the transcendent Christ.

Bonhoeffer appealed not to *imitatio Christi* but to the *Gestalt Christi* as his basis for paradoxical obedience. Thurneysen declared following Jesus never means imitating him; only 'false prophets' confuse discipleship with imitation. Städeli insisted there can be no *imitatio Christi* on the supposition there is no analogy between Christ's 'way' and our own. Behind these negative reactions lies the common assumption that *Nachfolge Christi* invariably must degenerate into 'legalistic,' self-conscious, self-righteous *imitatio 'Spielerei,'* an impotent game that too cheaply neutralizes the infinite paradox of the ideal.

Nevertheless, the idea of the imitation of Christ as "a way of making explicit what *kinds* of divine activity should be imitated by men, and how, and why, and in what circumstances"[12] is too deeply rooted in the Christian tradition to be repudiated by anti-Catholic polemic.[13] Paul professed being an "imitator of Christ" (1 Corinthians 11:1), and Peter, who had received the call, "Follow me" (Mark 1:17; John 21:22), referred to Christ's "leaving you an example, that you should follow in his steps" (1

---

[12]C. H. Dodd, *Gospel and Law*, 42.

[13]Clearly, in acknowledging the example and teaching of Jesus as our normative, vital guide, *Imitatio Christi* does not exclude our creative initiative in conforming to the will of God as interpreted by Jesus.

Peter 2:21). They appealed to Jesus as our model and example in human relations whether regarding treatment of slaves, promotion of famine relief (2 Corinthians 8:9), reconciliation between brothers (Romans 14:10), or relation to persecutors (Romans 12:14). This understanding of *imitatio Christi* accords with Jesus' saying, "For I have given you an example, that you also should do as I have done to you" (John 13:15). *Nachfolge Christi* is central to the gospels in general which describe its context (ἀκολουθέω recurs more than 70 times to characterize the disciples' relation to Jesus) and to the Sermon on the Mount in particular, which articulates its content.

To avoid any 'legalistic' misunderstanding of *imitatio Christi* it is of fundamental importance to understand Christian discipleship in the Jewish context of the idea that human beings should imitate God.[14] Jeremiah proclaimed God's word to Jerusalem: "I remember the devotion of your youth, your love as a bride, *how you followed me* in the wilderness" (Jeremiah 2:2). Israel was called to participate in the perfections of God and do the works of God: to plant Canaan as God planted Eden, to clothe the naked as God clothed Adam, to visit the sick as God visited Abraham, to comfort the bereaved as God comforted Isaac, and to bury the dead as God buried Moses. To be God's people meant to be committed by a solemn covenant

---

[14]Unfortunately, C. H. Dodd (*Gospel and Law*, 52-53, 61) refers to *imitatio Dei* as "a very dangerous maxim" to be used only "with very great caution, because we really do not know how to translate our conceptions of divine perfection into canons of human behaviour"—when this was precisely what Jesus in his Sermon undertook to do. Dodd rejects the demands of Jesus as "simply not suitable . . . as a plain guide to conduct" and therefore concludes they were evidently "not intended for such use" and are meaningful only "as providing the material for an intelligent act of 'repentance,' " whereas the precepts of Paul which are based on these demands he regards as straightforward general maxims which may be taken quite literally as they stand. For example, Jesus' saying, "When you give alms, do not blow your trumpet," could not possibly, thinks Dodd, refer to a musical instrument. However, as it is obvious that a literal reference preceded the allegorical idiom "blowing your horn" to mean ostentatious conduct, it is therefore not at all improbable to assume Jesus drew attention to the conspicuous association between the priest's sixfold blast on the shofar announcing the approach of the Sabbath and the ostentatious parading of the official alms-collectors immediately preceding this bugle call every Friday evening. Dodd surmises whimsically, "What hopeless confusion would result!" if someone were so misguided as to try to apply literally the drama of Matthew 5:25-26 apart from its cultic context, whereas he observes no such difficulty with Paul's injunction, "Bless those who persecute you," which (apart from having its precedent in the Sermon on the Mount) could by the same logic be discredited as ludicrously impracticable in view of the cultic embarrassment of trying to stage an ordination service for one's persecutor.

to a pattern of living in conformity with God's holy will.[15] The injunction to "follow in his steps" therefore means to "be imitators of God" (Ephesians 5:2) in a divine pattern made comprehensible and imitable by the teaching and example of Jesus. "Hence, the imitation of Christ," C. H. Dodd wrote, "being the imitation of God Himself as far as God can be a model to His creatures, becomes a mode of absolute ethics."[16]

Seen in the context of *imitatio Dei, imitatio Christi* is not just an ideal for admiration but the standard for conformation. Jesus' demands reflect God's nature: the prohibition of anger is an expression of his conciliation, the prohibition of adultery is rooted in his holiness, the prohibitions of divorce and swearing are based on his covenantal faithfulness and integrity, the prohibitions of retaliation and enmity are manifestations of his longsuffering[17] and mercy, the prohibition of anxiety is based on his providence, the prohibition of judging reflects his impartiality, and so on. Whether we think of the Beatitudes, Similes, Antitheses or any other precepts of the Sermon on the Mount, the entire ethic of Jesus is conceived as response to the nature of God, a correlation Jesus made most explicit in his demand to love as God loves, to forgive as God forgives, and to be perfect as God is perfect. God's will is rooted in God's nature. To love God is to imitate him. *Imitatio Christi* means obedience to the Law as interpreted by Jesus. He who loves God keeps his Law, "for this is the love of God that we keep his commandments. And his commandments are not burdensome" (1 John 5:3).

Nevertheless, theologians insist that his commandments are not only burdensome but impossible. How shall we be holy when we have none of the making of holiness? How shall we love God and neighbor when we are without divine charity? How shall we make bricks without straw? Did not Paul speak of another law which is at war with the Law of God and keeps us from fulfilling it? Origen ascribed the "law of sin" according to Romans 7 to Paul's pre-Christian Jewish life, but, since in that context Paul

---

[15]Gerhard Kittel, ed., *Theologisches Wörterbuch zum Neuen Testament* (Stuttgart: Kohlhammer Verlag, 1933) 1:210, and *Die Religion in Geschichte und Gegenwart* (Tübingen: J.C.B. Mohr, 1960) IV:1286-87.

[16]C. H. Dodd, *Gospel and Law*, 42.

[17]Jesus did not demand that we love our enemies because the time is so short (as Weiss and Schweitzer presumed) but because God's lovingkindness endures forever (Matthew 5:44-45).

was hardly living "without the law" (Romans 7:9), Augustine, the Reformers, and most of their descendants refer this carnal law to some aspect
of the Christian life. On that basis they then rationalize the impracticability
of full obedience to the law of Christ. Since it is alleged, on the authority
of the Apostle Paul, to be impossible to observe Christ's demands on account of the weakness of human nature, it was left to the ingenuity of theologians to answer Tolstoy's question: "Why should Christ have given us
such clear and good precepts, applicable to us all, if he knew beforehand
that the keeping of them was impossible by man in his own unaided
strength?"[18] This challenge has been brilliantly met in the most incredibly
diverse, imaginative, and contradictory ways, ranging from the eschatological approach that ascribed to the Sermon an apocalyptic temperature
which it did not possess to the sacramental approach that equates "Follow
me" with "Take, this is my body,"[19] thereby reducing ethics to nourish-
ment.

After indicating on what various grounds the validity of Jesus' demands must be restricted, each theological school has proffered its own
equally incredible consolation by explaining in circuitous ways in what
sense Jesus' impossible demands are nonetheless relevant as an illusory
ideal that is not altogether uninfluential in inspiring in us an impracticable
aspiration for an unattainable good. We do not intend to say: All other
interpretations are wrong;[20] Tolstoy alone represents light and truth! But
neither can we share the assumption that the Sermon on the Mount is only
part of an extended introduction to the passion narrative. "No 'Christology,' " Günther Bornkamm has written, "no matter how true to the scriptures and to the faith, can or should diminish the pressure placed upon those
who hear the Sermon on the Mount."[21] Harnack posed two alternatives:
either identify the gospel with its earliest form (in which case he alleged
that it came with its time and departs with its time) or extrapolate what is
eternally valid (in which case its Jewish 'husk' is abandoned and only its

---

[18]Tolstoy, *What I Believe*, 8.

[19]"There at last Christian life is defined in its completeness;" William Manson, *The Way of the Cross* (Edinburgh: Hodder & Stoughton, 1958) 76.

[20]Indeed "Jesus was richer and more many-sided than any one-sided theology can be, though at the same time he was also more elementary and less reflective than we are"; Windisch, *The Meaning of the Sermon on the Mount*, 43.

[21]Bornkamm, *Jesus of Nazareth*, 108-109.

sublime and sentimental 'kernel' remains). If "salvation is from the Jews" (John 4:22), the hope of theology cannot lie with Harnack in rejecting what God elected.

Typical of Jewish piety is the belief that, if Israel will obey the commandments, God will be with his people, forgiving and healing them. "The law is not ruined by the disillusioning actuality of sin," Hans-Joachim Schoeps wrote. "Rather God is the more earnestly implored to further graciously, by His commands, the sanctification of men."[22] Human beings are not considered pitifully helpless and waiting only to be embraced by the boundless grace of God. They stand under oath to observe the Law and their lives depend on it (Leviticus 18:5). God's blessing or curse is made dependent on whether the people observe or transgress the conditions of the covenant (Deuteronomy 28). Jewish religion is active rather than passive and demands the will to conquer life ethically. The foundation of life remains a mystery, but the *way* of life is revealed. What is concealed belongs to God, but what is revealed belongs to human beings that they may act and live (Psalm 119:92-93). "Quantitatively it becomes a task laid on man and an appeal to him to do as much as possible," Schoeps observed. "Qualitatively it is a challenge to man's constantly renewed self-examination to see that he does the law with the right faith and disposition—which is the Jewish counterpart to Paul's insistence on faith."[23] In Judaism, faith is not an alternative to ethical action. The Jewish solution to the tension between law and faith is not vicarious atonement but renewed self-commitment and obedience to the will of God (Deuteronomy 10:12-13) by the power of God (Isaiah 40:29) in the fear of God (Ecclesiastes 12:13) which obviates the question regarding the practicability of the commandments of God (Deuteronomy 30:11-14). Without faith it is impossible to take a step into the future. Faith is a struggle against fate rather than a sweet repose in predestination. "There is no faith without effort."[24] Faith is the passionate clinging to God as with Abraham who was bound to God beyond his destiny, and it is the extreme of human striving exemplified by Jacob

---

[22]Schoeps, *Paul*, 282.

[23]Ibid., 284.

[24]Abraham Joshua Heschel. *The Insecurity of Freedom* (Philadelphia: Jewish Publication Society, 1966) 197.

wrestling the angel for a blessing.[25] In Judaism there are no religious experiences without ethical tasks and no ethical tasks without religious experiences. Its highest ideals are expressed in ethical action. Judaism agrees with Jesus that a man could do the good if he would while Christianity argues with Paul that a man would do the good if he could.[26]

Despite all ethical rigorism, the sanctification of man intended by the Law as the earthly embodiment of the holy is not, in the last analysis, accomplished by human attempts to keep the commandments but by God himself. Though the human side to every free and responsible moral action may not in any way be minimized, the divine side is in every sense prior:

> It is not the law which makes man righteous, but God, the Lord of the covenant and the Founder of the law as a system of polity. Hence, in the first place it is not the meticulous fulfilling of the law which is the main point but the fulfillment of an adherence to the law in the faith that it is the expression of the will of the God of the covenant.[27]

"The good was His before it was ours," Donald M. Baillie wrote. "That comes first, and in a sense covers the whole. It is not as though we could divide the honors between God and ourselves, God doing His part, and we doing ours."[28] And yet our action and responsibility are not delimited by the grace of God, otherwise we would be reduced to automatons.

If God's righteousness is not diluted, how is his purpose to be realized? In its despair of life, Jewish apocalyptic envisioned a heavenly city coming down by fiat of the Almighty, a hope born of historical disillusionment that had paralyzed the springs of life and eliminated human involvement in the realization of the divine purpose. The other extreme is that of secular optimism which envisions the realization of the ideal by a feat of Baron Münchhausen. Unlike the former, Jesus did not despair of the historical process, and, unlike the latter, his hope was not in 'superman.' The confidence with which Jesus proclaims the demands of the Almighty is the

---

[25]Cf. Sholem Ash, *The Nazarene*, ET M. Samuel (New York: Pocket Books, 1956), 32-35.

[26]"Like Moses at the end of his great speech about the Law in Deuteronomy 30:19f., Jesus places a choice before his hearers, a choice of life or death, blessing or curse, admittance or exclusion. A man's fate depends on his obedience to the will of God as it has been newly revealed." Windisch, *The Meaning of the Sermon on the Mount*, 28.

[27]Schoeps, *Paul*, 282.

[28]Baillie, *God Was in Christ*, 116.

confidence that "all things are possible with God" (Mark 10:27), a divine optimism rooted in the power of God and realized in the human obedience of all who seek to do His will.

It is commonly assumed that Jesus' ethic was too high to be woven into the fabric of life in this world, that his teaching was too lofty for ordinary people in usual circumstances, and that his demands are therefore intended essentially for the original disciples transfigured by the divine aura of their Master, for metamorphosed believers elevated into an otherworldly existence, and possibly for beatifed monks reposing in celestial bliss on holy mountains. To correct this misunderstanding, it should be noted first of all that, despite Jesus' demand to "be perfect," Matthew depicts the disciples as very *im*perfect (Matthew 14:31, 16:8, 17:20, 21:21, 28:17). Judging from its content, we conclude that the Sermon on the Mount is evidently not addressed to the best of all possible worlds (as was the "metaphysico-theologo-cosmolo-nigology" of Dr. Pangloss in Voltaire's *Candide*) but rather to a world in which there are very deep personal and spiritual needs. The words of Jesus address a world: where there is unreconciled anger and litigation, adultery and divorce, where speech has lost its integrity, where there is persecution and retaliation, where coats are stolen and cheeks are slapped, where hatred of enemies is sanctioned, where hypocrisy parades in the guise of piety, where people trespass against each other and against God, where thieves break in and steal, where there is danger of the whole body being full of darkness, where people are preoccupied with material cares and are anxious about the future, where they condemn each other and profane what is holy, and where the majority are on the way to destruction. Surely it is unrealistic to assume that the Sermon on the Mount applies only to an otherworldly apocalyptic or monastic ideal where these conditions presumably do not apply.

Whether the demands of the Sermon on the Mount apply more properly to the Church than to those outside its fold depends on the extent to which its people are committed to the realistic meaning of that Cross which stands between the Kingdom of God and the human process and do not confuse its existential skandalon along the via dolorosa of discipleship with its dogmatic interpretation in the creed[29] nor with its symbolic presentation

---

[29]"The fact is that the Sermon on the Mount is not in our creeds. . . . Suppose we had

between two candlesticks in the liturgy. It is the task of the Church to proclaim the Law of God interpreted by Jesus as the universal law of life, whose field of application is as wide as creation itself and whose ethical precepts, while infinite in their ultimate range, are nevertheless capable of our conscientious observance at every level of relevance.

> Questions like: where shall we land, if we try to govern and fashion the world with these directions? What happens to my inalienable rights? Shall evil not triumph? But all these questions become of secondary importance before the recognition that what is said here is true. The first thing required of the hearer of the Sermon on the Mount is not the questioning of the possibility of its fulfilment but rather the acknowledgment of the reality of God's will.[30]

Though the Sermon on the Mount contains no political program of the kind Ragaz proposed and prescribes no sociological lineaments for a new *corpus christianum*, we would miss its social intentions if we assumed with Naumann and Baumgarten that it is inconsequential for the actual structures of life. The Sermon on the Mount takes issue with the fundamentals of institutional life including (1) the protection of life in accord with the equity of *lex talionis* ("an eye for an eye") and the social binding of the collective ego ("love your neighbor and hate your enemy"), (2) the preservation of the family (by prohibiting adultery) and its social control ("give her a certificate of divorce"), (3) the confirmation of the religious oath ("you shall not swear falsely . . . "), (4) the public scrutiny and social approval of exemplary behavior patterns involving charity, piety, and asceticism (alms, prayer, fasting), (5) the social control implemented by reciprocal surveillance, mutual censure, and democratic correction to conform with established custom and convention (you will be judged as

---

written it in our creeds and had repeated each time with conviction: 'I believe in the Sermon on the Mount and in its way of life, and I intend, God helping me, to embody it!' What would have happened? . . . The history of Christianity would have been different. With emphasis on doctrines which left unaffected our way of life the Christian Church could accept Constantine as its prize convert. And yet Constantine, after his alleged conversion, murdered his conquered colleague and brother-in-law Licinus; sentenced to death his eleven-year-old nephew, killed his eldest son, Crispus; brought about the death of his second wife. . . . Yet he was canonized by the Greek Church and his memory celebrated 'as equal to the apostles.' He talked and presided at the opening of the Council of Nicaea, which was called to frame a creed, and he was hailed as 'a bishop of bishops.' Could this have happened if the men who gathered there had made the Sermon on the Mount an essential part of the Creed?'' E. Stanley Jones, *The Christ of the Mount*, 12-13.

[30]Bornkamm *Jesus of Nazareth*, 107.

you judge and get what you give), (6) the social ownership of public property ("treasures on earth"), and (7) the economic provision of life's necessities (concerning food and clothing).[31] These rudimentary elements on which the social and cultural viability of primary institutions depend are the very ones Jesus' Antitheses systematically challenge in the name of a higher level of personal consciousness and a deeper sense of social responsibility.

Central to this new relational pattern is Jesus' didactic triad on alms, prayer, and fasting, according to which an individual becomes authentic in his consciousness before God and himself apart from social approbation or control. This reorientation to the Father in heaven rather than to the social approval of the religious establishment enables a new integrity in relation to God when one prays, to the recipients of charity when one gives alms, and to oneself when one fasts. The one-relational grid fixed by social convention is replaced by a multi-relational pattern based on authentic confrontation. Now charity is no longer a matter of social prestige ("in order to be seen") nor a guaranteed reciprocity of mutual benefits ("they have their reward"). Prayer is no longer performed with an eye to public scrutiny, and fasting is no longer an exercise in public relations. Charity, piety, and asceticism now assume intrinsic meaning and acquire real character. Relational patterns within an institution are entirely predictable in that they are fixed by convention. They are, therefore, objectively calculable and as such legally enforceable—in effect, deliberately producible. The multi-relational "Kingdom of God" authenticity involves a fundamental transition of all relationships of life "from the limited to the unlimited, from the fixed to the mobile, from the expected to the unexpected, from calculation to hope, from that which can be secured by force, to that which can only be requested."[32]

Point by point Jesus confronts the fixed institutional structures with a new understanding of one's place before God and man in a new kind of relationship characterized as the "Kingdom of God." Jesus' first antithesis transcends the enforcement of capital punishment with an invitation to the would-be accuser to become one's brother at the altar of thanksgiv-

---

[31]For these insights I am indebted to the sociological analysis of Dietrich von Oppen. *The Age of the Person: Society in the Twentieth Century*, ET Frank Clarke (Philadelphia: Fortress Press, 1969).

[32]Ibid., 14.

ing. The prohibition of killing is recast into a positive act of reconciliation. Beyond the legal constitution and dissolution of marriage as a social institution, Jesus looked to the personal intention in that relationship and in a blunt and graphic way declared that a human being must exercise self-control over his natural drives if he is to be a person. Instead of solemnizing the institutional formality of truth-speaking with its respective adjudications for calibrated degrees of falsification, Jesus commended the unambiguous "Yes" and "No" so as to restore to speech its integral function. Not resisting the evildoer and instead turning the other cheek and going the second mile are so revolutionary because they transcend the calculated reciprocity of measured institutional judgments.

The crucial threat and test of the new outlook is the new relation to the stranger and enemy. The institution by the defined rules of its existence excludes and repulses the nonmember as a stranger and enemy and assumes no positive responsibility for him. In loving the outsider and outcast, Jesus builds a bridge of personal trust to the enemy so that he may be the recipient of blessing rather than curse. In contrast to the institution's economic security investiture for its members, the level of personal responsibility to which Jesus appeals is not established by material tenure claims. "Treasure in heaven" is an open-ended investment in a different kind of time not measurable by interest rate percentages. The institution insures its perpetuation into the future in continuity with its past while he who seeks the Kingdom of God and his righteousness lives in the eternal Now. His is not a disconnected, solitary, uncommitted, irresponsible, momentary existence but one filled with spontaneously vital meetings with God and other human beings. Jesus assumed the essential nature of man to be structural openness because any programmed depersonalized fixation of his relationships thwarts his spiritual potential and interferes with the "way that leads to life" by stifling the life of the spirit.

Despite the contrast between institution and person, they were meant to coexist. The goal of the Sermon on the Mount is not a utopian escape from social existence. Law and prophets are to be fulfilled not through abolishing all institutions and exploring purely personal ways of conduct that lead directly to life eternal but rather by reifying and reauthenticating the corporate forms of human existence so as to fulfill God's covenantal intentions for all his people. This penetration of the disciple's personal influence into the fabric of social togetherness is likened by Jesus to the salt of the earth and the light of the world.[33] The presence of personal openness challenges institutional fixation from within by creating an intolerable tension which eventually forces it open, relativizes its absolute authority, and qualifies its unconditional validity. In the process of its revitalization, the institution, however, develops an inevitable hostility against the free spirit who surmounts it, resulting in a confrontation which in its crudest form eventuates in crucifixion.[34]

What then are the chances of realizing the level of personal relation the Sermon on the Mount exemplifies? Is it possible in this world for such personal integrity to prevail? Jesus predicts that those who find his narrow and hard way will always be few (Matthew 7:13-14). According to the Beatitudes however, the prospect this new way opens up transcends every pessimism as the divine paradox of their realization unfolds the meaning of the historical process.[35] Yet the same difficulties prevail: the majority is still tied to institutional standards, institutions still trample under foot the pearls of the new freedom, the turmoil that results still threatens to devour those who cause it. Furthermore, the effect of those forces that have throughout all time threatened the destruction of the person is greatly compounded by advanced technological ways of literally exterminating people or of reducing their personhood to a programmed function. Nevertheless, there are signs that a new age is dawning, and there are intimations that a new consciousness is emerging. There is a growing awareness that all material and financial security is provisional and conditional and therefore unstable and uncertain. The responsible person of today increasingly re-

---

[33]"The salt does not take the place of food, nor does the light take the place of the house it illumines; both are additions, but their effect is to stimulate and open up. They complete, 'fulfill,' the food and the dwelling; for food without salt is insipid and incomplete, and a building without light is no home." Ibid., 22.

[34]"Time and again the institution claims to be an absolute, and will tolerate no attempt to make it relative. It thinks to gain strength through absoluteness, and does not know that (as the Sermon on the Mount says) the only institution that stands on a rock is one whose validity is conditional—provided that any curtailment of its authority arise from personal responsibility before God." Ibid., 22.

[35]We concur with Bornkamm (*Jesus of Nazareth*, 108) that "there exists . . . no gulf which cannot be bridged between the Beatitudes and the demands of the Sermon on the Mount. To live in the presence of God and in the expectation of his future is the blessing which Jesus' Beatitudes promise, which is no less the blessing of his commandments. The door which Jesus opens with the Beatitudes is not closed by him like the angel with the sword of fire."

alizes that to become authentic one must be guided by something higher and deeper than the vacillating whim and fancy of public opinion. If one applies to oneself the standards of the Sermon on the Mount, one will be able to counteract one's own depersonalization by the institutional mentality and discover instead a new kind of structural openness in relation to persons of other societies and cultures and so transcend institutionalized enmity between people.

Cf. the forthrightness with which the German TV journalist Franz Alt in *Peace Is Possible. The Politics of the Sermon on the Mount,* ET Joachim Neugroschel (New York: Schocken Books, 1985) applies Jesus' teaching directly to our political existence. Alt contends we have too long assumed the Roman dictum: "If you want peace, prepare for war." Consequently, the present American-Soviet arsenal now exceeds a million times the destructive capacity of Hiroshima with sixty tons of explosives to overkill every inhabitant of every country in NATO or the Warsaw Pact. The holocaust looming ahead threatens to destroy everything. "An atomic war will leave no winners and no losers, just corpses. Only the weapons will win" (37). Formerly, nuclear weapons were justified as "deterrents"—for "intimidation." What if intimidation fails? Then nuclear warfare results "with the aim of annihilating the enemy" (47). The super death powers have prepared for this eventuality with their capacity to kill one another at least twenty times over. Yet we keep up the arms race despite the awareness that we are planning suicide and preparing to destroy creation!

The alternative is to want peace and prepare for it unconditionally in accord with the politics of Jesus. The peace Jesus promises is possible IF we really want it and are willing to work for it. The policy of peace does not seek victory, but reconciliation. Nor does it spend 700 billion dollars a year on armaments while a million human beings starve to death (34). "It is a promise of life, an experiment in love, a chance for humanity to become mature" (22). "Love of enemies does not mean glossing over conflicts: it means bridging them so that opponents can come together. . . . Today, love of enemies has become the logic of survival" (86). It demands intelligence, courage, and inner freedom to take the first step without anxious calculation and selfish insistence on being right (88). There is no love, no hope, and no peace without risks. "Without courage and imagination, no salvation is possible" (97). The Sermon on the Mount invites us to overcome fear and to create trust in the nonviolent struggle for justice and freedom through disarmament and negotiation. Peace is possible. "For the past 170 years, neither Sweden nor Switzerland has fought a single war" (109). Either we have peacetime or no time. Either we conquer war or it will conquer us. Either we abolish nuclear weapons or they will abolish us. Franz Alt challenges us to become ambassadors of peace committed to the work of healing and saving the world in the spirit of Jesus according to the Sermon on the Mount.

V
CONCLUSION

CONCLUSION

In reviewing the imaginative variety of modern interpretations of the Sermon on the Mount, one cannot evade the disconcerting impression that they are for the most part motivated by the dubious aim of restricting the scope of its meaning, qualifying the sense of its validity, and limiting the context of its relevance. The demands of Jesus, we are informed, request *only* a new *Gesinnung* (Herrmann), apply *only* to the uncultured Orient (Naumann), refer *only* to an otherworldly bliss (Weiss), are valid *only* within an apocalyptic framework (Schweitzer), make sense *only* in a non-Jewish way (Müller), involve *only* the inner, personal life (Baumgarten), concern *only* the twelve disciples (Bornhäuser), stand *only* as corrected by nature (Wünsch), intend *only* our salutary despair (Stange), determine *only* to destroy our self-confidence (Kittel), are relevant *only* existentially (Bultmann), can be regarded *only* as religious attitudes (Windisch), represent *only* symbolic expression (Dibelius), allow *only* paradoxical obedience (Bonhoeffer), are fulfilled *only* by Christ (Thurneysen), constitute *only* gospel (Jeremias), derive *only* from cultic contexts (Städeli), and denote *only* nonliteral illustrations (Hunter), hyperbole (Barton), or counsels of perfection (Scott). This polymorphic "only" by the ingenious diversity of its recurrence throughout the hermeneutical history of this text appears highly suspicious.[1] These professional qualifications, modifications, and limitations of Jesus' demands dispute, refute, and confute the articulation, intensification, and radicalization intended by his Antitheses.[2]

---

[1] "Again and again it became a shock absorber, which made the real meeting with Jesus' word bearable and therefore illusory, and which, in advance, dissolved this meeting into historical and theological reflections." Bornkamm, *Jesus of Nazareth*, 225.

[2] "All these antitheses contain one sustained theme which may be summarized in these few words: 'Not only—but even. . . . ' Even wrath, even the lustful look, even the 'legal' divorce, even the mere oath (by which *one* word is singled out above others as true), even the kind of retaliation which remains within the limits prescribed by the law, even the kind of love which yet excludes the enemy, are against God's will." Ibid., 103.

With astounding ingenuity Christendom developed an amazing variety of hermeneutical reasons why one could not or should not obey the commandments of Jesus. Though an analysis of these various views reveals profound elements of truth in each, most of them nevertheless appear to imply (1) that either Jesus did not mean what he said or did not say what he meant or (2) that what he said applies either to a different time than now or in a different way than then. Our analysis substantiates the observation of Günther Bornkamm that

> we find ourselves faced with the question whether the times when the Sermon on the Mount has had special historical significance were not always those in which men allowed themselves to be challenged by Jesus' demand and commandment in a radical and direct fashion, and sought, with the most thoroughgoing personal decision, to put the Sermon on the Mount into practice, quite literally in their own day—in their refusal to take an oath, by their renunciation of personal property, their "no" to military service. Were not these the truly historical moments, in which the attack upon this world was actually launched and in which the crumbling foundations of its supposedly sacred political, social, moral, and religious traditions were shaken; where the volcano of the Sermon on the Mount erupted, or at least where its menacing glow of fire became visible, whose light revealed the precarious ledge upon which Christianity had settled down to a comfortable existence, and upon which unconcernedly it let the flocks of its faithful graze?
>
> In these moments the attack was always directed towards a Church which, with its sophisms and theologisms, sanctioned the existing world and its "orders," and which had put the dynamic power of the Sermon on the Mount, so to speak, under lock and key. We are reminded in this connection especially of Tolstoi's exposition of the Sermon on the Mount. . . . Time and time again Christianity, especially with the assistance of its theology, has known so well and still knows how to intercept, so to speak, the thrust of Jesus' challenge, to divert it and to settle down peacefully in spite of it.[3]

The Sermon on the Mount has always been an embarrassment to the Church. Catholicism took the burden of Jesus' demands off the shoulders of its believers by delegating it to professionals in supererogatory accomplishment. In this way the mandatory nature of these demands was circumvented and at the same time left intact to be fulfilled vicariously 'for' all by a few purist saints like Francis of Assisi, whose decisive influence is

---

[3]Ibid., 221-23.

credited less to his radical obedience to the will of God than to his humble compliance with the authority of Rome. Nevertheless, a place was provided within Catholicism for the ethic of Jesus. It was, though, a very modest place indeed, procured at the price of institutionalizing the division between the ordinary and the extraordinary, between the worldly ethos which normally applies and the Jesus ethic which applies exclusively to the holiest profession in whose ranks only those few are permitted who are unfit to bear the world's necessary compromises.

Meanwhile, Protestant exegesis in prolific variety concluded that the words of Jesus do not really mean what they say. If the logic is more subtle, it establishes that Jesus never intended in the first place that we do what he says. Protestant theologians almost invariably concur that one should in any case not always or not completely presume to obey Jesus' demands because, apart from proving inconvenient, inappropriate, and impracticable, doing so would imply a despicable regression to the legalism of Catholicism, of the Anabaptists, or of Tolstoy. Time and again the Protestant Church has gone on record lauding the Sermon's lofty ideals and resolving to take them ultimately seriously in any other than a merely legalistic way. It has exalted the Sermon on the Mount as the incomparable, incomprehensible, and unattainable perfect will of God as though God's will were an object of spiritual admiration, pious ecstasy, and pure worship. Jesus' demands in the Sermon have been elevated to the level of the supraholy and relegated to the realm of the suprareal. They are seen to require the casuistic function of interpretation, application, and adaptation of their incomprehensible ideas and inaccessible ideals to our lower real world in calculated, prudential, and fully enlightened ways commensurate with our social, cultural, and political responsibilities as citizens of a modern age.

All eloquence has been commanded to establish the infinite worth, eternal validity, and universal relevance of Jesus' unfathomable precepts on the subtle supposition that his intention could never have been to legislate so deliberately, prescribe so pedantically, or demand so legalistically as to imply that the actual cases of prohibiting anger, lust, divorce, retaliation, and war should or could be taken literally. Rather these 'examples' are made to serve a far nobler function as picturesque Oriental illustrations of a much broader, more profound, more universal, more natural, more humane, more responsible, and more Christological principle than that which Jesus himself had in mind. This sophistical comedy perpetuates itself in virtually a thousand commentaries whose function it is to explain by the arts of theological science why the plain words of Jesus mean the opposite of what they say. And this is called interpretation and passes for hermeneutical learning.[4]

The Church has too long been divided over the great Either/Or—Faith *or* Ethics—instead of realizing the one through the other. The truth of the matter lies in the admission that ethics is of the essence of the religion of Jesus—if you will, an expression of his faith. Unfortunately, the claims of ethics have been considered a mere supplement to the doctrine of substitutionary atonement, an appendix of secondary importance.[5] Luther underscored Paul's emphasis on grace over against works and declared that the gospel admits of no law. The Reformers and their descendants eloquently defended the splendor of this gospel of grace as the sole basis of Christianity over against all Jewish, Catholic, and sectarian "heresy." They insisted that Christ fulfilled the Law for us, that is, in our stead by his sacrificial death, and that we consequently need not fulfill it but only need believe in him who has fulfilled it. And the Christianity that developed from this Pauline emphasis focuses on Jesus Christ as a heavenly being become man, in whose transcendent resurrected reality a mortal can share by the power of heavenly grace experienced through the sacraments to effect redemption from earthly guilt and death and to inspire eternal life and blessedness. Seen in this context, the good is lifted out of the struggle of life and appropriated essentially in a metaphysical sense of the incarnation that confronts us without making moral demands upon us. The good remains the object of fascination and awe and tends to captivate our fantasy and emotion rather than affect our will and life.

---

[4]"What confronts us is not a contradiction between the ideal and reality—that is essentially human—but the romantic discord of text and sermon, of word and will, the triumph of romantic irony over the ideal. . . . The opposition between speech and action, between teaching everything and fulfilling nothing, easily leads to the result that everything ethical becomes ambiguous; and then ethics becomes a mere matter of words, a matter of interpretation." Leo Baeck, "Romantic Religion," 264-65.

[5]Jesus intended for us to do the will of God—that was his only creed. "Even when he says: 'Whosoever shall confess me before men, him will I confess also before my Father which is in heaven,' he is thinking of people *doing as he did*; he means confession which shows itself in feeling and action. How great a departure from what he thought and enjoined is involved in putting 'Christological' creed in the forefront of the Gospel, and in teaching that before a man can approach it he must learn to think rightly about Christ. That is putting the cart before the horse. A man can think and teach rightly about Christ only if, and in so far as, he has already begun to live according to Christ's Gospel." Harnack, *What is Christianity?*, p. 110.

Once it has been firmly ingrained in the human psyche that one can do no good work and that original sin is the all-pervading ontological reality of human being, then all ethics has been eliminated on principle as an expression of that original sinfulness on account of which man is caught up in the cosmic drama of supernatural redemption. Supernaturalistic explanations for why Jesus died and how his death saves us, however, largely evade the historical implications of messiahship and discipleship along the via dolorosas of life. To the extent that the teaching of Jesus appears irrelevant and inaccessible for our life it has in the lectionaries and liturgies of the great churches been replaced by dogmatic creeds taught and read as prayers. The emphasis has been not on the didachē *Of* Jesus but on the kerygma *About* Christ. Jesus' teaching of the WAY (ὁδός) of the Cross has been replaced by Paul's proclamation of the Word (λόγος) of the Cross with the effect that the offense of the Cross has been transferred from the existential to the epistemological plane so that the authoritative command to *Follow* Jesus has become an intellectual problem of *Believing* in Christ. That following Jesus is presumptuous and unnecessary is implicit in the logic of most atonement theories.

The sum of the matter is that the meaning of Jesus is to be sought in his teaching. In this conclusion we concur with W. D. Davies that "it is the penetrating precepts of Jesus as they encounter us in the Sermon on the Mount, and elsewhere, that are the astringent protection against any interpretation of that person, life, death, and resurrection in any other than moral terms."[6] Consequently, Davies concludes,

> to interpret the faith of the New Testament only, or even mainly, in terms of a rigid understanding of the Pauline antithesis of Grace and Law is to ignore not only the tumultuous, tortuous nature of Paul himself (a fact which alone should make us chary of making his experience in any way normative), and not only the exaggerations engendered by the historical controversy out of which the antithesis arose, but even more, [it is to ignore] much of the evidence pointing to a 'law' which remains in the new covenant of grace, and indeed, especially there, and which is rooted in the words of Jesus Christ himself.[7]

The truth of God's love and will "is not too hard for you, neither is it far

---

[6]*The Setting of the Sermon on the Mount*, 435.

[7]Ibid., 439-40.

off. It is neither in heaven nor beyond the sea. It is in your mouth and in your heart, so that you can do it" (Deuteronomy 30:11). The transcendence that the Sermon on the Mount attests was meant to happen immanently within the context of our real life.

Dogmatic Christianity insists that "Christ is the end of the law" (Romans 10:4), while Judaism lives on in the belief that "every commandment through which God speaks to man . . . has its own infinity."[8] For Judaism, the endlessness of God's law is the basis for man's continuing life. "Thy word is a lamp to my feet and a light to my pathway" (Psalm 119:5).[9] "The commandment of God . . . leads into the future and involves a mission which, in the words of the Bible, 'continues from generation to generation.' "[10] To be a Jew is to identify with the hope of this mission as the ground of one's whole being. Jesus differed from other men in the way he fully embodied this mission in his calling and vocation as Messianic teacher of God's law.[11] The conflict that brought him to the cross developed over his teaching. Those who rejected him did so because they could not identify with his teaching. Christians hold to his person despite the fact that they do not live by his teaching. Jews and Christians still ask the same unbelieving questions: How can a nation triumph if it becomes pacifist? How can a state endure if it abolishes the oath? How can a culture prosper if its investors are condemned for being camels that cannot squeeze through the needle's eye of austerity? How can a people survive if its eunuchs are idolized? What these questions really ask is: Why use the name of God in this world? The only answer that meets this question on its level lies beyond the limit of human reason and cannot be forced by logic. It is the call to *Imitatio Dei* that issues from the Mosaic Torah and finds its fulfillment

---

[8]Baeck, "Romantic Religion," 179.

[9]In the Old Testament God's "word" refers to God's commandments. The Ten Commandments are, for example, never spoken of as law but are always called "the Ten Words."

[10]Baeck, "Romantic Religion," 179.

[11]"He was himself the complete embodiment of the commandment of love and the love commanded within our human existence, and as such He constitutes in Himself the ultimate source of the inner relation between commandment and love and the creative ground of all true Christian service. This is particularly apparent in the Sermon on the Mount, which is at once the self-portrait of our Lord in His life on earth as Son of Man and the promulgation of the will of the Father as unconditionally binding on all men." T. F. Torrance, "Service in Jesus Christ," *Service in Christ: Essays presented to Karl Barth on his 80th Birthday*, J. I. McCord and T. L. Parker, eds. (London: Epworth Press, 1966) 3.

in the Messianic Torah as an invitation to *Imitatio Christi* in the faith and love, freedom and foolishness, joy and agony, grace and mercy that characterize the Christian way.[12]

There is actually nothing that should or could keep us from following Jesus except our instinctual responsibility to defend our 'self-respect,' theologically or otherwise. So long as we insist on this 'inalienable right,' we see in the Sermon on the Mount only our own theological problems. But, if we resolve to pursue with unconditional openness the path that opens up to us, we come in contact with the same source that inspired it. Through the Spirit we are endowed at the horizon of our new being with the identifiable continuity of his consciousness with our own. The Word of God, which in its indicative and imperative form calls us to the imitation of God by following in his way, may not be dissolved into the free-floating subjectivity of our own self-understanding. Nor may God's law be evaporated into the feeble sentimentality of the Augustinian maxim, "Love and do as you please."

In obeying his call and responding to it in the love of God which constitutes the whole of religion and ethics, we realize, however, that he leaves us with something less tangible, less arguable, less teachable, and more vital than Torah. To understand this is also to know why it is not enough to preserve the sayings of Jesus in their original purity in order to hand them down unaltered from generation to generation like mandatory yoga exercises for spiritual formation. Truth is not a static possession but a dynamic inspiration. To truly hear the Sermon on the Mount is to be inspired by the spirit and will of Jesus to venture our own way illumined by its light.

---

[12]"The springs of revelation are not dried up. The living Christ is there to lead the way for all who are prepared to follow him. . . . So the Christian ideal lies before us, not as a remote and austere mountain peak, an ethical Everest which we must scale by our own skill and endurance; but as a road which we walk with Christ as guide and friend." T. W. Manson, *Ethics and the Gospel*, 68.

BIBLIOGRAPHY

BIBLIOGRAPHY

Asch, Sholem. *The Nazarene*. Translated by M. Samuel. New York: Pocket Books, Inc., 1956.

Asmussen, Hans. *Die Bergpredigt. Eine Auslegung von Matth. Kap. 5-7*. Göttingen: Vandenhoeck & Ruprecht, 1939.

Bachmann, Phil. *Die Sittenlehre Jesu und ihre Bedeutung für die Gegenwart*. Leipzig: A. Deichertsche Verlagsbuchhandlung, 1904.

Baeck, Leo. "Romantic Religion," *Judaism and Christianity*. Translated by Walter Kaufman. ("Meridian Books.") Cleveland and New York: The World Publishing Co. of America and The Jewish Publication Society of America at Philadelphia, 1961.

Baillie, Don M. *God was in Christ*. London: Faber & Faber, 1947.

Barnette, Henlee. "The Ethic of the Sermon on the Mount." *Review and Expositor* 53 (1956): 23-33.

Barth, Karl. *Church Dogmatics*. Volume II, part 2; volume III, part 4. Edinburgh: T. & T. Clark, 1957, 1961.

Barton, George A. "The Royal Law" of Matthew 5:21-48. *Journal of Biblical Literature* 37 (1918): 54-65.

Batdorf, Irvin. "How Shall We Interpret the Sermon on the Mount?" *Journal of Bible and Religion* (1959): 211-17.

Bauman, Clarence. *Gewaltlosigkeit im Täufertum. Eine Untersuchung zur theologischen Ethik des oberdeutschen Täufertums der Reformationszeit*. Leiden: E. J. Brill, 1968.

──────────. "Luther and the Turks: An Interpretation of Christian Responsibility from Within the Two-Kingdoms Doctrine." *Christus Victor* (London: International Fellowship of Reconciliation) number 107 (December 1959): 3-15.

──────────. "The Theology of 'The Two Kingdoms': A Comparison of Luther and the Anabaptists." *Mennonite Quarterly Review* 38 (January 1964): 37-49, 60.

Baumgarten, Otto. *Bergpredigt und Kultur der Gegenwart*. Religionsgeschichtliche Volksbücher für die deutsche christliche Gegenwart. VI. Reihe, 10/12. Heft. Tübingen: Verlag J.C.B. Mohr, 1921.

Ben-Chorin, Schalom. *Jesus im Judentum*. Schriftenreihe für christlich-jüdische Begegnung, Band 4. Wuppertal: Theologischer Verlag Rolf Brockhaus, 1970.

──────────. "Possibilities and Limits of our Dialogue." *The Jews and Ourselves*. "Judaism and Christianity in the World Today," volume II, number 4 (Autumn 1964): 127-32.

Berner, Ursula. *Die Bergpredigt. Rezeption und Auslegung im 20. Jahrhundert.* Göttinger theologische Arbeiten, Band 12. Göttingen: Vandenhoeck & Ruprecht (1979) 1983.

Bethge, Eberhard. *Dietrich Bonhoeffer. Theologe. Christ. Zeitgenosse.* München: Chr. Kaiser Verlag, 1967.

Beyer, H. W. *Der Christ und die Bergpredigt nach Luthers Deutung.* München, 1933.

Beyschlag, Karlmann. *Die Bergpredigt und Franz von Assisi.* Gütersloh: C. Bertelsmann Verlag, 1955.

Blumhardt, Joh. Christoph. *Die Bergpredigt (Mt. 5-7).* Basel: Karl Werner, 1944. [Originally published in 1871.]

Bonham, Tal. D. *The Demands of Discipleship.* Pine Bluff AR: Discipleship Book Co., 1967.

Bonhoeffer, Dietrich. *The Cost of Discipleship.* Translated by R. H. Fuller. New York: Macmillan, 1961.

_____. *Ethics.* Translated by N. H. Smith. New York: Macmillan, 1962.

_____. *Gesammelte Schriften.* Edited by E. Bethge. Volume 1. München: Chr. Kaiser Verlag, 1958.

_____. *Prisoner for God. Letters and Papers from Prison.* Translated by R. H. Fuller. New York: Macmillan, 1961.

Bornhäuser, Karl. *Die Bergpredigt. Versuch einer zeitgenössischen Auslegung.* Beiträge zur Förderung christlicher Theologie, 2. Reihe, 7. Band. Gütersloh: Druck u. Verlag von C. Bertelsmann, 1923.

Bornkamm, Günther. "The End-Expectation and the Church in Matthew." In *Tradition and Interpretation in Matthew,* edited by Günther Bornkamm, Gerhard Barth, and Heinz J. Held, 15-51. London: SCM Press, 1963.

_____. *Jesus of Nazareth.* London: Hodder & Stoughton, 1960.

_____. Barth, Gerhard, and H. J. Held. *Tradition and Interpretation in Matthew.* Translated by P. Scott. Philadelphia: Westminster Press, 1963.

Bousset, W. *Jesu Bergpredigt in ihrem Gegensatz zum Judentum. Ein religionsgeschichtlicher Vergleich.* Göttingen: Vandenhoeck & Ruprecht, 1892.

_____. *Jesus.* Translated by J. P. Trevelyan. Crown Theological Library, volume 14. Williams & Norgate; New York: G. P. Putnam's Sons, 1906.

Braaten, Carl E. *History and Hermeneutics.* New Directions in Theology Today, volume 2. Philadelphia: The Westminster Press, 1966.

Brunner, Emil. *The Mediator. A Study of the Central Doctrine of the Christian Faith.* Translated by O. Wyon. London: Lutterworth Press, 1937.

Buber, Martin. *Kampf um Israel.* Berlin, 1933.

_____. "Königtum Gottes," *Werke,* volume II. München: Kösel-Verlag and Heidelberg: Verlag Lambert Schneider, 1964.

Bultmann, Rudolf. *The History of the Synoptic Tradition.* Translated by John Marsh. Oxford: Blackwell, 1951.

_____. *Jesus and the Word.* Translated by Louise P. Smith and Erminie H. Lantero. London & Glasgow: Collins, 1958.

Carson, D. A. *The Sermon on the Mount. An Evangelical Exposition of Matthew 5-7.* Grand Rapids: Baker Book House, 1978.

Chafer, Lewis Sperry. *Systematic Theology,* volumes 4 and 5. Dallas, Texas: Dallas Theological Seminary Press, 1948.

Chestov, Leo. "The Last Judgment, Tolstoy's Last Works." In *In Job's Balances.* London, 1932.

Craufurd, Alexander H. *The Religion and Ethics of Tolstoy.* London, 1912.

Cullmann, Oscar. *Christ and Time.* Translated by F. G. Filson. London, 1951.

Davies, W. D. *The Sermon on the Mount.* Cambridge: Cambridge University Press, 1966.

_____. *The Setting of the Sermon on the Mount.* Cambridge: Cambridge University Press, 1964.

Dibelius, Martin. *The Sermon on the Mount.* New York: Charles Scribner's Sons, 1940.

Dimitroff, Stojan. *Der Sinn der Forderungen Jesu in der Bergpredigt.* (Bern dissertation.) Sofia, 1938.

Dodd, C. H. "Eschatology and History." An appendix to *The Apostolic Preaching and its Developments.* New York and London: Harper & Brothers, 1954.

_____. *Gospel and Law. The Relation of Faith and Ethics in Early Christianity.* Cambridge: Cambridge University Press, 1953.

_____. *A New Testament Triptych on Christ's Coming, His Gospel, His Passion.* Cincinnati OH: Forward Movement Publications, 1955.

_____. *The Parables of the Kingdom.* Third edition. London, 1936.

Dostoevsky, Fyodor. *The Brothers Karamazov.* Translated by C. Garnett. London: William Heinemann, 1913.

Eichholz, Georg. *Auslegung der Bergpredigt.* Biblische Studien, Heft 46. Neukirchner Verlag des Erziehungsvereins GmbH., 1965.

Fascher, E. "Bergpredigt II: Auslegungsgeschichte." *Religion in Geschichte und Gegenwart,* third edition, 1:1050-53.

Fiebig, Paul. *Jesu Bergpredigt. Rabbinische Texte zum Verständnis der Bergpredigt, ins Deutsch übersetzt, in ihren Ursprachen dargeboten und mit Erläuterungen und Lesarten versehen.* Forschungen zur Religion und Literatur des Alten und Neuen Testaments, Neue Folge. 20. Heft. Göttingen: Vandenhoeck & Ruprecht, 1924.

_____. "Der Sinn der Bergpredigt." *Zeitschrift für systematische Theologie* 7 (1929-1930): 497-515.

Fisher, Fred L. *The Sermon on the Mount.* Nashville: Broadman Press, 1976.

Flusser, David. *Jesus.* Translated by Ronald Walls. New York: Herder and Herder, 1969.

Fox, Emmet. *The Sermon on the Mount. A General Introduction to Scientific Christianity in the Form of a Spiritual Key to Matthew V, VI, and VII.* New York: Grosset & Dunlap, 1938.

Freud, Sigmund. *Civilization and its Discontents.* Great Books of the Western World, series 3, volume 1. Chicago: The Great Books Foundation, 1961.

Friedlander, Gerald. *The Jewish Sources of the Sermon on the Mount.* London: Routledge & Kegan Paul, 1910.

430   THE SERMON ON THE MOUNT

Gilmour, S. MacLean. "Interpreting the Sermon on the Mount." *Crozer Quarterly* 24 (1947): 47-56.

Gore, Charles. *The Sermon on the Mount: A Practical Exposition.* London: John Murray, 1900.

Guelich, Robert A. *The Sermon on the Mount. A Foundation for Understanding.* Waco TX: Word Books, 1982.

Harder, Günther. "Jesus und das Gesetz (Matthäus 5:17-20)." In *Antijudaismus im Neuen Testament? Exegetische und systematische Beiträge.* Abhandlungen zum christlich-jüdischen Dialog. Hrsg. von Helmut Gollwitzer, Band 2. München: Chr. Kaiser Verlag, 1967.

Häring, Bernard. *What Does Christ Want?* London: Geoffrey Chapman, 1968.

Harnack, Adolf. *What is Christianity?* Translated by T. B. Saunders. Fifth edition. London: Ernest Benn, 1958.

Heim, Karl. *Die Bergpredigt Jesu in ihrer praktischen Gegenwartsbedeutung.* Hamburg: Furche Verlag, 1959.

Heinrici, C. F. G. *Die Bergpredigt (Mt. 5-7, Lk. 6: 20-49) quellenkritisch und begriffsgeschichtlich untersucht.* Beiträge zur Geschichte und Erklärung des Neuen Testaments, II u. III,1. Leipzig, 1900, 1905.

Heinzelmann, Gerhard. "Das richtige Verständnis der Bergpredigt." *Theologische Studien und Kritiken,* N. F. III, 6. Heft, 108 (1937-1938): 458-71.

Hermann, Rudolf. *Die Bergpredigt und die Religiös-Sozialen.* Leipzig / Erlangen: A. Deichertsche Verlagsbuchhandlung [W. Scholl], 1922.

Herrmann, Wilhelm. *Ethik.* Tübingen und Leipzig, 1901.

_____. *The Moral Law. As Understood in Romanism and in Protestantism.* London and New York, 1904.

_____. *Die sittliche Weisungen Jesu. Ihr Mißbrauch und ihr richtiger Gebrauch.* Second edition. Göttingen: Vandenhoeck u. Ruprecht, 1907.

Heschel, Abraham Joshua. *Between God and Man. An Interpretation of Judaism.* New York: The Free Press / London: Collier-Macmillan Ltd., 1959.

_____. *The Insecurity of Freedom.* Philadelphia: The Jewish Publication Society of America, 1966.

_____. *The Prophets.* New York, 1962.

Heuss, Theodor. *Friedrich Naumann, der Mann, das Werk, die Zeit.* Second edition. Stuttgart und Tübingen: Rainer Wunderlich Verlag Hermann Leins, 1949.

Hochgrebe, Volker, Hrsg. *Provokation Bergpredigt.* [Mit Beitr. von J. Blank, E. Käsemann, J. Moltmann, O. H. Pesch, R. Roessler, L. Schottroff, L. Schwarz, M. Stöhr, K. Walf, J. Zink.] Stuttgart: Kreuz Verlag, 1982.

Huber, Hugo. *Die Bergpredigt. Eine exegetische Studie.* Göttingen: Vandenhoeck und Ruprecht, 1932.

Hunter, Archibald Macbride. *Design for Life; An Exposition of the Sermon on the Mount, its Making, its Exegesis, and its Meaning.* London: SCM Press, 1965.

Ingalls, Jeremy. *The Galilean Way.* New York: Longmans, Green & Co., 1953.

Jäger, Hans Ulrich. "Die Begründung der Sozialethik bei Leonhard Ragaz." *Reformatio* (October 1965).

——————. "Die sozialische Funktion des Reichgottesglaubens bei Leonhard Ragaz." *Evangelische Ethik* (Juli/September 1968).

Jeremias, Joachim. *New Testament Theology. The Proclamation of Jesus.* New York: Charles Scribner's Sons, 1971.

——————. *The Sermon on the Mount.* Translated by Norman Perrin. Philadelphia: Fortress Press, 1963.

Jones, E. Stanley. *The Christ of the Mount: A Working Philosophy of Life.* Toronto: McClelland & Stewart, 1931.

Jordan, Clarence. *Sermon on the Mount.* Valley Forge PA: Judson Press, 1952.

Kepler, Thomas S. *Jesus' Design for Living.* New York: Abingdon, 1955.

Kissinger, Warren S. *The Sermon on the Mount: A History of Interpretation and Bibliography.* ATLA Bibliography Series, number 3. Metuchen, N.J.: Scarecrow Press, 1975.

Kittel, Gerhard. "Die Bergpredigt und die Ethik des Judentums." *Zeitschrift für systematische Theologie* (edited by Carl Stange; Gütersloh) 2 (1925): 555-94.

——————. "Nachfolge." *Theologisches Wörterbuch zum Neuen Testament,* 1:210ff. (Stuttgart: Kohlhammer Verlag, 1933).

Klausner, Joseph. *Jesus of Nazareth. His Life, Times, and Teaching.* Translated from the Hebrew by H. Danby. London: Allen and Unwin, 1925.

——————. *The Messianic Idea in Israel from its Beginning to the Completion of the Mishnah.* Translated from the Hebrew by W. F. Stinespring. London: Allen & Unwin, 1956.

Knörzer, Wolfgang. *Die Bergpredigt. Modell einer neuen Welt.* Stuttgart: Verlag Katholisches Bibelwerk, 1970.

Kraus, Oskar. *Albert Schweitzer, his work and his Philosophy.* London: Adam & Charles Black, 1944.

Kümmel, George. *Promise and Fulfilment. The Eschatological Message of Jesus.* Translated by D. M. Barton. Studies in Biblical Theology, number 23. London: SCM Press, 1957.

Lanwer, P. Bernhard. *Jesu Stellung zum Gesetz. Matth. 5: 17-48 auf dem Hintergrunde des Alten Testaments und Spätjudentums.* (Den 3. Teil einer Inauguraldissertation der Katholisch-Theologischen Fakultät der Universität Münster.) Hiltrup: Herz-Jesu-Missionshaus, 1933.

Lapide, Pinchas. "Die Bergpredigt—Theorie und Praxis." *Zeitschrift für Evangelische Ethik* 17. Jahrgang, Heft 6 (November 1973): 369-72.

Laurila, K. S. "Leo Tolstoy und Martin Luther als Ausleger der Bergpredigt." In *Suomalaisen Tiedeakatemian Toimituksia.* Annales Academiae Scientiarum Fennicae. Sarja / Ser. B, Nid. / Tom. LV, 1. Pp. 1-92. Helsinki: Suomalaisen Kirjallisuuden Seuran Kirjapainon Oy., 1946.

Ligon, Ernest Mayfield. *The Psychology of Christian Personality.* New York: Macmillan, 1961.

Lindeskog, Gösta. *Die Jesusfrage im neuzeitlichen Judentum.* Uppsala, 1938.

Lindsay, Alexander Dunlop. *The Moral Teaching of Jesus*. London: Hodder & Stoughton, 1937.

Ljungman, Henrik. *Das Gesetz Erfüllen (Mt. 5:17ff. u.* 3:15). Lund: Gleerup, 1954.

Lohse, E., et al. "Nachfolge Christi," *Religion in Geschichte und Gegenwart* (edited by K. Galling; Tübingen: J.C.B. Mohr, 1960) 4:1286ff.

Luck, Ulrich. *Die Vollkommenheitsforderung der Bergpredigt*. Theologische Existenz heute, Nr. 150. München: Christian Kaiser Verlag, 1968.

Lundström, Gösta. *The Kingdom of God in the Teaching of Jesus, A History of Interpretation from the Last Decades of the Nineteenth Century to the Present Day*. Translated by Joan Bulman. Edinburgh and London: Oliver and Boyd, 1963.

Mann, Thomas. "Goethe and Tolstoy." In *Three Essays*. London, 1932.

Manson, T. W. *Ethics and the Gospel*. London: SCM Press, 1960.

_____. *The Teaching of Jesus*. Cambridge: Cambridge University Press, 1959.

Manson, William. *Jesus the Messiah. The Synoptic Tradition of the Revelation of God in Christ: with special Reference to Form-Criticism*. London: Hodder & Stoughton, 1943.

_____. *The Way of the Cross*. Edinburgh: Hodder & Stroughton, 1958.

Marriott, Horace. *The Sermon on the Mount*. New York / Toronto: Macmillan, 1925.

Mathews, Shailer. *Jesus on Social Institutions*. New York: Macmillan, 1928.

_____. *The Social Teaching of Jesus*. New York: Macmillan, 1897.

Mattmüller, Markus. *Leonhard Ragaz und der religiöse Sozialismus*. Volume 1. Zollikon: Evangelischer Verlag AG., 1957.

Maude, Aylmer. *Tolstoy and His Problems*. London, 1902.

McArthur, Harvey K. *Understanding the Sermon on the Mount*. London: The Epworth Press, 1961.

Miller, John W. *The Christian Way. A Guide to the Christian Life based on the Sermon on the Mount*. Scottdale PA: Herald Press, 1969.

Moltmann, Jürgen, Hrsg. *Nachfolge und Bergpredigt*. [Mit Beitr. von H. Gollwitzer, R. Heinrich, U. Luz, W. H. Schmidt.] München: Kaiser, 1981.

Montefiore, C. G. *The Synoptic Gospels*. Volume 2. London: Macmillan & Co., 1927.

Müller, Johannes. *Die Bergpredigt verdeutscht und vergegenwärtigt*. München: Oskar Beck, 1906.

Naumann, Friedrich. *Asia*. Berlin-Schönberg: Verlag der "Hilfe," 1899.

_____. *Aspects of the New Theology*, containing selections from *"Die Hilfe."* Translated by J. Miller. London: Elliot Stock, 1915.

_____. *Briefe über Religion mit Nachwort "Nach 13 Jahren."* Sixth edition. Berlin: Druck u. Verlag Georg Reimer, 1916.

Niebuhr, Reinhold. *An Interpretation of Christian Ethics*. New York and London: Harper, 1935.

Nietzsche, Friedrich. "Der Wille zur Macht. Versuch einer Umwertung aller Werte." In *Nietzsches Werke*, volume 15. Leipzig, 1901.

Ohrn, Arnold T. *The Gospel and The Sermon on the Mount*. New York: Fleming H. Revell Co., 1948.

Oppen, Dietrich von. *The Age of the Person. Society in the Twentieth Century*. Translated by Frank Clarke. Philadelphia: Fortress Press, 1969.

Pentecost, J. Dwight. *The Sermon on the Mount. Contemporary Insights for a Christian Lifestyle*. Portland OR: Multnomah Press (1975) 1980.

Perrin, Norman. *Rediscovering the Teaching of Jesus*. London: SCM Press, 1967.

Pokorný, Petr. *Der Kern der Bergpredigt. Eine Auslegung*. Hamburg: Herbert Reich Evangelischer Verlag, 1969.

Prabhavananda (Swami). *The Sermon on the Mount According to Vedanta*. London: George Allen & Unwin, 1964.

Preisker, H. "Die Art und Tragweite der Lebenslehre Jesu." *Theologische Studien und Kritiken*, (1919): 1-45.

Ragaz, Leonhard. *Die Bergpredigt Jesu*. Bern: Verlag Herbert Lang & Cie, 1945.

——————. *Die Botschaft vom Reiche Gottes, ein Katechismus für Erwachsene*. Bern, 1942.

——————. *Die Geschichte der Sache Christi. Ein Versuch*. Bern: Verlag Herbert Lang & Cie, 1945.

——————. *Der Kampf um das Reich Gottes in Blumhardt Vater und Sohn—und weiter!* Erlenbach-Zürich: Rotapfel-Verlag, 1922.

——————. *Du Sollst. Grundzüge einer sittlichen Weltanschauung*. Freiburg i.B.: Paul Waetzel, 1904.

——————. *Mein Weg*. Volume 2. Zürich: Diana Verlag, 1952.

Rasmussen, Larry L. *Dietrich Bonhoeffer: Reality and Resistance*. Studies in Christian Ethics. Nashville & New York: Abingdon Press, 1972.

Rauschenbusch, Walter. *A Theology of the Social Gospel*. New York: Macmillan, 1927.

Redpath, Theodore. *Tolstoy*. London, 1960.

Reimarus, Hermann Samuel. *Fragments*. Translated by R. S. Fraser. Lives of Jesus Series. Philadelphia: Fortress Press, 1970.

Rénan, Ernest. *The Life of Jesus*. London: Watts & Co., 1904.

Rich, Arthur. "Leonhard Ragaz, Eine Skizze von seinem Denken und Wirken." *Evangelische Ethik* (Juli/September 1968).

Roubiczek, Paul. "The Struggle for Virtue." In *The Misunderstanding of Man, Studies in European Thought of the Nineteenth Century*, chapter 9. London: Routledge and Kegan Paul Ltd., 1949.

Schabert, Arnold. *Die Bergpredigt. Auslegung und Verkündigung*. München: Claudius Verlag, 1966.

Schnackenburg, Rudolf. "Bergpredigt." *Lexikon für Theologie und Kirche* (second edition, 1958) 2:223-27.

Schneider, Johannes. *Der Sinn der Bergpredigt. Von der Grundordnung christlichen Lebens*. Band 12 der Sammlung: Aus der Welt der Bibel. Berlin: Furche Verlag, 1936.

Schneller, Ludwig. *Die Bergpredigt*. Leipzig: H. G. Wallmann, 1924.

Schoeps, Hans-Joachim. *Paul, The Theology of the Apostle in the Light of Jewish Religious History*. Translated by H. Knight. London: Lutterworth Press, 1961.

Schweitzer, Albert. *Civilization and Ethics*. Translated by C. T. Campion. London: Adam & Charles Black, 1946.

_____. *The Kingdom of God and Primitive Christianity*. Translated by L. A. Garrard. London: Adam & Charles Black, 1968.

_____. *My Life and Thought, An Autobiograhy*. Translated by C. T. Campion. London: Allen & Unwin, 1933.

_____. *The Mystery of the Kingdom of God. The Secret of Jesus' Messiahship and Passion*. Translated by W. Lowrie. London: Adam & Charles Black, 1925.

_____. *The Mysticism of the Apostle Paul*. Translated by W. Montgomery. New York: Henry Holt & Co., 1931.

_____. *Paul and his Interpreters*. Translated by W. Montgomery. London: Adam & Charles Black, 1912.

_____. *The Philosophy of Civilization*. New York: Macmillan, 1950.

_____. *The Quest of the Historical Jesus. A Critical Study of its Progress from Reimarus to Wrede*. Translated by W. Montgomery. London: Adam & Charles Black, 1910.

Schweizer, Eduard. *Die Bergpredigt*. Göttingen: Vandenhoeck & Ruprecht, 1982.

_____. ''Mt. 5:17-20. Anmerkungen zum Gesetzesverständnis des Matthäus.'' *Theologische Literaturzeitung* 77 (1952): 479-84.

Scott, Ernest F. *The Ethical Teaching of Jesus*. New York: Macmillan, 1925.

Seeberg, Reinhold. *Zur Ethik der Bergpredigt*. Schriften des Instituts für Sozialethik und Wissenschaft der Inneren Mission an der Universität Berlin, Heft 4. Leipzig: A. Deichertsche Verlagsbuchhandlung, D. Werner Scholl, 1934.

Shears, H. *Christ or Bentham? A Criticism of Dr. Gore's Work on the Sermon on the Mount*. London: Williams and Norgate, Ltd., 1927.

Shinn, Roger L. *The Sermon on the Mount*. Philadelphia: United Church Press, 1962.

Smith, Morton. *Tannaitic Parallels to the Gospels*. Journal of Biblical Literature Monographic Series, volume 6. Philadelphia: Society of Biblical Literature, 1951.

Soiron, Thaddäus. *Die Bergpredigt Jesu. Formgeschichtliche, exegetische und theologische Erklärung*. Freiburg im Breisgau: Herder, 1941.

Stadland-Neumann, Hiltrud. *Evangelische Radicalismen in der Sicht Calvins. Sein Verständnis der Bergpredigt und der Aussendungsrede* [dissertation]. Beiträge zur Geschichte und Lehre der Reformierten Kirche. Neukirchener Verlag des Erziehungsvereins GmbH., 1966.

Städeli, Walter. ''A Study of Christian Perfection in the Context of the Sermon on the Mount.'' Ph.D. dissertation, Faculty of Divinity, University of Edinburgh, 1964.

Stange, Carl. ''Zur Ethik der Bergpredigt.'' *Zeitschrift für systematische Theologie*, 2. Jg., 1. Vierteljahrheft (1924): 37-74.

Staudinger, Josef. *Die Bergpredigt*. Wien: Herder Verlag, 1957.

Stendahl, Krister. *The School of Matthew and its Use of the Old Testament*. Second edition. Philadelphia: Fortress Press, 1968.

Stöger, Alois. *Ich aber sage euch. Die Bergpredigt lebendig gemacht*. München: Pfeifer, 1952.

Thielicke, Helmut. *Life Can Begin Again*. Translated by John W. Doberstein. Philadelphia: Fortress Press, 1963.

Thurneysen, Eduard. *The Sermon on the Mount*. Translated by W. C. Robinson and J. M. Robinson. Richmond VA: John Knox Press, 1964.

Tilborg, Sjef Van. *The Jewish Leaders in Matthew*. Leiden: E. J. Brill, 1972.

Tolstoy, Leo. *My Confession* [1879-1882] and *The Spirit of Christ's Teaching*. London: Walter Scott, n.d.

—————. ''The Kingdom of God is Within You.'' In *The Kingdom of God and Peace Essays*. Translated by Aylmer Maude. The World's Classics, number 445. Fourth edition. Oxford: Oxford University Press, 1951.

—————. *On Life, and Essays on Religion (1887-1909)*. Volume 12 of *The Works of Leo Tolstoy*. Oxford: Oxford University Press, 1934.

—————. *What I Believe*. Translated by C. Popoff. London: Elliot Stock, 1885.

Torrance, T. F. *Conflict and Agreement in the Church*. Volume 1. London: Lutterworth Press, 1959.

—————. ''Service in Jesus Christ.'' In *Service in Christ. Essays presented to Karl Barth on his 80th Birthday*. Edited by J. I. McCord and T. L. Parker. London: Epworth Press, 1966.

Traub, Friedrich. ''Das Problem der Bergpredigt.'' *Zeitschrift für Theologie und Kirche*. N. F. 17 (1936): 193-218.

Trilling, Wolfgang. *Das Wahre Israel. Studien zur Theologie des Matthäusevangeliums*. Erfurter Theologische Studien, Band 7. Leipzig: St. Benno-Verlag, 1962.

Troeltsch, Ernst. *The Social Teaching of the Christian Churches*. Translated by O. Wyon. London: Allen & Unwin, 1931.

Vermes, Geza. *Jesus the Jew. A Historian's Reading of the Gospels*. London: Collins, 1973.

Vidler, Alec R. *Christ's Strange Work. An Exposition of the Three Uses of God's Law*. London: SCM Press, 1963.

Walker, Thomas. *Jewish Views of Jesus*. London: George Allen & Unwin, 1931.

Waylen, Hector. *Mountain Pathways: A Study in the Ethics of the Sermon on the Mount*. London: Sherratt & Hughes, 1909.

Weiss, Johannes. *Die Predigt Jesu vom Reiche Gottes*. Göttingen: Vandenhoeck und Ruprecht, 1900.

—————. *Die Nachfolge Christi und die Predigt der Gegenwart*. Göttingen: Vandenhoeck und Ruprecht, 1895.

Wellhausen, Julius. *Einleitung in die drei ersten Evangelien*. Berlin: Georg Reimer, 1905.

White, Ellen G. *Thoughts From the Mount of Blessing*. Mountain View CA: Pacific Press, 1956.

Wilder, Amos N. *Eschatology and Ethics in the Teaching of Jesus*. New York: Harper & Brothers, 1950.

Windisch, Hans. *The Meaning of the Sermon on the Mount: A Contribution to the Historical Understanding of the Gospels and to the Problem of Their True Exegesis*. Translated by S. MacLean Gilmour. Philadelphia: The Westminster Press, 1951.

Wood, James. *The Sermon on the Mount and its Application*. London: Geoffrey Bles, 1963.

Wrege, Hans-Theo. *Die Überlieferungsgeschichte der Bergpredigt*. Wissenschaftliche Untersuchungen zum Neuen Testament, Band 9. Tübingen: J.C.B. Mohr, 1968.

Wünsch, Georg. *Die Bergpredigt bei Luther. Eine Studie zum Verhältnis von Christentum und Welt*. Tübingen: J.C.B. Mohr, 1920.

_____. *Evangelische Wirtschaftsethik*. Tübingen: J.C.B. Mohr, 1927.

_____. *Theologische Ethik*. Sammlung Göschen 900. Berlin und Leipzig: Walter de Gruyter & Co., 1925.

INDEXES

NAMES

Alt, Franz, 414
Aquinas, Thomas, 3, 149, 165
Anabaptists, 57, 150, 171-72, 279, 285, 293, 419
Asch, Sholem, 395, 408, 427
Asmussen, Hans, 174, 427

Bachmann, Phil., 92, 427
Baeck, Leo, 387-88, 420, 422, 427
Baillie, Donald M., 408, 427
Barnette, Henlee, 6, 427
Barth, Karl, 3, 37, 270, 286-89, 373-74, 427
Barton, George A., 3, 35, 417, 427
Batdorf, Irvin, 6, 427
Bauman, Clarence, 174, 427
Baumgarten, Otto, 139-51, 161, 167, 214, 224, 225, 355-56, 357, 358, 361, 372, 383, 397, 410, 417, 427
Beck, Tobias, 154
Bell, George, 267
Ben-Chorin, Schalom, 269, 393, 427
Bengel, 154
Bergson, Henri, 54
Berner, Ursula, 7, 338, 428
Bethge, Eberhard, 266, 272, 428
Beyer, H. W., 6, 428
Beyschlag, Karlmann, 185, 428
Bitzius, Albert, 54
Blumhardt, Joh. Christoph, 54, 285-86, 428
Bonham, Tal D., 7, 338, 428
Bonhoeffer, Dietrich, 249-74, 363, 384, 398, 403, 417, 428
Bornhäuser, Karl, 3, 153-61, 225, 228, 356-57, 362, 383, 397, 417, 428
Bornkamm, Günther, 29, 385, 389-90, 402, 406, 410, 413, 417-18, 428
Braaten, Carl E., 375, 428
Brunner, Emil, 289, 428
Brunner, Robert, 289

Buber, Martin, 378, 380, 382, 428
Buddha, 120, 135, 312
Bultmann, Rudolf, 4, 37, 166, 167, 213-14, 216, 225, 254, 359-60, 362, 373-74, 380, 383, 398, 417, 428

Calvin, 54, 209, 211, 278, 285
Carlyle, 54
Carolsfeld, Schnorr von, ix, 79
Carson, D. A., 7, 338, 429
Catholic, Roman, 68, 150, 179, 185, 211, 285, 418-19
Chafer, Lewis Sperry, 4, 127, 429
Chelcický, Peter, 338
Chestov, Leo, 32, 33, 429
Chrysostom, John, 20, 21
Commenius, Johannes A., 338
Craufurd, Alexander H., 30, 34, 429
Cremer, Hermann, 154
Cromwell, Oliver, 306

Davies, W. D., 338, 388, 389-90, 391, 421, 429
Denck, Hans, 4
Dibelius, Martin, 3, 213-14, 224, 225, 226, 229-48, 294, 362-63, 374, 398, 417, 429
Dodd, C. H., 374-75, 380, 387, 403-405, 429
Dostoevsky, Fyodor, 192, 241, 276, 402, 429

Eichholz, Georg, 331-32, 365, 429

Fascher, E., 6, 429
Fiebig, Paul, 391, 429
Fisher, Fred L., 338, 429
Flusser, David, 391, 429
Fox, Emmet, 3, 311-17, 365, 398, 429
Francis, St., 3, 64, 76, 185, 349
Freud, Sigmund, 402, 429

Gandhi, Mahatma, 4, 267, 346
Gilmour, S. MacLean, 6, 430

Gollwitzer, Helmut, 329, 389, 430
Gore, Charles, 151, 430
Gregory, Casper René, 241-42
Grundvig, 54
Guelich, Robert A., 7, 338, 430
Häring, Bernard, 338, 430
Harder, Günther, 389, 430
Harnack, Adolf, 3, 138, 349, 355, 370, 374, 392, 396, 406-407, 420, 430
Heidegger, 207
Heim, Karl, 4, 6, 430
Heinzelmann, Gerhard, 6, 430
Hensius, Wilhelm, 285-86
Hermann, Rudolf, 73, 430
Herrmann, Wilhelm, 3, 37-51, 52, 55, 57, 151, 160, 161, 166, 171, 179, 199, 213, 214, 224, 347-49, 355, 357, 369, 383, 397, 403, 417, 430
Heschel, Abraham J., 33, 393, 407, 430
Heuss, Theodor, 77, 430
Hochgrebe, Volker, 329, 430
Hunter, Archibald Macbride, 4, 6, 296-97, 417, 430
Hus, John, 57, 338

Ibsen, 70
Ingalls, Jeremy, 321-22, 365, 399, 430

Jäger, Hans Ulrich, 66, 69, 71, 431
Jeremias, Joachim, 7, 291-96, 364, 385, 394, 396, 417, 431
Jones, E. Stanley, 3, 307-11, 365, 394, 410, 431
Jordan, Clarence, 319-21, 365, 399, 431

Kähler, Martin, 154, 348-49
Kant, Immanuel, 3, 49, 73, 112, 114, 166, 171, 179, 181, 247, 349
Käsemann, Ernst, 372
Kautzky, 143
Kepler, Thomas S., 298, 431
Kierkegaard, Søren, 54, 78, 150, 241, 254
Kissinger, Warren S., 7, 338, 431
Kittel, Gerhard, 3, 187-95, 214, 216, 225, 226, 359, 360, 361-62, 383-84, 405, 417, 431
Klausner, Joseph, 369, 378, 380, 387, 431
Knörzer, Wolfgang, 7, 338, 431
Kraus, Oskar, 121, 431
Kümmel, Werner, 381, 431

Lao-tze, 188
Lapide, Pinchas, 289, 431
Lenin, 346
Ligon, Ernst M., 323-25, 365, 399, 431
Lindsay, D. A., 175, 432
Lohmeyer, Ernst, 338

Luck, Ulrich, 332-35, 365, 431
Lundström, Gösta, 370-71, 432
Lüthi, Walter, 289
Luther, Martin, 40, 41, 55, 163, 171, 176, 179, 182, 185, 209, 211, 278, 285
Lutheran Zwei-Reiche-Lehre, 68,141,165-66, 171, 172, 173, 174, 253-54, 263, 264, 358, 420
Luz, Ulrich, 329

McArthur, Harvey K., 7, 338, 395-96, 432
Machiavelli, 29
Mann, Thomas, 28, 32, 33, 432
Manson, T. W., 375-76, 396, 423, 432
Manson, William, 381, 396, 406, 432
Marx, Karl, 28, 29, 54, 346, 402
Mathews, Shailer, 347, 432
Mattmüller, Markus, 66, 70, 432
Maude, Aylmer, 12, 13, 28, 31, 34, 432
Merezhkovsky, 31
Miller, John W., 329, 399, 432
Mohammed / Koran, 171
Moltmann, Jürgen, 329, 432
Montefiore, C. G., 389, 390, 392-93, 396, 432
Müller, Johannes, 354-55, 370, 372, 383, 396, 397, 417, 432

Naumann, Friedrich, 3, 37, 49, 51, 54, 57, 67, 75-93, 151, 161, 167, 214, 224, 226, 350-51, 354, 355, 357, 370, 372, 383, 397, 410, 417, 432
Niebuhr, Reinhold, 4, 250, 432
Nietzsche, Friedrich, 54, 135, 140, 145, 232, 256, 387, 401-402, 432

Oetinger, 154
Ohrn, Arnold T., 399, 432
Oppen, Dietrich von, 411-13, 433
Origen, 405

Paul, St., 24, 59, 65, 107, 112, 125, 126, 160, 161, 185, 209, 211, 214, 215, 216, 217, 225, 254, 284, 354, 386-88, 405-407, 420, 421
Pentecost, J. Dwight, 338, 433
Perrin, Norman, 381, 433
Pestalozzi, 54
Plato, 33, 345
Plekhanov, 28, 346
Pokorný, Petr, 7, 336-38, 361, 433
Prabhavananda, Swami, 4, 325-29, 365, 399, 433
Preisker, H., 6, 433
Prophets: Isaiah, Amos, Jeremiah, 188
Rabbis: Hillel, Akiba, Eleazer, Jochanan, 189

Ragaz, Leonhard, 4, 53-73, 143, 160, 278, 346, 349-50, 354, 372, 383, 398, 410, 433
Rasmussen, Larry L., 249, 433
Rauschenbusch, Walter, 347, 433
Redpath, Theodore, 28, 433
Reimarus, Hermann Samuel, 371, 433
Rénan, Ernst, 3, 345, 352, 433
Répin, 34
Rothe, Richard, 54, 166
Rich, Arthur, 68, 433
Ritschl, 37, 54, 96, 167
Roubiczek, Paul, 28, 31, 433
Rousseau, 28, 345
Russell, Bertrand, 402

Schabert, Arnold, 185, 433
Schlatter, Adolf, 154
Schleiermacher, Friedrich, 166
Schnackenburg, Rudolf, 339, 433
Schneider, Johannes, 6, 266, 433
Schneller, Ludwig, 93, 433
Schoeps, Hans-Joachim, 378-80, 382, 386-87, 393, 407-408, 433
Schweitzer, Albert, 4, 5, 49, 66, 72, 91, 111-27, 151, 160, 199, 211, 225, 226, 227, 244, 245, 246, 277, 292, 352-55, 357, 361, 370-72, 374, 375, 376, 377, 383, 397, 417, 434
Schweizer, Eduard, 338, 385, 394-95, 434
Scott, Ernest F., 50, 417, 434
Seeberg, Reinhold, 317-19, 365, 398, 434
Shears, H., 152, 434
Shinn, Roger L., 298, 402, 434
Socrates, 25, 33, 55
Soiron, Thaddäus, 7, 339, 434
Spinoza, Baruch, 54
Stadland-Neumann, Hiltrud, 285, 434
Städeli, Walter, 4, 299-304, 364, 403, 417, 434
Stange, Carl, 3, 196, 214, 216, 224-26, 292, 358-59, 362, 383, 417, 434
Staudinger, Josef, 6, 339, 434

Stöger, Alois, 335, 434
Strecker, Georg, 7, 338-39
Thielicke, Helmut, 195, 435
Tholuck, 37
Thoreau, Henry David, 346
Thurneysen, Eduard, 3, 6, 275-85, 363-64, 384, 398, 403, 417, 435
Tersteegen, 150
Tilborg, Sjef Van, 386, 390, 435
Tolstoy, Leo, 4, 11-35, 37, 42, 43, 49, 51, 54, 55, 57, 69, 70, 72, 76, 88, 113, 131, 136, 150, 157, 161, 179, 180, 181, 183, 192, 203, 241, 244, 278, 279, 294, 305, 312, 343-47, 354, 383, 398, 406, 418, 419, 435
Torrance, T. F., 5, 422, 435
Traub, Friedrich, 51, 435
Troeltsch, Ernst, 143, 146, 163, 224, 344, 355, 399-401, 435
Twain, Mark, 403

Vidler, Alec R., 384, 399, 435
Vinet, Alexander, 54
Voltaire, 317, 409

Waylen, Hector, 4, 305-307, 346, 365, 435
Weber, Max, 76
Weiss, Johannes, 3, 66, 95-110, 151, 160, 211, 246, 277, 292, 351-52, 354, 357, 361, 370, 372, 397, 403, 417, 435
Wellhausen, Julius, 369-72, 435
White, Ellen G., 35, 342, 435
Wilder, Amos N., 380, 435
Windisch, Hans, 3, 6, 35, 209-26, 292, 295, 360-62, 376-77, 383, 384, 395, 396, 398, 406, 408, 417, 435
Wood, James, 152, 435
Wrede, Wilhelm, 121, 371
Wrege, Hans-Theo, 335-36, 365, 385, 436
Wünsch, Georg, 4, 49, 161, 163-74, 224, 358, 397, 417, 436
Wycliffe, 57
Zwingli, 54

THEMES

BEATITUDES [MT 5:3-12], 58, 97, 100-101, 115-17, 134-35, 144-45, 155, 168, 219-20, 258, 279, 287, 300-301, 303, 309, 312-13, 323-24, 326-27, 331, 336, 377, 413

SALT AND LIGHT [MT 5:13-16], 59, 159, 212, 284-85, 293, 301-302, 313, 376

JESUS AND TORAH [MT 5:17-20], 20, 136, 145, 156, 180, 183, 184, 191, 193, 214, 259-60, 276-77, 280, 282, 284, 287, 296, 309, 324, 331, 336, *383-96*

ANTITHESES [MT 5:21-48], 200, 212, 214, 277, 288, 296, 302, 309, 319, 336, 344, 357, 389

MURDER AND WRATH [MT 5:21-26], 21-22, 59, 136, 146, 156, 200, 260, 310, 313-14, 327, 376

ADULTERY AND DIVORCE [MT 5:27-32], 21-22, 60, 107, 136, 146, 156-57, 173, 178, 184, 189-91, 232, 236, 288, 294, 297, 305, 306, 310, 331, 352, 376, 389

SWEARING OF OATHS [MT 5:33-37], 21, 22-23, 60, 72, 93, 136, 146, 169, 173, 178, 189, 236, 260-61, 297, 310, 314-15, 324, 340, 376, 389

NONRESISTANCE AND FEINDES-LIEBE [MT 5:38-48], 11, 16, 20, 21, 23-24, 34, 35, 45-49, 56, 60-63, 72, 80, 93, 103-104, 136-37, 140-42, 144, 146, 147, 157-58, 168-70, 190, 203, 222, 223, 224, 234-35, 245-46, 256, 261-74, 294, 296-97, 306, 310, 322, 323-24, 328, 336, 338, 339, 345-46, 348, 356, 358, 363, 376, 389

'PERFECTION' [MT 5:48], 35, 178, 180, 184, 208, 279, 294-95, 302, 309, 315, 328, 332-33, 365

ALMS, PRAYER, FASTING [MT 6:1-18], 50, 120, 190, 202, 280, 293, 310, 318, 334, 376, 390

TREASURES AND CARES [MT 6:19-21, 25-34], 38, 56, 63-64, 80, 84-86, 93, 101-102, 108, 111, 147-48, 159-60, 168, 173, 190, 199, 202, 213, 222, 224, 233, 236, 244, 256, 348, 350, 352, 376

SINGLE EYE / TWO MASTERS [MT 6:22-24], 202, 287

On JUDGING [MT 7:1-5], 18-20, 64, 72, 199, 236, 336, 377

The HOLY / The GOLDEN RULE [MT 7:6, 12], 206, 281, 376

GOD'S ANSWERING OF PRAYER [MT 7:7-11], 199, 220, 376

TWO WAYS / FRUITS [MT 7:13-20], 50, 64, 183, 201, 219, 281, 310, 321, 329, 336, 377, 413

Saying: 'LORD, LORD' [MT 7:21-23], 284, 289, 376

IMITATIO CHRISTI / NACHFOLGE, 42, 43, 67-68, 106-107, 109-10, 185, 282-83, 338, 347, 349, 350, 352, 357, 363, 384, 388, 397-414 esp. 403-405, 417-23 esp. 422